Stephen Rapawy

The Culmination of Conflict

The Ukrainian-Polish Civil War and the Expulsion of Ukrainians After the Second World War

Stephen Rapawy

THE CULMINATION OF CONFLICT

The Ukrainian-Polish Civil War and the Expulsion of Ukrainians After the Second World War

ibidem-Verlag
Stuttgart

Bibliographic information published by the Deutsche Nationalbibliothek
Die Deutsche Nationalbibliothek lists this publication in the Deutsche Nationalbibliografie; detailed bibliographic data are available in the Internet at http://dnb.d-nb.de.

Bibliografische Information der Deutschen Nationalbibliothek
Die Deutsche Nationalbibliothek verzeichnet diese Publikation in der Deutschen Nationalbibliografie; detaillierte bibliografische Daten sind im Internet über http://dnb.d-nb.de abrufbar.

ISBN-13: 978-3-8382-0895-4

Printed in the United States of America

Table of Contents

List of Charts

List of Tables

Acknowledgements

My desire to write a book about the historic Polish-Ukrainian conflict and the post-World War II deportations comes from a longstanding and deeply personal interest in the topic. In 1947, when I was twelve years old, my family and I were deported from the Ukrainian districts in southeast Poland and resettled in western Poland during "Operation Vistula". Because my parents were American citizens, I was able to emigrate to the United States after the deportation. Over the years I considered writing about these events, and even considered this as a dissertation topic in graduate school. However, the available information at the time was derivative in nature, and because I had a full-time career, I had insufficient time to conduct on-site primary research. After retiring from the U. S. Census Bureau, I finally found the time to begin researching and writing. It was also a fortuitous time to start working on this topic since both Polish and Ukrainian archives became accessible after the collapse of communism. I had visions of spending years in Polish and Ukrainian archives but serendipity again came to the rescue. After the archives became accessible, Yevhen Misylo began a systematic search of Polish archives related to the expulsion of Ukrainians from the eastern districts in Poland. The collected documents were published in three volumes with numerous helpful annotations. At about the same time, Volodymyr Serhiichuk searched Ukrainian archives on the same subject and published his findings in a large compendium. Both scholars made significant contributions to my understanding and provided this researcher with necessary and readily available documents.

Once I began writing the manuscript, it quickly became a cooperative affair. Therefore, I wish to express my gratitude to a number of people who assisted me in this enterprise. My wife Luba spent countless hours stoically typing the handwritten manuscript with numerous changes, while my son Michael assisted me with various computer issues. Jacqueline Nolan, a cartographer in the Geography Division at the Library of Congress, graciously prepared two maps in the manuscript. Artist Jon Coulter enhanced the cover photograph that depicts villagers being deported during Operation Vistula in April 1947, and graphics artist Oleh (Alex) Gyba enhanced many other photos that appear in the book. Most of all, I wish to express my deep appreciation to Corinna Wengryn

Caudill not only for editing the manuscript, but also for reading it carefully and making numerous suggestions that significantly improved the quality of the book. Finally, I wish to thank the staff of ***ibidem*** Press for preparing the manuscript for printing.

Preface

In recent years, there have been several English-language publications on the subject of the post World War II deportations of Poland's Ukrainians. It has only been during the last two decades that the subject could finally be discussed openly, and state archives have been accessible to scholars regardless of their political viewpoints. Since then, a number of monographs and conference materials have been published in numerous languages and with varying interpretations. For Polish and Ukrainian authors, the interpretation of events greatly varies and usually falls along ethnic lines, with individual polemics corresponding to the nationalities of their authors. With respect to the history of Ukrainians in Poland after World War II, the most comprehensive treatment was given by Grzegorz Motyka in his Polish language book *Tak Bylo w Bieszczadach (It Happened in the Bieczczady)* that describes the pre-war conflict, partisan warfare, and the deportations. Additional valuable information is provided in a 10-volume collection of conference papers entitled *Polska-Ukraina: Trudne Pytannia* (*Poland-Ukraine: Difficult Questions*.) These essays were produced through conferences attended by Polish and Ukrainian scholars between 1999–2006 who examined the partisan warfare in that period as well as various aspects of the deportations.

More recent publications provide a great deal of useful information that debunks the communist narratives of the past. The authors typically discuss the events of the Second World War and provide detailed descriptions of the mechanics of the deportations. However, most tend to omit important historical details. Since these works are usually focused on the twentieth century and emphasize the rise of modern Ukrainian nationalism in Poland and Ukraine, the lengthy history of internecine warfare between Poles and Ukrainians is often treated with only a cursory discussion. The growth of nationalism, the formation of national states, and widespread deportations have moved many scholars to see a close relationship between all three phenomena. As a result, none have comprehensively examined the events as part of a longer historical process that has occurred between the Polish and Ukrainian ethnic groups in Europe.

Until the collapse of communism in 1991, the mass deportation of Poland's Ukrainians after World War II was a topic that generally received only cursory treatment in the historical literature of both Poland and Ukraine. When it was mentioned in periodicals or other sources, both Poland and the Soviet Union presented the accepted communist party line as such: an agreement existed between the two countries; the resettlements had been voluntary; resistance to the resettlement was conducted by UPA, who had been Nazi collaborators; and the Soviet Union and Poland had taken necessary measures to reduce ethnic internecine violence along the border.

The exception to this lack of examination was a lengthy monograph published in 1973 that was co-authored by Antoni Szcześniak and Wiesław Szota. The two Polish writers examined Ukrainian-Polish relations between the wars, the internecine conflict during the war, and the several years of fighting in the post war period before the Ukrainian insurrection in Poland was suppressed and the Ukrainian population was removed. Although the writers advanced the standard communist viewpoints, Szcześniak and Szota provided detailed information on the topic, frequently using archival materials that were not available to other writers at that time. Regardless of the authors' ideological biases, three important observations in the monograph reveal that the insurgency was the result of a popular uprising against Soviet and Polish communist rule in post-war Poland. First, the insurgency in post-war Poland lasted for more than three years, which could only have been possible with the support of the local Ukrainian population. Second, the insurgency was a sizeable force rather than merely the work of a few malcontents. Third, the monograph elucidates the Polish government's *prima facie* justification for Operation Vistula (*Akcja "Wisła"*): UPA could not be destroyed without the removal of the Ukrainian population. One of the most important works is American political scientist John Armstrong's book *Ukrainian Nationalism,* first published in 1955, which takes a detached view in describing the development of Ukrainian nationalism in the twentieth century and the formation of the Ukrainian Insurgent Army during the Second World War. The book, which was subsequently updated in several editions, is still valuable and informative despite the fact that it was published before much of the current archival material became available. Norman Davies' *God's Playground: A History of Poland, Vol. II, 1795 to Present*, first published in 1982, provides valuable information on the formation of the Polish underground during the war and the communist takeover of Poland in the post-war period.

Because Ukraine emerged as a political entity in the twentieth century, many scholars limit the discussion of the Polish-Ukrainian conflict to the period of modern states, viewing it as a struggle between national entities rather than a longstanding and deeply entrenched conflict between Polish and Ukrainian interests. In Philip Ther and Ana Siljak's edited compilation *Redrawing Nations: Ethnic Cleansing in East-Central Europe, 1944–1948*, several contributing authors, including Orest Subtelny and Marek Jasiak, used archival materials to describe the forcible transfers of the Ukrainian population of southeast Poland after the war. Their examinations include the initial deportations into the Soviet Union, and later, the expulsions into Western Poland as part of Operation Vistula. Ther noted "...the specific interaction of the growth of the modern states with the development of the idea of the 'nation' created the precondition for cleansing of the minorities."[1] In *The Reconstruction of Nations*, American historian Timothy Snyder described the deportations in the context of building modern Ukrainian and Polish nation states and also analyzed the mutual conflicts and deportations. He attributes the Polish-Ukrainian conflict to the Ukrainian integral nationalism that required "ethnic homogeneity" to establish a Ukrainian state.[2] In addition to the publications that describe and analyze the deportations of Ukrainians, a number of other studies provide valuable information related to the topic. Norman M. Naimark's *Fires of Hatred: Ethnic Cleansing in Twentieth Century Europe* surveys the deportations of numerous ethnic groups during the twentieth century and relates these events to the rise of modern nationalism. Naimark sees ethnic cleansing in the twentieth century as "...a product of the most 'advanced' stage in the development of the modern state." [3]

In contrast to the views of these scholars, Andrew Bell-Fiolkoff, a historian who specializes in historical ethnic conflicts, presented a wider-ranging viewpoint on the historical practice of deporting populations in

---

1 Philip Ther and Anna Siljak, *Redrawing Nations* (Lanham, Md.: Rowman & Littlefield, 2001), 44.

2 Timothy Snyder, *The Reconstruction of Nations*, (New Haven: Yale University Press, 2003), 168.

3 Norman Naimark, *Fires of Hatred,* (Cambridge: Harvard University Press, 2001), 8.

his 1996 book *Ethnic Cleansing*. He examined the practice of mass deportation throughout the ages, delineating deportation practices into three historic periods: Antiquity, the Middle Ages, and the Modern Period, tracing the origin of the practice to the Assyrians.[4] He notes that the best documentation of the ancient deportations is that of the upper strata of Hebrew society in the sixth century BC to Babylon after the conquest of Jerusalem.[5] His examination demonstrates that various peoples were expelled for a variety of reasons, including economic purposes and religious conflicts. Over time, ethnic factors became a major motivator for dominant groups to expel unwanted minorities, although the rhetoric surrounding such actions was usually couched in religious terms. For example, the seventeenth century expulsion of the Irish from Ulster "...although still a religious expulsion, it can still qualify as the first ethnic cleansing of modern times."[6]

The core of the study is based on a variety sources. In addition to reviewing the literature published on the topic in the post-communist period, I have made use of numerous primary sources located in Polish and Ukrainian archives made available after the establishment of democratic republics in Poland (1990) and Ukraine (1991). These resources include approximately 450 documents published in three volumes by Eugeniusz Misiło, who searched archives in Poland and subsequently published three volumes of archival material generated by the Polish communist government, its military, and some captured Ukrainian underground documents that relate to the deportation of Ukrainians and the military operations against the Ukrainian underground in southeastern Poland. The documents issued by the Polish civilian authorities deal largely with deportation of the population while the military documents describe military operations against the partisans. The collection includes instructions, reports, and summaries of conferences conducted by civilian and military authorities. The Organization of Ukrainian Nationalists (*Orhanizatsiia Ukrains'kykh Nationalistiv*—OUN) and the Ukrainian Insurgent Army (*Ukrains'ka Povstans'ka Armiia*—UPA) generated most of the Ukrainian material, and there were also numerous memoirs and recollections that were published after the events took place.

---

4 Ibid., 52.

5 Andrew Bell-Fialkoff, *Ethnic Cleansing* (New York: St. Martin's Press, 1996), 7.

6 Ibid., 18.

A comparable archival search was undertaken in Ukraine after the collapse of the Soviet Union. In 1997, Ukrainian historian Volodymyr Serhiichuk published a collection of relevant documents in a 438-page compendium consisting of correspondences between Soviet party officials, appeals of Ukrainians in Poland to the Soviet officials, and reports from the Soviet population exchange commission in Poland. The reports describe the attitudes of Polish officials concerning the deportations, the Polish national resistance to the pro-Soviet government in Poland, and UPA attacks on the transportation network. Particularly valuable was Mykhailo Romashchenko's lengthy report included in the compendium. Romashchenko headed the Soviet deportation commission in Poland and published his report on February 14, 1947. The report provides details that were previously not reported (or were underreported) in both Ukrainian and Polish sources and in documents detailing the operations of the population exchange commission.

Examining archival sources alone would fall short of providing comprehensive insight into the events of the post-war period since many important points were not adequately described in the available material. Official government documents and correspondences typically recorded only cursory comments concerning specific events or operations and often omitted background information dealing with the reasons for the deportations and the mutual hostilities. Polish correspondences among and between civilian and military officials were often summarized rather than reported verbatim, and occasionally the comments of some officials present at the conference do not appear in the protocol. The underground publications, more so than the government correspondence and reports, provide insight into the fluid political and tactical environment in which the insurgency operated, the ideological drive of the underground, the impact and relationship of the underground with the Ukrainian civilian population, and the fundamental conflict between Ukrainian interests and those of Poland and the Soviet Union

Although it's likely that the majority of the prolific underground correspondence perished in well-concealed bunkers during and after the destruction of the insurgency in Poland, much of it did manage to survive. It was subsequently organized into a large series of volumes entitled *Litopys Ukrains'koyi Povstans'koyi Armiyi* (*Chronicles of the Ukrainian Insurgent Army*), a series of archival compilations organized and edited by the Ukrainian historian Peter Potichnyj and his associates, many of whom had been members of the Ukrainian underground. The available literature provides a great deal of information concerning the perspectives and operations of the Ukrainian underground, including OUN and UPA, since it is largely comprised of correspondence generated through the organization's extensive communications network. After the insurgency was organized in Poland, OUN and UPA instructed their lower level organizations to establish archives, usually in underground bunkers in the forest, in order to chronicle the insurgency's struggle for purposes of posterity. In addition to the archives, OUN issued five different publications that included brochures and newspapers that described current local events, foreign news, and the ideological position of the underground. The publications were designed to gain the support of the civilian population, maintain morale among the insurgency's personnel and military cadre, and were also used as instruction material for the partisan units. The insurgents were also keen on informing the outside world about their activities, and to that end, many publications were sent to the U.S. Embassy in Warsaw, which were subsequently forwarded to the United States and preserved in the U.S. archives. In addition to these publications, local OUN organizations received instructions from superior organizations and in turn wrote reports about the events that were happening in their districts. The reports describe civilian attitudes toward the underground and the deportations, the number of people deported, and also include details that were not recorded in the archives concerning large-scale Polish atrocities against civilians. With the exception of the brochures, most underground communications were cryptic and transmitted clandestinely in order to avoid enemy interception while simultaneously ensuring that superiors were apprised of the general situation.

In addition to the extensive amount of documentation and literature produced by OUN, UPA also created a sizeable archive that resulted from a monthly reporting system. Every month, the commanders of company-sized units were required to submit operational reports to their respective battalion commanders, therein enumerating all activities and events that had occurred during that period. In some cases, these reports included diagrams of battles and the operational status of units. The battalion commanders summarized these reports and forwarded them to the military district commander who commanded UPA operations in Poland.

Finally, personal memoirs included in the literature of the insurgency provide some additional insight into the events that transpired, although most were written years after the events that the authors describe. Typically, many such publications provide a patriotic and one-sided account of events, omitting important details and therefore limiting their historical value.

By comparing Polish and Ukrainian archival materials in tandem with the literature of the Ukrainian underground, I endeavored to provide a more comprehensive analysis of the Polish-Ukrainian conflict in the post-war period, particularly as it pertains to the actions of the insurgency and the deportation of Ukrainians first to the Soviet Union and later, to the northern and western provinces of Poland during Operation Vistula.

Introduction

The rise of modern nationalism was undoubtedly a major factor that exacerbated the longstanding historical Polish-Ukrainian conflict to its culmination in the twentieth century; however, it was one of many factors rather than the singular factor that is often the focal point of discussion in recent historical publications. A thorough examination of Ukrainian and Polish relations from all available sources reveals that the conflict in the post-war period was infused with the same political undertones that had existed between the two groups for centuries: deeply ingrained cultural and religious divisions combined with incompatible claims to mutually settled territories.

This study examines the post-World War II conflict through lens of the broader historical relationship between Polish and Ukrainian interests. In the first chapter, I endeavored to provide a brief overview to Polish-Ukrainian relations dating back to the tenth century Polish claim to lands that now comprise modern western Ukraine. It was this territorial claim along with the Polish imperative to assimilate the Ukrainian population in those territories that ultimately determined Polish policy until the twentieth century and resulted in various episodes of conflict between the two ethnic groups. My examination of the conflict takes into consideration centuries of ethnic strife, the population shifts that resulted from foreign conquests, and the formation of national states on multiethnic territories as the pre-conditions for the events that occurred in the years following World War II. The discussion of the post-war period is limited largely to events that occurred in southeastern Poland, where the Ukrainian nationalist insurgency clashed with Polish and Soviet forces in a violent struggle to control territories that both Ukrainians and Poles viewed as their historical inheritance. Ultimately, the Polish state would prevail in the mid-twentieth century through a series of deportation operations that would destroy the insurgency and end the centuries-long Ukrainian presence in the region. In doing so, Poland would finally bring about the end of the historic conflict between the two groups.

The historic conflict between Poles and Ukrainians is deeply rooted in the religious and cultural divide that has existed since the introduction of eastern and western Christianity in Eastern Europe. During this period in history, religion and church rituals unified people in the same manner in which the notion of "nationalism" would influence political actors in the twentieth century. Given their religious and cultural differences as well as their close geographic proximity, the first few centuries of Polish-Ukrainian relations were marked by intermittent conflicts that were characteristic of the middle ages. Each side sought to expand its domain at its neighbors' expense. The major turning point of Polish-Ukrainian relations occurred in the fourteenth century, when the Kingdom of Poland, with the aid of the Hungarian Kingdom, conquered the Galicia-Volhynia Principality, the westernmost dominion of the Rus' polity (territories that now comprise western Ukraine.) Polish control eventually extended as far eastward as Kyiv. As Poland began incorporating territory that is presently in western Ukraine, Polish elites faced a fundamentally different society with its own laws, customs, and above all—a well-entrenched Orthodox Church. Initially the newly acquired territory was designated as the Kingdom of Rus' which suggested the possibility of a federative arrangement. This policy, however, was not pursued and instead, the new Polish government decided to eliminate the distinctive character of the region. This was to be achieved by eliminating the previous administrative apparatus and local laws, restricting religious observances, and ultimately assimilating the population through conversion to Roman Catholicism. To permanently incorporate the old Rus' territories into the Polish state, the Orthodox religion had to be eliminated or modified, and the associated population (the noble class in particular) had to be assimilated or, at a minimum, acculturated to Polish society.

In 1569, the Union of Lublin united the Kingdom of Poland and the Grand Duchy of Lithuania, creating the Polish-Lithuanian Commonwealth and annexing the Orthodox Rus' lands in the process. In 1596, Polish agents encouraged the hierarchs of the Orthodox Church to accept religious union with Rome in an effort to strengthen control over the conquered territories and foster acculturation and assimilation of the Orthodox people into the Commonwealth. Under this state pressure, along with the desire to improve their own position within the Polish societal structure, some bishops from the Orthodox Church of Rus' broke relations with the Patriarch of Constantinople and declared allegiance to the papacy in Rome in an arrangement that would come to be called the Union of Brest. The former orthodox structure did not simply convert to Roman Catholicism; instead, a hybrid church was created that was called

"Uniate," having shifted its allegiance from Constantinople to Rome while retaining the original orthodox liturgical traditions (including use of the Julian calendar and the ability of clergy to marry) and also retained old Slavonic (rather than Latin) as its liturgical language.

Over time, the Commonwealth experienced a slow and torturous economic decline that can be partially attributed to the persistence of a feudal economy. In contrast to western Europe's evolving industrial growth which gave rise to urban industrial centers, the Commonwealth's ruling nobility instead placed a heavy emphasis on agriculture and investment in their own rural plantations. Over time, they increased their exactions from both the state and the peasantry in order to meet the demands of the increasingly competitive international grain trade. These conditions delayed Poland's modernization and the increasing exactions incited a violent Ukrainian reaction against Poland's ruling nobility. The seventeenth century Cossack Rebellion shook the Commonwealth to its foundation and it was forced to cede some territory, including Kyiv, to Russia. The following century, Russian troops were needed to quell the peasant rebellion on the west bank of the Dnieper under Polish control. These uprisings and rebellions eroded the Commonwealth's ability to provide for its own state defense.

It was under these circumstances that the Commonwealth met its demise with the partitions of Poland at the end of the eighteenth century, when Russia, Austria and Prussia seized and divided the Commonwealth's territory in three partitioning actions. In 1772, during the first partition, the empire of Austria annexed the western Ukrainian lands, which became part of the new Austrian province called "The Kingdom of Galicia and Lodomeria." After the Napoleonic Wars, Austria retained Galicia and Empress Maria Theresa and her son Joseph II introduced the policies of "enlightened absolutism" which sought to improve economic conditions and increase the educational level of the ethnically diverse population. Key developments in this period were generally positive toward the cultural ascendency of Ruthenians living within the empire, although Poles retained a much higher socioeconomic and cultural position because of the presence of a robust Polish noble class that had developed during the Commonwealth period. Nevertheless, the feudal burden of the peasantry was reduced and Ruthenians received greater legal protection than they had previously enjoyed under the Commonwealth,[7] although on the local level, these protections were frequently curtailed because the Polish landlord class and their supporters administered the local offices and courts.

Polish-Ukrainian animosities were compounded after World War I, when the three continental empires, Austrian, German, and Russian, collapsed and were replaced by national states on these ethnically heterogeneous territories. As it had done in the middle ages, Poland once again emerged as a multinational state, acquiring all of Galicia as well as the Ukrainian province of Volhynia, a large portion of Belarus, and some ethnic Lithuanian territory.[8] Unlike the middle ages, however, this was an age of nationalism. Minority groups, which comprised about one-third of the population, were in a nation-building mood. The situation was especially tense in Galicia, where Ukrainians had lost a bloody six-month war with Poland in a failed attempt to obtain independent statehood. The Allied powers obligated the Polish interwar government to provide extensive religious, cultural, and civil rights for the minorities, to be supervised by the League of Nations and the World Court (which would later be renamed the International Court of Justice.) These rights, as later discussion will reveal, were severely abridged. Rather than reaching a meaningful accommodation with the non-Polish citizenry, the new Polish government instead instituted a policy of rapid Polonization, and closing Ukrainian churches and schools were among the policy measures taken. As a result, the conflict with ethnic Ukrainians living within the borders of the Polish state continued during the interwar period.

Within its new borders, Poland had large minority groups whose loyalty to the new state was questionable, and it once again became imperative for state security to assimilate and de-nationalize them. The large Jewish minority was dispersed throughout the state living mostly in towns. Ethnic Germans, who lived mostly to the north and west of the country, were also a sizeable group but did not form compact districts. The Ukrainian and Belarusian minorities, however, were settled in compact rural areas in the eastern part of the country that bordered with the

---

7 Orest Subtelny, *Ukraine: A History* (Toronto: University of Toronto Press, 1988), 216.

8 In much of the Ukrainian historical literature dealing with this period, Galicia and Volhynia are referred to as "Western Ukraine."

Soviet Union. During this period, most Ukrainians could not reconcile themselves to the Polish conquest and refused to take an oath of loyalty to the Polish state.

As Polish rulers had done earlier in history, the new Polish government considered the ethnic Ukrainian territory to be a part of historic Poland and sought to fully integrate these territories into the new Polish state. Their claim to the territory was based on two fundamental precepts. First, concerning the territories of modern western Ukraine, they viewed these areas as places that had been settled by ethnic Poles who had been incorporated into the Kyivan state by force of arms and then converted to Eastern Christianity. Second, they viewed the territory as having been for centuries an integral part of the Polish state where Poles had played a leading role in administering the land. Besides these claims of questionable validity, many Poles had in fact lived on the territory for centuries, although some were assimilated Ruthenians and naturally considered it to be their land. Ukrainian nationalists rejected these claims. They considered themselves to be a separate nationality striving to form a national state on their ancestral lands. They viewed the territory as having been a part of the medieval Kyivan state prior to the Polish conquest in the fourteenth century, and a place where Ukrainians still comprised a large majority despite significant Polish migration and settlement.

To preclude possible future partitions of the new Polish state, the government instituted a Polonization policy that was much more severe than it had been during the Commonwealth era, and the more extreme politicians believed that the region could be fully Polonized within a twenty-five year period. The interwar government imposed repressive policies on the Ukrainian population; including the sharp curtailment of Ukrainian language education, an overall decrease in Ukrainian access to education, and also barred Ukrainians from access to government employment. These policies sought to retard the growth of an educated Ukrainian class that had advocated for independence and had therefore threatened Polish hegemony. In some areas where national identity was weak, the notion of regionalism was fostered or individuals were encouraged to embrace outright conversion to Roman Catholicism, which equated to Polonization. For example, in the western Lemko region, most Lemkos identified themselves as Rusyns or Rus'naks (Ruthenians.) The government encouraged the retention of the regional Lemko identity, supported Lemko language programs intended to preserve the unique dialect, discouraged the spread of Ukrainian nationalism through educational and ecclesiastical channels, and engaged in politics that exacerbated ideological divisions in the Greek Catholic church. In the Chełm and Podlesie districts, which had once comprised the western edge of the historic Volhynia Principality west of the Bug River, the Orthodox Church was targeted for virtual extinction. The government further initiated colonization, settling approximately 300,000 Poles on the Ukrainian territory, with the majority placed in Volhynia to increase the "Polishness" of the region. The settlers, many of whom were army veterans, were designated as colonists and some were provided with arms and ammunition. Their presence would incite a violent conflict with Ukrainians that would reach disastrous proportions during the Second World War.

By 1939, Polish-Ukrainian relations had severely degraded to the point that many Ukrainians living within Polish borders initially viewed the Germans as liberators from Polish oppression. As it became clear that the Germans had no intentions of allowing the formation of an independent Ukrainian state, Ukrainian nationalists organized a large partisan army. Throughout the war there were mutual small-scale attacks, but by 1943, the violence had significantly escalated on both sides of the Bug River. Poles attacked Ukrainians living west of the river and Ukrainians attacked Poles on the east. Sensing that the Germans were losing the war, Ukrainian nationalists correctly assumed that the postwar Polish state intended to retain control of the territory, a condition that would preclude the formation of a Ukrainian state. The local Poles, in the Ukrainian view, were a "fifth column" who had fought earlier against Ukrainian independence. They would need to be removed from Ukrainian territories if independence was to be secured in the future.

When the Red Army arrived in western Ukraine in the summer of 1944, they found a chaotic situation. Ukrainian partisans were driving Polish civilians out of Volhynia and battling Polish and Soviet partisans. The Soviet police and the army immediately became involved in the conflict and a leading Soviet general, Nikolai Vatutin, was ambushed and killed by Ukrainian partisans.[9] Soviet authorities had to resolve the conflict and stabilize the area. Although documents are not available con-

9 John Armstrong, *Ukrainian Nationalism* (Littleton: Ukrainian Academic Press, 1980), 293

cerning Stalin's view on the deportations, his motives can be deduced from examining Soviet actions. Beyond retaining the territories that had been gained through the 1939 Molotov-Ribbentrop pact, which projected Soviet power deeper into Europe, Stalin was keen on bringing all Ukrainians under his control. Establishing a Ukrainian state on all Ukrainian ethnic territory had been the primary goal of Ukrainians between the wars. When Ukrainians in Transcarpathia declared independence in 1938 as Czechoslovakia was disintegrating, many Ukrainians crossed the Carpathians to aid them, hoping to establish a piedmont that could be used to liberate the rest of Ukraine. Stalin groused that attaching Ukraine to Transcarpathia was the equivalent of "sewing an elephant to a button," but was sufficiently concerned about the developments to incorporate the territory into the Soviet Union in 1945. Deportations from the Soviet point of view resolved several issues, including the removal of a hostile Polish population and the quelling of Ukrainian-Polish ethnic conflict, although the Soviet fight with the Ukrainian underground would continue for another six years. This strategy further brought all Ukrainians under Soviet control, prevented a future irredentist movement on the Soviet border, and established a clear ethnic demarcation between the Soviet Union and Poland.

In July 1944, the Soviet Union installed a provisional government in Poland that was comprised of Polish communists from the Communist International in Moscow. The group was designated as the "Polish Committee of National Liberation" (*Polski Komitet Wyzwolenia Narodowego*, PKWN.) As one of the first orders of business, the PKWN and the Soviet Union signed a secret agreement that established a new Polish eastern boundary that left the Molotov-Ribbentrop boundaries in tact, therefore enabling the Soviet Union to retain them. The following September, the PKWN entered into a population exchange agreement with the Soviet Union that called for the "voluntary" exchange of Polish and Ukrainian ethnic populations in the borderlands. The agreement was modeled after the 1939 population exchange agreement between the Germany and the Soviet Union, which provided for Germans living within the newly acquired Soviet territory to emigrate to the German zone and allowed Ukrainians in the German Zone to resettle in Soviet Ukraine. The 1944 agreement stipulated that Polish nationals living within Ukraine's recently established border could emigrate to Poland and likewise, Ukrainians on the Polish side could relocate to Ukraine. At the end of the war, the international political climate was conducive to the strategy of exchanging populations as a means to create stability. At the Potsdam Conference on August 1, 1945, the Allies agreed to the wholesale removal of ethnic Germans from Poland, Czechoslovakia and Hungary, stipulating that the removal should be humane.[10] The massive ethnic cleansing was largely completed but was anything but humane. Large numbers of people were moved on foot, in carts, and via inadequate railroad transport. Many succumbed to the elements, were subjected to hostility and violence by Soviet troops, and endured the scorn and condemnation of local populations who assigned them collective blame for the wartime actions of the Nazi regime. As the war came to a close, over 13 million Germans were expelled from Eastern Europe.[11]

As in western Ukraine, the situation was chaotic in the Ukrainian districts of eastern Poland, with the partisan armies of both groups at war with each other. Both governments quickly established the requisite relocation apparatus and encouraged people to "voluntarily" relocate. Poles on the Soviet side left comparatively quickly under Soviet and Ukrainian pressures—some actually fled to Poland prior to the deportation because of Ukrainian partisan attacks. Ukrainians on the Polish side held out for several years because of a strong Ukrainian underground and a weak emerging communist government in Poland.

The Soviet distortion of the terminology apparently had some success since even some knowledgeable scholars are reluctant to consider Polish-Soviet removals as deportations or expulsions.[12] Although a small number of people voluntarily resettled to Ukraine, Polish officials had limited success between 1944–1945 since most people simply refused to leave their native territories. Because the exchange had been presented as being voluntary, the Polish Army resorted to terrorizing people in order to compel them to sign the required documents indicating that it was a voluntary departure. The Soviet Union sent its personnel to monitor removal at the deportation points and encourage Ukrainians to leave.

---

10 Walter LaFeber, ed. *Eastern Europe and the Soviet Union, Vol. II,* part of Arthur M. Schlesinger, gen. ed., *The Dynamics of World Power, A Documentary History of the United States, 1945–1973* (New York, Chelsea House Publishers, 1973), 101.

11 Joseph B. Schechtman, *Postwar Population Transfers in Europe* (Philadelphia: University of Pennsylvania Press, 1962), 363.

12 Bell-Fialkoff, 39.

Polish authorities were required to round up the people and bring them to the railroad stations. Since most people refused to leave, the army attempted to intimidate them to reconsider by raiding or burning villages and killing civilians, especially men, resulting in deportations that were usually more violent than most. Most of those who succumbed to the intimidation came from the Ukrainian districts in the Lublin Province where they had been subjected to vicious Polish partisan attacks between 1942–1945. Some left when the Red Army occupied the area, fearing for their safety. In the Galician counties to the south, Polish partisan attacks were fewer and the Polish Army forcibly removed most Ukrainians.

The Ukrainian Underground leadership adamantly opposed the expulsion of Ukrainians from Poland, viewing it as a loss of Ukrainian historic land, and responded by expanding both the OUN network and the UPA ranks to fight the removal. The UPA organization, totaling about 3,000 men, thwarted these efforts by attacking troops when they ventured into the Ukrainian countryside. They destroyed trains, railroad bridges, and occasionally railroad stations. At the approach of Polish troops, Ukrainian civilians fled when possible, usually to the forests. Those who lived within the Carpathians occasionally fled across the border to Czechoslovakia. Thus, the relocation that had begun in the autumn of 1944 continued for a year with limited success. Most Ukrainians simply refused to leave their native territories and a well-organized partisan force delivered staunch resistance.

In the autumn of 1945, Poland deployed three divisions of army troops to the Ukrainian districts and by that time, forcible deportation became the norm compared to earlier when it had been episodically applied. The process was prolonged by the Ukrainian population's adamant refusal to leave as well as the Ukrainian Insurgent Army's numerous attacks on the transportation infrastructure and authorities who were conducting the deportations. These conditions eventually convinced Polish authorities to increase the number of troops and treat the relocations as a military operation. In the spring of 1946, Operation Rzeszów was organized to expedite the deportations and to meet an extended deadline that had been arranged with the Soviets as the result of the shortfalls of "volunteers" in earlier relocation operations. At the conclusion of the operation in the summer of 1946, the authorities erroneously concluded that they had accomplished their objectives of removing almost all of the

Ukrainians and fatally damaging the Ukrainian insurgency. In reality, approximate half a million Ukrainians had been deported to the east, which constituted about three quarters of the total. Despite being damaged and reduced in numbers, the Ukrainian underground remained in tact.

Although the Kremlin orchestrated the deportations to the east, the deportation campaign to the west, known as Akcja "Wisła," was purely a Polish affair. When Ukrainians began returning to their villages from the forests and countryside after Operation Rzeszów, the authorities realized that large numbers of Ukrainians still remained in Poland. More disturbingly, they became aware of the fact that the insurgency's losses were not as extensive as had been previously estimated. As a result, both military and civilian officials again began discussing the need for another deportation. By that point, the Soviet authorities were unwilling to organize another deportation, leaving Poles with only one option: to send the expelled Ukrainians to the newly acquired German territories in the west and north of Poland, far away from the border of Soviet Ukraine. Although the ethnic German population had been removed by that time, ethnic Poles only sparsely populated the areas. After a bogus election in January 1947, the communists established more permanent control in Poland and preparations for another deportation began in earnest. More troops were sent to the Ukrainian areas and battles between the Poles and the partisans flared up once again.

In late March, an event occurred that would provide the Polish authorities with the perfect pretext to conduct a final campaign to remove the remainder of the Ukrainian population in Poland's border regions, an action that would destroy the Ukrainian insurgency by removing what remained of its support base. On March 28, 1947, the Deputy Minister of Defense, General Karol Świerczewski, was killed in an ambush near Baligród in the Carpathians while conducting an inspection of troops who were fighting the Ukrainian partisans. The Polish government seized upon this incident to justify the final deportation, and launched a propaganda campaign that used Soviet slogans to demonize the partisans and anyone else who opposed them. The deportation was billed as a necessary excision to cleanse the area of fascist "Nazi" elements. During the next month, various departments worked energetically to finalize the plans, and the army dubbed the campaign "Operation Vistula" (*Akcja "Wisła."*)

The deportations began at the end of April and were carried out over the next several months. Compared to Operation Rzeszów, Operation Vistula was more meticulously planned and executed, with more troops specifically dedicated to the task of deportation. Previously, troops had been dispersed along the 300-mile border with Ukraine and had attempted to simultaneously conduct the deportations and fight the partisans. In the planning of Operation Vistula, the Polish Army deployed significantly greater numbers of troops and changed their tactics. They began the expulsions in the three southeastern counties near the Carpathian Mountains where they flooded Ukrainian inhabited regions, surrounded villages in the pre-dawn hours, and gave people little opportunity to flee to the forests. Poland further reached an agreement with Czechoslovakia, which promised to deploy large numbers of troops along its border to prevent Ukrainian civilians and partisans from crossing as some had done in the past. With approximately 17,000 troops participating in the operation, the Polish Army's presence in most areas was roughly a 30-to-1 numerical advantage over the partisans. Once they had cleared each area, troops moved on to the next counties, working their way northward along the Ukrainian border. Overall, the operation was less chaotic and violent than had been the previous deportations to the east since there was no longer a charade about "voluntary" resettlement. People were simply rounded up, brought to railroad stations, and placed on the next available train.

The Ukrainians who were expelled from Poland experienced great privations during transport and endured significant hardships in the territories where they were resettled. Many were settled in areas in eastern Ukraine that had been heavily damaged during the war. The lack of decent shelter was the most immediate problem, but food shortages were also severe and became catastrophic between 1946 and 1947 when a severe draught combined with Soviet grain export policies resulted in a famine. Those who were shipped to the former German territories also faced significant difficulties. By the time they arrived, most of the habitable dwellings were occupied by Poles who had arrived earlier and many damaged buildings where Ukrainians were placed had not been repaired before the winter. In addition, many Poles in the region had been resettled from western Ukraine and were hostile and fearful of the new Ukrainian settlers.

Over a three-and-one-half year period, approximately 700,000 Ukrainians were expelled from their native territories in southeastern Poland, thereby ending centuries of concentrated Ukrainian settlement there. Thousands of Ukrainian villages were destroyed, depopulated or Polonized, and the Ukrainian Greek Catholic Church was outlawed and nearly destroyed. The Ukrainian partisans, who suffered heavy losses during Operation Vistula, were ordered to head to the American Zone in Germany or were instructed to cross the Ukrainian border and join the insurrection that continued in western Ukraine.

With the final expulsion of the Ukrainian population in the summer of 1947 and the end of the insurgency in Poland, the millennium-long Polish-Ukrainian struggle had finally concluded.

Chapter I: An Overview of Polish-Ukrainian Relations Before World War I

The Polish-Ukrainian conflict began in the tenth century and continued until the Second World War. During that lengthy period, the Polish State was usually on the offensive while Ukrainians fought to prevent encroachment. In the sixteenth century, Poland acquired all Ukrainian lands, a condition that precipitated the Cossack revolt in the following century. The revolt brought Russia into the conflict and ultimately forced Poland to cede some territory to Russia, including the city of Kyiv. This event began the slow decline of the Polish State until its dismemberment at the end of the eighteen-century. The territory was initially brought under Polish control by conquest, but Polish society began to view this land as Polish territory based on their lengthy domination and the growth of the Polish population. Some Poles had migrated with the conquests, and over time, they assimilated a segment of the local population. Despite the Polish inroads to historic Ukrainian territories, Ukrainians comprised a large majority of the population and generally rejected the Polish interpretation of history. The differing views precipitated centuries of conflict between the two groups.

The Rus' Period (981–1349)

Historians usually begin the discussion of the Polish-Ukrainian border territory with the 981 conquests of the Cherven (Red) cities and Przemyśl (Peremyshl)[13] by "Volodymyr the Great."[14] Documents and archaeological evidence, however, provide information on the region for approximately one hundred years prior to the conquest. During that period, the territory was under the control of Moravia and later Bohemia when Eastern Christianity was introduced to the region. The introduction of Eastern Christianity was an extremely significant event because the

13 When used the first time, Ukrainian towns in Poland are noted by their Polish names and the Ukrainian version is noted in parenthesis.

14 The *Kyivan Chronicle* renders the name as "Volodimer." Modern versions of the name are "Volodymyr" in Ukrainian, used here, and "Vladimir" in Russian.

subsequent acceptance of Western Christianity by the Polish Crown divided the territory between Poland and Rus' along religious lines.[15]

Eastern Christianity was introduced in the region in 863 by Byzantine missionaries Cyril and Methodius who came to the town of Nitra at the invitation of a local prince, Rastislav. In the late ninth century, there followed a rapid expansion of the Moravian State that "extended from the Elbe and the Saale to the upper Bug and Styr and in the east and south to the Tisza and the Danube with the fair prospect of annexing Pannonia."[16] The Byzantine Emperor Constantine Porphyrogentius referred to the newly expanded state as the "Great Moravian Empire." Great Moravia included Bohemia (which later played a dominant role in the state) and introduced Eastern Christianity north of Carpathians although it was eventually eliminated in Moravia under German pressure.[17] The disappearance of Eastern Christianity in Moravia, Bohemia, and later Poland indicates that the two churches were unable to coexist on the same territory, and animosities were further exacerbated by the 1054 Schism between Constantinople and Rome.

A century later, the Moravian state north of the Carpathians came into contact with the expanding Polish kingdom, which was under the rule of King Mieszko I. It was a relationship that was initially friendly. Mieszko realized that the German conquest of the Slavic lands was presented as an effort to bring Christianity to the so-called heathen Slav; he undercut the *raison d'etre* for the conquest by accepting Western Christianity, but from Bohemia rather than Germany. Boleslav I of Bohemia sent missionaries to Poland and gave Mieszko his daughter Dubravka in marriage. Around the year 966, both rulers requested that Pope John XIII "establish bishoprics in their countries." Thus, the acceptance of Christi-

---

15 Until modern times, the territory of present-day Ukraine was called Rus,'sometimes translated as "Ruthenia" or "Kyivan Rus'." Older terms are occasionally used when describing the earlier history of Ukraine.

16 Dvornik, Francis. *The Slavs*, 94.

17 The presence of the Eastern Church on both sides of the Carpathians is described in number of sources. See Lanckoronska, *Studies on the Roman-Slavonic Rite in Poland,* (Pont. Institutum Orientalium Studiorum, 1961) which provides the most detailed exposition, synthesizing medieval documents and modern studies. Additional discussion is provided in Kantor, Marvin, *Medieval Slavic Studies of Saints and Princes*. (University of Michigan, 1983); and in Dvornik, Francis, "The Significance of the Missions of Cyril and Methodius," in *Slavic Review*, Vol. 23, No. 2 (Jun., 1964), 195–211; and Dvornik, Francis, *The Slavs in European History and Civilization* (Rutgers University Press, 1962)

anity in Poland is dated from that year. To thwart the German conquest further, Mieszko made his state a vassal of the Papacy, reducing the chance of a possible incorporation into the German Empire. Cordial relations between Poland and Bohemia were brief since Boleslav I died in 967 and was succeeded by his son, Boleslav II. Unable to incorporate additional Slavic territories in the west that stretched beyond the Elbe River, Mieszko shifted his expansion to a softer target in the south and east, a policy that would be continued by Polish rulers throughout the following millennium. He attacked his brother-in-law's dominion and seized Silesia, Cracow, and White Croat territory on the Bug (Buh) and San (Sian) rivers, territories that included the Cherven cities and Przemyśl.[18]

Mieszko's conquest would only last a decade, as another ambitious prince would come to occupy the territory on the Bug and San rivers, adding it to the dominion of Kyivan Rus.' The *Primary Chronicle* notes that in the year 981, "Volodimer went to Liakhs taking their cities of Przemyśl, Cherven, and other cities which are in Rus' today."[19] Volodymyr's conquest preserved the Slavonic Rite in the region and in doing so, initiated centuries of violent conflict between Rus' and Poland. The cryptic entry in the *Chronicle* has inspired various interpretations of the event. Polish historian Henryk Paszkiewicz, for example, claimed that the *Chronicle* actually referred to the town of Peremil, a Galician town that was located much further to the east of Przemyśl.[20] Because more specific information is not documented, and also due to the absence of plausible evidence to the contrary, the *Chronicle* is generally accepted as being the most reliable historical account of the medieval period. Moreover, in 1018, when the Polish King Bolesław was returning from Kyiv in conjunction with the support of his son-in-law for the Kyivan throne, he captured Przemyśl and added it to his kingdom. This clearly indicates that during the reign of Volodymyr, the town and its adjacent territory had belonged to Kyiv.

A more serious controversy centers on the towns noted in the *Chronicle*: did Poles recently conquer them or were they ethnic Polish territories? Ukrainian historian Mykhailo Hrushevsky (1866–1934), among others, considered the area to have been under Polish control at

18 Dvornik, *The Slavs*, 113.
19 See Vol. I. of Hrushevsky, Mykhailo. *History of Ukraine-Rus*, 448.
20 Paszkiewicz, Henryk. *The Origin of Russia*, 82.

the time, but not ethnically Polish.[21] Polish historian Józef Widajewicz (1889–1954) wrote, "Polish scholars usually consider Volodymyr's conquest of 981 as a conquest of Polish lands in a political and ethnic sense."[22] The ethnicity issue remains unresolved, but despite the ambiguity, it became the basis for the Polish claim to the Ukrainian territories. The conquest of Przemyśl and adjacent territories thus inaugurated several centuries of intermittent warfare between Rus' and Poland. The princes of the Rurikid Dynasty ruled the principalities of Rus'. Since clear succession had not been established, the death of a Kyivan Grand Prince frequently resulted internal strife for the Kyivan Crown and drew the neighboring rulers into the conflict. An especially violent civil war occurred after Volodymyr's death in 1015, when his sons engaged in an internecine conflict over the Grand Prince's patrimony. When Iaroslav (referred to as "Iaroslav the Wise" in the *Chronicle*) defeated his brother Sviatopolk I in 1016, the latter fled to his father-in-law, King Bolesław I Chrobry of Poland. Bolesław's forces pushed Iaroslav to Novgorod, regained the Kyivan throne for Sviatopolk, and provided the Polish king with significant plunder during his short stay in Kyiv. Most importantly, Bolesław used the conquest to attach territories west of the Bug River to Poland. Over the next few years, a violent war waged between Iaroslav and Sviatopolk, during which time their other three brothers (Borys, Hlib and Sviatoslav) were assassinated, an action that the *Chronicle* attributes to "Sviatopolk the Accursed.") In 1019, Iaroslav finally defeated Sviatopolk and assumed control of Rus', taking the title "Grand Prince of Kyiv." He seized the opportunity to re-conquer lost territory and established his namesake city of Iaroslav (Jarosław) on the west bank of the San River. For almost two centuries, recurrent conflicts ensued between the Volhynian and Galician principalities, caused mainly by a Volhynian push to bringing Galicia under its control. The internal strife occasionally brought foreign countries into the fray, but subsided in western Rus' when the principalities of Volhynia and Galicia were finally united in 1199 after the death of the reigning Galician prince ended the Galician royal line. The boyars (nobles), who wielded considerable power in the united principality, invited Prince Roman Mstyslavych of Volhynia to rule as well. The unification of Volhynia and Galicia consolidated territo-

---

21 See Vol. I. of Hrushevsky, *History*, 488.

22 Widajewicz, *Południowo-Wschodnie Kresy Polski w X i XI wieku*, 54.

ries on the Bug and San rivers that formed a boundary with Poland (See Map 2.) Prince Roman's reign, however, was brief since he was killed in 1205 while attacking Polish territory on the west bank of the Vistula River.[23] His two infant sons, Danylo and Vasyl'ko Romanovych, were exiled along with their mother and the principalities fell into chaos for several decades. In 1245, the two brothers finally gained control of the principalities and reunited them, and the Galicia-Volhynia principality remained a strong state for about a hundred years. Events in the fourteenth century, however, destabilized it once again, eventually leading to its incorporation by Poland. The male line of the ruling Romanovych Dynasty ended in 1323 when two princes died in a battle with Mongols, and the principality came under Mongol vassalage. Nevertheless, it enjoyed autonomy and even prospered.

The boyars immediately selected Prince Bolesław, a Romanovych on his mother's side, but there was a major obstacle to his candidacy. He was a Roman Catholic and had to accept Eastern Christianity, taking the name "Iurii." Despite his affinity for the Roman church, he pursued the traditional foreign policy of his adopted principality by using its existing ties with the Teutonic Knights (a German crusading order) as a counterweight against Poland and Lithuania. Relations with Lithuania were improved in 1331 when Iurii-Bolesław (as he is noted by historians) married the daughter of Gediminas (Gedymin), the Grand Prince of Lithuania. The marriage, which took place eight years after he had acquired the throne, suggested that the prince was still a boy when he was chosen to be ruler of the principality. Interestingly, his bride was baptized in the Latin Rite and the wedding took place in the Mazovian town of Płock, west of Warsaw.[24] During Iurii's reign, he encouraged foreign merchants and artisans to settle in towns and Sanok (Sianik) was the first Ukrainian town to receive Magdeburg Law, or self-rule. The charter indicates that Germans, Poles, Hungarians and Ukrainians conducted business in the town.[25] He further adopted a Polish policy that had been in place for more than a century by encouraging German and Jewish merchants and artisans to settle in Polish towns and expand commerce and industry.

---

23 Perfecky, *The Galician-Volynian Chronicle*, 17.

24 See Vol. III of Hrushevsky, *History*, 127

25 See Chubaty, N. "The Medieval History" in Vol. I. of Kubijovyč, ed. *Ukraine; A Concise Encyclopedia*, 610.

Foreign merchants had always been present in Rus', but now they came in larger numbers and brought the Catholic Church with them. While this development was well-received by the prince, the changes disturbed the Eastern Church as well as the native merchants and artisans who suddenly faced stronger competition. The opponents undoubtedly exaggerated the effects of foreign penetration; nevertheless, the prince was accused of favoring the Roman Catholic Church and foreigners above his own people and soon fell out of favor with the boyars. Because they had accepted foreign Catholic kings in the past, it is unlikely that the boyars' resentment of Iurii-Bolesław resulted solely from his attachment to the Latin Church. It is more plausible that they disliked his foreign policy and used his foreign origin, Catholic sympathies, and relationships with foreign merchants to depose him. On April 7, 1340, Iurii-Bolesław was mysteriously poisoned. Shortly after his death, foreign merchants and artisans came under attack by the locals.

Ukrainian Territories under Polish Rule (1349–1795)

For several centuries, Poland and Hungary made numerous unsuccessful attempts to bring southwestern Rus' under their control, but in the fourteenth century, the effort was better coordinated. The Polish King Casimir III (Kazimierz Wielki) and his brother-in-law, the Hungarian King Charles I (Károly Róbert), met in Visegrád in 1339 to plan the conquest of the Galician-Volhynia Principality. Károly agreed to back the Polish conquest and in turn, Casimir agreed to give the Polish crown to Louis I, son of Charles I, in the event that he would not produce male heirs.[26] Following the death of Iurii-Bolesław, the boyars immediately selected Liubart Gediminovich, a Lithuanian prince who was married to a Ukrainian princess, as their next ruler. The fact that the selection was made so quickly after Iurii-Bolesław's death suggests that the boyar clique may have been in contact with Liubart while Iurii-Bolesław was still alive.

Perhaps a week after the poisoning, Poland and Hungary attacked Rus' simultaneously and swiftly. Information on Hungarian participation is not available other than the fact that it took place. Polish sources report that Casimir's forces burned L'viv and took a great deal in plunder, but it

---

[26] See Vol. III of Hrushevsky, *History*, 128–29.

is doubtful that he could have established much control over the territory in only a matter of weeks. Considering the fact that he had already returned to Cracow by May 1340, it is most likely that the campaign was a quick raid rather than a systematic invasion designed to add the territory to the Polish Crown.[27] Nevertheless, the brief raid is difficult to explain, unless Tatars had posed a threat and deterred the Poles from engaging in a more protracted invasion. When the Poles struck again in June 1340, a nobleman from the Przemyśl area named Dmytro Dedko, who controlled the Galician principality (and was therefore a major political figure), called upon the Tatars for assistance. Fearful of being caught in a hostile country by the Tatars, the Hungarians (who showed little enthusiasm for the enterprise) hastily retreated. Once again, Casimir had failed to seize the principality and was forced to make peace with Dedko, a nobleman rather than a prince. Dedko subsequently sent a letter to the Turin merchants, probably in 1341, inviting them to settle and do business in L'viv. Dedko attributed the latest conflict with Casimir to "the devil" and, in any event, peace had been restored. The peace did not last long, however, and by the end of the decade Casimir managed to take control of western Volhynia (west of the Bug River) and Galicia. He renewed the 1339 treaty with Louis of Hungary with an additional clause stipulating that Hungary could take Galicia even if Casimir produced a male heir, with the caveat that Poland would be compensated. After Casimir's death in 1370, Hungary continues the struggle while Poland was preoccupied with the succession. Eventually, Hungary was able to reoccupy western Volhynia while holding Galicia, and the death of Louis in 1382 brought forty years of conflict to an end.

The Polish conquest of Rus' was not conducted as a typical medieval transfer of a principality from one crown to another; rather, it was a clear attempt to change the religion and culture of the people. This policy of Polonizing the region continued in various forms for the next 600 years with Poland (in its various iterations) claiming the territories of Rus' as Polish lands. The tenth century cultural, legal and religious differences between eastern Slavs living on the San and Bug compared to western Slavs on the Vistula have been debated and remained unresolved; however, by the middle of the fourteenth century, the differences

[27] See Vol. IV of Ibid, 26.

were quite apparent. Separate identities evolved based on cultural, legal, and above all, religious differences, even after the establishment of Greek Catholic Church, "...Religion has at all times separated Poles and Ukrainians by an indelible line of demarcation. The question is not one of `Catholicism' and `Orthodoxy' in the technical sense: The Eastern Rite Catholic shares a spiritual-cultural tradition with his Orthodox compatriot, and feels distinct from his Polish neighbor, a Catholic of the Latin Rite." [28]

The Polish conquest of Galicia and the part of Volhynia west of the Bug River brought immediate changes, with the annexed territory designated as the Kingdom of Rus' and divided into six districts.[29] In addition to the administrative changes, a new legal system was introduced known as the Magdeburg Law, a legal framework for self-governance that was originally adopted by the city of Magdeburg, Germany and copied by other cities and municipalities throughout Europe. It was introduced in numerous towns such as L'viv (c. 1352) and Kamianets' Podils'kyi (1374), but applied only to Catholics. Nevertheless, the Ukrainian legal system managed to survive until 1434, despite the numerous inroads of German and Polish laws.[30]

The new Polish, German and Hungarian immigrants to Galicia and Volhynia brought the presence of the Roman Catholic Church, which enjoyed numerous privileges in the Polish kingdom. In 1375, a Catholic Archdiocese was established in Halych, the old capital of Galicia. The monastic orders, especially Franciscans and Dominicans, received large tracts of land and the Roman Church was frequently appropriated properties of the Orthodox Church by the civil authorities. For example, in 1442, King Jagiełło gave an Orthodox Cathedral in Przemyśl to the

---

28 Rudnytsky, Ivan L. "Polish-Ukrainian Relations: The Burden of History" in Peter Potichnyj, ed. *Poland and Ukraine: Past and Present* (Edmonton: Canadian Institute of Ukrainian Studies, 1980), 5.

29 The Volhynia region formed two districts, Chełm (Kholm) and Bielsk (Bels'k) and in Galicia, there were four: Przemyśl (Peremyshl'), Sanok (Sianik), L'viv and Halych; The Przemyśl' district included the western towns of Rzeszów (Riashiv), Przeworsk (Perevors'k), and Jarosław (Iaroslav). Volhynian districts included the towns of Zamość (Zamostia), Grodlo (Horodlo), Włodawa (Volodova), but northwestern towns, Bels'k, Mielnik (Mel'nyk), Drohiczyn (Dorohochyn) and Berestia remained under Lithuanian control.

30 See Starosolsky, J. "Ukraine Under Polish Domination in the Fourteenth to Eighteenth Centuries" in Vol. II of Kubijovyč, ed., *Ukraine*, 46.

Catholic Church.[31] The changes were accompanied by the steady erosion of the legal and economic position of the urban Ukrainian population, who were confined to the poorer sections of town and were limited in their trading rights. The disadvantages could be partially alleviated by accepting Catholicism and many chose that route, but the new converts frequently had fewer privileges than their Polish neighbors. Toward the end of the fifteenth century, the Kingdom of Rus' was renamed the Ruthenian Province and Latin became the official language of governance. The Polish legal system gave greater rights and fewer obligations to nobility provided that they were Catholic, a policy that prompted the assimilation of both Ukrainian nobles and urban dwellers, and which had the effect of isolating the peasantry. Since Polish influence was mainly confined to towns, the rural population, who were confined to the villages and influence of the Orthodox Church, retained their identity and language preference.

While Galicia and Volhynia were engaged in a losing struggle with Poland and Hungary, Lithuania annexed territories that would eventually comprise Belarus and the Dnieper region of Ukraine. The conquest was accelerated by Lithuanian Prince Algirdas (son of Gediminas) who captured Kyiv in 1362, defeated the Tatars in 1363, and reached the Black Sea by the end of the century. The rapid advance was possible because Lithuanians accepted Orthodox religion, Ruthenian law, customs, and language and co-opted local princes and nobility by leaving the socio-economic order of conquered territories intact. By mobilizing local resources, they were able to protect the population from predatory Tatar raids and consequently gained the support of the people. In Ukrainian historiography, Lithuanian rule is viewed as a quasi-indigenous state with the Gedimin Dynasty replacing the Rurikid Dynasty.

Although the Lithuanians rapidly brought a large amount of territory under their control, it became more difficult to defend, especially against the new rising powers in the east: Muscovy and the Tatars. To protect its conquest, Lithuania was forced eventually to form a union with Poland and Poland became the principal partner in the future Commonwealth. Casimir died in 1370 without leaving a male heir, ending the male line of the Piast dynasty, and thus Galicia became attached to the

---

31 See Polonska-Vasylenko, N, "At the Dawn of the Modern Age: Ukraine Under Polish and Lithuanian Domination" in Vol. I. of Kubijovyč, ed., *Ukraine,* 623

Hungarian Crown as specified in the Polish-Hungarian treaty. King Louis of Hungary appointed a viceroy to administer his new land until 1385 when his daughter, Jadwiga, became queen of Poland, which resulted in Hungary's transfer of the Galicia principality to the Polish Crown in 1387.

To acquire the Polish throne for his daughter, Louis had made a number of concessions to the Polish nobility. The king would no longer have the power of imposing war tax or requiring the nobility to provide troops. The nobility was exempted from taxation; provinces were to be governed by indigenous nobility; and only a nobleman could become *castellan* or *starosta*, a term that was later applied to provincial officials.[32] These concessions would have a disastrous impact on Poland's future, but in the short term, it enabled Poland to assimilate Ukrainian and Lithuanian nobility by bestowing upon them the rights and privileges of the Polish nobility. The cooperation and solidarity of this new political class enabled Poland to establish control over vast territories without encountering serious opposition. However, the nobility's ever-increasing exactions of privileges, which were at first limited to change of dynasties but later demanded of each new king, seriously hampered the ability of the kings to govern effectively. At the same time, neighboring states such as Austria, Russia and Prussia, were forming strong centralized monarchies while the authority of the Polish kings diminished, a situation that ultimately led to the demise of the Polish State. Jadwiga's ascendancy to the Polish throne had far-reaching consequences for the southwestern Rus' territories. In 1385, a treaty was concluded between the two states in the Belarusian town of Krevo, where Jadwiga consented to marry Władysław II Jagiełło, the Grand Prince of Lithuania. The union effectively made him the Polish king and began the Jagiełłonian Dynasty in Poland. Jadwiga's consent required Jagiełło to accept Catholicism both for himself and the Lithuanian people and to attach the Grand Principality of Lithuania (including an extensive amount of Ukrainian territories) to the Polish Crown. In Lithuania and the Ruthenian Orthodox lands (Belarus and Ukraine), opposition quickly mobilized against the union and in 1392, Jagiełło was forced to recognize his cousin Prince Vytautus Kiejstutavič as the ruler of a separate Grand Lithuanian Principality.

---

32 Magocsi, Paul Robert. *A History of Ukraine*, 132.

Since the Union of Krewo, Poland and Lithuania were united through a common king; however, the Polish side was dissatisfied with the arrangement and strove to annex the Grand Principality of Lithuania, including much of the Ukrainian territory. The matter finally came to a head in January 1569 when King Sigismund III of Lithuania called a joint session of the Polish-Lithuanian parliament in Lublin for yet another attempt to forge a stronger union. A number of developments then favored the union, especially since Lithuania was engaged in protracted and unsuccessful wars to halt Moscow's westward expansion. To the south, the newly formed Khanate of Crimea, together with the Tatar tribes in the Black Sea steppes, began raiding Ukrainian lands and sacked Kyiv in 1482. Raiding the sedentary population for booty was a time honored tradition in the region and by then, slaves had become a new commodity that was added to the conquest. Large numbers of people were captured during the frequent raids and brought to the Crimean Peninsula, which as a new vassal of Turkey, had access to the Middle Eastern slave markets. Hard pressed to defend their territory, Lithuanians increasingly relied on Polish military assistance. In addition to the military needs, there was growing support for the union among the lesser nobility who had shouldered the burdens of war but enjoyed fewer privileges compared to their Polish counterparts. Princes and wealthy nobles who were afraid of losing their privileges opposed the union, and commoners were not permitted to participate in the deliberations. On the Polish side, the nobility was eager to gain a foothold in the vast and rich eastern territories; therefore, Sigismund was intent on fusing the two lands into a strong centralized state.

Besides establishing a union, the Polish side sought to place the southern portion of Ruthenia (the Ukrainian provinces) under direct Polish control. Polish delegates attempted to provide historical and legal justification for the annexation by employing selective use and imaginative interpretations of distant historical events to make their case. The Polish claim to Kyiv, for example, was based on the aforementioned campaign of "Bolesław the Brave" and his son-in-law Sviatopolk, in which the former had captured and looted Kyiv in 1018 and then left the city after a short stay. The fifteenth century Polish historian Jan Długosz alleged that Bolesław had "imposed a modest tribute" on Iaroslav the

Wise.[33] The supposed tribute portrayed the Kyivan princes as having been subordinated to Poland, giving the Polish Crown a legal claim to the territory. With respect to the territory on the Polish border, the claims were somewhat less fanciful since some towns had changed hands during several centuries of warfare.

When the legislative session finally concluded, the Union of Lublin transformed the previous personal union between ruling heads to form what became a federal union, or Commonwealth (*Rzeczpospolita*). The two lands would have a single parliament and elect a common king, who at the same time, would serve as the Grand Prince of Lithuania. The newly created Polish-Lithuanian Commonwealth would adopt a single currency and a common foreign policy.[34] The Grand Principality retained the Lithuanian and Belarusian territories while Poland took the Ukrainian lands including Kyiv, Bratslav (located southwest of Kyiv), Podilia, and the lower Dnieper region. "The 1569 Lublin Union was thus a repartition of old Rus', on terms favorable to Poland."[35]

The formation of the Commonwealth and its extension to the east brought some elements of western learning to the region, which resulted in an invigorated Ukrainian culture and learning environment. At the same time, the vast territory was divided into Polish provinces that did not participate in the governance as a single entity. The Union of Lublin politically solidified the Commonwealth and the question arose once again about the unification of the church. Some bishops seized upon the idea of unifying the Eastern Church with Rome and acknowledging the Pope of Rome instead of the Patriarch of Constantinople, since they had more cultural contact with the west and doing so would provide some political advantages. The antecedents for unification, however, had been in place much earlier in history. Ukrainian princes occasionally established contacts with Rome in times of disturbance. For example, in 1247, after the Mongol invasion, Prince Danylo sought to create an anti-Mongol crusade and appealed to Pope Innocent IV for military aid through his papal delegate, Giovanni da Pian del Carpine (John of Plano Carpini). The

---

33 See Pelenski, "The Incorporation of the Ukrainian Lands of Old Rus into the Crown of Poland," in Lunt, Horace G., ed., *American Contribution to the Seventh International Congress of Slavists,* 39.

34 Polonska-Vasylenko, N. "At the Dawn of the Modern Age" in Vol. I. of Kubijovyč, ed., *Ukraine*, 623.

35 Snyder, Timothy, *The Reconstruction of Nations*, 105.

pope was receptive, hoping to bring the region under his control, but little came of the consultations since the Vatican had been unable to provide military aid. Nevertheless, Danylo received a papal crown from the pope and it's possible that his grandson, Iurii, may have received a crown as well. This incident became the catalyst for discussions concerning the relationship of the Orthodox Church and the papacy.

Another attempt at church unification was made in 1429, supported by "Metropolitan Isidore of all Rus'"[36] and Pope Eugene IV, which resulted in the Union of Florence. This union reconciled the theological differences and administrative practices of the two churches. Both churches were to be subordinated to the pope and enjoy equal rights. The union was never implemented, however, because the Catholic Church in Poland and Lithuania intended to Latinize the Ukrainian population and was therefore against granting equal status to the Eastern Church. There was little support among the Orthodox hierarchy as well since they feared that closer ties to the papacy would eventually obliterate the distinctiveness of their church. Nevertheless, the proposed union established a precedent and some agreements reached in Florence were incorporated later in the Union of Brest (1596). Despite the rejection of the Union of Florence, there were forces at work pushing the Orthodox Church to embrace the papacy. Since the conquest of western Rus', the Orthodox Church had been under siege, and secular rulers traditionally had a greater role in the administration of Eastern Church than in the West. The Grand Prince of Lithuania and the King of Poland had the right to appoint bishops or even metropolitans. Because the rulers were Catholics, and were often ardent supporters of Rome, their decisions did not always reflect the interests of the Orthodox Church. Local Polish authorities placed additional restrictions on the Orthodox Church and the urban population, conditions that resulted in the gradual polonization of the nobility, and thus the strata of society that normally provided material and intellectual stimulation to the church were falling by the wayside. To further complicate matters, the Protestant Reformation and the Catholic Counter Reformation further degraded religious tolerance in the region.

In an attempt to reverse the deteriorating position of the church, some Orthodox bishops and secular leaders, headed by Ukrainian Prince

---

[36] Polonska-Vasylenko, "The Ukrainian Church in the Lithuanian-Polish Realm and the Kozak Hetman State" in Vol. I. of Kubijovyč, *Ukraine,* 145.

Kostiantyn Ostrozky, sought to reach an accommodation with the papacy.[37] Other bishops were further agitated by unpopular changes in the church that had been instituted by Jeremiah II, the Patriarch of Constantinople who had placed all of the church brotherhoods under his authority, thereby removing them from the jurisdictions of the local bishops. The brotherhoods were organized in towns by merchants and artisans with the initial purpose of maintaining church buildings, but over time, they expanded their activities to providing care for orphans and widows, supporting hospitals, and establishing schools. As the influence of the brotherhoods increased, they attempted to raise the morals of the Orthodox bishops and the clergy, which brought them into direct conflict with the local hierarchy. In 1595, the growing political conflicts prompted four Orthodox bishops to establish contact with Polish officials and papal representatives for the purpose of establishing a new church union.[38] By the end of the year, the pope had approved the union, agreed that the new church would retain the Orthodox Rite and Old Church Slavonic as the liturgical language, but the pope would have the final authority in respect to dogma. When the secret negotiations became public, the union created an uproar with the laity as well as a number of bishops and priests. Some feared the complete domination of their church by the papacy while others, like Prince Ostrozky, who had earlier supported the union, resented the conspiratorial approach and organized an opposition movement.[39] The opponents contended that the matter should have been openly discussed in the Orthodox communities and in consultation with the Patriarch of Constantinople. In response to the opposition, the council of hierarchs held synod in the city of Brest where they set about resolving their differences, drafting 33 articles of union with the Roman Catholic Church. The Orthodox side had a larger representation at the council but ultimately could not prevail. Both sides appealed to King Sigismund III, who sided with the faction favoring the union in the interest of strengthening state unity. He promised to protect the Uniate Church, as it came to be known, and to grant the Uniate clergy the same rights enjoyed by the Catholic clergy, giving their bishops seats in the Senate.

---

37 Gudziak, Borys A. *Crisis and Reform*, 209.

38 Subtelny, Orest. *Ukraine: A History*, 100.

39 Snyder, *The Reconstruction*, 110.

Ironically, the Union of Brest increased religious animosities in the Ukrainian lands, where each church organization began accusing the other of treachery and deceit. Due to opposition from the Polish Government and the Polish Catholic Church, the Uniates did not receive all of the rights promised at Brest, and the Orthodox became enraged as more of their churches and ecclesiastical lands were being transferred to the Uniate church. The Orthodox Church continued to lose ground until the partition of Poland at the end of the eighteen-century when most Ukrainian lands were incorporated into the Russian Empire.

In addition to its impact on Orthodoxy, the consolidation of the Commonwealth brought about significant political, economic, and social changes. Under this new republic style of government, the process of selecting a sovereign became a lengthy, disruptive affair that would gradually erode royal authority and the ability of the king to effectively govern because much of the actual political power was concentrated in the upper strata of Polish nobility. Newly elected kings had to sign agreements with the nobility guaranteeing their prerogatives, and the demands increased with each successive election. The nobility comprised perhaps eight percent of the population, and all members of the noble class had equal rights and nominally governed the country, but the real power rested with a limited number of very wealthy nobles or magnates. The nobility as a class ranged from the magnates at the top, whose estates may have encompassed a territory the size of a county or in some cases even a province with towns and villages, to those at the very bottom whose economic situation did not differ much from the peasantry. The huge estates *(latifundia)*, were especially large in Ukraine: The Ostrozky family owned "l,300 villages, 100 towns, 40 castles, and 600 churches" and the Vyshnevts'kyi family owned nearly the entire Left Bank (east of the Dnieper River) of the Kiev palatinate (claiming 230,000 subjects), and in Volhynia, 13 noble families owned 57 percent of the land."[40] Their political and economic domination extended to towns and the urban population. Towns were deprived of the right to elect delegates to the Diet in 1505 and later restrictions were placed on their trading rights. Local merchants were taxed on their commercial activities and prohibited from engaging in foreign trade. The nobles, on the other hand, could buy goods

40 Magocsi, *A History of Ukraine*, 145.

from foreign merchants and export their own goods without taxation. The unequal tax burden and restrictions on trade impoverished urban residents, forcing many merchants and artisans to work for local lords on their estates.[41] In the declining towns, the urban Orthodox population suffered more than most since special restrictions were placed on them, such as being denied the right to participate in town's government or to join some guilds. Limits were usually placed on the number of urban dwellers permitted to live in towns, and those who made the cut were confined to special sections.[42] In religious matters, the Orthodox dwellers were required to contribute to the support of the Catholic clergy and their church processions were limited to the Ukrainian sections of towns.

The powerful social and economic pressures created in the Commonwealth made a significant impact on Ukrainian society, and forced much of the nobility and urban dwellers to change creed and assimilate into Polish society to avoid discrimination. Of all the societal strata, the Ukrainian nobility was most vulnerable to assimilation, since the Polish nobility enjoyed numerous privileges, had fewer obligations, and Polish culture was more refined than the indigenous culture. Understandably, the Ukrainian nobles were eager to join this privileged world, even at the price of abandoning their ancestral culture and religion. The choice was rarely presented in such stark terms because the abandonment was a slow, subtle process that began with acculturation. They imitated Polish dress, manners, customs, and began using the Polish language, and a more complete and final assimilation was usually accomplished after conversion to Catholicism, frequently through intermarriage. The church began to play a more prominent role in society, and religion was a more important distinguishing factor than ethnicity at that time. A new convert joined the Polish community by worshipping and socializing with the church members, a process that naturally led to intermarriage and assimilation. Intermarriages were given such importance that even kings encouraged and promoted them. The Roman Catholic Archbishop Pokhornyts'kyi of L'viv, himself of Ukrainian ancestry, wrote that the king encouraged the Polish nobility to marry wealthy Orthodox widows or single women, with marriage conditioned upon the Orthodox spouse

---

41 Subtelny, *Ukraine: A History*, 89.

42 Polonska-Vasylenko, "At the Dawn of the Modern Age" in Vol. I. of Kubijovyč, ed., *Ukraine*, 625.

accepting Catholicism.[43] Such royal matchmaking could not have affected many families, but this practice underscores the importance that Polish society placed on conversion, intermarriage, and assimilation.

Language became another instrument of assimilation since the Polish language was used in administration and in the upper strata of society. By the sixteenth century, considerable linguistic inroads were made along the western border of the former Galician-Volhynian Principality. A Polish atlas shows that the Ukrainian towns of Rzeszów (Riashiv), Jarosław (Iaroslav), and Krosno (Korosno) fell within the Polish speaking areas, but along the crest of the Carpathians, Ukrainians migrated westward into territories that eventually became the future western Lemko region.[44]

Although the urban population was subjected to political and economic discrimination, it managed to resist assimilation better than did the nobility. Urban residents petitioned the government to remove restrictions placed on them and demanded the same rights enjoyed by their Catholic neighbors. In the end, the petitions provided little relief, and people relied on their own resources. Some towns organized brotherhoods, which were fraternal organizations that supported churches, schools and other cultural activities. As a consequence of legal and economic impediments, the Ukrainian population became a minority in many towns due to both assimilation and the influx of Catholics encouraged by the Polish crown. The migrants were mostly Jews and Germans, who themselves were quickly Polonized, especially in such western towns as Krosno, Sanok, and Przemyśl. Jews, on the other hand, retained their religion and identity. The rural population, on the other hand, was largely shielded from the Polish influence and preserved its culture and religion better than other groups. Unlike the nobility and the urban people, serfs could not improve their political and economic position by changing religion. The peasants sought to protect their rights by petitioning the Crown, refusing to work on Polish estates, or resorting to violence, although such actions did not improve their situation. Because Polish influence was confined principally to urban areas, it resulted in the development of Polish towns and Ukrainian villages, essentially segregating the two groups along religious, linguistic and socioeconomic lines.

---

43 See Vol. VI of Hrushevsky, *History*, 238.

44 Czaplinski, Władysław and Tadeusz Ladogorski, eds., *Atlas Historyczny Polski*, 23.

Despite Polish acculturation and assimilation policies, Ukrainian resistance to Polish domination smoldered in Galicia and Volhynia for many years. The Polish State was incapable of reaching political accommodation with Ruthenians in the vast territory that included much of modern Belarus and Ukraine, and this inability continued into the twentieth century. The lack of Ukrainian political influence and the increasing exploitation of the peasantry eventually fueled the Cossack and peasant rebellions that contributed to the ultimate demise of the Commonwealth. The Cossacks had formed militarized settlements in the steppe lands by the sixteenth century as a defense against Tatar raids, eventually evolving into a quasi-military state along the Dnieper River. Most notably, the Cossack uprising of 1648, led by Bohdan Khmelnytsky, became a pivotal event in the history of Russia, Ukraine and Poland. The rebellion initially sought to increase Cossack rights in the Polish state, but as the campaign became more successful, Khmelnytsky's view of the struggle expanded into a national liberation campaign: "I shall fight to free the whole Ruthenian nation from Liakh bondage…I shall fight for our Orthodox faith."[45]

When the Cossacks advanced from the Dnieper and entered Galicia, uprisings broke out in Treboval, Ternopil', Kalush, Rohatyn, Drohobych, and other cities. The urban population, occasionally led by the clergy who comprised a sizeable share of the adult male population, joined forces with neighboring villages and offered considerable opposition.[46] The rebellion enjoyed early successes, as Khmelnytsky was able to forge a powerful force consisting of Cossacks and peasants that reportedly had over 120,000 men as they advanced toward L'viv in western Ukraine.[47] Initial victories, however, could not be sustained as permanent gains, and he was eventually forced to form an alliance with Moscow. In 1658, Khmelnysky's agreement with the Tsar of Moscow brought the Muscovites into the conflict. By 1667, when the conflict finally ended, Russia acquired all the territory east of Dnieper, as well as the city of Kyiv and the surrounding environs, but the Cossack lands on the Dnieper were

45 The Liakhs were a Polish tribe that inhabited the upper Vistula, but Ukrainians applied the term to all Poles and it eventually acquired a pejorative connotation. See Vol. VIII of Hrushevsky, *History*, 521.

46 See Vol. VI of Hrushevsky, *History*, 260–62.

47 Ibid, 478.

placed under joint Russian-Polish control. Russia had gained a foothold in Ukraine that eventually led to an incorporation of most Ukrainian lands into the Russian Empire.

Despite the failure to gain independence, Ukrainian historians claim that Khmelnytsky's efforts laid the foundation for building a modern Ukrainian State.[48] The rebellion marked the decline of the Polish-Lithuanian Commonwealth as the polity sustained large material and population losses; the old feudal system was not established on the Dnieper for decades.[49] Polish nobility and Jews were primary targets of the Cossacks, and the local population joined the revolt and attacked both groups, occasionally using farm implements. Jews were an important cog in the Polish feudal system, especially in Ukraine where huge estates required Jewish business expertise.[50] Leaseholding (*arenda*) was the principal mechanism that involved Jews in the economic activity of the country. The system was pervasive since "fixed assets, such as land, mills, inns, breweries, and distilleries, or special rights, such as the right to collect customs duties and taxes" were leased.[51] Roughly half of the Polish-Lithuanian crown lands in the Ukrainian territories had been leased by 1616.[52] The system exploited the peasantry to the fullest and the common people rarely had contact with the landlords or property owners, but came in contact with their Jewish agents on a daily basis. In times of upheaval, the outrage of the common people was transferred to the Jews who were much more vulnerable than their Polish masters. A Jewish chronicler wrote that Ukrainians "...were looked upon as lowly and inferior beings, and became the slaves and handmaids of the Polish people and the Jews..."[53]

Despite the fact that the Khmelnytsky revolution may have introduced the concept of a national state, it was a disaster for Ukraine in almost every other way. A good part of the country was devastated by the prolonged warfare, another dominating power (Moscow) had been

48 Subtelny, 1988, p.138, citing Viachyslav Lypynsky.

49 Historian Timothy Snyder places Commonwealth losses at about one-third out of an estimated 10 million people. See Snyder, *The Reconstruction of Nations*, 114

50 For an excellent discussion of the Jewish economic activities in Poland, see Rosman, 1990.

51 Magocsi, *A History of Ukraine*, 147.

52 Subtelny, *Ukraine,* 124.

53 Cited in Snyder, *The Reconstruction of Nations*, 112.

brought to Ukraine, and the Orthodox Church faced great difficulties. Under Cossack protection, Kyiv developed into an important educational and ecclesiastical center, but after the conclusion of hostilities, the city was placed under Russian control and eventually subordinated to the Patriarch of Moscow. The Orthodox Church in the Commonwealth was cut off from the support of the Orthodox Metropolitan in Kyiv and continuously lost ground to the Uniate Church. Eventually, one eparch in Belarus was all that remained of the Orthodox church in the Commonwealth. The invigorated Uniate Church, on the other hand, gained status as a separate church within the Catholic Church, although it was still susceptible to Latinizing influences since much of its hierarchy was Polonized. Nevertheless, the church nurtured indigenous Ukrainian culture and promoted education spearheaded by religious orders.

While the seventeenth century Cossack rebellion seriously weakened the Commonwealth, political and economic conditions in the next century further precipitated its demise. The government was a decentralized political structure comprised of an elective monarchy and a parliament run by a noble class (*szlachta*) which had expanded over time, progressively weakening the Polish crown and the economy. In contrast to Western Europe's evolving industrialization which gave rise to urban industrial centers, the Commonwealth nobility placed a heavy emphasis on agriculture and rural manufacturing on plantations, which had the effect of limiting urbanization and rendering the Commonwealth a backward agrarian country.

As Polish landlords sought to bring increasingly more land under their control for cultivation, they enticed the peasantry to migrate deeper into the steppe by suspending corvée (feudal) obligations for a period of time (usually a decade or two). The Ukrainian frontier had always been a volatile and dangerous region since it lacked the natural topographical protection offered by mountains and forests, therefore making it susceptible to Tatar raids. The native frontiersmen were accustomed to freedom, and could not be readily transformed into docile serfs. Likewise, peasant settlers had become accustomed to handling arms to defend themselves from raids, and were therefore less inclined to be subservient compared to serfs in the interior lands.

Ukrainian rebellions during this period were usually extremely violent given the fact that the people were oppressed as a nationality as well as religiously and economically. Moreover, most uprisings were not centrally organized and directed with specific objectives; rather, much of the fighting was conducted by enraged local mobs that frequently engaged in brutal, senseless slaughters. In the eighteenth century, after the corvée suspension period expired for peasants who had migrated to the steppe, the obligation was again re-instituted. This prompted a number of peasant revolts on the west bank of the Dnieper, with rebels called the Haidamaks engaging in hit-and-run tactics. The most serious rebellion occurred in 1768 when a small group led by the Zaporizhian Cossack Maksym Zalizniak was able to attract a large peasant following as the Cossacks made their way west through the Kiev palatinate and into Podolia and southern Volhynia. During these raids, Zalizniak's band engaged in brutal attacks on the population, targeting Polish landowners as well as Roman Catholic and Uniate clergy.[54] Their numbers had increased to about 2,000 by late June, when they attacked the fortified town of Uman. Ivan Gonta, a Cossack officer in the Polish service in Uman, defected to the rebels and joined his forces with Zalizniak's. Together, they mercilessly slaughtered the town's Poles and Jews, and Uman quickly fell to Haidamak control. The chaos and instability prompted Russia's Catherine II to dispatch Russian troops from Podolia to eliminate the Haidamaks.[55] After the rebels were defeated, about 5,000 to 7,000 were killed by the Poles. Zalizniak was sent to Siberia, and Gonta, considered a traitor, "...was brought to Warsaw and tortured, his dismembered body was put on public display."[56]

As a result of both the Cossack and peasant uprisings, Russia's influence on the Commonwealth increased militarily and politically. It began interfering in the elections of Polish kings and assumed the right to protect the Orthodox population in the Commonwealth. By that time, Poland was no longer a viable state and Prussia feared that the Commonwealth would be absorbed by Russia. Accordingly, a plan was jointly devised by Prussia and Russia to partition Poland, and Austria was invited as the third participant. [57] During the three partitions, which occurred in 1772, 1793, and 1795, the Commonwealth was divided among the three

[54] Magocsi, *A History of Ukraine*, 299–300.
[55] Subtelny, *Ukraine*, 193.
[56] Magocsi, *A History of Ukraine*, 300.
[57] Ibid, 301.

participating countries and the Polish State effectively ceased to exist. Ukrainian lands were distributed between the Russian and Austrian empires with most of the Ukrainian territory annexed to Russia. Austria gained Galicia and retained Bukovyna and Transcarpathia.

Ukrainian lands on the San and Bug Rivers that had shared a common history since Grand Prince Volodymyr's tenth century conquest were suddenly partitioned between the two empires. As a result, they would experience very different political realities for the next century and-a-half.

Volhynia under Russian Rule

After the partitions, Russia introduced its administrative structure in the acquired territory and the Medieval Volhynian Principality became just another province in the empire. The new province, which included adjacent lands in Ukraine and Belarus, had a large Uniate population as well as a sizeable Polish population that continued to exercise considerable influence. To blend the new lands with the rest of the empire, Russia had to tackle the problem of religious affiliation, which still served as a marker for ethnic identity. During the next century, Polish rebellions and the gradual conversion of the Uniates dominated the events in the province. In 1795, Catherine II replaced the Uniate bishoprics with Orthodox bishoprics and issued decrees urging the Uniates to join the Orthodox Church. During her reign, approximately two million Uniates in Ukraine and Belarus converted to Orthodoxy. The Polish insurrection of 1830–31 provoked Russia to curtail the rights of the Uniate Church, which effectively occurred in 1839. Despite the Uniates' very minimal support for the rebellion, the church continued to function under the close supervision of a viceroy. Later, in the second Polish rebellion (1863–1864) some Uniate clergy and seminarians participated in an insurrection that ultimately resulted in Russia's decision to eliminate the Uniate Church within its borders and to institute Russification policies.

The 1905 Russian Revolution brought about significant political changes, which especially impacted the Kholm and Podlachia regions. Tsar Nicholas II issued a decree on religious toleration, permitting people to change their religion. The toleration decree did not, however, lift the ban on the Uniate Church and many former Uniates who had previously been forced to join the Orthodox Church began converting to Roman Catholicism. In the Kholm region, approximately 170,000 of the Orthodox population of 450,000 converted to Catholicism, and in southern Podlachia, 58 percent chose the Roman Catholic Church.[58] In Ukrainian communities, hostilities developed over the mass conversion and the Orthodox faithful began calling the new converts "turncoats" (*kalakuts*) since conversion to Catholicism essentially amounted to becoming a Pole. To stem the tide, the Russian Holy Synod established a separate Orthodox eparchy for the region and appointed a less dogmatic bishop as its administrator. Some local liturgical practices (derived from Catholic practices) were permitted and sermons were allowed to be conducted in the Ukrainian language.

The newly instituted policies of religious tolerance paved the way for improvements to educational access and the development of a secular Ukrainian intelligentsia. Elementary schools were established in large numbers and teachers were trained in several local seminaries. The more liberal atmosphere and increased literacy stimulated the revival of a secular culture, promoted largely by teachers. The Enlightenment Society (*Prosvita)* was organized in 1868 in L'viv to promote Ukrainian language and culture. It established a branch in Kholm and published books, a weekly newspaper, and a magazine. Private individuals augmented the publishing activities and the Kholm Orthodox brotherhood was formed in 1885. In 1912, it began publishing a daily newspaper, *Kholmskaia Rus'.* The increased national awareness prompted local leaders, especially brotherhood organizations, to demand a separate province (*guberniia*) for the Ukrainian population. The issue, which was seen as a way of reducing Polish influence, was debated in the Russian *Duma* (parliament), but was opposed by Polish delegates, delegates of other minorities, and the socialists. Nevertheless, the Duma eventually approved the formation of the new *guberniia* and Nicholas II issued the necessary decree on June 21, 1912. The borders of the new *guberniia* were based on ethnographic studies and consisted of six counties within the Podlachia and Kholm regions, which encompassed 4,037 square miles with a population of 841,800 by 1914. Of that population, Ukrainians comprised the majority with 53.2 percent, Poles 23.9 percent, Jews 15.4 percent and Germans

---

58 Kubijovyč, Volodymyr. "Kholm region" in Vol. II of *Ukraine*, 481 and "Podlachia" in Vol. IV of Ibid, 60.

and Russians 3.7 percent each.[59] The province was placed under the auspices of the Ministry of Internal Affairs and the schools were supervised by the superintendent of the Kyiv school system. Although the establishment of the guberniia was a significant step forward for the formation of Ukrainian secular society, the subsequent outbreak of World War I in 1914 and the Polish occupation after the war would curtail its development.

Ukrainians in Austrian Galicia

In 1772, during the first partition of Poland, the empire of Austria annexed most of the territories of the old Rus' principality of Halych-Volhynia but ultimately retained only Galicia.[60] The Austrian annexation improved the situation for the Ukrainians (called *Ruthenians* by the Austrians.) Key developments in this period were generally positive toward the cultural ascendency of Ukrainians living within the empire, although Poles retained a much higher socioeconomic and cultural position due to carry-over of the robust Polish noble class that had developed during the Commonwealth period. Nevertheless, the feudal burden of the peasantry was reduced and Ukrainians received greater legal protection than they had enjoyed under the Commonwealth.[61] On the local level, however, protections were frequently curtailed because the Polish landowning class and their supporters generally administered the local offices and courts. Nevertheless, while Ukrainians in Podlachia and Kholm regions continued to endure exploitation and discrimination within the Russian Empire, the situation of their compatriots in Galicia had significantly improved under Austrian rule during the reign of Maria Theresa and her son Joseph II. The Habsburg rulers introduced the principle of enlightened absolutism, an ideology that advocated for more benevolent treatment of the common people in the empire. Joseph II sought to improve condition of the peasantry, expand industry, and establish compulsory education using local vernacular languages. To further bind the various national and religious groups to the empire, a large army was maintained and a

---

59 Kubijovyč, Volodymyr. "Kholm Gubernia" in Vol. II of Kubijovyč, ed. *Ukraine*, 480.

60 Later, after the Napoleonic Wars in the early nineteeth century, Austria retained only Galicia while Volhynia was annexed by the Russian Empire.

61 Subtelny, *Ukraine*, 216.

centralized bureaucracy was established to improve government operations, giving Vienna greater control over the outlying regions.

The most immediate and welcomed changes for the peasantry included restrictions on the corvée requirements, which had previously amounted to five or six days of work per week and per household were suddenly reduced to three days with an annual limit of 156 days. Peasants were given legal possession of the plots they cultivated, the right to marry and change residence without their landlord's permission (provided that a suitable replacement was found) and the right to sue their landlord if their rights were violated. In religious matters, the changes were even more fundamental.

Religious differences between Roman Catholic Poles and Uniate Ukrainians had always been a contentious issue. To improve relations, Austrian Empress Maria Therese renamed the Uniate church as the "Greek Catholic Church," a tribute to its Byzantine Orthodox origins and a nominal step toward providing parity with the Roman Catholic Church. In additional to the nominal changes, the Greek Catholic clergy received government stipends and the Austrians established the first state-sponsored Greek Catholic seminaries in an effort to raise the educational level of the clergy, an action that also raised their social and material status. However, real equality was never achieved because the powerful Polish nobility backed Roman Catholics. (The Greek Catholic clergy, for the most part, represented Ukrainian serfs.) To sever any relations between the metropolitan of Kyiv and the Galician church, Vienna re-established the metropolitinate of L'viv, which had been abolished four centuries earlier. The act made the Greek Catholic Church in Galicia the de facto national autonomous church. In time, the Greek Catholic clergy became the principal literate segment in Ukrainian society and would play a leading role in the cultural and national revival of Ukrainians in Galicia at the beginning of the nineteenth century.

During the early years of Austrian rule in Galicia, the educated class among Ukrainians consisted largely of the clergy, and the Greek Catholic Church had two clerical groups: a monastic order (monks) who comprised the hierarchy, and parish priests who were permitted to marry. The latter provided education for their children who in turn played a major role in cultural and political affairs of the province. Educational opportunities were extended to the common people as well, and as elementary and secondary schools were established, the Ukrainian vernacular was permitted as a language of instruction. Expanding the school system met numerous difficulties and opposition from local government administrations, which were administered largely by Poles. Thus, despite the fact that Vienna's reforms raised the overall economic and educational levels among the Ukrainian population, they remained comparatively lower than those of the Polish population.

In time, the Austrian school reforms (although never fully implemented) managed to produce a larger pool of educated Ukrainians in both the clerical and secular spheres. Scholarly interests among the population began to expand beyond church matters into topics such as language and ethnography, and a number of studies were produced on these subjects.[62] However, the studies, which were written either in Latin, German or Polish, had little effect on the larger society because of the problem of widespread illiteracy among the Ukrainian population. The impetus for the new interests came from several sources, including the Romantic Movement, which emanated from the German lands and emphasized national language and culture, cultural revivals among other Slavs in the Habsburg Empire, and competition with Poles who used their own national language in cultural affairs. The romantic glorification of the common folk, their language, and culture became especially popular with the budding Ukrainian intelligentsia, most of whom were only a generation or two removed from the village.

The 1830–1831 Polish rebellion in the Russian Empire prompted Poles in Galicia to demand a greater role for Polish language and culture in the province, with the vision of eventually establishing a new Polish State within the pre-1772 boundaries. Numerous conspiratorial groups were formed to promote these demands and many young Ukrainians joined them and in the process became politicized. When Poles organized an Association of the Polish People, Ukrainians demanded that the name be changed to the "Association of the Polish People and the Ruthenian People": however, the Poles refused to make the change.[63] This disagreement raised the question about the place of Ukrainians in the reconstituted Polish State that stretched (in the Polish parlance) from the Baltic Sea to the Black Sea. The Poles sidestepped the contentious issue by

62 Magocsi, *A History of Ukraine*, 400–401.

63 Kozik, Jan. *The Ukrainian National Movement in Galicia*, 128.

denying that Ukrainians were a separate people. In their view, they were a regional variant of Poles who spoke a Polish dialect, but accepted Eastern Christianity, the only substantive distinction.[64] The inability of Poles to accept Ukrainians as a separate people was necessitated by the Polish concept of a "Historical Poland." The Polish national state could not conceivably stretch "from sea to sea" if Ukrainians were to be acknowledged as a separate people, and this fundamental issue would be a source of conflict for the next one hundred years.

A turning point in the development of Ukrainian national awareness occurred in 1848 with a series of political upheavals throughout Europe that came to be known as the "Springtime of Nations." These revolutions marked the first continent-wide collapse of traditional authority and had the effect of spreading nationalist ideas throughout Europe, including Galicia. The revolutions began in Paris in February and reached Vienna by March where liberal-minded professionals and students began agitating for civil and political reforms including the abolition of serfdom. The demonstrators forced the resignation of Prince Klemens von Metternich (architect of the old order at the Congress of Vienna in 1815) and compelled the Emperor to undertake liberal reforms.

The news of events in Vienna reached L'viv on March 19 and galvanized the Polish community to action. They petitioned the Emperor demanding extensive political rights for Poles and organized a Polish National Council in L'viv on April 13, followed by the establishment of regional councils. Poles assumed then, as they had done in 1830, that Galicia was a Polish province and invited Ukrainians to join the council. The revolution pushed a small group of educated Galician Ukrainians, whose intellectual interests had previously been confined to folklore and linguistic problems, into the political arena.[65] Having by that time reached a greater level of national awareness and organizational skill, they petitioned the Emperor on April 19. They declared their loyalty to the Austrian crown and asked for the use of Ukrainian language in education and government, access to government employment, equal rights for Greek Catholic clergy, and the recognition of Ukrainians as a separate people. The petition was followed by organizational activities similar to that of Poles. Bishop Iakhymovych called a meeting on May 2 at the St. George

[64] Ibid, 129.
[65] Subtelny, *Ukraine*, 247.

Cathedral in L'viv to consider the current developments. Over three hundred individuals representing all strata of Ukrainian society except the peasantry assembled that evening. In addition to founding the "Supreme Ruthenian Council," which consisted of sixty-six members, the participants organized an administrative apparatus consisting of an executive board and departments for correspondence, finance, national affairs, constitutional issues, education, and religious matters.[66] In the following weeks, the council was able to organize thirteen regional and fifty local councils with the support of the Greek Catholic Church. These political activities of the Church, coupled with its educational and cultural work, demonstrated that "the Greek Catholic clergy became the pioneers of the Galicia's Ukrainian renaissance."[67] The Council established the first Ukrainian newspaper, the Galician Star *(Zoria Halyts'ka)* on May 15 and initiated contacts with Ukrainian leaders in Bukovyna and Transcarpathia. Besides the organizational work, the council prepared a proclamation, which reviewed the history of Kyivan Rus' and its collapse, and emphasized that the Galician Ukrainians were part of a 15 million-person nation with its own separate language. It pledged loyalty to the Emperor and the Austrian State, and reflected the Ukrainian view of the Austrian crown as the guarantor of Ukrainian progress in Galicia. The remainder of the document dealt with the protection of the Greek Catholic Church and the clergy, the expanded use of the Ukrainian language in education, publishing, and in government. The proclamation was published in three languages in the *Galician Star*, with 3,000 copies in Ukrainian, 2,000 in Polish, and 1,000 in German. Despite the massive distribution, the proclamation did not extend much beyond the issues raised in the April 19 petition.

The council's activities were greatly aided by Austrian Count Franz Stadion, who was appointed governor of Galicia in 1846 after another unsuccessful Polish revolt that year in the Cracow region.[68] The new governor realized that Ukrainians who perceived Poles as exploiters could blunt Polish revolutionary activities, and the 1848 Revolution gave him the opportunity to implement his policy. After Poles issued their proclamation, the governor urged Ukrainians to present their demands to

---

66 Kozik, Jan. *The Ukrainian National Movement*, 195.

67 Himka John Paul. *The Greek Catholic Church and Nation-Building in Galicia*, 442.

68 Rudnytsky, Ivan I. *The Ukrainians,* 31.

the Emperor in a document similar to his proposal submitted to Vienna in 1847.[69] In addition to the advice and encouragement, Stadion helped financially to launch the *Galician Star* and requested that the Austrian government provide funds to support Ukrainian activities. At the same time, he assured Vienna that the Ruthenian Council would not seek union with Russia, but instead would oppose the activities of the Polish Council. Stadion further urged the government to abolish serfdom in Galicia as a way of undermining the position of the Polish radicals who also demanded abolition and to gain support of the peasantry. By the Emperor's decree, serfdom was abolished in Galicia on April 23, 1848, several months before it was eliminated in the rest of the Empire. This act gained the gratitude of the Ukrainians who now viewed Vienna as their protector against the rapacious Polish nobility. Stadion's Polish opponents, on the other hand, charged that he had invented Ukrainian separatism.

While the struggle in Galicia was political in nature, an armed struggle appeared in Hungary, headed by Lajos Kossuth, a liberal politician who was later credited as being the "Father of Hungarian democracy." The Hungarians were aided by Polish émigrés, commanded by General Bem who had fought with Napoleon in his Russian invasion and in the 1830–31 Revolution, and also by many Poles who crossed the Carpathians when the revolt broke out in Hungary. Governor Stadion, suspicious of Polish loyalty, forbade the formation of military units. The Hungarian insurrection prompted Vienna to organize territorial units, the so-called national guards, which forced the governor to reverse his policy in Galicia. Throughout the summer there was a great deal of backstage maneuvering on the guards issue, and after some initial indifference, the Ruthenian Supreme Council began a strong campaign to organize the guards in Eastern Galicia, a proposal that was opposed by Poles and the newly appointed Polish governor, Count Agenor Gołuchowski. During the autumn of 1848, as the Hungarian insurrection grew more ominous, the military began to form national guard units, including a number of company sized units of approximately 100–200 men in Galician towns.

69 Prior to the Revolution, there were two administrative units, the Cracow Republic and Galicia. Because Cracow was the center of the rebellion, the territory was added to Galicia in 1846, the two areas were frequently called East and West Galicia. Adding Polish territory to Galicia reduced Ukrainian influence in the province and gave the impression that there were two Galicias; one Polish and one Ukrainian.

Their function was to preserve order in the province and prevent Polish sympathizers from crossing the Carpathian Mountains to aid the Hungarians. The guards actually had little influence on the events in Hungary and were disbanded on January 10, 1849. In addition to the guard units, the Council campaigned, with encouragement from the Austrian military, to organize a battalion of Mountain Riflemen that would seal the Hungarian border and prevent possible Hungarian incursions to Galicia. At the beginning of April 1849, 3,460[70] men volunteered and eventually a battalion of six companies, 1,400 men, was formed and sent to Hungary in September. By then, the Hungarians surrendered as Russia intervened at the request of Vienna. The battalion returned to Przemyśl in 1850 and was deactivated despite the Ruthenian Supreme Council's strenuous efforts to preserve the unit, which was the first Ukrainian military formation since the disbandment of the Ukrainian Cossacks in the Russian Empire. More importantly, it would later serve as a model for organizing similar units during the First World War that would in turn play a significant role in the Ukrainian struggle for independence.

Despite the Polish insurrection and Ukrainian loyalty, Vienna favored Polish interests over Ukrainian, viewing Poles as an important element in preserving the empire and so accordingly gave them de-facto control of Galicia. The Polish nobility, who played a major role in the imperial administration, promoted this attitude. It was further augmented by Polish propaganda that characterized Ukrainians as untrustworthy, alleging that in the event of a conflict with Russia, Ukrainians – especially Ukrainian military units—would be loyal to the Russian side. The 1869 decree specified that the viceroys of Galicia must be Poles, and a few years later, a minister without portfolio[71] was established for the province and given to the Poles. At the federal level, the Polish presence was extensive and included several premiers and numerous cabinet ministers.[72] Vienna obtained their support not only by giving them important positions in the province and also by raising the specter of a possible partitioning of Galicia into Polish and Ukrainian parts. The western part was

70 Kryp'iakevych, Ivan. *Istoria Ukraiyinskoho Viis'ka,* 288

71 This refers to a minister who did not administer a specific ministry but instead held an advisory position.

72 Wandycz, Piotr. "The Poles in the Habsburg Monarchy" in Markovits and Sysyn, eds. *Nationbuilding and the Politics of Nationalism: Essays on Austrian Galicia,* 69–70 and 85.

overwhelmingly Polish, except for a large Jewish presence, while Eastern Galicia was ethnically diverse. In 1849, Ukrainians in Eastern Galicia comprised 71 percent of the population, Poles 20 percent, and Jews almost 8 percent. Poles, despite their minority status, dominated political, economic, and cultural life because they comprised the landlord class and administered local government. To gain control over their part of the province, Ukrainians began petitioning Vienna to divide Galicia along ethnic lines. Vienna demurred, but the demand frightened Poles who were attached to Galicia more than any other Ukrainian territory and who considered it to be an important component in the future Polish State. "The possibility of the division of the province into two parts was real, and it hung as a Damoclean sword over the head of the Poles."[73] To prevent that possibility, Poles were determined to impede the overall educational level and national awareness among Ukrainians.

The Revolution initially generated an upsurge in political activities among Ukrainians, but they became complacent as the rebellion was quelled and reforms were halted or rescinded. The Reichstag was abolished in March 1849 and the Ruthenian Council voluntarily dissolved itself in 1851. During the 1850's, the reforms were largely abandoned and the province was at first governed by martial law and later by a viceroy, and the empire did not return to a constitutional form of governance until 1861. The newly elected diet consisted of 150 delegates elected by several legally defined *curia* (economic groups): the landlord class received 44 delegates, the Chamber of Commerce 3, the towns 28, and villagers 74.[74] The peasantry was clearly underrepresented and Ukrainians who comprised nearly one half of the population were even more underrepresented with only 49 delegates. For the remainder of the century, the Ukrainian share in the provincial diet continued to decrease after each successive election due to changes in the electoral law and Polish machinations, finally dropping to a low point of having only 11 delegates in 1883. Besides being deprived of equal representation, the Polish majority routinely ignored Ukrainian demands, which exacerbated tensions between the two groups and would eventually erupt in violence. In 1908 another election was held for the provincial diet and some Ukrainian peasants were killed. In retaliation, a Ukrainian student killed Governor Potocki, further

73 Ibid., 81.

74 Subtelny, *Ukraine: A History*, 314.

raising hostilities. Fights began breaking out between Polish and Ukrainian students at the University of L'viv, and a Ukrainian student was killed. Unable to gain influence within the existing political structure, Ukrainians began organizing political parties that advocated radical solutions. The Ukrainian Radical Party, formed in 1890, initially proposed the adoption of socialism in order to improve conditions in the province, but a few years later called for the unification of all Ukrainian lands and an establishment of a Ukrainian state. Their agenda failed to gain significant support, and the National Democratic Party replaced them in 1899. The new party sought to gradually accomplish similar objectives by working within the existing system, and it remained the most influential Ukrainian party until the war. [75]

Besides representation, education was another contentious issue between the Ukrainian and Polish establishments. The reforms of Maria Theresa and Joseph II had extended secular education to the Ukrainians, several types of elementary schools and secondary schools were proposed, and the University of L'viv was founded in 1784. As with other reforms in the empire, school reforms were difficult to implement and Ukrainians and Poles were soon mired in controversies over the language of instruction. Despite fitful progress, 2,132 different elementary schools were established by 1843, teaching in several languages.[76] In the second half of the century, elementary schools were taught from one to seven years, depending on the size of enrollment, but authorities did not favor seven-year schools in Ukrainian villages, and hence most children in rural areas received only one or two years of schooling. Obtaining a secondary education was even more difficult because these schools were not state-funded and most Ukrainian children came from poor rural families who could not afford to pay the tuition. Many had not achieved even the four years of elementary education required to enter a secondary school. For those few who did manage to obtain it, a secondary education consisted largely of *gymnasia* where students received eight years of education, were taught Greek and Latin, and were eligible to enter university after graduation. Alternatively, after four years of schooling, a student could enter *realschulen* (a type of German secondary school), which of-

---

75 Magocsi, *A History of Ukraine,* 446–7.

76 Herasymovych, I. and Terletsky, O. "Ukrainian Lands Under Austria-Hungary." In Vol. II of Kubijovyč, ed. *Ukraine,* 328.

fered a seven-year course without the classical languages. *Realschulen* graduates could enter an institution of higher learning, but not a university. Before World War I, there were 102 public *gymnasia* in both parts of Galicia: Poles had 96 and there were six Ukrainian gymnasia. The poor Ukrainian showing was due to the low social and economic position of Ukrainians and the reluctance of the school authorities to increase educational opportunities in Ukrainian settlement areas. Ukrainians were able to partially counteract the official bias by establishing 13 private secondary schools before the war. The growing ethnic tension and disparity between the two groups was most notable at the University of L'viv, which had been a German language institution until 1867. After the introduction of Polish and Ukrainian as languages of instruction, the faculty positions were to be filled by individuals proficient in Polish or Ukrainian. The provision gave Poles the opportunity to Polonize the university. Out of 80 faculty positions, only 12 were eventually filled by Ukrainians. This prompted Ukrainians to campaign for a separate Ukrainian university, which the Austrians finally agreed to establish by 1916, but the war precluded implementation.

The realization that Vienna no longer supported them, the nullification of many of the early reforms, and the Polish takeover of the province were all factors that forced Ukrainians to rely on their own resources and reconsider their attitude toward Austria. To mobilize their own community, however, a clear national identity and a national language remained to be forged. Ukrainians in the Austrian Empire used a medieval name *Rusyn* (Ruthenian), while those in the Russian Empire were officially designated as *Malorusy* (Little Russians), an artificial name contrived by the Patriarch of Constantinople in the middle ages and adopted by the Russian Crown. The term Ukraine (*Ukrayina*—derived from the word for border or edge) was mentioned in the medieval chronicles, and referred either to a specific territory or a borderland. Cossack leaders and chroniclers in the seventeenth century used the term to describe Cossack territories on the Dnieper and in the broader sense, the territory of all Ruthenians, i.e., Ukrainians. During the national revival in the nineteenth century, the new name was widely adopted by Ukrainian writers in the Russian Empire and applied to the people and the country. The switch from *Rusyn* to *Ukrainian* established a clear difference and removed the confusion between the two peoples since the adjective for Rusyn in Galicia was *Rus'kyi,* compared to *Russkiy* for a *Russian,* and the language was called *rus'ka mova* compared to *russkiy iazyk* in Russian. The new terminology not only established a clear demarcation but also was part of a new wave of nationalism sweeping across Eastern Europe. A Ruthenian or Little Russian belonged to an ethnic group without a clear and distinctive identity, but a Ukrainian had a clear national identity that was frequently coupled with a political agenda. The political agenda included the name change and the belief that the language spoken by the common people should be elevated to the literary language and used in schools and publishing. It was a development that served to fragment Galicians.

For secular purposes, Galicians used a hybrid language consisting principally of the Church Slavonic with borrowings from the Galician vernacular and Russian. The artificial language was not standardized and was confusing, especially to the school children. The *starorusyny* (Old Ruthenians), as they were now called, faced difficulties in attracting readers with this language and decided to limit its use to popular publications, while scholarly publications were published in standard Russian. Their approach to the language question was losing ground to the populists, *narodovtsi*, as the Ukrainophiles were known at the time. The latter switched to vernacular, with borrowings from Dnieper Ukrainian that used a simplified phonetic alphabet. This gave them a tremendous advantage because the language was comprehensible to the common people, and a phonetic spelling enabled people with minimal education to read it. At the same time, many outstanding writers in eastern Ukraine and Galicia began writing in a modern form of Ukrainian. Because of the restrictions placed on the use of the Ukrainian language in the Russian Empire, L'viv became the principle center for Ukrainian language publications.[77] At the outbreak of World War I, approximately three quarters of the existing Ukrainian language literature was published in L'viv, and many Ukrainian writers and scholars from the Russian Empire also pub-

---

77 The use of the Ukrainian language in publications began toward the end of the eighteen century in the Ukrainian lands of the Russian Empire. As the Ukrainian national revival began to take on political coloration, Tsar Alexander II issued a secret decree on June 18, 1876 the forbidding use of Ukrainian in print and education. See Luckyj, George, Sn.N. "Between Gogol' and Ševčenko: Polarity in Literary Ukraine, 1798–1847." *Harvard Series in Ukrainian Studies*, Vol. 8., 38–57. See also Boroschak, Elias. "Ukraine in the Russian Empire in the Nineteenth and Early Twentieth Centuries, 1800—1917." In Vol. I. of Kubijovyč, ed. *Ukraine,* 684.

lished in Galician journals. The Shevchenko Scientific Society, modeled after the Vienna Academy of Science, was formed in L'viv using modern Ukrainian in its extensive research and publication program and eventually became the de facto Ukrainian Academy of Sciences. These developments gave Galician Ukrainians a great advantage vis-à-vis their rivals, the *starorusyny* ("Old Ruthenians" who resisted Ukrainianization). The latter were beginning to disappear as supporters joined either the Ukrainians or the Russophiles (Muscophiles or *novokursnyky*). The Russophiles considered themselves to be a branch of the Russian people, a view advocated by the Russian government, and used Russian in their publications. The Ukrainian language gained widespread acceptance among the people as well as recognition by the Austrian Government as a language of instruction in schools and for official functions,[78] however limited, and the Russophile influence steadily diminished.

The Polish-Ukrainian struggle since the 1848 Revolution energized the Ukrainian community and the tension was heightened by the influx of nationalism from the West, which posited that defined ethnic groups had the right to form their own state. The growing Ukrainian educated class provided the necessary political leadership, and numerous political battles with Poles had made the Ukrainian peasantry more politically active and savvy than their educational and economic attainments would suggest. In 1902, for example, about 10,000 Ukrainians refused to harvest grain on Polish estates unless wages were raised. Their demands were eventually met, but more importantly the strike demonstrated their organizational skill and discipline. More ominously, the struggles now were no longer between a Ukrainian peasant and a Polish landlord, but evolved into ethnic strife between Ukrainians and Poles. Polish workers and peasants tended not to cooperate with their Ukrainian class equals because national interest took precedent over their economic interests. Diametrically opposite and strongly held views by both groups on major issues set the stage for future struggles.

78 Magocsi, Paul R. "The Language Question as a Factor in the National Movement in Eastern Galicia" in Markovits and Sysyn, eds. *Nationbuilding and the Politics of Nationalism*, 234.

Chapter II:
The Interwar Years

Because of its location along the border of the Austrian and Russian empires, the territory of western Ukraine became the battleground of the Eastern Front from the early days of the First World War. From 1914 to 1918, the Russian, Austrian, and German armies advanced and retreated over the land, displacing people, inflicting staggering casualties, and damaging infrastructure. In the aftermath of the war, the final collapse of the Austrian and Russian empires incited a more intense struggle between the Ukrainian and Polish national movements as both sought to establish nation states. The biggest point of contention centered around which side would obtain the former Habsburg province of Galicia, where the diverse ethnic composition included a significant number of Polish and Ukrainian settlements, as well as a long history of territorial disputes between the two groups. The Polish claim was not so much based on ethnicity but rather the assertion that it was historically Polish territory. Since the fourteenth century conquest, the Poles had gradually moved their ethnic boundaries over 30 miles to the east in some areas by assimilating Ukrainians and creating Polish settlements in the former territories of Rus' which had a Ukrainian majority. To the east of that belt, Ukrainians formed the majority but there were a significant number of Polish enclaves, especially in the towns. While Ukrainians claimed only those districts where they still formed a majority, the Poles demanded the territory of all of western Ukraine regardless of ethnic composition based on the notion that it was part of "historic Poland." In 1918, this conflict culminated in an almost yearlong war with Ukrainians that came to be termed "The Ukrainian-Polish War of Independence." The Polish conquest of Volhynia (which had been a part of the Russian Empire) was comparatively quick, but it would take more than six months to occupy Galicia and several years to solidify Polish control and gain international recognition for the conquest.

In 1923, the League of Nations finally assigned the territory of Galicia to the new Polish government, a decision that was partly based on the fact that the Poles had occupied the territory since 1919. The decision did not bring tranquility since many Ukrainians resented what they viewed as the new Polish occupation, and Polish policies toward Ukrainians only intensified this reaction. Based on the terms of the Versailles Treaty, minority groups were to receive extensive cultural autonomy in the new Polish state, but Poland failed to observe and implement the agreements and without the restraining hand of Vienna, conditions for Ukrainians in Galicia rapidly deteriorated. The Polish government did not seek political accommodation and ignored the fact that the lengthy struggle for independence had intensified Ukrainian patriotic fervor. Haunted by past partitions, Polish officials were anxious to implement a process of rapid Polonization to eliminate future divisions along ethnic lines, a policy that some ideologues believed was achievable within 25 years. These policies, which included colonization, educational repressions and other measures, provoked strong and sometimes violent Ukrainian resistance to which Polish authorities responded with pacification measures. The mutual hostilities continued to escalate during the interwar years.

World War I: Ethnic Conflicts and the Growth of Ukrainian Nationalism

The First World War was sparked by the 1914 assassination of the Habsburg Archduke Franz Ferdinand, the presumptive heir to the Austrian imperial throne, by a young Bosnian revolutionary in Sarajevo. The Archduke's assassination provoked the empire's declaration of war on Serbia and pitted the Central Powers (Austria-Hungary and the German Empire) against Serbia and its allies (Russia, England and France.) Austrian troops went on the offensive first by advancing east from Galicia, and the Russians mounted a swift counterattack on August 5, reaching L'viv on September 3 and quickly occupying the remainder of Galicia. The retreating Austro-Hungarian Army attributed the defeat to the spread of Russophilism among the local Ukrainian population; a view promoted by local Polish officials, and commenced their campaign of terror against individuals suspected to Russian sympathizers. Initially the repression was directed against Russophiles but it was later expanded to Ukrainians in general, regardless of their political views. Many were executed without trial and thousands were sent to detention camps in Austria. Thalerhof, the largest and the most infamous of the camps, had about 30,000 prisoners and many died of diseases contracted in the camp. Thalerhof was finally abolished by the Austrian parliament in 1917.

The outbreak of the war produced a flurry of activity among Ukrainian political leaders in Galicia who sought to protect Ukrainian interests in the coming conflict. The major political parties formed the Supreme Ukrainian Council in L'viv on August l, 1914, an organization that was headed by Kost' Levyts'kyi. The Council declared loyalty to Austria and urged Ukrainians to join a united struggle against autocratic Russia as a way of achieving independence for Ukraine in the Russian Empire. The Council further established a Ukrainian Military Board to handle military matters, and issued a call for volunteers to serve in Ukrainian units. Over 28,000 volunteered, mostly young men from sports clubs and the Boy Scouts, but only 2,500 were accepted as Poles urged Vienna not to organize Ukrainian formations, a propaganda tactic used to frighten Austrians with unfounded claims that Ukrainian sympathies would lie with Russia in the event of war.[79]

As Russian troops advanced westward in the autumn of 1914, many Ukrainian leaders from Galicia and Bukovyna fled to Vienna and on May 4, 1915, formed the General Ukrainian Council to promote Ukrainian interests. The Council advocated the creation of an independent Ukrainian State on ethnic Ukrainian territory in the Russian Empire, the partition of Galicia into Ukrainian and Polish halves, and political autonomy for Ukrainian Galicia and Bukovyna. Austria looked favorably on attempts to establish a Ukrainian State on the Dnieper since it would weaken Russia. Concerning the lands of the Russian empire, they supported the eastern Ukrainian émigrés who formed the "Union for the Liberation of Ukraine" in Vienna; however, with respect to the province of Galicia, their attitude was quite different. The Austrian monarchy sought Polish support and favored Polish interests over Ukrainian interests within the province, and since Poles were adamantly opposed to the partition, Vienna ignored the Ukrainian demand for partitioning the province. In November 1916, Germany and Austria proposed establishing a Polish kingdom on the Polish territory in the Russian Empire,[80] but as to their plan for Galicia, both parts of the province were to remain as Austrian crown

---

[79] Subtelny, *Ukraine: A History*, 340.

[80] Gieysztor, et. al. *History of Poland*, 527.

lands, although they would receive greater political autonomy. For Ukrainians, this meant greater Polish control. In protest, the Council resigned and Ukrainian delegates to the Austrian parliament formed the Parliamentary Club, headed by Ievhen Petrushevych, to continue the work of the defunct Council.

Ukrainian political activities were paralleled by efforts to organize a Ukrainian military unit within the Austrian army. The unit, called the Sich Riflemen, was formed at the beginning of the war and its name was based on that of a paramilitary organization of the same name founded in L'viv in 1913.[81] At the outbreak of the war, Austrians permitted 2,500 men to join the unit, which was organized into two battalions. In September, the battalions fought Russian troops in the Carpathian Mountains and in August 1915 were reorganized into a regiment of 1,700 men. Over the next two years, the unit participated in a number of battles and by all accounts performed well, but the Austrians refused to increase the size of the unit or even to replace its losses. In September 1916, the organization was renamed the Ukrainian Legion and by that point consisted of only a single battalion. The Austrian attitude toward the Legion was not based on military considerations; rather, it was the result of a Polish lobby to avoid creating Ukrainian military formations. The Poles continued to assert that such formations could side with Russia. The Austro-Hungarian Army was a multilingual conglomerate where German-speaking officers had difficulty communicating with their non-German soldiers. At the same time, large numbers of Ukrainians were scattered throughout the Austrian Army, and while transferring these men to a proven Ukrainian unit would have certainly increased their value, political considerations prevailed over military efficiency.

Although the Legion's role on the Eastern Front was insignificant, this organization would evolve to form the nucleus of the Ukrainian Galician Army of World War I, and later played an important role in eastern Ukraine. As the Russian Empire disintegrated, Sich Riflemen who were captured by Russians and other Ukrainian captives from the Austrian Army formed a Volunteer Battalion of Sich Riflemen in November 1917. Eventually, the battalion accepted eastern Ukrainians and became the

---

81 *Sich* was a name of Cossack stockades on the islands in the Dnieper River, and the Sich Riflemen extensively adopted Cossack military terminology.

most reliable unit in the army of the Ukrainian National Republic that formed in Kyiv on November 20, 1917.

The northwestern territory, which became the newly formed Kholm Province, saw heavy combat throughout the war, but would soon enter a new phase of history. The news of the collapsing Russian monarchy, the first dynastic casualty of the war, reached Kyiv on March 13, 1917. In the next several days, three major political groups were formed: The Executive Committee of the Council of Combined Social Organizations; the Kyiv Soviet of Workers' and Soldiers' Deputies; and the Central Rada. The Executive Committee, which supported the Provisional Government in Petrograd, represented government officials, some political parties, and various organizations and institutions in the city of Kyiv. The Kyiv Soviet of Workers' and Soldiers' Deputies, on the other hand, was a radical leftist organization supported by Russians and Russified Ukrainian industrial workers who supported the Bolshevik party in Russia. The Central Rada[82] represented a pro-Ukrainian moderate leftist view initially advocating autonomy for Ukraine within Russia, but as the struggle continued, it eventually sought to establish an independent Ukrainian state. When the Provisional Government fell in 1917, the struggle in Kyiv was between the Rada and the Soviet. Although the Rada had a greater following, the Communists had the support of the Bolsheviks in Russia, which ultimately proved decisive. Aided by local communists, Soviet Russian forces invaded Ukraine on December 25, 1917 and brought much of the territory under their control. On the same day, the Central Powers (Germany, Austria-Hungary, Turkey, and Bulgaria) signed a treaty with Russia and the new seceding states of the Russian Empire (the Baltic states of Estonia, Latvia, Lithuania; and Finland, Poland, and Ukraine).[83] In addition to nine eastern Provinces, Ukraine received the Kholm Province and southern districts of the Grodno Province, including the city of Brest-Litovsk, and a portion of the Minsk Province where Ukrainians formed a majority. Ukraine's generous treatment was due to Germany's desire to terminate the Eastern Front, shift troops to the west, and the desperate need for Ukrainian grain to feed its starving population. The Brest-Litovsk Treaty brought Volhynia under Kyiv's control

[82] In the Ukrainian language, *Rada* refers to a council and is equivalent to the Russian term *Soviet*.

[83] Wheeler-Bennett, John W. *Brest-Litovsk,* 406–7, Article VI.

and a national revival was encouraged in the backward and extensively Polonized region. A local administration was established for the area located in Brest-Litovsk and emphasis was placed on education, designating Ukrainian as the language of instruction. This policy evoked hostilities from the Poles, and the fledgling independence movement was finally halted the following year when Polish troops occupied the territory.

As the war continued into 1918, it became apparent that the Habsburg Austro-Hungarian Empire would collapse and the numerous ethnic groups living within its territories were making preparations to establish their own national states. In the Ukrainian case, the leading political and church leaders met on October 12, 1918 and made plans to organize a constituent assembly. Emperor Charles I of Austria (Charles IV of Hungary), who succeeded Franz Josef I in 1916, issued a decree on October 16, 1918, calling for the reorganization of the Empire into a federative state and urging ethnic groups to form their own administrative units. The Ukrainian leaders of Galicia and Bukovyna formed the Ukrainian National Council on October 18, headed by Ievhen Petrushevych, and declared their intention to unite all Ukrainian ethnic territories. According to their plan, Eastern Galicia, Bukovyna, and Transcarpathia, then under Hungary, would form a single administrative unit, but their intended relations with Vienna were left vague. At the same time, Polish nationalists were working to establish a Polish State and did not rescind their intention to incorporate Eastern Galicia, rendering conflict with the Ukrainians inevitable. At the end of September, Ukrainian officers in the Austrian Army organized the Central Military Council in L'viv and preparations were made for the coming conflict.

On October 31, Ukrainians demanded that the Austrian governor, Karl Huyn, hand over administrative control of Galicia, which the governor refused. In the early hours of November l, over 1,200 Ukrainian soldiers occupied the city. In the morning, L'viv's residents found Ukrainian flags flying over the public buildings and declarations posted on the walls informing them that a Ukrainian State had been formed on the territory of the former Austrian Empire, with L'viv established as the capital.[84] The Ukrainian occupation caught Poles in the city by surprise, especially since they had themselves been preparing to stage a coup and

84 Stachiw and Sztendera. *Western Ukraine at the Turning Point*, 106–111.

had already assembled some 1,500 armed men for the cause. Fighting broke out immediately—the Poles were better armed, more numerous, familiar with the city, and had the support of the Polish population in Galicia. The Polish contingent in the city was reinforced from the west and Ukrainians were finally forced to abandon the city on November 22 but retained control of rural areas surrounding the city. The Polish-Ukrainian war had begun.

The Polish-Ukrainian War: A Struggle for Independence

Following the retreat from L'viv, the armed conflict between Ukrainian and Polish nationalists continued for the next few months, with bloody fighting along the Przemyśl'-L'viv railroad corridor. Although Poles comprised only about one-fifth of the population in Eastern Galicia, they had a number of advantages over the Ukrainians. They were better educated, had more numerous and better-trained officers, and controlled major transportation and communication junctions. Typically, Poles were the majority ethnic group in most towns, followed by a large Jewish minority and a small share of Ukrainians. Since Jews had remained neutral in the struggle, Poles were frequently able to seize a town and its adjacent villages since many of them were heavily settled by Poles and Polonized Ukrainians.

Because the Polish units were located in more compact areas (towns and suburban areas) as opposed to Ukrainians (who were spread out through the villages), they were able to mobilize quickly, hold more transportation and communication points, and could more effectively defend themselves. Ukrainians had neither the numbers nor the tactical training and weaponry to engage Polish units in urban warfare with house-to-house fighting, a difficult feat for any army. The Polish military advantage is best exemplified in the capture of a railroad line between the city of Przemyśl and L'viv. At the time, Przemyśl, located on the River San about 55 miles west of L'viv, had a population of approximately 50,000 people, with Poles comprising nearly half and a politically active Ukrainian community amounting to about one-fifth of the total population. Initially, the Ukrainians seized the city, but by the middle of November, a Polish regiment of about 2,000 men supported by artillery and an armored train recaptured the town. With the aid of Polish residents in the towns along the line, a Polish corridor was established between the two cities. During this phase of fighting, Poles were also able to control several counties in the north and west while Ukrainians held the rest of Galicia, establishing their capital in the southeastern town of Stanislaviv, now called Ivano-Frankivsk.

For the next several months, the struggle continued between the Ukrainians and the local Poles, who were occasionally reinforced by troops from Poland. After much maneuvering among Polish factions, the Polish parliament enacted the "Little Constitution" in February 20, 1919, giving itself the power to govern and promptly appointing Józef Pilsudski as the head of the Polish State.[85] Establishment of a central authority enabled the Poles to launch an offensive at the beginning of March and re-establish their control over the Przemyśl-L'viv corridor by March 19. In April, the offensive intensified with the arrival of a 100,000-man field army commanded by General Józef Haller.[86] The army consisted of six infantry divisions totaling with 60,000 men, along with artillery, tank and aviation units and other supporting elements.[87] The army was organized in France largely from the Polish POWs of the Austrian and German armies, and Polish émigrés including those from the United States. The units were well trained and armed, and had a contingent of French officers. Per the agreement with the French, the army was to be used only against the Russian Bolshevik Communists; however, the Poles claimed that Ukrainians had attacked first and directed the troops against them.[88] The additional troops enabled the Poles to break the Ukrainian encirclement of L'viv by the end of April and push the Ukrainian Galician Army further east. The following month, the Poles launched an offensive in Volhynia, which was under the control of the Ukrainian National Republic, and also launched a separate offensive in Galicia. The fortified town of Lutsk in Volhynia was taken on May 16 and fell back to the southeastern portion of the province. By the beginning of June, the Ukrainians had regrouped and launched an unexpected

---

85 Gieysztor, et. al. *History of Poland*, 547.

86 Magocsi, *A History of Ukraine*, 516.

87 Valasek, *Haller's Army in France*, 15–16 and Jonca, *Polish Tracks & Wheels,* 1.

88 Vytvytsky, S. and Baran, S. "The Renascence of Ukraine: The Ukrainian State, 1917–1920." In Vol. I. of Kubijovyč, ed., *Ukraine,* 775.

offensive from the town of Chortkiv, re-capturing much of Galicia, but the lack of ammunition halted the offensive. At that point, the Allied Powers authorized Poland to occupy East Galicia up to the Zbruch River, which had marked the Austro-Russian boundary before the war. Simultaneously, pending a formal treaty with the Western Powers, Poland was permitted to introduce its administrative system before there was formal international agreement to acquire the province.[89] The Polish counteroffensive forced the Ukrainian Army out of Galicia; the Galician Army, 120,000 strong at its peak, crossed the Zbruch River in the middle of July to fight alongside the troops of the Ukrainian National Republic against the Bolsheviks. [90] As Timothy Snyder notes, "...The war cost Galician Ukrainians fifteen thousand men, created a generation of frustrated veterans, and confirmed a prevailing belief that Poland was the main enemy of Ukraine."[91]

The military campaigns were paralleled by the diplomatic activities of the two warring powers and the Entente.[92] The initial diplomatic efforts were confined largely to arranging a cessation of hostilities, although attempts were usually rejected by one side or another or simply not implemented after nominal acceptance. The Ukrainians were not willing to accept any peace proposal unless their control of Galicia was guaranteed, but the Polish goal was to occupy Eastern Galicia and to use any cessation of hostilities as an opportunity to reorganize and re-supply their troops. Most western powers favored the Polish national cause over that of the Ukrainians, and France openly supported the formation of a strong Polish State to replace Russia on the German eastern boundary, a situation that required Polish annexation of Ukrainian territory.

In addition to brokering truces between Poles and Ukrainians, the Allied Powers attempted to establish a permanent eastern boundary of Poland and protect minority rights not only in Poland but also in other newly established East European countries. The establishment of a permanent Polish eastern boundary took several years because of the conflicting claims of Poles, Ukrainians, and Lithuanians, as well as the un-

---

89 Paneyko, Basil. "Galicia and the Ukrainian Problem." 579.

90 Motyka, Grzegorz. *Tak było w Bieszczadach*, 25.

91 Snyder, Timothy. *The Reconstruction of Nations*, 138.

92 The official designation for the Western Powers at the end of the war was "Allied and Associated Powers consisting of Great Britain, France, Italy, the United States, and Japan."

settled situation caused by the 1917 revolution in Russia. During that period, Poland signed number of treaties and conventions guaranteeing extensive cultural and political rights to the numerous minorities who amounted to about one-third of the population in the new Polish State. The Treaty of Versailles, the first and most important treaty, was signed on June 28, 1919, establishing Poland's borders with the neighboring states with the exception of the eastern border. On that subject, Article 87 specified that the boundaries not established by the treaty "will be subsequently determined by the Principal Allied and Associated Powers."[93] Article 93 obligated Poland "...to protect the interests of inhabitants of Poland who differ from the majority of the population in race, language, or religion."[94] Finally, Article 116 required Germany to abrogate the Treaty of Brest-Litovsk, which gave Volhynia to the Ukrainian National Republic.

The Western Powers and Poland had signed a second treaty on the same date, June 28, amplifying minority rights granted in the Treaty of Versailles. The treaty, frequently called the "Minority Treaty," was proposed and signed largely through the efforts of Jewish organizations in Western Europe and the United States. The Committee of the Jewish Delegation at the conference requested that Allied Powers grant political and cultural autonomy to an estimated nine million Jews in Eastern Europe. The request was forwarded to the New State Committee for study and the committee issued a report concluding that political autonomy "...would seriously undermine the authority of the Polish State."[95] The Allied Powers, therefore, rejected demands for political autonomy but granted extensive legal, cultural, and religious rights to the Jews and other national groups.[96] With respect to native languages, the Polish State was forbidden to restrict their use in private conversations or communications, publishing, business, public gatherings, or in courts. Moreover, non-Polish groups were given the right to organize and manage their religious, social, and educational institutions at their own expense. In compact ethnic areas, the state was obliged to establish and finance elementary native language schools, although Polish language would be taught

93 Schonfield, Hugh J. *The Treaty of Versailles*, 34.
94 Ibid, 40.
95 Horak, Stephen. *Poland and Her National Minorities, 1919–39*, 63.
96 An abridged version of the treaty is published in Horak, 188–91.

as a subject. Article 12, the last article of the treaty, designated the League of Nations as the guarantor of the minority rights specified in the treaty. Any member of the Council of the League of Nations had the power to bring any infraction of the treaty before the entire council. If they perceived that their minority rights had been violated, Ukrainian representatives could approach the Council, which would then determine the validity of the claims. If the claims were determined to be valid, they would approach the government in question. Any further legal disagreement between the plaintiffs and the defendant (in this case, the Polish Republic) would then be adjudicated at the Court of International Justice, based at The Hague. As the guarantor of minority rights, the League received a steady flow of complaints during the interwar period since the new Polish State ignored many provisions in the treaty. Many Poles were against the treaty at the time but since the fate of the emerging Polish State was largely in the hands of the Allied Powers, Poland ratified the treaty on January 20, 1920. The Allied Powers signed the treaty with Austria at St. Germain-en-Laye on September 10, 1919 which disposed of numerous ethnic territories of the former Austro-Hungarian Empire and established state boundaries in the region.[97] The treaty dealt directly with the Ukrainian Northern Bukovyna (now the Chernivtsi Oblast in Ukraine.) This was territory acquired Austria had acquired from Turkey in 1774 and assigned to Romania pending final approval of the treaty. The other province, Transcarpathia, had been under Hungarian rule since Hungarians had settled the Pannonian Plain in the Middle Ages and remained part of Hungary within the Habsburg Empire. According to the terms of the treaty, the territory was assigned to the newly established Czechoslovak State and was granted extensive local autonomy. The status of East Galicia remained unresolved as the Allied Powers acquired legal authority over the territory (per Article 91), but the territory remained under Polish occupation.

While the Allied Powers wrestled with Poland's eastern borders, events in the east would prove decisive. As civil war raged in the Russian Empire, Ukrainians and many other nationalities sought to break away from Russia and establish their own independent states. The situation in Ukraine was especially chaotic as Ukrainians fought the Communists

97 Israel, Fred L. *Major Peace Treaties of Modern History, 1648–1967, Vol. III.*, 27–29.

from the north and the White Russians from the south, while independent guerrilla bands roamed the countryside looting and switching their support among the contending forces. By the end of 1919, Ukrainian forces were driven out of Ukraine along with their leader Symon Petliura, and they retreated to Poland. During the winter, an understanding was reached between Petliura and Józef Pilsudski to launch an attack against the Soviet forces and capture Belarusian and Ukrainian territories. The Poles never gave up their desire to re-establish the "Historic Poland" with the eastern boundaries on the Dnieper River, and in the latest version of that concept, Poland planned to establish client states between itself and Russia. Petliura and the Poles signed a treaty in Warsaw on April 21, 1920, relinquishing East Galicia and most of Volhynia to Poland in return for the Polish recognition of a Ukrainian State on the remaining Ukrainian territory.[98] The joint offensive enjoyed early success and on May 6th, 65,000 Polish troops and 15,000 Ukrainian troops entered Kyiv.[99] As Poles entered Ukraine, Petr Wrangel, the last White Russian general, was bottled up in the Crimea seeking Polish alliance against the Communists, but was spurned by the Poles.

The Polish victory was short-lived. The Red Army counterattacked at the end of May, eventually forcing Polish forces to abandon Kyiv on June 11. Under the command of Mikhail Tukhachevsky, the main Soviet force advanced across Belarus toward Warsaw. The left flank moved across northern Ukraine, commanded by Aleksandr Yegorov and Semen Budyenny with Josef Stalin as the political commissar. As the Red Army approached the Polish frontier, heated discussions ensued at the Politburo as to whether or not they should enter Poland or stop at the Polish ethnic frontiers and incorporate Belarusian and Ukrainian territories into the emerging Soviet State. Leon Trotsky and several other Politburo members opposed a Soviet occupation of Poland, fearing a spirited patriotic resistance by the Poles; however, Vladimir Lenin and the majority, including Stalin, favored occupying Poland. Lenin counted on the support of the Polish workers and by installing a Soviet regime in Poland, he hoped to aid German Communists and spark Communist uprisings in Western Europe. To that end, a Polish Communist government headed

98 The treaty is reprinted in Reshestar, John S. Jr. *The Ukrainian Revolution: 1917–1920*, 301–302.

99 Subtelny, *Ukraine: A History*, 375.

by the Polish communist leader Julian Marchlewski was organized in Białystok and readied itself for installment in Poland.

The West was alarmed at the so-called "Red Peril" from the east, and the Allied Powers authorized Great Britain to negotiate a truce between Poland and the new Soviet Russia. Britain was chosen because the Allied Powers had no contact with Moscow, but a Soviet delegation headed by Leonid Krassin and Lev Kamenev was visiting London and provided a suitable link. The British foreign secretary, Lord George Curzon, telegraphed Moscow on July 11 urging an armistice between the two warring powers and proposing a demarcation line that ran approximately along the Polish and Belarusian-Ukrainian ethnic frontier but favored Poland in terms of territorial gains. Nevertheless, neither the Poles nor the Soviets accepted the plan. The Soviets were not interested in halting their army as it was making rapid progress toward Warsaw, and the Poles would not relinquish L'viv and other territories located to the east of the line. At that point, the Soviet left flank, contrary to Tukhachevsky's orders, turned southwest to capture L'viv leaving his main force exposed. Poles massed their troops on the Soviet left flank and launched an attack on August 14. As Budyenny attempted to close the gap, he was checked at Hrubieszów (Hrubeshiv). The Poles now turned north, rolled up behind Tukhachevsky's left flank and attacked from the rear, sending the Red Army into a headlong retreat. The Soviet debacle, which Poles called the "Miracle on the Vistula," ended Lenin's dream of seeing a Communist Europe during his lifetime.

During the conflict, Polish-Soviet discussions continued without success in Minsk, but after the defeat on the Vistula, Soviet Russia was ready to negotiate. On September 2, both parties agreed to transfer the conference to the neutral city of Riga in Latvia and negotiations were resumed on September 21. An agreement was reached on October 12 and ratified on November 2, but not signed until March 18, 1921. There were two major provisions in the Treaty of Riga: the demarcation of the boundaries (Article II) and the rights of minorities (Article VII).[100] The treaty further transferred the property of the Russian government to the

---

[100] The treaty is printed in this brochure: "Traktat pokoju miedzy Polska a Rosja I Ukraina." Ministerstwo spraw zagranicznych. Warszawa: F. Hoesick, 1921.

Polish government, including some lands of the Orthodox Church that had been legally owned by the Russian government.[101]

The provision on minorities gave minority groups broad cultural, legal, and religious rights on both sides of the Polish-Ukrainian border. Ukrainians in Poland, just as Poles in Ukraine, had the right to propagate their native language and to maintain schools and cultural organizations. Each side agreed not to interfere in the religious matters of nationalities whose churches had the right to own property. Given the behavior of both sides on the minority provisions, it was a cynical agreement that neither the Poles nor the Soviets intended to implement. The treaty had settled the matter of the Polish eastern boundaries with the emerging Soviet State except for East Galicia, which had nominally remained under the control of the Allied Powers. That matter was finally resolved at the Conference of Ambassadors on March 15, 1923, as the Allied Powers recognized Polish control of the province and the existing Soviet-Polish boundary agreement. Ultimately, the Second Polish Republic would include territory to the east of Lord Curzon's proposal. The so-called Curzon Line would henceforth be forgotten until the Second World War, when Stalin would push the United States and Great Britain to accept it as the new boundary between Poland and the Soviet Union.

The Interwar Years

The newly formed Second Polish Republic became a multi-national state, similar to the Polish Commonwealth that had been partitioned at the end of the eighteenth century. After the war, Poland conducted two censuses, in 1921 and 1931, reporting a larger share of Polish population compared with the earlier Russian and Austrian censuses. Many questioned the accuracy of the figures. A Polish scholar named Andrej Chojnowski examined the census data and concluded that the nationality figures had been falsified. He estimated that the non-Polish groups totaled over 30 percent in the Polish State, with Ukrainians comprising 15–16 percent, Belarusians 4–6 percent, Jews 8–10 percent, and Germans 2–3

[101] The agreement was signed by Poland and the Soviet Socialist Republic of Russia, the latter acting on behalf of Belarus and Ukraine. The Soviet Union was not formally created until December 1922.

percent.[102] Germans were scattered in the west and north of Poland while Jews were found throughout the Polish State, almost exclusively in towns, and both groups formed minorities comprising a small share of the population in any area. In respect to the Ukrainian territories, Volodymyr Kubijovyč, a Ukrainian geographer who specialized in studying the Ukrainian population, adjusted the 1931 census figures and concluded that out of 9,198,000 people living in western Ukraine (Galicia and Volhynia), Ukrainians amounted to 64.5 percent, Poles (including Ukrainian-speaking Roman Catholics) comprised 25 percent, Jews 9.8 percent, and others 0.7%.[103]

The revived Polish state, as earlier, would have a large non-Polish population and therefore, much of the discussion among Polish elites during the nineteenth century centered on future policies toward minority groups. By the turn of the century, two proposals for a minority policy emerged. The first called for an eventual assimilation of the minorities and the second advocated a formation of a federal state where non-Polish groups would have a voice in matters of governance. The assimilation view held that Poles should have a leading role in the state while other groups were to enjoy fewer rights with the goal of eventually assimilating them through civic and political pressures. The two east-Slavic groups, Ukrainians and Belarusians, were primary targets because they occupied large tracts of land bordering a foreign state and were culturally and linguistically closer to Poles than other groups such as Jews or ethnic Germans. Elites rationalized the assimilation as a natural process of political Darwinism, viewing their failure to establish their own states as prima-facie evidence that the groups were unfit to govern themselves. This extreme nationalistic view was advocated by the National Democrats and propagated by their chief ideologue, Roman Dmowski.[104] The second and much more moderate proposal, the formation of a federal state, was far more nebulous and did not attract as much support, although the popular World War I hero Josef Pilsudski was associated with it. Polish literature falsely maintained that the federal state was not formed because Po-

---

102 Chojnowski, Andrej. *Koncepcje polityki narodowościowej rządów polskich w latach 1921–1939.* (Wrocław: Akedemiia Nauk, 1979), 6.

103 Latinates totaled 480,000. See Kubijovyč, Volodymyr. "Ethnic Composition of the Population" in Vol. I. of Kubijovyč, *Ukraine,* 210–11.

104 Chojnowski, *Koncepcje polityki,* 18–20.

land failed to extend its eastern boundary to the Dnieper, and the eastern territories were too small to form a federal system. However, the territory east of the Curzon Line (approximate to the post-World War II boundary between Poland and the Soviet Union) comprised 47 percent of the territory and was home to some 34 percent of the population in interwar Poland, certainly a sizeable region to support a federative system.[105] Nevertheless, the concept of a federal Polish State failed to gain significant support, and some used the Soviet conquest of the territory sought by Poland as an excuse to abandon the idea.

The Polish Nationalities Policy

The new Polish State adopted a simplistic approach to assimilation. Long-term socioeconomic factors that normally produced change were eschewed, and instead, assimilation would be achieved by administrative methods. In the 1930s, the Polish government introduced a more aggressive nationality policy that hadn't worked since their fourteenth century conquest of Rus.' Throughout the interwar period, Ukrainians experienced significant repressions that directly resulted from the Polish nationality policy: Polish colonization of Ukrainian lands, denial of political rights, religious persecution, repression of Ukrainian culture and education, and encouragement of regional differences. From the Ukrainian point of view, none of these contentious issues was more inflammatory and dangerous than colonization. The influx of large numbers of Poles would alter the ethnic composition of the population, thereby strengthening Polish claims to the territory and creating further difficulties in establishing a future Ukrainian State. As part of the agrarian reforms, the Polish government approved legislation on December 19, 1920 to settle Polish war veterans in parts of Belarus and Volhynia. The homesteads were to be between 30–111 acres and not subject to partitions for 25 years.[106] The lands subjected to colonization were those that were previously owned by the Tsarist government, the Orthodox Church, or non-Polish nobility who had neglected to claim the ownership of the land by

[105] Kirkien, L. *Russia, Poland and the Curzon Line.* (London: Cadra House Publishers Ltd.,1944), 47.

[106] Land could not be transferred, divided or sold off within the 25-year period.

April 1, 1921.[107] The last category consisted of Orthodox landlords and others who had fled either during the First World War or during the Russian Civil War. The provision did not apply to Roman Catholic landlords and was clearly designed to expropriate the lands of non-Polish minority groups without compensation. Government officials rationalized the seizures of Orthodox estates as the repossession of Polish estates taken in the Polish rebellions of the nineteenth century. Of course, not all of the lands owned by the Orthodox Church had been previously owned by Polish nobility. In reality, the policy was designed to provide land for Polish settlements and was in fact a colonization process being undertaken "with the view of forced Polonization of these territories..."[108] The colonists were former war veterans who strongly supported the Polish government's policies. Their presence would form a bulwark against local nationalism and endeavor to further Polish assimilation. There was even a discussion to form permanent "native" cavalry regiments from among the settlers, a throwback to the Cossack era. More than half (59 percent) of the settlers were officers and non-commissioned officers who besides receiving almost a combined million acres of land, were given material incentives, including two billion Polish marks, seeds, farm implements, construction material, as well as arms and ammunition. By the beginning of 1923, land had been allocated for 8,732 Polish homesteads, with 3,548 in Volhynia alone, but only 5,557 families settled permanently. Others who received land elected to lease it out and frequently became local government officials.[109]

To underscore the impact on the Ukrainian population, the colonization must be considered in the context of a severe land shortage. The growing rural population, unable to find work in towns or emigrate, continued to subdivide their already small land holdings. Farms with less than two hectares of land comprised 42 percent of the households in Galicia and Volhynia, those with 2–10 hectares accounted for 53 percent, and only five percent of the population had more than 10 hectares (25

---

107 Madajczyk, Czesław. *Burzuazyno Obszarnicza reforma rolna w Polsce (1918—1939)* (Ksiazka i Wiedza, 1956), 173.

108 Ibid.

109 Chojnowski, *Koncepcje polityki narodowościowej rządów polskich w latach 1921–1939,* 46.

acres).[110] There were few Polish estates in Volhynia, but in Galicia, the Polish nobility had thrived under the Habsburgs and accumulated "…about 2,000 large estates, owned by Poles and sometimes consisting of 10,000–20,000 acres, controlling close to 25 percent of the land."[111] When the land reforms were introduced, the local peasantry in Volhynia hoped to become owners of the land they had tilled during the Tsarist period. The reforms, however, allocated the prime land, and well as the bulk of it, to the Polish arrivals. The partitioning of the old estates deprived the local minority populations of supplementary earnings. The reforms further reviewed the legal status of pastures and woodlands that had been used in common since the abolition of serfdom in the nineteenth century. The review reduced the common land to approximately one-quarter of its former size,[112] further impoverishing the already poor peasantry. As K. Srokowski wrote in his memoirs, "...masses of peasants in western Ukraine and western Belarus were not only oppressed as a nationality, but also destroyed economically."[113] Besides economic losses, the local population was incensed at the aggressive behavior of the military colonists. Polish settlers formed armed units and arguments erupted between the settlers and Ukrainians which occasionally resulted in Poles killing Ukrainians without consequences. Ukrainian locals responded in kind and violence spread throughout the countryside. As one eyewitness described, "Partisan units attacked not only the police, the military, and the estates but also military settlers. In Brest County, for example, the mayor, a military settler, was shot and killed and there were numerous beatings of other settlers."[114] The rural population also organized strikes throughout Poland. Faced with the opposition, the government replaced some military settlers with civilian settlers, a move that hardly appeased the local population, and the violence continued. Land reforms and the colonization of eastern territories still continued until World War II, alt-

110 Vytanovych, I. "Agriculture in Western Ukraine Between 1914 and 1939." In Vol. II of Kubijovyč, Volodymyr, ed. *Ukraine*, 859.

111 Subtelny, *Ukraine: A History*, 433.

112 Madajczyk, *Burzuazyno Obszarnicza reforma rolna w Polsce (1918—1939)*, 176.

113 Ibid. Srokowski published a monograph on the nationality problems in eastern Poland and was a government official who, at the request of the Prime Minister Sikorski, prepared a report on Slavic nationalities in Poland.

114 Ibid., p.175. See also Chojnowski, *Koncepcje polityki,* 46; and Snyder, *The Reconstruction*, 148. Snyder cites sources claiming that in the early 1920s, Soviet authorities organized raids against Poles in Volhynia.

hough this happened at a slower pace. Throughout the interwar period an estimated two million acres of land, 800,000 hectares, was redistributed to Poles in western Ukraine. Although most of the redistributions occurred in Volhynia, a sizeable portion took place in Galicia, coming to about 200,000 hectares by the end of 1920.[115] An estimated 300,000 Poles moved to Volhynia and Galicia, with some 200,000 settling in rural areas and the remainder in towns.[116] While the new immigrants increased the "Polishness" of the territory, one of the Polish government's goals of land distribution, their presence did not significantly alter the overall ethnic composition of the region. Nevertheless, the policy exacerbated an already tense situation between the two groups that would again turn violent during the next war. The colonists would become the primary targets of local Ukrainian civilian attacks after the collapse of the Polish State in 1939, and the violence would be most severe in Volhynia where the colonization was most extensive.

Administrative Changes

In addition to colonization, the Polish government introduced administrative changes designed to Polonize the Ukrainian territories even before receiving international recognition for the recent conquest. To the south, the historic name of Galicia was abolished and renamed Eastern Little Poland, *Wschodnia Malopolska*, in March of 1920. Later that year, the territory was divided into three provinces (*Wojewodztwa*): Lwów (now L'viv), Tarnopol (now Ternopil'), and Stanislawów (now Ivano-Frankivsk), and the Austrian local administrative system was abolished. On September 30, 1921, the Polish government conducted a census of the population, and elections were held in November for both chambers of the national parliament. Most Galician Ukrainians boycotted both the census and the elections fearing that participation would jeopardize their chances of establishing an independent state since the final status of Galicia was still under consideration by the Allied Powers. The situation in Volhynia was even more chaotic, as the Tsarist administration collapsed during the Bolshevik Revolution and was temporarily replaced by the short-lived Ukrainian National Republic. Regional administrations were

---

115 Vytanovych, *Agriculture,* 858.
116 Subtelny, *Ukraine: A History*, 429.

formed in Kholm, Podlachia, Polisia, and eastern Volhynia, but all were abolished after Poland took control. The Ukrainians in those regions, unlike the Galicians, participated in the 1922 parliamentary elections and elected 25 members to the Polish parliament and five to the Senate. After presenting issues of great concern to Ukrainians, the legislators were outvoted by their more numerous Polish colleagues. In the end, Ukrainian participation in the parliament produced few tangible gains other than providing a platform for presenting and publicizing grievances.

Because of the government's policy of "Polonization through Catholicization," religious issues were extremely contentious in the interwar period as the state sought to minimize the influence of Ukrainian churches in order to expedite assimilation. Poland confronted two churches on Ukrainian territory: the well-organized Greek Catholic Church in Galicia and the Orthodox Church in Volhynia. Polish intrusion into church affairs was underscored in 1923, when Andrii Sheptytsky, the Metropolitan Archbishop of the Ukrainian Greek Catholic Church, was detained in Poznan after returning from a visit to the Ukrainian communities in the Americas. The Metropolitan was finally released through the intercession of Pope Pius XI. To normalize relations, an agreement was reached between the Vatican and the Polish State. The Greek Catholic Metropolitinate was again affirmed and the Metropolitan exercised authority over the internal affairs of the church. Nevertheless, the Polish government still managed to continue their intrusion on church matters since churches held the function of providing vital statistics to the government. All births, marriages, and deaths in a parish were recorded, and if a priest issued a birth certificate in Ukrainian or signed his name in Ukrainian, he was subject to prosecution for falsifying an official document.[117]

In the south, the government was unable to make gains against the well-organized Greek Catholic Church since it was protected to some extent by the Vatican; however, the Ukrainian Orthodox Church in the north was much more vulnerable because it had just been established in the wake of the Russian Revolution. The revolution had not only stimulated the desire to establish an independent Ukraine but had similarly inspired churchmen to form an Orthodox Church independent of the Patri-

---

117 Vytvytsky and Baran. "Western Ukraine Under Poland." In Vol. I. of Kubijovyč, *Ukraine*, 847; and Lencyk. "The Ukrainian Catholic Church Since 1800." In Ibid, 191; see also Magocsi, *A History of Ukraine*, 595.

arch of Moscow: The Ukrainian Autocephalous Orthodox Church. After a great deal of struggle with occasional successes, the Autocephalous Church finally created its own hierarchy, and in October 1921 had begun expanding, but by 1924, the church's inroads were still quite small with only 1,100 parishes established,[118] since most people continued to attend churches subordinated to the Moscow Patriarchate. The new church struggled not only against the Muscophile religious orientation but more so against secular authorities; specifically, the self-avowed atheistic government in Moscow which was keenly involved in church matters. To preserve the unity of the new state, the Soviet government preferred the Moscow Patriarchate because it emphasized previous ties to the government and the All-Russia view compared to the independent Ukrainian church, which emphasized Ukrainian distinctiveness. The embattled church was therefore vulnerable to Polish ambitions to eliminate it, which was especially the case on the western edge of the historic Volhynia where national awareness was comparatively weak and Roman Catholicism had expanded during the Tsarist period. Some officials advocated the rapid Polonization of the territory between Wieprz and Bug rivers, a strip of land approximately 50 miles in width.[119] The Polish government embraced this view and began the process of administratively dismantling the church.

In Belarusian and Ukrainian territories, the Polish government encouraged and supported the Ukrainian Autocephalous Church, severing ties with Moscow. This was an important consideration since in the past; Russian tsars had interfered in Polish internal affairs under the guise of protecting the Orthodox population in the Commonwealth. In 1921–22, shortly after gaining international recognition for the newly occupied territories, the Polish government had removed bishops favoring ties with Moscow and replaced them with church leaders advocating the formation of the Autocephalous Church. Iurii Iaroshevsky, a Ukrainian priest, received a title of Exarch from the Patriarch of Moscow but in January 1922 convoked a synod of Orthodox bishops in Warsaw to establish an Orthodox Church in Poland, severing ties with Moscow in the process. The Synod, under the auspices of the Polish government, adopted

---

118 Bociurkiw, B.R. "The Orthodox Church in Ukraine Since 1917." In Kubijovyč, *Ukraine,* Vol. II., 170.

119 See Kuprianowicz in Isaievych et al., 2003, 101.

"...provisional rules on the relationship of the government and the Orthodox Church in Poland."[120] The rules minimized the role of the clergy and laity in the church and gave the new government considerable influence in selecting its hierarchy and promoting the Polish language within the church. With the help of the Polish government, the church received a charter and blessings from the Patriarch of Constantinople, as well as approvals from the patriarchs of the Orthodox countries in Europe. The church encompassed "five dioceses: Warsaw-Kholm, Volhynia, Vilnius, Grodno, and Polisia..."[121] Secular interference in church affairs escalated and in 1938, and the Polish government issued a regulation "giving the state the power of sanctioning all ecclesiastical appointments from bishops to sextons" and making Polish "the official language in the Church..."[122]

Seizure of Ukrainian Church Property

Disputes over church property became another burning issue in Volhynia, where the religious beliefs of the population were manipulated more than on any other Ukrainian territory. In the pre-partitioned Poland of the eighteenth century, large tracts of land had been given to the Monastic orders and Roman Catholic parishes despite the presence of a relatively small number of Catholics, and in some cases Orthodox Churches were even turned over to the Catholics. In the aftermath of the nineteenth century rebellions, Russian authorities had reversed the process and most Uniate Church properties and some belonging to the Catholic Church were transferred to the Orthodox Church with the government retaining the titles to the properties.[123] After World War I, the Polish State sought to repossess Church properties that had been seized by Russia in the nineteenth century, and the repossession (*rewindykacja*) naturally favored the Roman Catholic Church and claimed lands of former Catholic and Uniate churches. The latter claim was based on the assumption that the Uniates would have become Roman Catholics except for the interference of the Russian government, ignoring the fact that the Uniate Church

---

120 Chojnowski, *Koncepcje polityki,* 51.

121 Korowytsky, I. "The Orthodox Church in Poland," in Kubijovyč, *Ukraine*, Vol. II, 179.

122 Ibid.

123 Chojnowski, *Koncepcje polityki,* 52.

in Galicia became a de facto Ukrainian national church and directly contributed to the growth of Ukrainian nationalism. Not withstanding public rhetoric, this implication was clearly understood by the Roman Catholic hierarchy as it opposed the re-introduction of the Uniate Church for fear that the population would be Ukrainianized.[124] By a decree issued December 16, 1918, the Polish government took possession of all church properties, lands, and buildings of the Orthodox Church. The Treaty of Riga enhanced the claim by transferring all Russian State property on the territory of the new Polish State to the Polish government.[125]

The religious conflict over church property was especially intense in the Chełm and Podlasie districts. The state took possession of all Ukrainian Orthodox Church properties through the laws of December 1918 and June 1919; some were given to the newly formed Polish Orthodox Church, others to the Catholic Church, and the remainder was held by the state pending future disposition.[126] At the beginning of 1923, the status of 260 pre-war Orthodox Churches in the Lublin Province, which included the Chełm district, was as follows: 109 churches remained closed, 86 had been given to the Roman Catholic Church, 39 were transferred to the Polish Orthodox Church, 23 had been designated as destroyed during the war (presumably damaged), and three had been converted for secular use.[127] In 1924, the distribution of Orthodox properties was halted, apparently in anticipation of mass conversions to Catholicism. Not only did the conversions fail to materialize, but the Orthodox Church was energized by the arrival of church and secular leaders who had fought for Ukrainian independence in the east. At the same time, the struggle for independence in Chełm, as on other Ukrainian territories, stimulated patriotism and national assertiveness among the laity. Nevertheless, the 32,000 Orthodox faithful in the district received only nine churches,[128] 3,500 parishioners per church, an extremely high number for a rural area. Therefore, there was a genuine need for additional Orthodox Churches. According to historian Konrad Sadkowski, "For the clergy, the elimination of as many of the Orthodox Churches in the

---

124 See Sadkowski, Konrad in *Slavic Review*, Number 4, (1998), 817, Footnote 11.

125 Much of the land in possession of the Orthodox Church was nominally owned by the Russian State. See Chojnowski, *Koncepcje polityki,* 52–3.

126 Sadkowski, 818.

127 Ibid, 819.

128 Ibid, 825.

state's possession as possible became the only real option if it were to 'contain' Orthodoxy and hope to one day eliminate it from the Chelm region."[129] By the mid-1930s, the Polish government became more reactionary as the Catholic Church pushed for the elimination of the remaining Orthodox Church and the military advocated for more rapid Polonization for security reasons. The military worked with the clergy to force conversion to Catholicism as the first step toward Polonization and began the physical destruction of the Orthodox Church. The military, with the support of the Catholic hierarchy (which did not wish to be publicly identified with the destruction), demolished or burned 127 buildings of the Orthodox Church; including 91 churches, 10 chapels, 26 prayer halls, and transferred three churches to the Catholic Church in 1938.[130] For many Ukrainians, the seizure of the churches was considered to be the most tragic example of Polish interwar policies toward Ukrainians.[131]

Educational Restrictions

Polish policies in education, as in other spheres, were designed to promote assimilation by reducing the number of educated Ukrainians who were in the forefront of national revival, and to that end the government significantly decreased the number of Ukrainian schools. The two Ukrainian lands differed considerably in educational attainment and national awareness. Volhynia had few schools before the war and none were taught in Ukrainian; however, during the war, Austrian and German forces occupied much of the area during which time the establishment of Ukrainian schools was permitted. The school staffs were comprised of former Ukrainian prisoners of war who had served in the Tsarist army, educated members of the local population, and graduates of special courses organized in Brest. According to I. Herasymovych and O. Terletsky, "Between the winter of 1916 and the autumn of 1918 there were approximately 250 schools in the lands occupied by the Austrians."[132] The number increased to 500 Ukrainian elementary schools when Poles occupied the region after the war; in Galicia the educational system was

129 Ibid, 823

130 Sadkowski, 836.

131 Chojnowski, *Koncepcje polityki,* 53–4.

132 Herasymovych, Terletsky and Kubijovyč. "Education in Western Ukraine in 1919–44." in Kubijovyč, *Ukraine*, Vol. II., 371.

much more developed with 2,500 Ukrainian elementary schools operating throughout the region in 1914.

After consolidating control of the territory, the Polish State began centralizing and altering the existing educational system. The system went through several reforms, and the last was based on a law issued on March 11, 1932 extending compulsory education to seven years, ages 7–14. The elementary grades were divided into three levels, grades 1–4, 5–6 and the seventh grade.[133] The reforms did not provide seven grades of education for all pupils, especially in the rural Ukrainian areas. Typically, children spent a year in the first and second grades, two years in the third grade, and three years in fourth grade, but the low quality of the curriculum prompted many to spend less than three years in the fourth grade since they were not learning anything new. Secondary education was not compulsory and consisted of four years of gymnasium. Graduates who wished to continue their secondary education could also enter a special two-year academic secondary school or a lyceum, a two-year curriculum which also provided semi-professional training. Additionally, vocational schools and pedagogical schools provided secondary education and prepared graduates to teach in elementary schools. The number of elementary schools increased in Galicia from 4,030 schools in 1911 to 4,998 in 1937; in Volhynia and Polisia the increase was greater, from approximately 1,000 schools to 3,101 in the same period.[134] By 1937, 85 percent of the children in Ukrainian areas, seven to thirteen years of age, attended school compared to 90 percent for Poland as a whole. While the elementary school network increased, the number of Ukrainian schools decreased drastically. In 1911, Galicia had 2,420 Ukrainian elementary schools, but between 1937–1939, the number had dropped to 352 schools. A similar pattern followed in Volhynia as 443 schools in 1922 were reduced to eight schools by 1937. In Chełm and Podlasie districts, where Polonization was especially intense, Ukrainian language instruction was banned after 1924. The decrease of Ukrainian schools was largely the result of legislation by Prime Minister Stanisław Grabski in 1924, which established bilingual schools. The law combined Polish and Ukrainian schools, and the language of instruction was to be determined by parents through a referendum vote. The cumbersome procedure was

133 Ibid, 372.

134 Volhynia and Polisia figure includes Belarusian area in Polisia. See Ibid.

administered by local Polish officials who were considerably more hostile to Ukrainian education than were the central authorities. Through various machinations by the school authorities, the bilingual schools became the de facto Polish schools. Instructions were usually conducted in Polish and many Ukrainian teachers were either dismissed or transferred to ethnic Polish areas. Ukrainians responded by campaigning to have some Ukrainian content in bilingual schools and by organizing private Ukrainian schools under the auspices of the *Ridna Shkola* ("Native School") organization. Ridna Shkola had limited success because it relied on private donations in underdeveloped areas and, more importantly, it faced numerous obstacles from local Polish authorities who were intent on restricting the growth of the private Ukrainian school system. By 1937, there were 41 Ukrainian schools located in Galician cities with an enrollment of 6,400 students, as well as two schools in Volhynia where authorities were even more adamant against permitting private Ukrainian schools. The informal education of the youth was supplemented through the reading rooms of the *Prosvita* (Society for Enlightenment), which were frequently headed by parish priests and teachers. Reading rooms developed into important social and educational organizations for the young, especially those living in the villages. Most reading rooms had some books and subscribed to Ukrainian newspapers and magazines. Members would socialize and discuss Ukrainian history, current events and other educational topics. Discussions were frequently augmented by organizing choral groups, musicals, and skits. While it is difficult to determine whether Prosvita's efforts significantly raised the literacy of the population, since reading and writing were not formally taught, there is little doubt that the Society was instrumental in raising national consciousness among the younger generations.

The struggle for Ukrainian higher education was especially intense during the interwar period. Under the Austrian rule, L'viv University remained a mainly Polish institution, but Ukrainians were able to acquire 10 departments by 1914 through constant pressure, Austrian authorities eventually agreed to establish a Ukrainian University by 1916. During the interwar period, the Polish government sharply curtailed Ukrainian language education and restricted the admission of Ukrainians to all schools, reducing the possibility for Ukrainians to obtain higher education at any institution in Poland. At the L'viv University, Ukrainian departments were abolished in 1919 with the exception of the Ukrainian language department where the chair remained vacant until a Polish linguist was appointed in 1927. Admission to the university was limited to Polish Army veterans.[135] Ukrainians reacted to the restrictions by organizing university level courses at Ukrainian research and teaching institutions. In 1920, the government banned the courses and the following year, a Ukrainian underground university was established and had an enrollment of 1,500 and a faculty of 63, but due to government pressure, it lasted only until 1925. On the political front, Ukrainians petitioned the League of Nations in 1922, and the Polish government responded by passing legislation calling for the establishment of a Ukrainian University by 1924. The law was never implemented because the Council of Ambassadors approved the incorporation of Galicia to the Polish State in March 1923, effectively removing any incentives for the Polish government to comply with international requirements. The Theological Academy of L'viv was established in 1928, based on the existing Theological Seminary, and became the sole Ukrainian institution of higher learning for the duration of the interwar period. The two Greek Catholic Seminaries in Galicia provided additional religious training. There was also an Orthodox Seminary in Kremianets, and Orthodox Theology courses were offered in Polish at the University of Warsaw. With Ukrainian schools limited to seminaries, Ukrainians tried to enroll in Polish language institutions but the results were meager. In 1937, nearly 3,000 were receiving higher education, about six percent of the total enrollment in Poland but almost a third of that number (about 800) were receiving theological training in preparation for priesthood.[136] Because of the restrictions in Poland, Ukrainians who were intent on obtaining a higher education often studied abroad, especially in Czechoslovakia where a number of schools were organized after the war, including three that provided higher education. Foremost among them was the Free Ukrainian University in Prague. The university was modeled after the Charles University and even received some financial aid from the Czech government. The new Polish State sought to prevent the crystallization of Ukrainian identity and to that end Ukrainian language education became a primary target. The state further pursued a policy of limiting Ukrainian access to any ed-

---

[135] Ibid, 377.
[136] Ibid, 378.

ucation or governance, effectively marginalizing Ukrainian influence in Polish society.

Fostering Regional Differences

Polish policies designed to stifle Ukrainian cultural and national development were augmented by measures to foster regional differences, especially among the Hutsuls and Lemkos, regional groups in the Carpathian Mountains who practiced Eastern Christianity (most were Greek Catholic.) Many Lemkos and Hutsuls considered themselves to be a subset of the Ukrainian people and therefore identified with the Ukrainian national cause. The Polish government's administrative measures in these regions were designed to undercut the growing assertiveness among the Ukrainian population and make the two areas more pro-Polish with the intent of eventual Polonization. Hutsuls are located in the southeastern portion of the Ivano-Frankivsk Oblast with Kolomiya as the principal city and have a distinct dialect and material culture that bears the imprint of Romanian and Balkan influence. The Polish military, concerned with the Soviet threat, took the lead in 1933 and established the Society of the Friends of the Hutsuls, headed by General Jan Kasprzycki. The Society developed publishing plans and hoped to settle Poles in the area, but the efforts remained largely unrealized.[137]

The campaign in the Lemko territory was pursued much more energetically as the chances of success were greater. Lemkos lived on both sides of the Carpathians, although those on the southern slopes usually considered themselves to be "Rusyns" (Ruthenians) rather than Lemkos. After World War I, the Lemko settlement land was partitioned, with the territory on the southern slopes given to Czechoslovakia (specifically to Slovakia) and the northern half went to Poland. The ideological differences between the two northern Lemko regions became apparent after the collapse of the Habsburg Empire. Upon learning that Ukrainians had seized L'viv and proclaimed a Western Ukrainian National Republic on November 1, 1918, Father Ponteleymon Shpylka of Wisłok Gorny (Upper Wisłok, Sanok County) quickly organized a meeting and proposed that similar liberation efforts should begin in the county. The following day, over 70 delegates representing more than 30 neighboring villages at-

---

137 Chojnowski, *Koncepcje polityki,* 198–99.

tended the meeting. They formed the Ukrainian National County Council, sometimes referred to as the Lemko Republic or Komańcza (Komancha) Republic since the last battle with Poles had taken place in that village. The attendees approved the formation of a local militia to be formed largely from men returning from the Austrian Army who had military training and combat experience. Andrii Kyr of Komańcza, a former non-commissioned officer in the Austrian army, was selected to command the militia. The militia reportedly had over 300 men and skirmished with local Poles until the Polish Army arrived and captured Wisłok on January 23, 1919. The seat of the Council, Komańcza, fell the following day. Similar events were unfolding on the western end of the Lemko region, and a Western Lemko Republic headed by Iaroslav Kachmarchyk was proclaimed in the village of Florynka on December 5, 1918. Unlike Lemkos in the east who hoped to join the Ukrainian Republic, those in the west had to find a suitable partner. Leaders made contact with the Prešov (Priashiv) National Council on the south side of Carpathians and held a joint meeting on December 21, 1918 in Košice, Slovakia. Both parties expressed a desire to join Russia, but since that was to prove geographically unrealistic, a delegation was sent January 23, 1919 and asked the Czechoslovakian government to annex the Lemko region north of Carpathians to the Czechoslovak Republic. Since a satisfactory answer was not given, another delegation visited President Tomas Masaryk with the same proposal in May. The Czechs did not wish to exacerbate the conflict with Poland so they declined the offer, and Poland quickly occupied the territory.[138]

The growing ethnic and religious discord among the Lemkos gave the Polish government an opportunity to manipulate the differences to its own advantage. From the Polish point of view, the Lemko region, which stretched along the Carpathians to about 55 miles southeast of Cracow, was steadily being Ukrainianized. To counter the trend, the Polish government in the region formed a Lemko Provincial Committee. The Committee consisted of representatives from several ministries, adminis-

---

[138] The description of the two republics is based largely on the discussion in Hvat, I. "Istoriia pivnichnoii Lemkivshchyny do vyhnannia lemkiv" in Struminsky, *Lemkivshchyna,* 179–186. Additionally, Fr. Shpylka described the events. See Shpylka in *Lemkivskiy Kalendar* (1967), 19–45 and Moklak in *The Lemko Region*, 24–32. Events in the western Lemko region are also discussed in Tarnovych, Iulian. *Iliustrovana istoriia Lemkivshchyny (L'viv*, 1936), 246–258.

trators of Cracow and L'viv School Districts, the Society for the Development of Eastern Lands, and members of the "Old Ruthenians", a contingent who claimed that Lemkos were not Ukrainian but a separate ethnic group. The Committee concentrated on political, educational and religious issues. In political matters, the government allied itself with the Old Ruthenians to block the spread of Ukrainian nationalism.[139] To implement the policy, educational and cultural activities received considerable attention, Ukrainian teachers were largely removed, and schooling was conducted in the Lemko dialect. A Lemko primer was provided for schools and some educational material was introduced in the dialect using the Latin alphabet. Because Lemko dialect has many Polish cognates and a Polish accentuation pattern, the school material left the impression that there was little difference between Poles and Lemkos with the exception of religious differences.

In religious matters, the Committee supported the pro-Orthodox movement as a way of checking a pro-Ukrainian view of the Greek Catholic Church. Conservatism and claim by some Lemkos that they were a part of the Russian nation, dubbed Muscophiles by Ukrainians, generated a desire by some to re-introduce the Orthodox Church. To that end, Old Ruthenians from the village of Tylawa (Tyliava) sent a delegation to Kyiv in 1911, with the hope of receiving help in establishing an Orthodox Church in their area. In the early 1920's attempt to introduce Orthodoxy was resumed with much greater effort in order to counter growing Ukrainian nationalism.[140] By the early 1930's, 15 villages, mostly to the south of Gorlice, turned Orthodox, their parishioners numbering approximately 18,000 to 25,000 people.[141] To counter the growth of the Orthodoxy, the Vatican, at the urging of the Polish Roman Catholic Church and secular authorities, established the Lemko Apostolic Administration in February 1934 with its administration encompassing most of the Lemko territory. The rural population at the time was either illiterate or barely literate, and village teachers and parish priests were influential figures. Besides their professional activities, they were natural community leaders that were consulted on various matters and promoted whatever cultural activities existed in the villages. Not surprisingly, the primary

139 Chojnowski, *Koncepcje polityki,* 198–99.

140 Hvat, 188.

141 The lower figure appears more plausible. See Ibid, 189–90.

movers in organizing the two Lemko republics were parish priests. After the war the newly ordained young priests reflected the changing political attitude of their generation that promoted common Ukrainian identity. Older conservative members of the church hierarchy who sought to maintain Old Ruthenian orientation faced a difficult task in organizing Apostolic Administration. The new administration was organized not only to prevent the spread of Orthodoxy but more importantly to prevent the Ukrainianization of Lemkos. The new administrator, Father Vasylii Matsiukh, forbade priests "to sing Ukrainian religious and patriotic songs or to subscribe to Ukrainian periodicals. Those who did not obey the new regulation were punished by having their salaries reduced or were not paid at all. An attempt was also made to remove the most active pro-Ukrainian clergymen as Matsiiuch (sic) searched for fifty new priests."[142] During the German occupation, the policy was reversed and the subsequent post-war deportations ended the existence of the Apostolic Administration. It should be noted, however, that Rusyns (Ruthenians) were not Polonizers; they considered Lemkos to be separate people whose identity was threatened by Ukrainian nationalism. This development forced their alliance with the government as a way of thwarting the more immediate threat: Ukrainianization.[143]

The Growth of Ukrainian Opposition

For Ukrainians, the conquest of western Ukraine generated hostilities against the new Polish regime that were further exacerbated by policies of rapid Polonization and the government's unwillingness to provide them with cultural and economic opportunities. The Ukrainian opposition took two forms: those who organized legal political parties in the hope of improving conditions for Ukrainians and preparing them for an eventual statehood, and those who advocated violence as a way of destabilizing the Polish State and gaining independence. The first group was by far the largest contingent, but the inability to achieve meaningful gains through legal means reduced its influence. As a result, those who advocated a violent solution continued to gained more followers, and by the outbreak of World War II, they became a dominant force in Ukrainian politics. The

142 Horbal, *Lemko Studies*, 259.

143 Estimate of the population in the Lemko region is presented in the Appendix I.

first Polish election was held in 1922 and Ukrainians in Volhynia formed an electoral bloc with other non-Polish groups, intending to work toward Ukrainian independence in the future, but in the meantime cooperate with the government to improve conditions for Ukrainians. The internationally sanctioned transfer of Galicia to Poland led to the establishment of numerous Ukrainian parties in the province that eventually united on July 11, 1925, to form the Ukrainian National Democratic Association (Ukrayins'ke Natsional'ne-Demokratychne Obiednannia - UNDO). UNDO considered itself more of a movement than a political party, as it was neither registered as a political party nor did it charge dues, but it nevertheless functioned as a political party in other ways. The Association was headed by Dmytro Levyts'kyi and included most of the Ukrainian political leaders of prewar Galicia. The Association was liberal and democratic, advocating cooperation with the government while strengthening the Ukrainian community through education and economic growth. The party participated in the 1928 elections, received 600,000 votes, and sent 23 delegates to the Polish parliament and eight to the Senate where it formed its own parliamentary club, establishing itself as the leading Ukrainian political party.

At the same time there were unsuccessful attempts, both in the east and west, to establish a Ukrainian State, displacing many Ukrainian soldiers who would come to dominate right wing Ukrainian politics between the wars. At the conclusion of the hostilities, approximately 20–25,000 soldiers of the Army of the Ukrainian National Republic were interned in camps throughout Poland. The remnants of the Ukrainian Galician Army, perhaps half as large as that of the Polish Republic's army, were interned in Czechoslovakian camps.[144] The veterans, especially officers, were motivated to encourage others to continue the struggle; partly because of their unwillingness to accept defeat but also due to a lack of opportunity to establish a meaningful civilian life. By the summer of 1920, the more militant members had formed an underground organization, the Ukrainian Military Organization (*Ukrains'ka Viis'kova Orhanizatsiia*, UVO.)[145] The actual date of UVO's establishment is uncertain, but on September 2, 1920, the organization issued UVO Order No. 1, indicating its existence and the UVO Executive Collegium was formed at

144 Motyl, *The Turn to the Right*, 94.

145 Subtelny, *Ukraine: A History*, 443.

the beginning of September in L'viv. The organizational structure was expanded with the return of Colonel Ievhen Konovalets', the board was renamed the Executive Command, and they appointed Konovalets' as their commander on July 21, 1921. Galicia formed the base for the organizations, and the UVO divided the province into 13 military districts and 50 counties, assigning each military district and county a separate command.[146] The operation of the organization, as well as its successor, the Organization of Ukrainian Nationalists (Orhanizatsiia Ukrayins'kykh Nationalistiv—OUN) was directed by Konovalets' until his assassination by a Soviet agent in Rotterdam on May 23, 1938.[147]

Having lost the struggle on the battlefield, UVO prepared to wage an underground war for Ukrainian independence. A few raids were conducted inside the borders of Soviet Ukraine, but were ineffective and impractical due to the combination of strong resistance by the Red forces and Soviet economic and cultural policies that were favorable to Ukrainians at the time. Ukrainians in the west, by contrast, had a heightened Ukrainian national awareness due largely to Polonization policies, which created a favorable milieu for terrorist activities. The UVO hoped that this course of action would precipitate an eventual collapse of the Polish State. The first few years of UVO's existence were devoted to organizing, collecting arms and explosives, and making preparations for an underground war. The first serious operation occurred in L'viv on September 25, 1921, when UVO agents attempted to assassinate Józef Pilsudski, the head of the Polish State, in L'viv.[148] The act was part of the campaign to resist the Polish occupation and entice Ukrainians to openly resist Polish authorities. To that end, the UVO urged Ukrainians not to take the oath of allegiance to the Polish State and to boycott the November 1921 population census as well as the November 1922 parliamentary elections. Young men were urged not to serve in the Polish Army when Poles be-

---

146 Knysh, Z. "Ukrainian Military Organization." In Struk, ed. *Encyclopedia of Ukraine,* Vol. V., 400.

147 As the Russian Empire disintegrated, Konovalets', a lieutenant in the Austrian army, escaped from the Russian internment camp on the Volga and reached Kyiv. There, he was instrumental in organizing other Galician POWs into a Sich Riflemen Battalion. The unit expanded by recruiting eastern Ukrainians and emerged as the most effective detachment of the Ukrainian National Republic. Between the wars, national unity and establishment of a Ukrainians State became for him an all consuming passion.

148 Subtelny, *Ukraine: A History*, 443.

gan drafting Ukrainians in December 1922. Most of these policies were supported by large numbers of Ukrainians, especially in Galicia.

In the spring of 1922, the UVO began systematic acts of sabotage; including burning military warehouses, bombing police stations, and cutting telephone and telegraph wires. In the summer and fall of that year, the attacks were directed against the estates of Polish nobility and the holdings of recent colonists; including the burning of some 2,300 estates and farm buildings. Acts of arson were committed; some by individuals and others by organized guerrilla bands which sometimes numbered up to 50 men.[149] Besides directing their attacks against Poles, Ukrainians who did not support the UVO policies were denounced and retaliated against, sometimes with extreme violence. In one case, Sydir Tverdokhlib, a writer who advocated cooperation with the Polish state and organized the Ukrainian Agrarian Party with the financial aid of the government, was assassinated. In L'viv, Polish groups retaliated by burning Ukrainian cultural institutions. Soon after, the Polish government initiated a vigorous campaign against the organization, during which time they captured and executed some guerrilla leaders and arrested many activists. At a meeting near Danzig (now Gdańsk) in early 1923, UVO decided to move the executive command headed by Konovalets' to Berlin, and the Home Command in L'viv was taken over by Andrii Mel'nyk. Mel'nyk had previously been a company commander of the Sich Riflemen of the Austrian Army, during which time he was captured and interned near the Volga. He had fought alongside Konovalets' in Kyiv, eventually rising to the rank of colonel and becoming his close ally.

Ukrainian nationalists at the time came under the influence of an ideology known as *integral nationalism*, a concept developed by French political thinkers at the turn of the century. Despite the lack of a clear definition for this ideology, it has certain noticeable tenets. A main tenet espoused that the interest of the nation was above that of any individual or institution, and all persons of a given nationality must support the national cause because they were biological and historical products of the nation. To that end, emotional romanticism was placed above the rational. The ideology, which had elements of social Darwinism, was based on the integral notion that a capable, strong-willed leader coupled with a

---

149 Mirchuk, *Narys istorii Orhanizatsii Ukrains'kykh Natsionalistiv,* Vol. I., 26–30.

single party was the necessary formula to best achieve the goals of the nation. Thus, war and violence were justified to assure that only the strong would survive.[150] Integral nationalism did not gain many followers in most countries of Western Europe, but attracted a considerable following among hard-core nationalists in Eastern Europe as well as in Italy and Germany. Since the interwar period was not a favorable season for democracy, evidenced by its nonexistence in some countries and a struggle to survive in others, the political climate was favorable to more radical authoritarian political thinking. Moreover, the authoritarian regimes, both of the left and right, were headed by strong-willed leaders who triumphed over the opposition because they were supported by disciplined and committed groups. For those Ukrainians who had devoted their lives to the establishment of the Ukrainian State, the democratic approach had already been attempted without success, and by contrast, the authoritarian approach appeared more promising and was therefore adopted.

The UVO's ideology and policies were disseminated throughout several journals. The *Literary Scientific Herald* was revived in 1922 and *The Glow* was founded in May 1922. Dmytro Dontsov edited both journals, and these activities were the beginning of his long association with the Ukrainian nationalists. Born on August 29, 1883 in Melitopol, located just north of the Sea of Azov, Dontsov studied law in St. Petersburg and became active in Ukrainian political circles in the capital. Because of his political activities and strong anti-Russian attitude, he was jailed and finally fled to Galicia in 1908. Like many others, he was influenced by integral nationalism and admired the Italian Fascists for their accomplishments. Though not a sycophantic admirer of either ideology, he studied Fascist and Bolshevik successes to see how their methods could be applied to the cause for Ukrainian independence, a process which led him to conclude that both approaches had succeeded because they were "'anti-democratic', 'populist', 'uncompromising', and were led by an 'initiative-minority.'"[151] Like other Ukrainian nationalists, he saw the peasantry as the only class that had preserved national identity and possessed the numerical strength and vitality to organize a national state.

While the nationalists glorified the Ukrainian language and culture, they eschewed the Polish government and embraced an exaggerated ro-

---

150 Armstrong, *Ukrainian Nationalism*, 20, and Motyl, *The Turn to the Right*, 162–3.
151 Motyl, *The Turn to the Right*, 68.

manticism for the cause as well as a willingness to condone acts of terrorism. Despite infatuations with extreme ideologies such as those in Italy and Germany, most of the Ukrainian nationalists' ideas came from indigenous sources.[152] The nationalistic romanticism reached fanatical levels for those on the right and the left, and had some important utilitarian aspects for Ukrainians. Faced with enemies that possessed advantages in numbers and materials, success was possible only if the followers were prepared to sacrifice everything for the cause. In the struggle to achieve some political rights and improve material conditions, Galicians in the Austrian Empire stressed reliance on their own strength and resources, and nationalists enshrined this notion as a guiding principle. The emphasis on national exclusivity was exacerbated by vehement opposition to Ukrainian independence by large Polish and Russian minorities. These two groups arrived in Ukraine as part of the occupation army and continued to identify themselves with their respective ancestral countries, comparable to the European colonists in Asia and Africa. Since they ruled Ukraine, other groups tended to assimilate, or at least acculturate, to one of the two groups. For the nationalists, ethnic Ukrainians were the only reliable element while other groups were viewed as a threat to their objectives. The multitude of parties, petty ambitions, and the ensuing chaos led to an emphasis on strong leadership and a clear ideology. In the end, the "Ukrainian Nationalism was as organically Ukrainian a phenomenon as any other Ukrainian political current of the 1920s."[153]

The ongoing conflict with other Ukrainian groups and a significant number of arrests reduced UVO's ranks. As a result, the weakened local organizations were unable to conduct terrorist activities, a task now assigned to a mobile band of members called the "Flying Brigade." The Brigade continued to assassinate government officials and added a new activity that was termed the "expropriation acts." The "acts" consisted of robbing post offices and mail trucks as a means of intimidating Polish officials, gaining necessary funds, and perhaps to show domestic and foreign supporters that the organization retained élan.[154] UVO exploited Poland's tense relations with foreign countries such Czechoslovakia, Germany, and Lithuania over border issues and as a result, stronger and mu-

---

152 Ibid, 172.
153 Ibid, 173.
154 Ibid, 122.

tually beneficial relationships developed between Ukrainians and the neighboring foreign powers. UVO acquired safe havens to direct operations in Ukraine, established publishing facilities, and received specialized training and financial support. The foreign supporters, on the other hand, had access to the organization's intelligence and sabotage capabilities. The free city of Danzig soon developed into an important operational center because of support from anti-Polish German groups and its comparatively easy access to Poland. A six-month officer training course was conducted in the eastern portion of Czechoslovakia, now the Transcarpathian Oblast of Ukraine.[155] Publishing activities centered on the journal *The Trumpet,* which was first published in Berlin in 1927 and moved to Kaunas, Lithuania in 1928. The change of venue was designed to show that the organization was an independent entity and not an arm of the German government as the Poles had claimed.[156] About 10,000 copies of the journal were published in a single run for readers abroad and in Ukraine, and copies destined for Ukraine were printed on thin paper to facilitate smuggling through Danzig, Teschen (Cieszyn) in Silesia and through Transcarpathia.

In addition to the UVO, other militant groups formed during the 1920s and later in the decade, they coalesced to form a single organization. At the beginning of 1929, the First Congress of Ukrainian Nationalists was held in Vienna and the Organization of Ukrainian Nationalists (Orhanizatsiia Ukrayins'kykh Nationalistiv--OUN) was formed, headed by Konovalets'. Half of the thirty delegates attending the Congress were eastern Ukrainians. Most lived abroad and were professionals, and twelve were in the military during the struggle for independence.[157] The divisive issue of the relationship between the UVO and the OUN ended in a compromise: the UVO would remain within the OUN and continue armed struggle, eventually to be absorbed by the latter. The Congress approved a program describing the administrative structure as well as the social, political, and economic policies of the future Ukrainian State. The ideology of OUN reflected the views of the organizations that formed it. The OUN committed itself to the formation of a Ukrainian State on all ethnic Ukrainian territories through revolutionary means under the guid-

---

155 Mirchuk, *Narys istorii*, 34.

156 Motyl, *The Turn to the Right*, 124.

157 Ibid, 150.

ance of the nationalist dictatorship. The proposed state would introduce land reforms and an economy based on state capital, private capital and cooperatives. The cultural and educational level of the population was to be raised principally through the introduction of compulsory education financed by the state. The program decreed that the OUN would be organized along military lines, and militaristic obedience was expected of all members. In Ukraine, the OUN was divided into 10 organizations; each were divided into five districts with 10 regional organizations allocated to members living abroad. Ukrainians as young as eight years of age could be admitted to the organization, but only those 21 years or older could become regular members.[158] Despite the agreement on major issues, a rift began developing between the older leadership living abroad and the younger members in Ukraine. Youthful members were made more militant due to several factors directly impacting them; such as the discrimination against Ukrainians in Poland, the Polonization of Ukrainian schools, and the lack of economic opportunities caused in part by the worldwide depression. Stalinist repressions in eastern Ukraine pushed youth even more to the right. The leaders abroad, on the other hand, were less prone to violence having matured in less strident pre-war times and because they had not personally been subjected to the oppressive policies of the Polish government.

In February 1929, the newly established OUN formed the Western Ukrainian Territorial Executive to conduct military activities against the Polish establishment.[159] At the beginning of 1930, when members of the Polish parliament proposed intensifying the colonization of eastern territories, Ukrainian and Belarusian delegates protested the proposed policy to no avail. When the Polish government began moving large numbers of Poles into Ukrainian lands, there was an intensely emotional reaction among Ukrainians which frequently devolved into violence. Ukrainians were fearful that in a comparatively short time, the Polish state would attain its assimilationist goal and cause a large portion of Ukraine to be permanently lost. As a response to the mounting concerns, the OUN decided to take more direct action, implementing tactics designed to fright-

---

158 Mirchuk, *Narys istorii,* 100–101.

159 Yurkevich, "Organization of the Ukrainian Nationalists" in Struck, ed. *Encyclopedia of Ukraine*, Vol. III, 708

en potential Polish settlers.[160] The campaign began in the autumn of 1930 and according to the official Polish sources, 191 acts of terror were committed by the UVO,[161] most of them involving arson. 172 of those cases were committed against the properties of Polish colonists, with the remaining attacks carried out on telephone and telegraph lines, railroads, and police stations.

The Polish government responded with pacification measures that were even more violent than the UVO's attacks. Pilsudski stated that arson, sabotage, raids, and violence would not be tolerated and urged repressive police action. Some suggested that one aim of the pacification, limited to Galicia, was to undermine the opposition in the upcoming parliamentary elections scheduled for November 1930.[162] Beyond the immediate political gains, the pacification was designed to drive the Ukrainians into submission. As noted by the Polish historian Andrej Chojnowski, "The scope of the operation and the manner in which they were carried out...made it clear that the Polish government was responding to more than just the UVO threat. In effect, the pacification was comparable to a pogrom against Ukrainians initiated, sanctioned, and executed by the Polish State authorities."[163] In a campaign that was inaugurated on September 9, Pilsudski ordered his minister of interior to send troops and police to the districts believed to be supporting the underground, resulting in the arrests of five Ukrainian deputies.

The actual operations began on September 21 and ended on October 16. Pilsudski's task force consisted of about 1,000 policemen, commanded by Bronisław Pieracki, Deputy Minister of the Interior, and supported by cavalry units. The operation, based on the notion of assigning collective guilt, was intended to cleanse 450 villages in 16 counties of Galicia. The "cleansing" consisted of searching buildings, trashing their interiors, occasionally destroying entire buildings, and beating the occupants. The searches were not only limited to private dwellings but also included cooperatives and cultural institutions where books, national customs, and other folk art items were destroyed. At the same time the army requisi-

---

160 Mirchuk, *Narys istorii*, 233.

161 Chojnowski, *Koncepcje Politiky*, 157.

162 Chojnowski, "Pacification." In Vol. III. of Struk, ed. *Encyclopedia of Ukraine*, 747.

163 Ibid, 747. See also Budrowycz, Bohdan in *Canadian Slavonic Papers, XXV, 4*. Toronto. (1983): 486–7.

tioned grain, presumably to feed horses. During the searches, some arms and explosives were found and according to Ukrainian sources, seven people died as a result of the beatings, although the government claimed that only two people had died. Besides the deaths, 970 people were arrested, of which 538 were released and the remainder turned over to the courts for prosecution. In the end, the courts released over three-quarters of the detainees due to a lack of evidence. Searches of UNDO offices resulted in establishing contact between the party and the underground, and this directly led to the arrests of several party leaders. In the aftermath of the pacifications, secondary schools in several Galician towns were closed and *Plast*, the nationalistically oriented Ukrainian scouting organization, was banned. The Polish pacification measures were reported extensively and strongly condemned by the presses in Western Europe and the United States. The Ukrainians took their case to the League of Nations, the guarantor of minority rights in Poland, and while complaints were received sympathetically, the League was ultimately unwilling to condemn the Polish actions. After much behind the scenes political maneuvering, the League concluded in 1932 that the Polish actions were justifiable in view of Ukrainian terrorist activities.

The pacifications provoked demonstrations and meetings among Ukrainians and likewise provoked the UVO/OUN to escalate their terrorist activities. Over the next several years, OUN (at this time UVO merged with the OUN) engaged in acts of sabotage, attacked post offices and banks to raise money, and conducted over 60 assassination actions,[164] although not all were successful. Attacks were directed largely against government officials, especially police, as well as Ukrainians who were suspected of collaborating with Polish authorities. With respect to the government officials, the most sensational case was the 1934 assassination of Bronisław Pieracki, Pilsudski's Minister of Internal Affairs in Warsaw, whom the underground held responsible for the 1930 pacifications. More disturbing to the Ukrainian population was OUN's assassination of Ivan Babii, the respected director of a secondary school and a former officer of the Galician Army. For Babii's alleged crimes, OUN tried him in absentia, judged him to be a police informant and summarily ordered his assassination. Most Ukrainians were disturbed by

164 Yurkevich, *Organization,* 708.

the underground's policy of arbitrarily assassinating Ukrainians for alleged disloyalty and many were against the terrorist activities committed against the Polish government. In their view, OUN's terrorism had not only failed to weaken the Polish State, but it had provoked even more repressive measures against the Ukrainian population. The Ukrainian legal press frequently condemned OUN's actions, and this sentiment was echoed in the pastoral letters of the Ukrainian Catholic Metropolitan Archbishop Andrii Sheptytsky, the most respected Ukrainian in Galicia. After the Pieracki assassination in June 1934, the government began a massive campaign of arrests among OUN leadership, virtually destroying its network in Galicia. Much of the leadership, including Stepan Bandera and Mykola Lebed, were confined in Bereza Kartuska, a newly built prison for political prisoners in the Brest region. Later, it became apparent that police had infiltrated the OUN.

As the violence subsided in the wake of the OUN suppression, the government and legal Ukrainian parties attempted to normalize the situation and reach an accommodation. Ukrainian parliamentarians presented their demands and concessions to the Ministry of Internal Affairs, which included a halt to the Polish colonization of western Ukraine, the expansion of education in Ukrainian language at all levels, Ukrainian access to government employment, and the release of political prisoners. For their part, the Ukrainians promised to end the vehement opposition to the government, but refused to take a loyalty oath to the Polish State as the government demanded. From the Ukrainian perspective, they had never accepted nor acquiesced to the post-war boundaries of a new Polish state, and therefore had not developed any loyalties to the new government because they considered this to be an occupation. During the war, Poles viewed Ukrainian cooperation with Germans as a treasonous collaboration; however, Ukrainians viewed the Germans as the latest occupier and their destruction of the political order in Eastern Europe raised the possibility of organizing a Ukrainian State. Despite the refusal to take a loyalty oath, Minister Marian Zyndram-Kościałkowski agreed to consider the Ukrainian demands and proposed a new electoral scheme, where both Poles and Ukrainians would elect their own parliamentary delegates in the 15 electoral districts of Galicia with the caveat that the government had the right to disqualify any Ukrainian candidate. Some Ukrainian parties rejected the offer because the government was given the right to determine the suitability of Ukrainian candidates and similar rights were not extended to Ukrainians in Volhynia. UNDO, the largest party, concluded that better terms could not be extracted from the government and therefore accepted the proposal. Elections were held in September 1935, with 14 Ukrainian delegates elected to the parliament in Galicia and five to the senate, Volhynia elected five to parliament and one senator. The new members formed their own parliamentary club to advance their aims, and Vasyl Mudry, head of UNDO, was elected Deputy Speaker. One of the points of contention centered around the fact that although the Polish government had released most political prisoners and extended credit to the Ukrainian cooperatives, their demands for increased Ukrainian education were ignored.[165]

After Pilsudski's death in 1935, the more conservative government, supported by a right wing coalition called the Camp of National Unity, advanced a more authoritarian system of governance that reduced minority rights and intensified Polonization activities. Poles in western Ukraine, who were resented by the local Ukrainian population, became vociferous advocates of the new policy, viewing increased rights for Ukrainians as a threat to their own prerogatives. Their increased hostilities resulted in some mob attacks on Ukrainian institutions and individuals. The military, concerned with the security of the eastern border, was at the forefront of the drive to Polonize the region. At this time a pamphlet was published wherein the author, taking a creative approach to genealogy, discovered that 880,000 western Ukrainians (approximately 15 percent) were actually descendants of the Polish nobility.[166] In the prepartitioned Polish state, the nobility was thought to comprise about eight percent of the population and a very small share would have been of Ukrainian ancestry. During the new Polonization drive that began in Chełm region following the conference of September 1935, representatives of the Second Military district urged the immediate assimilation of Ukrainians in the area. Specifically, "Speakers urged the state to restrict excessive development of the Orthodox Church network to the numbers necessary for religious needs and remove Ukrainians from the position of gamekeepers, forest wardens, road maintenance workers, teachers, rural

---

165 Budrowycz, *Poland and the Ukrainian Problem,* 491.

166 Chojnowski, *Koncepcje Politiky*, 228.

administrators, railroad workers..."[167] To implement the policy, a Coordinating Committee was organized in December 1936, headed by General Mieczysław Smorawinski, commander of Military District II. The committee, in keeping with a widespread attitude at the time, considered Ukrainians in Chełm to be "Ruthenianized Poles" and divided them into three groups. Those who could be converted to Roman Catholicism, strong Orthodox believers influenced by Ukrainian nationalism, and finally a third group which was totally committed either to Ukrainian nationalism or communism. Different approaches were developed for dealing with each group. The first group was to be proselytized with the expected conversion to Roman Catholicism. The second group was subjected to gradual assimilation pressures with the hope of future religious conversions, and the third group was to be dispersed among Polish settlements and insulated from the outside political currents. Armed local groups who frequently resorted to violence aided the new propaganda campaign. The program was to be implemented in the next several years, but, in fact, showed modest results except for the destruction of some Orthodox religious buildings. Ukrainian nationalism and the church in Galicia were much more militant and also drew the attention of the military. The Greek Catholic Church played an important role in Ukrainian national life, but the final assault, as had occurred in Chełm, was not possible because the Church was well organized and its subordination to Rome offered considerable protections. Rather than attempting to threaten the existence of the church, the Polish government efforts focused on influencing internal practices that would bring it closer to the Latin Rite. On the secular side, about 40,000 rural Ukrainians in Galicia and Volhynia believed to be of Polish descent were organized into 450 groups, usually under the auspices of the military.[168] Lectures and summer camps were organized for the groups in an attempt to Polonize them. Border Corps conducted these activities and organized a paramilitary group called The Riflemen from local Polish youth. The Riflemen, familiar with the local conditions, were to aid regular police in maintaining order, but its chauvinistic and ill-disciplined members frequently attacked Ukrainians. The unfortunate practice of using armed local Poles to

---

167 Ibid, 230.
168 Ibid, 229.

harass Ukrainians pushed ethnic hatred to the extreme and contributed to the tragic events that would unfold during the Second World War.

The second Polish pacification mobilized Ukrainians to defend their rights, and a coordinating committee of political parties and civil organizations was formed to discuss the course of action against the new threat. UNDO representatives in the parliament presented their demands for territorial autonomy, but the party was split because many members doubted that cooperation with the government would accrue any real benefits for Ukrainians. The disintegration of Czechoslovakia also began to affect the attitudes of Ukrainians. Before its total dismemberment, the Prague government had granted regional autonomy to Slovakia and Carpatho-Ukraine in 1939.

Events in Czechoslovakia prompted Ukrainians to demand autonomy for the "Galician-Volhynian Land," their proposed concept for a new autonomous region. Regional officials would conduct all government activities with the exception of foreign policy, military and financial matters, with Polish and Ukrainian as the official languages.[169] The government rejected the proposal and in the winter of 1939, they began a new Polonization drive by sending more Polish administrative and technical personnel to the region, encouraging Ukrainian emigration, expanding the Polish school system, and promoting the growth of Polish civic and paramilitary groups.[170] Both Ukrainians and Poles followed the events leading to the Czechoslovak State's collapse, but for different reasons. On March 14, the Ukrainians declared an independent Carpatho-Ukrainian state, and many young Ukrainians crossed the Carpathians to join a hastily organized Carpathian Sich, which consisted of a force of approximately 5,000 poorly trained and poorly armed men. Carpatho-Ukraine offered the nationalists a base to be used for the liberation of other Ukrainian territories, although nationalism there was only beginning to develop. For Poland, the situation was grave: if the new state continued to exist, it would serve as a base for the Ukrainian irredentist movement; however, if it were to be annexed by Germany, an additional threat from the south would develop. To the chagrin of Ukrainians and the delight of Poles, the territory was occupied by Hungary within several days of the declaration. In reality, the fate of the new state had been determined earlier when Hitler, in order to secure Hungarian support in the coming war, gave the territory to

169 Budrowycz, 496.
170 Ibid, 498–99.

Hungary, since the province had been part of the Hungarian State for centuries and was viewed by Hungarians as their land.

By the end of the interwar period, the Ukrainian struggle for independence, although unsuccessful, had generated strong patriotism and a widespread desire to establish an independent Ukrainian state. The Polish government's uncompromising attitude toward Ukrainian demands combined with their radical tactics, created an atmosphere of intense ethnic hostilities between Poles and Ukrainians in Poland. As the Second World War approached, many Polish communities had formed paramilitary units with the support of the state to maintain order. This further exacerbated ethnic tensions, and the 1939 German invasion and subsequent collapse of the Polish State ushered in an unprecedented period of violence.

Chapter III:
World War II, The Nationalist Movement, and the Ukrainian-Polish Civil War

On August 23, 1939, the German and Soviet governments signed a nonaggression treaty what would become known as the Molotov-Ribbentrop Pact. The agreement was named after Soviet foreign minister Vyacheslav Molotov and German foreign minister Joachim von Ribbentrop. In addition to stipulations of non-aggression between Germany and the Soviet Union, the treaty included a secret protocol dividing several eastern European countries, including Poland. The Soviet Union would annex Lithuanian, Belarusian, and Ukrainian ethnic territories that had been a part of pre-war Polish state and Germany would occupy the remaining territory of Poland. The German-Soviet boundary in the Ukrainian area was anchored on the Bug and San rivers.

On September 1, 1939, Germany invaded Poland, an action that started World War II. The Germans annexed ethnic Polish territories that had comprised the western portion of the Polish state as well as a strip of land in southeastern Poland on the west bank of the two rivers—an area which contained a mixture of Poles, Ukrainians, and Jews. On September 17, a few weeks after the German invasion, the Red Army invaded Poland from the east and annexed the historic Ukrainian territories of Galicia and Volhynia,[171] which had formed Poland's eastern frontier during the interwar period. The Soviet portion in Galicia included lands between the San and Zbruch rivers in the east, with territory that now forms three oblasts (provinces) in Ukraine: L'viv, Ternopil' and Ivano-Frankivsk, all of which were heavily populated with Ukrainians but had sizeable Polish and Jewish populations. To the north, the Soviet Union annexed Volhynian territory east of the Bug River, now comprising the Luts'k and Rivne oblasts, with a population as diverse as that of Galicia.

At the beginning of 1939, the Ukrainian districts on the German side encompassed over 6,000 square miles and had a population of over 1.2 million people. The territory stretched along the demarcation line like

---

171 This refers to the medieval principality of Halych-Volhynia as discussed in Chapter 1.

a ribbon, broken in several places, for almost 400 miles, from the Carpathian Mountains northward. Ukrainians totaled 695,000, but 170,000 of that number had been Polonized,[172] and most spoke Polish but their confession remained either Greek Catholic or Orthodox. Ukrainians largely populated the countryside, although Polish rural settlements were more numerous compared to regions further east. In the Carpathians, the Lemko region differed from other districts, as it stretched westward about 70 miles from the San River toward Cracow and had a width of 20–25 miles, covering a total of approximately 1,500 square miles.[173] The towns, as in other parts of Galicia, were thoroughly Polonized and the Ukrainian population was minimal. Before the Polish conquest in the fourteenth century, the region had two principal towns: Krosno and Sanok. The old Polish-Ukrainian border ran west of Krosno, but by World War II, the town was surrounded by Polish villages and had only a few Ukrainian inhabitants. Sanok was located further east, just inside Ukrainian ethnographic territory, and had a total population of approximately 15,400 of which 1,450 were Ukrainians, but 650 spoke only Polish. To the north in the San River valley are two major towns, Jarosław and Przemyśl, and the latter had been an important political and commercial center in the early history of Galicia. Over the centuries, the town was gradually Polonized and by 1939, the Polish presence was dominant. Out of the population of 54,200, Poles numbered 26,470, Jews numbered 18,400, and Ukrainians totaled only about 9,230 (including about 2,000 who considered Polish to be their native language.) The old town, which was the principal part of the city, was located on the east bank of the San River and the new suburban portion was located on the west bank. Because the German-Soviet line in this area ran along the San River between 1939 and 1941, Soviets occupied the major portion of Przemyśl. To the north, on the west bank of the river, is Jarosław, which was founded in 1031 by the Grand Prince of Kyiv, Iaroslav the Wise. In 1939, the town had a total population of 24,000; Ukrainians totaled 3,500 (about 2,500 spoke only Polish,) Poles numbered 13,700, and Jews 6,700.[174] North of Jarosław were the Ukrainian districts Bilogray (Bi-

---

172 Kubijovyč, *Ukraintsi v Heneral'nii Hubernii*, 20

173 Ibid, 21

174 Population data for the two cities are reported in Kubijovyč, Volodomyr, *Ethnic Groups of the Southwestern Ukraine*, 55, 109.

lohrai), Zamość (Zamostia), and Hrubieszów (Hrubeshiv), which had a combined Greek Catholic and Orthodox population of 182,000, and of which 52,000 were linguistically Polonized.[175] Further north were the Chełm and Podlasie districts, located on the western edge of the medieval Volhynia Principality, which had been part of the Russian Empire until World War I. The districts encompassed approximately 4,000 square miles and had a total population of 720,000; Ukrainians totaled 380,000, with 160,000 of them Polonized.[176] Although this group had converted to Roman Catholicism, most spoke Ukrainian as their primary language and continued to observe Ukrainian customs.

The collapse of the Polish State brought about profound changes to the political and civic order in the region. At the conclusion of hostilities and territorial adjustments after the 1939 invasion, Germany divided Poland into several districts. The Baltic region and western Poland formed two separate districts annexed and administered directly by Germany, while central Poland and the adjoining Ukrainian districts formed the *Generalgouvernement,* an administrative region that was established by Hitler on October 12, 1939. Those living in the eastern part of Poland found themselves in the newly annexed territories of the Soviet Union and faced "Sovietization," which included the arrests of real and imaginary opponents, nationalization of businesses, and the collectivization of farms. In the Generalgouvernement, anti-German acts would bring about brutal reprisals, but unlike the situation in the Soviet zone, the socio-economic order was left in tact and Ukrainians in the region gained much greater cultural autonomy than they had enjoyed under Polish administration in the interwar period.

In early 1940, soon after the German occupation, Ukrainians formed the Ukrainian Central Committee (*Ukrains'kyi Tsentralnyi Komitet,* UTsK), a cultural and political organization that promoted native language education, economic improvements, and rendered aid to refugees and the indigenous population. For Ukrainians in Poland, the German occupation meant that Ukrainians were free from two decades of repressive policies that had targeted cultural and religious activities. Compared to the Polish government of the interwar period, the Generalgouvernement administration in Poland was comparatively more tol-

175 Kubijovyč, *Ukraintsi*, 32.
176 Ibid, 26.

erant of Ukrainian religious and cultural activities. It was partly for this reason that Ukrainians initially viewed the German occupation as a positive political development, welcoming the Germans as liberators and viewing them as an ally against a common Polish enemy. In reality, the German perspective was strictly pragmatic, since German racial ideology viewed all Slavic peoples as *untermenschen* (subhuman) and plans for developing Ukraine into Hitler's *lebensraum* ("living space") were already underway. To that end, the Germans used Ukrainians as a counterweight against Poles,[177] their implacable enemies from World War I, and regarded Ukrainians as the more trustworthy contingent. Under the Germans, Ukrainians suddenly enjoyed considerably more cultural autonomy, and were able to open schools, cultural centers, and even obtain administrative jobs and other professional positions within German civic and military organizations. Since the Germans lacked the manpower to carry out all of the administrative functions of the new district, they employed local people in lower level administrative positions, keeping them under strict supervision. Under these conditions, Ukrainian community leaders sought to replace local Polish officials and police, not only to gain jobs but also as a means of Ukrainianizing the region and preparing it for the eventual formation of a Ukrainian state.

Throughout the Generalgouvernement, the appointment of pro-Ukrainian German officials contributed to the comparatively better treatment of Ukrainians vis-à-vis Poles. One such official was Dr. Hans Koch, the Director of the Institute for Eastern Europe at the University of Wrocław. Dr. Koch was also a former captain of the Ukrainian Galician Army, and he had been an officer in *Abwehr*, the German intelligence agency in charge of Ukrainian affairs. Known for being sympathetic to the Ukrainian people, he "…helped Ukrainians a lot, especially in respect to refugees and political prisoners."[178] Koch was appointed to the German-Soviet exchange commission in L'viv where he helped many Ukrainians leave the Soviet Zone under the pretense that they were of German ancestry. In Cracow, he was replaced by his colleague from the Institute, Dr. Theodor Oberländer, also an Abwehr officer and a former colonel of the Galician Army with similar pro-Ukrainian views. Another key official in the Generalgouvernement administration was Alfred

177 Ibid, 48.

178 Ibid, 59–60.

Bysanz, a German-Galician landowner and former Lt. Colonel in the Galician Army (at the end of World War I, a handful of Austrian and German officers served in the Galician Army). During the German occupation, Bysanz held a rank equivalent to Colonel in the German Army but was attached to the civilian government in charge of Ukrainian affairs, where he displayed a sympathetic disposition toward Ukrainians. Finally, Dr. Fritz Arlt, author of a brochure on ethnic Ukrainian groups, directed an office on population and welfare. He was also known for his strong Ukrainian sympathies. As noted by Volodymyr Kubijovyč, a leading Ukrainian academic and the head of the Ukrainian Central Committee during World War II, "We found in him a genuine supporter."[179] These Germans all contributed to softening Nazi policies toward Ukrainians in the Generalgouvernement and encouraged positive German policies with regard to the growth of Ukrainian schooling and nationalism. Their policies, combined with the zeal of Ukrainian activists, increased national awareness in the western districts during the war. Polish historian Grzegorz Motyka noted that when Ukrainians arrived from the east and began organizing and tutoring Ukrainians in the Zamość region, "...national awareness of Ukrainians proceeded quickly". [180] The comparatively favorable position of Ukrainians in the German Generalgouvernement, and the increased emphasis on patriotic education and self-help made the local Ukrainian population more nationalistic and assertive during the war years, a condition that increased anti-Ukrainian hostilities among many Poles.

The Ukrainian Central Committee (UTsK)

The onset of World War II and the resulting new order quickly generated large numbers of refugees from the east, including an estimated 30,000 Ukrainians who entered the Generalgouvernement from territories that had been annexed by the Soviet Union. Most were fleeing the advancing Red Army, some were political prisoners who had escaped as the Polish State was disintegrating, and others were Ukrainians in the Polish Army who had been interned in German POW camps. To provide for the refugees and to enhance community life in Ukrainian districts,

---

179 Ibid, 61.

180 Cited in Motyka, Grzegorz. *Tak Bylo w Bieszczadach*, 88.

numerous ad-hoc committees were established, including the Ukrainian National Association (UNO), which was created in 1939 and headquartered in Cracow, making the city a major Ukrainian political center during the war. The UNO coordinated the efforts of numerous committees and represented Ukrainian interests in the Generalgouvernement, which also had organs of its administration located in the city. The principal organizer of the UNO, Col. Roman Sushko, nominated Ukrainian geographer Volodymyr Kubijovyč to head the umbrella organization. In addition to being widely recognized as a leading Ukrainian scholar, Kubijovyč had many other qualities that made him ideal for the position, including his fluency in German. As the Soviets may have objected to a Ukrainian political refugee heading an organization in the German zone, Kubijovyčh's leadership did not pose a threat to German-Soviet relations since he was from the small town of Nowy Sącz (located east of Cracow and well to the west of the German-Soviet border). In addition to being fluent in German, Kubijovyč also possessed excellent diplomatic skills, which helped to foster positive relations between Germans and Ukrainians in the Generalgouvernement district. Under his leadership, the UNO functioned for the next eight months, aiding refugees and establishing cultural and educational organizations without official permission from the Germans. The Germans, careful to avoid antagonizing the Soviet Union, permitted the Ukrainian organizations to function on the Soviet border, but stopped short of formally legalizing them.

The Association had two immediate tasks, finding housing and employment for the refugees and reviving commerce. Some refugees, especially laborers, went to work in Germany, while others found work in the Generalgouvernement administrative system, in Ukrainian schools, or in commerce and manufacturing. At this stage, the war had inflicted little physical or property damage in the region, but the Germans began removing Jews from the towns on the Soviet border and restricting their commercial activities elsewhere. These actions undermined the region's economy since Jews had been heavily involved in commerce and ran the majority of stores, shops and other important services in the towns. As a result, the Association encouraged Ukrainians to establish stores, especially small shops selling consumer items, and to expand the existing network of cooperatives. Beyond meeting the immediate material needs, an emphasis was placed on expanding Ukrainian schools, providing for adult education, and aiding the church in the western districts of Volhynia. Since there were few qualified local Ukrainians from the German zone, the influx of refugees from the east supplemented the workforce. Some were returning Ukrainian teachers who had earlier been sent to the Polish districts, and others were former political prisoners and political activists. The last two groups were reasonably well educated and many plunged into community activities with missionary zeal, providing the necessary services and raising national awareness through education.

While the UNO was created primarily to provide Ukrainians with relief and education, its activities were also directed toward much broader political goals, one of which was to install Ukrainians in administrative positions in the Generalgouvernement. Despite the fact that Germany had destroyed the Polish state, former officials of the defunct Polish government still controlled the administration of local affairs, including municipal services, schools, and public safety. The Association maneuvered to replace these officials with Ukrainians as a way of eliminating Polish influence in the Ukrainian districts and providing employment for Ukrainians. Public safety was a particularly sensitive issue for the Germans, who were unwilling to detach troops for routine police duty and therefore had to rely on staffing those positions with locals whom they did not trust. To resolve the dilemma, both Poles and Ukrainians were accepted for police duties under strict German supervision. In that arrangement, not every policeman had a rifle and for those who did, only 10 rounds of ammunition were issued. The police service was not especially popular among Ukrainians. After the German occupation of western Ukraine, the force was projected to reach 6,000 in the district, but due to the lack of volunteers only 5,000 were recruited.[181] Some volunteered because of pay, meager though it was, and prestige was also a draw since Ukrainians, as a rule, had been prohibited from serving in the Polish police force during the interwar period. Still others joined for patriotic reasons with encouragement from the Ukrainian nationalists, since having Ukrainians in the police force provided opportunities to wrest control from the local Poles. Moreover, the Ukrainian nationalist movement placed great emphasis on organizing an army, and by joining the German

---

181 Shankovsky, L. "Ukrainian Auxiliary Police" in Vol. V. of Struk, ed. *Encyclopedia*, 354.

police; young Ukrainian men could obtain some military training and a rifle, thus laying the foundation for future Ukrainian military formations.

Another goal of the Association was to inculcate patriotism and a strong sense of common identity among those ethnic Ukrainians who had previously been "denationalized," a process that would enable the organization to convert some areas into Ukrainianized districts that would be ready to support efforts for independence. To that end, it was important to develop support among the local population and eliminate Russophile influence, a condition that was particularly prevalent in the western Lemko region. To accomplish that goal, Ukrainian nationalists proselytized their ideology among Lemkos, whom they considered to be Ukrainian, with some success. On July 23, 1940, the Association was renamed the Ukrainian Central Committee (UTsK) and it absorbed the Ukrainian Aid Committee and its network. It was now allowed to provide the types of social and educational services that had been previously provided by Ukrainian organizations, but which had been nominally banned after the German occupation. In an apparent attempt to avoid ruffling Soviet sensibilities, the newly renamed organization was not legalized until Poles were allowed to organize Main Relief Councils, and Jews to establish Jewish Social Self-Reliance Organizations.[182] Without Ukrainian consultation, the German authorities drew up the UTsK statute, and the organization was to continue providing relief for destitute Ukrainians and to work with foreign relief organizations through the German Red Cross. The German statute contained numerous ambiguities and even contradictions, giving Ukrainians the opportunity to interpret these provisions in their favor; the Committee functioned throughout the war and expanded to Galicia after the German invasion and occupation in 1941.

Besides addressing the immediate economic needs and the refugee problem, the work of the committee extended to education, publishing, and even religious affairs. The need for these services was especially pressing in the Chełm and Podlasie regions where the interwar Polish government had restricted and virtually eliminated the Orthodox Church. By petitioning the Germans, Ukrainians were able to regain some religious rights, including the repossession of the Orthodox cathedral in Chełm which had been taken by the Poles in 1918 and converted to a

---

182 Kubijovyč, *Ukraintsi*, 98.

Roman Catholic Church.[183] The church was reorganized and renamed the *Autocephalous Orthodox Church*, and it consisted of three dioceses with 175 parishes—the Cracow-Lemko region had 35 parishes, and the Warsaw diocese about 10. In addition to the physical expansion, the church was infused with more vigorous leadership and clergy. Part of the clergy came from Northern Bukovyna (now the Chernivtsi Oblast of western Ukraine) which had been under the auspices of Romania in the interwar period.[184] Bukovyna was Orthodox, and Ukrainian patriotism there was comparable to that of Galicia. By and large, the refugee priests, fleeing Soviet occupation, were better educated and more patriotic than the local clergy, and their presence and involvement infused the Ukrainian orthodox church in the German zone with greater dynamism. Since religion and nationalism merged in the region, the Polish underground began attacking the revived Orthodox parishes as well as Ukrainian activists, both religious and secular.

Culture and political education presented another pressing need because most of the major Ukrainian newspapers and publishing houses were located in the Soviet zone. To rectify the problem, Ukrainians began petitioning the Germans for permission to establish publishing houses within the Generalgouvernement. On December 27, 1939, a meeting was held in Cracow, and the Cracow News (*Krakivs'ki Visti)* was established, premiering as a bi-weekly newspaper. Ukrainians sought to include "Ukrainian" in the title but the Germans refused that request for fear of antagonizing the Soviets. The paper was not allied with any Ukrainian political faction and sought to serve all Ukrainians despite its heavy German censorship. The paper was also required to publish official German decrees without compensation. Since the Germans treated foreign news with the utmost circumspection, Ukrainian presses were forbidden to broach some topics; including the OUN split, partisan activities in general, and life of Ukrainians in the USSR or abroad. An article published in January 1940 on the Soviet-Finnish War, based on official German sources without adding any political commentary, resulted

183 Kubijovyč, "Kholm region" in Vol. II of *Encyclopedia*, 483.

184 In 1940, when the Soviet Union annexed Northern Bukovyna as a result of the Molotov-Ribbentrop Pact, the territory formed much of the western portion of the Soviet republic of Ukraine. During that period, many Orthodox priests left the area and relocated to the Chełm and Podlesie territories in the Generalgouvernement zone to escape Soviet repressions.

in the editor's forced resignation.[185] Despite censorship and limited resources, the paper thrived, coming out three times weekly between May 1 and October 1940 and then daily after November 1, 1940 until the end of 1944. During that period, the paper's circulation increased from 6,000 to 27,000. Besides the newspaper, a weekly magazine was published under the same title and a regional variant was published in Chełm. Other magazines published through the same press addressed specific audiences; including a monthly magazine for children, another for youth dealing with sports and nature, and a monthly publication on literature and culture. Despite the limitations and censorship imposed, the newspaper and other publications were "...able to reflect a considerable range of Ukrainian life and thought. As a result, [they were] an invaluable witness of the events of the war years."[186] The publication of books, especially textbooks, became the major publishing activity of the Central Committee as it worked to revive and expand Ukrainian schools. By the summer of 1941, 195 titles had been published, with approximately 4,250 copies per title. The prodigious output was possible because about 80 percent of the books were either reprints or edited versions of pre-war publications. In 1940, 735,500 copies of 132 titles were published for 550,000 Ukrainians compared to 1,362,200 copies of 448 titles, published in 1937 for almost six million Ukrainians in Poland, the last year for which data are available.[187]

The publishing effort supported what became a significant expansion of adult educational institutions and Ukrainian language schools, despite German efforts to limit schooling to elementary education and vocational training. The Germans formally abolished the existing educational societies, including *Prosvita* ("Enlightment") in Galicia and *Ridna Khata* ("Native Hearth") in the Chełm region. The societies were, however, permitted to function, and the German authorities eventually established the Ukrainian Educational Society, which absorbed the two organizations. In March 1940, a convention was held in Cracow to organize additional Ukrainian schools, taking advantage of the German policy that granted Ukrainians more rights to promote education compared to the rights that had been granted by the Polish interwar government.

---

185 Kubijovyč, *Ukraintsi*, 274

186 Armstrong, *Ukrainian Nationalism*, 52.

187 Kubijovyč, *Ukraintsi,* 265.

The Ukrainian nationalist movement emphasized Ukrainian language education as a vehicle for inculcating patriotism and a strong common identity among the people and the UTsK pursued this policy vigorously. The task was daunting, since only 18 Ukrainian schools were fully functioning and the remainder of schools attended by Ukrainians used both Polish and Ukrainian languages. Since most teachers in those schools were Poles, they were considered to be de facto Polish schools, and there were no Ukrainian schools in the Chełm and Podlasie regions. Summer kindergartens were organized in most villages, frequently taught by village girls who possessed only an elementary school education and who had been provided with literature on pre-school education. Nevertheless, the expansion of elementary schools was significant, and by 1941, the numbers grew to 929 schools with 91,700 pupils and 1,415 teachers, with most being state schools.[188] In mixed Ukrainian-Polish villages, Ukrainians organized a total of 18 private schools. Virtually every Ukrainian child attended some type of Ukrainian school, and almost all of the children attending those schools were either Orthodox or Greek Catholic, with very few Roman Catholic Ukrainian children. The shortage of qualified teachers was met in part by transferring Ukrainian teachers from Germany, the Czech lands, and from other areas in Poland. However, approximately one-third of the teachers were not certified professional teachers. Some were students in higher educational institutions or secondary schools.

Organizing Ukrainian secondary schools was particularly difficult since none had existed on this territory prior to the war, when Ukrainian education at its best had been limited to elementary education. Nevertheless, three secondary schools were established in the Generalgouvernement zone, including two gymnasiums (high schools) that offered curriculum for grades 6–13, as well as a four-year pedagogical school for elementary school teachers. The gymnasiums were located in Chełm and Jarosław, while the pedagogical school was established in the western Lemko town of Krynica (Krynytsia). In March 1941, the three schools had a combined enrollment of 1,161, with females comprising 42 percent of the student body. In addition to the secondary academic schools, 31 schools totaling over 3,000 students were established in 1941 to provide

188 Ibid, 205.

vocational or semi-professional technical training. The Germans favored these schools, since they were designed to provide trained workers for agriculture, commerce, and industry.

Although the Ukrainian Central Committee did not organize institutions of higher learning, they made efforts to place qualified students in Czech, Austrian, and German universities. In 1941, about 400 students received some form of financial aid. Most were refugees from the Soviet Zone, since compared to Ukrainians in the Generalgouvernement, those on the Soviet side tended to be educated political refugees who could meet the prerequisites for university admission. Formal education placed an emphasis on national awareness and vocational skills for youth. Organizations were formed for young people in several age categories: children between 7–14 years of age, youth between 14–18 years, and young adults of 18–24 years, with the emphasis placed on educating youth and young adults.[189] The latter two groups were especially valued since they tended to be more active and idealistic compared to other segments of the population, and were usually not burdened with family obligations. To promote patriotism, lectures and discussions were organized on Ukrainian literature, history, and geography, with special courses available for those who were not literate in Ukrainian and for the barely literate. Courses were also established on the topics of agriculture, driving, and health to provide basic information and stimulate interest in a variety of professions. Youth were encouraged to participate in community service, cultural parades were encouraged, and clubs held competitions and public observances of events. These activities were designed to encourage solidarity, raise the morale of the participants, and to impress the public with the influence and strength of the organizations.

By the time Germany invaded the Soviet Union in 1941, the UTsK's accomplishments were impressive. Approximately 80 percent of the villages had established adult education organizations and another 50 percent had youth clubs.[190] With the German conquest of Ukraine, many activists returned home, but by then the organizations had been established and continued to work throughout the war with the local cadre and with those who stayed behind. In 1941, after Germany attacked the Soviet Union, Ukraine was added to German occupied territory and the Germans

---

[189] Ibid, 240.

[190] Kubiiovych, *Meni 70*, 44.

annexed territories in the southeast, including the oblasts of L'viv, Ternopil' and Stanislaviv (now Ivano-Frankivsk) to the Generalgouvernment district in order to provide German contact with Romania,[191] although a contributing factor may have been the fact that these territories had been part of the Austrian province of Galicia for 146 years. For the remaining Ukrainian territory, the German government set up a separate administrative district that they called *Reichskommissariat Ukraine*. There was significant difference in the treatment of Ukrainians in the Generalgouvernement district compared with those living in the Reichskommissariat, partly because a fanatical anti-Ukrainian Nazi named Erich Koch administered the latter. One of Koch's first actions as *Reichskommissar* was to close Ukrainian schools in the district, declaring, "...Ukrainian children do not need schools. What they will need to learn will be taught to them by their German masters."[192] His brutal mentality toward Ukrainians was evident in his famous remark: "If I meet a Ukrainian worthy of being seated at my table, I must have him shot."[193] The situation in Volhynia was especially difficult, exacerbated by the growing presence of Soviet partisans and ever-increasing hostilities between Poles and Ukrainians, prompting Ukrainian nationalists to organize a partisan movement in the province.

OUN Split: The Bandera and Mel'nyk Factions

The new developments under German administration had the unintended effect of increasing Ukrainian national awareness and patriotism, particularly in districts west of the Bug and San rivers, located close to the Ukrainian border. Nevertheless, despite the Generalgouvernment's comparatively tolerant policies toward cultural awareness and activities, its administration took a great deal of care to limit Ukrainian assertiveness to the extent that German rule would not be threatened. For this reason, Ukrainian political parties and organizations were prohibited. The pre-war membership in these organizations had been small, in any event, and during the war, many were affiliated with or working for the Central Committee. The exception was the OUN, whose members had fled in

---

191 Armstrong, *Ukrainian Nationalism*, 105.
192 Wistrich, *Who's Who in Nazi Germany*, 142–143.
193 Berkhoff, *Harvest of Despair*, 37

large numbers from the Soviet Zone to the German Zone in 1939. Though the Germans never formally legalized OUN in the Generalgouvernment, the organization was permitted to operate and maintained close relations with the German administration in the first few years of the war, with members augmenting the administration at lower levels, including the police force. However, as time went on, German actions raised doubts in some OUN circles, particularly among the younger, more militant members who grew distrustful of German intentions and came to advocate a more independent policy for pursuing Ukrainian independence. In their view, the German government had taken several actions that made them an untrustworthy ally, including their concession of Carpatho-Ukraine (*Zakarpattia*, Ukraine's Transcarpathian oblast) to Hungary in 1939, and the fact that they had formed an alliance with the Soviet Union, an enemy of the Ukrainians. However, the OUN leadership in Berlin steadfastly advocated the thesis that Ukrainian independence could be achieved only with foreign help, and to that end, allying with Germany seemed a pragmatic course of action.

The rift in OUN began in 1938, after the assassination of OUN leader Ievhen Konovalets' by a Soviet agent in Rotterdam. As the principal organizer of the OUN and a war hero, his leadership had not been challenged within OUN circles, but his replacement, Andrii Mel'nyk, was a less well-known figure who lacked the considerable political and diplomatic skills that had enabled Konovalets' to negotiate differences in the organization and avoid a split. Both the leadership change and the war forced internal political differences to the surface. Individual temperaments, political ambitions, and policy differences between the younger members at home in western Ukraine and the older leadership in Germany all factored into inciting the OUN split.

On February 10, 1940, some insurgents held a conference in Cracow to form a "Revolutionary Faction" of the OUN that claimed to represent the entire organization. Mel'nyk attempted, without success, to heal the growing rift that would ultimately lead to a permanent split. In April 1941, the Bandera faction, named after its leader Stepan Bandera, convened the "Second Extraordinary Congress" in Cracow, declaring the 1939 OUN Rome Congress that elected Mel'nyk as having been illegal.[194] The Cracow gathering was attended by 68 delegates, including 16 from western Ukraine and 52 from abroad, and the group elected Stepan Bandera as its leader. The Congress also passed a resolution affirming the basic tenets of the 1929 conference that had established the OUN. Henceforth, Bandera's group was called either the OUN (r) for revolutionary or OUN (b) for Bandera and Mel'nyk's group was called OUN (m) for Mel'nyk. The designations remained in place throughout the war, but the two groups were colloquially referred to *Banderivtsi* (Banderites) and *Mel'nykivtsi* (Mel'nykites) by the people. In 1941, as Germany prepared to invade the Soviet Union, the militant nationalist movement split and the internal struggle for support began, culminating in violence. Later, some of Mel'nyk's leading lieutenants were shot under mysterious circumstances, prompting the Mel'nyk organization to accuse the Bandera faction of committing political assassinations. Both factions began cooperating with the Germans, who appreciated Mel'nyk's greater reliability and his less radical views, but the Bandera group was more prone to military action and had a better organized network at home, making them more tactically valuable to the Germans in their impending war with the Soviet Union.

Unlike the Mel'nyk wing, which opposed the use of guerrilla warfare on the grounds that it would bring Soviet retaliation against the civilian population, the Bandera wing favored the militarization of the OUN and had a preference for conducting partisan warfare on the Ukrainian territory of the Soviet Union.[195] In addition to the partisan issue there were other differences as well, although they were not necessarily germane to the goal of creating an independent Ukrainian state. The Banderites favored the formation of a Ukrainian legion, which they planned to send to Finland in the event that the Finns would gain support from the west. Mel'nyk opposed involvement in the war for fear of antagonizing Germany, which had allied with the Soviet Union, and he insisted that Ukrainians should not fight unless it was clearly in their national interest. Finally, the Bandera faction proposed that the OUN headquarters should be relocated from Berlin to a neutral country where Ukrainian interests could be better pursued independent of Germany and would be better

194 Yurkevich, *Organization of Ukrainian Nationalists,* 709. See also Armstrong, *Ukrainian Nationalism*, 62.

195 Torzecki, *Kwesta Ukrainska*, 197.

represented in the international arena. To that end, they recommended the establishment of three branch centers; one in Germany, another in a neutral European country, and the third either in the United States or Canada since both countries had large Ukrainian diaspora communities. The Mel'nykites countered that there was little interest among western countries in Ukrainian matters and moving OUN elsewhere would not accomplish anything.[196] Their point was based on the fact that Ukrainian representatives abroad had worked to gain support among the western Allies for the Ukrainian cause. The Allies, preoccupied with containing Germany, had historically sought to have a strong German opponent in the east (which meant either Poland or the Soviet Union) and both would require Ukrainian manpower and resources. The Bandera wing also called for a purge of the existing leadership, whom they considered incompetent and in some cases perhaps traitorous, whereas Mel'nyk was unwilling to purge his own associates. On the surface, the policy differences between the Bandera and Mel'nyk factions appeared substantial, but in practice their differences were minimal. At the time, Ukrainians needed foreign assistance to secure independence and that assistance could come only from Germany. Ironically, both factions were unaware that Hitler planned to colonize Ukraine with Germans, precisely the same type of colonization policy that Poles and Russians had long been practicing and which the nationalists had been fighting against so vehemently.

Between 1939 and 1941, the Germans had permitted the Ukrainians to organize military units. The first such unit was formed by Col. Roman Sushko, Mel'nyk's supporter, who dubbed the unit the "Legion of Ukrainian Nationalists," a name later adopted by other formations. The Legion was organized in Austria and its membership mainly consisted of former Carpathian Sich members who had been released from Hungarian prisons by German request. On September 3, 1939, the Legion's two battalions moved to the Prešov region in northeastern Slovakia, then crossed the Polish border with the German army. Because of the rapid collapse of the Polish Army, the unit was not required to engage in combat and was instead stationed north of the Carpathians in the Dukla and Krynica regions to perform police duties. By the end of the year, the unit had been split

196 Ibid.

into two groups, with one group sent to guard industrial plants and the second to perform police duties.[197]

As the Germans prepared to attack the Soviet Union in 1941, additional Ukrainian units were again permitted to organize, with the Bandera faction taking the lead on that occasion. Under the direction of Dmytro Hrytsai, enough young Ukrainian men living in German-occupied Europe were recruited to form two infantry battalions. One battalion, dubbed *Nachtigall*, was trained in Silesia and commanded by a German officer, Lieutenant Hans-Albrecht Herzner under the advisement of the high-level Nazi officer Theodor Oberländer. The second battalion, *Roland*, trained in Austria and was commanded by a Ukrainian, Major Ievhen Pobihushchyi. At the outbreak of Operation Barbarossa in June 1941, *Nachtigall* accompanied the German Army and pushed through L'viv into central Ukraine. The unit was later renamed the Second Battalion of the Brandenburg Regiment No. 800, and commanded by another German officer, a Major Heinz. That unit was sent to the front lines in the Khmelnytsky and Vinnytsia regions.[198] The Roland battalion went through Northern Bukovyna and Moldova, reaching the Ukrainian territory west of Odesa at the end of July without engaging in any combat. Besides the two battalions, both factions organized Expeditionary Groups (*pokhidni hrupy*) consisting of approximately 2,000 young men and women. The groups followed the German Wehrmacht into Ukraine, not to fight, but to organize local groups among nationalistically-minded Ukrainians. At the outbreak of the German invasion, Bandera supporters staged attacks on Soviet troops and police in parts of Galicia: "The Ukrainian militia took over police functions and dissolved collective farms before the German arrival."[199]

Cooperation between the Germans and the Ukrainian nationalists was hardly harmonious since each side had its own political agenda. Confusion and misunderstandings were compounded by the differing and inconsistent attitudes of the German factions toward Ukrainians. The military was less racist and more rational than political circles and was prepared to make concessions to the Ukrainians. The primary concern of

---

197 Szcześniak and Szota, *Droga do nikad*, 69.

198 Sodol, P. "Legion of Ukrainian Nationalists" in Vol. III of Struk, ed. *Encyclopedia*, 72.

199 Armstrong, *Ukrainian Nationalism*, 76–7.

the Wehrmacht was to secure the rear and, to that end, the Germans welcomed any additional help from the Ukrainian nationalists in their struggle against the Red Army. However, the Nazi Party itself was divided on the issue. Alfred Rosenberg, the Reichsminister for the Occupied Eastern Territories, favored accommodation with Ukrainians. Familiar with the national sentiments in Eastern Europe, he was prepared to use nationalistic currents to dismember the Soviet Union and in doing so, remove the danger to Germany from the east.[200] Despite the fact that Rosenberg held a high status and position in the Nazi party as a theoretician, his views were not shared by Hitler, who planned to eventually settle Ukraine with Germans and enserf the local population. The nationalists, unaware of Hitler's ultimate plans and eager to rely on the Germans for support, were inclined to accept the views of Rosenberg and the military. In June 1941, at the news of the German invasion of the Soviet Union, the Bandera faction worked feverishly in Cracow to organize a framework for the Ukrainian State. The Ukrainian National Committee was formed by the Bandera wing and included many prominent Ukrainians.

On June 30, the Wehrmacht had reached L'viv along with the Nachtigall Battalion and Iaroslav Stets'ko, Bandera's lieutenant. Bandera himself was not permitted by the Germans to enter Ukraine, but Stets'ko and his aids were sent to proclaim a Ukrainian State and organize support.[201] The Ukrainian population in the city had been traumatized by the Soviet occupation, especially from the behavior displayed by the retreating Soviet Army and police. Thousands of people held in jails were either shot or deported, with many of the deportees having been shot along the route. Those who did manage to reach the concentration camps rarely returned. According to German reports, four thousand Ukrainian political prisoners were found shot in the L'viv jails alone.[202] As a result, the German arrival was greeted with relief and enthusiasm from a people who were finally delivered from the "Red Terror." Because a Ukrainian unit had arrived with the Wehrmacht and Ukrainians worked easily with German officers, many came to believe that Stets'ko's activities had official German support. In reality, Stets'ko and his entourage had come to Ukraine illegally and the Germans had never sanctioned the proclama-

---

200 Ibid, 104.

201 Yurkevich, *Organization of Ukrainian Nationalists,* 709.

202 Armstrong, *Ukrainian Nationalism*, 77.

tion. The undertaking was entirely the work of the Bandera faction, which sought to capitalize on the fluid situation and present the Germans with a *fait accompli.* Stets'ko organized a small gathering dubbed the "National Assembly," and read the act of proclamation that announced the renewal of the Ukrainian State under the auspices of the OUN with Stepan Bandera designated as its leader. More importantly, on the evening of June 30, he read the same proclamation on the L'viv radio station.[203] The German Army took no immediate action, but within several days an SS *Einsatzgruppe* task force arrived in the city to clear the occupied areas of undesirable elements, primarily Jews, but also communists, nationalists, or anyone who might oppose German rule. The SS arrested Stets'ko and his aid Mykola Lebed in L'viv on July 9, and Bandera and his aids were arrested in Cracow and brought to Berlin. When they refused to recant the proclamation, they were placed under house arrest, but Bandera managed to maintain contact with his leading associates on the outside and thus continued his political activities from his confinement in Germany.

While the top leadership was treated mildly, their followers in the succeeding months were given the usual SS treatment, including summary executions and deportations to extermination camps. Various groups that sprang up in eastern Ukraine either independently or with help of Expeditionary Groups were also repressed, but Bandera's followers bore the harshest treatment. Two of Stepan Bandera's brothers, Vasyl' and Oleksa, died in the Auschwitz concentration camp. Mel'nyk's groups were not spared either, as their followers in many areas of eastern Ukraine received similar treatment, with the Kyiv group enduring the most severe brutality. "Over forty leading members of OUN (m), including the poetess Olena Teliha, were shot and the popular newspaper, *Ukrainske Slovo* [the Ukrainian Word] was shut down."[204]

The two Ukrainian battalions were also affected by the swiftly changing German attitude toward the nationalists. *Nachtigall* was sent to Cracow in August, subsequently disarmed and its members interned in Germany, and Roland was also disarmed and returned to Austria. The men were reorganized into a special police battalion of 600 men, divided into four companies, and led by 22 Ukrainian officers under the com-

---

203 Ibid, 80.

204 Subtelny, *Ukraine*, 465.

mand of Maj. Pobihushchiy. The future UPA commander, Roman Shukhevych, led one of the companies. The special battalion was contracted for one year and sent to Belarus to protect transportation lines and factories. At the expiration of the contract, the battalion refused to prolong the service and was disarmed. Ukrainians who had joined in the belief that they would form the nucleus of the future Ukrainian Army and secure independence, were not willing to serve as guards in Belarus. At the same time, the harsh German treatment of Ukrainians provoked anger in the ranks, and Ukrainian officers protested to the German authorities. The enlisted men were sent home and the Gestapo in L'viv imprisoned the Ukrainian officers where only a few, including Shukhevych, managed to escape. In the end, the longstanding contacts between Ukrainians and Germans brought about little benefit for either side, as Hitler was no more interested in establishing a Ukrainian State than was Pilsudski or Stalin. The German formation of small units and police were of marginal benefit to Ukrainians, nor did the Germans receive much in the way of meaningful intelligence information. The rapid German occupation of Poland and later of western Ukraine precluded any valuable aid or information that the Ukrainians might have been able to provide.

The Ukrainian Insurgent Army (UPA)

While the two wings of the OUN organized military units in Galicia under German auspices, an independent guerrilla force began to form in Volhynia. Before the war, a Ukrainian National Rebirth Party had formed in the region and cooperated with the exiled Ukrainian National Republic (UNR) in Warsaw, headed by President Andrii Livyts'kyi. After the Soviet occupation in 1939, the organization went underground but maintained contacts with the Livyts'kyi group. Taras Borovets', a leading member of the party, traveled clandestinely to Warsaw and conferred with UNR members, reaching a decision to organize a partisan movement in Volhynia.[205] Borovets' and his supporters developed elaborate plans to create a nationwide guerilla movement with each region forming its own *Sich*. Borovets' assumed the pseudonym of *Taras Bulba*, named after the fictional Cossack chieftain from Nikolai Gogol's novel. At the beginning of 1941, the partisan movement began organizing and as-

---

205 Armstrong, *Ukrainian Nationalism*, 98–99.

sumed the name *Polisian Sich*, and that regional name was used until the end of 1941 when the name was changed to *Ukrains'ka Povstans'ka Armiia* (UPA, the Ukrainian Insurgent Army), although the original name still remained in use.

During the organizational stage, and up until the German invasion occurred, the guerrillas refrained from engaging Soviet police or troops. After the invasion, one German group went through central Belarus heading toward Moscow and another through northern Ukraine to Kyiv. The swampy, wooded area along the Prypiat River, called Polisia, was largely bypassed by the Wehrmacht, and it was there that Red Army stragglers, Soviet officials, police and NKVD trekked eastward to avoid capture by the Germans. These groups were not an organized partisan movement although they were usually referred to as such; in actuality, they were separate groups of armed men, avoiding combat and trying to survive.

The first major engagement between the Ukrainians and the Soviets reportedly took place in the Sarny region (now the Rivne Oblast), and the Sich partisans captured arms and ammunition that were stored in magazines throughout the forest. At that point, the Sich was officially renamed the Sarny District Police with German permission.[206] This prompted Borovets' to propose to General Karl Kitzinger, the local German commander, that the Sich be reorganized into a regular Ukrainian Army unit. The general refused to approve the proposal, claiming that only the German political authorities could authorize the formation of a Ukrainian Army, but Kitzinger conceded that the partisans could operate as a quasi-military organization.[207] As German control of the region expanded, the partisans withdrew to the more remote areas in order to avoid conflicts with the Germans.

The lack of trained officers was a major problem for the *Sich,* and in July, Borovets' traveled to L'viv with the hope of obtaining assistance from the OUN. The Bandera group responded by demanding control over the militia as the price for aid and the two sides failed to reach an agree-

---

206 Borovets' claimed that at that time, his partisans at this time totaled almost 10,000 men although his critics state that the actual figure was only several hundred men. See Bulba-Borovets', Taras Otaman. *Armiia Bez Derzhavy.* (Winnipeg: Society of Volyn, 1981), 122–3. See also Petrenko, Roman. *Slidamy Armii Bez Derzhavy.* (Kyiv-Toronto: Doslidnyy Instytut "Studium," 2004).

207 Bulba-Borovets', *Armiia*, 125.

ment, but the Mel'nyk people sent some officers without imposing any demands, drawing Borovets' close to OUN (m). Meanwhile, the remnants of the Red Army and police were beginning to form cohesive units, and with the help of the Belarusian self-defense units, the Sich launched an attack against the Red partisans on August 20 and entered the town of Olevs'k the following day. During the succeeding days, a triangular piece of territory that included the towns of Pinsk, Olevs'k, and Mozyr was cleared and the so-called "Olevs'k Republic" was established.[208] A Ukrainian civil administration was put into place, but in the middle of November, the *Sich* was forced to demobilize. The territory soon came under the authority of the Reichskommissar Erich Koch, who would not tolerate Ukrainian military units. General Kitsinger proposed that about 1,000 men could be transferred to fight the Red partisans in Chernihiv, a province between Kyiv and Kharkiv, since that area was under the control of the German army. Borovets' refused the offer, the *Sich* began demobilizing and hiding their better weapons, and he retired to the forest with a small group of his men.

The region remained comparatively peaceful during the first half of 1942, as the Borovets' partisans avoided contacts with the Germans. The second half of the year, however, brought dramatic changes as large bands of organized Red partisans began arriving from Belarus. A three-way struggle flared up in Volhynia among the Reds, the Ukrainians, and the Germans, intensifying in the autumn when a large group of Soviet partisans arrived, commanded by Sidor Kovpak. Kovpak's partisans enjoyed initial success and captured several towns, but the German counterattack forced them back to the Prypiat marshes in the north. As the Germans began to lose control over the region, their tactics against the Ukrainians became more draconian as they attempted to prevent support for the Soviet partisans, although their concerns had little foundation in reality. The communist sympathies among the people had never been strong in Volhynia even before the war (although they were stronger there than in Galicia), but almost two years of brutal Soviet occupation had managed to destroy even this limited support. Moreover, the Red partisans further antagonized people by forcibly taking food and other

---

[208] Much of this area, including the districts of Berestia and Kobryn was transferred to Belarus after the war although it was settled by Ukrainians.

supplies. Nevertheless, the German actions were indiscriminate, and the brutal German repressions increased Ukrainian hatred toward them

By 1942, a number of small Ukrainian partisan formations operated in Volhynia consisting of Borovets partisans, a group organized by Oleksandr Iatseniuk, and small Bandera and Mel'nyk units.[209] In December 1942, the Bandera wing ordered its units to consolidate and expand their operations. The following year, from February 17–23, 1943, OUN (b) held the Third Conference and proclaimed the party's intention to establish a Ukrainian state through an armed struggle. To accomplish the goal, a large partisan army had to be organized to fight "German and Muscovite imperialists"[210] and during that year, all Ukrainian partisans in Volhynia came under the control of the Bandera faction. This significant change of policy was considered necessary because of increased German repressions that included the forcible requisitioning of grain, the capture and deportation of young people for forced labor in Germany, and the ever-increasing number of executions. At the same time, many young Ukrainian men had fled to the forest to avoid deportation, and some were captured by the Reds and forced to join them. In order to offer some protection to the population and maintain a Ukrainian presence in the area, OUN (b) considered large military formations to be essential.[211] The German presence was augmented by Ukrainian guards and police who were reluctant to engage in repressive measures against their own people, and as a result, the Germans began to disarm some units and did not hesitate to execute individuals who refused to carry out orders. At the same time, nationalists penetrated the police force where many OUN police members, especially from the Bandera wing, carried out propaganda work and frequently became the de facto unit leaders.

On OUN orders, there was a massive Ukrainian desertion of the police between March 15 and April 10, 1943. About four to five thousand Ukrainians deserted German positions, and even those who were ambivalent about the desertion went underground for fear of being disarmed and arrested by the Germans.[212] The new recruits, who were armed and provided with military training, formed the initial core of the expanded par-

---

209 Armstrong, *Ukrainian Nationalism*, 151–152,

210 Lebed', *UPA, Ukrainska Povstans'ka Armiia*, 40, 44–45.

211 Armstrong, *Ukrainian Nationalism*, 148.

212 Shtendera and Potichnyj, eds. *Litopys* Vol. 5, 19.

tisan movement, which adopted the name *Ukrainska Povstans'ka Armiia* (UPA), a name that was first popularized by Borovets'.[213] After expanding the UPA, the OUN (b) group sought to quickly bring all Ukrainian nationalist partisan groups under its control. Negotiations began with Borovets', who proposed the formation of an All-Ukrainian Front that would include the Ukrainian National Republic group headed by Andrii Livyts'kyi from Warsaw, the Mel'nyk group, and the newly formed Ukrainian National Democratic Party, which had a small but devoted following. The Bandera group considered this coalition too cumbersome and proposed that Borovets' be an overall UPA commander, but with the caveat that his position should fall under the political direction of the OUN (b), a proposal that Borovets' refused.[214] Unable to reach an agreement, the Bandera group began forcibly disarming and absorbing other Ukrainian groups, approaching the task with the minimal use of force necessary. This move could be accomplished because the ideological differences among the groups were tactical and personal rather than substantive, and all of them fundamentally supported the establishment of an independent Ukrainian State. Both Borovets' and OUN (m), for example, advocated organizing small groups that could operate clandestinely, while the Bandera wing favored larger military formations. The OUN (b) had also gained considerable influence among the rural youth by establishing a secret political network in the countryside. As a centralized militant organization, it had the capacity to move quickly and decisively. Borovets' and Mel'nyk's partisans, as well as a small group organized by Oleksandr Iatseniuk, were already engaged in heavy fighting with Reds, and did not offer resistance when they found themselves suddenly surrounded by the Bandera partisans. Most of the rank and file partisans did not understand the subtle political differences among various factions, which enabled many to switch sides without much difficulty. During the summer of 1943, all Ukrainian partisans in Polisia and Volhynia were subsumed into the UPA and placed directly under the control of the Bandera wing.

As UPA quickly expanded in 1943, volunteers alone could not staff the organization and conscription was introduced, whereby approximate-

---

213 Grzegorz Motyka claims the out of about 12,000 policemen, 5,000 went to the forest. See Motyka, *Tak Bylo*, 109.

214 Armstrong, *Ukrainian Nationalism*, 150–51.

ly 50 percent of the UPA soldiers served "...on the orders of the Ukrainian Government."[215] The degree and the form of coercion used cannot be determined from the available data, but it is clear that many young men living in the areas controlled by OUN(b) did not join voluntarily. A former company commander recalled that many recruits who appeared healthy were claiming medical problems during their physical examinations. The commander and his officers conducted interviews with the new men and about a quarter were released because they did not wish to serve.[216]

The UPA, as other partisans that formed in Eastern Europe during the war, can best be described as an irregular army or militia. Most dressed in some sort of military garb and fought as units in quick hit-and-run raids that were especially frequent at night, and ambushes were a favored tactic. Per UPA policy, partisans strove to avoid engaging the enemy in or near villages so as to minimize enemy retaliations against civilians. Despite the fact that it was a guerrilla force, the UPA adopted an organizational structure similar to a regular army. A squad consisted of about a dozen men, several squads formed a platoon, and several platoons normally formed a *sotnia* (company).[217] A sotnia was a basic operational unit of about 100–125 men. Several sotnias, which normally operated independently, formed a *kurin* (battalion) and occasionally operated jointly. In a few cases, several battalions were combined into a *zahin*, a unit that was roughly the size of a regiment, for special operations.

In addition to line units, several training schools and support units were organized. The UPA had a severe shortage of trained commissioned and non-commissioned officers since Ukrainians, as a rule, had not been permitted to be commissioned in the Polish Army during the interwar period. Although there were some former Red Army officers and World War I officers among UPA's ranks, most officers had to be trained from the basic level. In the spring of 1943, larger units began a three-week training course for non-commissioned officers, and the graduates of those courses would go on to serve as either military instructors or squad leaders. An officer training school called *Druzhynnyky* ("Companions") was organized in July and provided three to four months of training, and

215 See Shtendera and Potichnyj in Vol.5 of *Litopys*, 23.

216 Ibid, 74.

217 The term “sotnia” literally means “one hundred.”

many former Ukrainian Red Army officers served as instructors.[218] Officer candidates were required to have completed or have come close to completing secondary education, and the school managed to graduate and commission 120 men by October of that year.[219] Graduates with previous command experience or outstanding grades served as officers while others became noncommissioned officers and squad leaders. A second school was opened in October and provided an abbreviated course that ended in January 1944. When the Red Army began occupying the area, the Druzhynnyky school was transferred to the Carpathian Mountains and renamed *Oleni*.

The lack of weapons, especially ammunition, was another pressing need. Many who joined the underground brought their own Russian, Polish, German, or Hungarian weapons, but had little ammunition. At times, there were only 20 rounds per rifle and commanders were frequently instructed not to engage the enemy unless there was a possibility to capture weapons and ammunition. The rifle was the standard weapon, and most soldiers used German and Soviet rifles, possessing more of the latter as the insurgency progressed. Some were armed with automatic weapons, but these consisted of mostly captured Soviet submachine guns that fired pistol-size ammunition. Sotnias normally had between two to five light machine guns in their possession, as well as one or two grenade launchers. In addition to the infantry, some cavalry units were formed and training was provided for sappers and demolitions specialists. Mortars and a handful of light artillery pieces augmented small arms weapons. The few light tanks that were captured could not be used due to the lack of trained personnel and maintenance facilities. The UPA, therefore, was confined to conducting attacks and ambushes in wooded areas or late at night and avoided fights on open fields, especially against well-armed enemies.[220] As the front moved through western Ukraine in 1944, Soviet and German arms and ammunition were collected from the battlefields and stored. During the next five years of its existence, UPA was well armed and usually possessed an adequate supply of ammunition.

The growing army also required a wide range of support services, and the OUN worked energetically to meet the need. The organization's

---

218 *Druzhyna* was a princely retinue in Kievan Rus'.

219 Shtendera and Potichnyj, in Vol. I. of *Litopys,* 30.

220 Ibid, 31.

large clandestine network enabled it to procure meager local resources that satisfied some basic requirements; such as the need for food, clothing, ammunition and medical supplies. Few needs were more pressing than medical services. Even before the war, medical care in the area was meager and the war only exacerbated the situation. Moreover, the remaining medical facilities were in towns controlled by Germans and therefore inaccessible to the UPA soldiers. As a result, the underground had to build medical facilities in remote areas, form their own Ukrainian Red Cross, and recruit medical personnel-a particularly difficult undertaking since many of the qualified doctors in the region had been Jewish, and some of the Ukrainian doctors had already been arrested or relocated. Most of the Jewish medical personnel had either perished, were confined to ghettos, or had been taken to concentration camps. Of the small pool of Ukrainian doctors in the area, some joined the UPA to alleviate the personnel shortage. Around the same time, OUN launched a campaign to attract Jewish doctors, enabling some, with their families, to be spirited out of confinements in the ghettos.[221] This approach increased the number of doctors, although shortages still remained, causing UPA to rely on nurses and assistant doctors to administer many medical treatments that would normally be provided by qualified physicians. Courses were instituted to train individuals to become field nurses, but it was a task that proved difficult due to the shortage of instructors as well as the generally low educational attainment of the rural women receiving training. A severe shortage of medical supplies compounded the difficulties, although that problem was somewhat mitigated by purchases on the black market or theft. A substantial share of the supplies obtained were received from Galicia, where the shortages were less severe and a better organized OUN network was able to obtain more supplies to send clandestinely to Volhynia. Under the circumstances, wounded partisans received very rudimentary treatment, and frequently recuperated in private homes or silos, visited by doctors or nurses.

Supplying troops and politicizing both the partisans and the population was yet another high priority. OUN formed an economic section in order to provide food, weapons, ammunition and clothing to UPA partisans. The section could reportedly draw on about 10,000 people who

---

[221] Ibid, 34

were engaged in the collection and distribution of food. Food was carted over long distances from the more richly populated districts in the south to the swampy, sparsely populated areas in the north where most partisans operated. Much of the supplies, weapons, and ammunition were provided by the combat units themselves, acquired through raids on German warehouses and stores, or from stocks of weapons that had been captured on the battlefield. Taking up collections among the local populations augmented these efforts, but the results of such collections were meager since most Ukrainians were too poor to provide clothing and generally reluctant to part with weapons that might be needed for self-defense. Finally, a number of shops were organized to repair weapons, manufacture simple spare parts, make mines and explosives out of artillery and mortar shells, and to produce incendiary grenades. Political education was conducted largely through printed material, and OUN established printing shops to publish information; including newspapers and other literature on the current political situation, technical military literature, and poetry focused on current events, and even a humorous publication devoted largely to ridiculing both the Soviets and the Germans. The two primary target audiences were the Ukrainian civilian population and the UPA, where the material was used in political lectures. OUN publications emphasized the importance of the UPA's armed struggle, which was focused entirely on the eventual establishment of an independent Ukrainian State.[222]

The expanding UPA in Volhynia often came into conflict with the Soviet partisans, Germans, and especially Poles, which intensified during the German occupation. In the early stages of the war, ethnic conflicts were generally limited to Ukrainians attempting to wrest control of the local administration from Poles, and violence during that period was sporadic. Chełm and Podlasie, the two Volhynian districts west of the Bug River, presented an exception since the Polish underground began attacking Ukrainians there in 1941, and in the following year, the violence became more systematic. The Polish attacks there were not random, and they were carefully designed to decapitate Ukrainian communities by eliminating community leaders. The sporadic attacks escalated to large-scale partisan warfare on both sides of the Bug in 1943. In the east, the

---

222 See Shtendera and Potichnyj, eds. in Vol. 2 of *Litopys*, 159.

armed struggle occurred in 1943 as the Polish government in-exile worked mightily through diplomatic channels to preserve the pre-war boundaries of the Polish State, a policy that was completely unacceptable to Ukrainians. The pre-war policy of rapid Polonization, if it had continued for an extended period of time, might have turned western Ukraine into a Polish speaking territory, but the German invasion had brought such activities to a halt and severe ethnic hostilities remained in place. Ukrainian nationalists were well aware that the realization of Polish assimilation policies in those regions would result in a sizeable loss of territory in Volhynia and especially Galicia, the most nationalistic part of Ukraine. The former Habsburg province was considered a Ukrainian Piedmont, an area that had spearheaded the Ukrainian drive for independence after World War I and was likewise expected to play a similar role in the future. Ukrainians, especially OUN, were determined to prevent the fruition of the Polish agenda. Polish efforts, moreover, were not limited to diplomatic lobbying, but also included the establishment of a political and military underground among Poles who were living on the Ukrainian territory. Even before the German occupation had been completed, the Polish military, headed by General Michał Karaszewicz-Tokarzewski, had prepared plans to organize a large partisan movement. Within months, hundreds of clandestine groups formed in the German and Soviet zones of occupation.[223] The principal underground group and the military arm of the government-in-exile went through some name changes before February 14, 1942, when the Polish partisan force was officially designated as the *Armia Krajowa* ("Home Army") better known by its initials, AK. At its height, AK was perhaps the largest partisan formation in German-occupied Europe, although most of the men were held in reserves or operated as self-defense units. Along with AK, there were also a number of other underground formations organized by different political parties. The largest among them were the Peasant Battalions (*Bataliony Chłopskie*, BCh) formed by the Peasant Party to oppose German confiscations and deportations in rural areas, and this group worked closely with the AK, with a combined strength totaling perhaps 400,000 men. The National Armed Forces (*Narodowe Siły Zbrojne*, NSZ) and the National Military Organization (*Narodowa Organizacja Wojskowa*,

223 Korbonski, Stefan in *East European Quarterly* (1978), 16.

NOW) were much smaller and advocated more nationalistic views, while the left organized a pro-Soviet Peoples Guard (*Gwardia Ludowa*, GL), totaling about 10,000 men at the maximum.[224]

The regional organizational structure of AK was modified over time, attaining its final form in 1943. The AK divided pre-war Poland into three regions: The Western Region, the Warsaw Region (known as the Białystok Region during the German occupation) and the Lwów Region. AK also established a number of independent districts. With regard to the Ukrainian territory, the Lwów Region encompassed Galicia and was divided into three districts: Lwów, Tarnopol and Stanisławów (now Ivano-Frankivsk), and this district demarcation was based on the three pre-war provinces of the same name. Separate districts were established for Polisia and Volhynia, and the Ukrainian territory west of the San River was included in the Cracow district.[225] The active strength of the Polish underground is difficult to precisely determine, but it was relatively small until the mobilization in 1944. At the beginning of 1942, the Polish underground decided to strengthen its presence in western Ukraine and ordered the formation of cells throughout the area, especially in Volhynia. By October 1942, a network of cells had spread throughout Volhynia, and Polish partisans began operating in the forest.[226] Their efforts coincided with the OUN (b)'s policy of organizing large partisan units in Polisia and Volhynia. What had been occasional violence between Ukrainians and Poles during the interwar period had severely intensified during the war. The sporadic violence escalated into an open conflict between the two groups in early 1943 and OUN (b) ordered the Polish population to leave Volhynia and Polisia.[227]

The Ukrainian-Polish Civil War

The events leading to the carnage between UPA and the Poles are confusing, since both sides accused each other of initiating attacks and produced lists of atrocities to buttress their contentions. The Ukrainian underground literature provides little in the way of detailed information on the conflicts with the Polish civilian population, and memoirs of indi-

224 Davies, Norman. *God's,* 466.

225 Bor-Komorowski, *Armia Podziemna,* 173.

226 Torzecki, *Kwesta Ukrainska*, 295.

227 Sokhan and Shtendera, eds. in Vol. 2 (New Series) of *Litopys UPA*, XXXIX & XL

viduals who were in the area at the time are equally brief. Many Ukrainian authors gloss over the details with little or no nuance in discussions concerning UPA's attacks on Polish civilians. Descriptions of the events in Polish and Ukrainian sources differ so radically that they cannot be considered as reliable accounts. To date, no official OUN documents have been found that outline the reasons for the expulsion of Poles in Volhynia, or the exact date and the means of implementation, although the related primary sources and secondary literature casts some light on Ukrainian motives. In his book *UPA,* Mykola Lebed', a principal UPA organizer, cites a section from a document issued by the second OUN conference in 1942. The document detailed OUN's recognition of the Polish right to an independent state, but beseeched the Poles to respect Ukrainian rights to the western Ukrainian territory.[228] In his analysis, Lebed' underscores the Ukrainian resolve to fight Polish designs on the territory and Polish policies of dominating the economic and administrative organizations in the region. In July 1943, as the struggle raged, a pamphlet printed in Polish was issued to the Polish population and fragments are cited by Lebed':

> "The Ukrainian people were always convinced that the pre-condition for permanent and independent existence of both peoples—Ukrainian and Polish— requires common understanding based on mutual respect... The current Polish policy is strange and incomprehensible, the Polish people groan under the German imperialist yoke and Russia is planning new occupation of Poland, but Polish imperialists declared a merciless struggle against the Ukrainian people, denying them the right to an independent national existence...We have no hostile intentions toward the Polish people and do not want an inch of the Polish territory."[229]

An OUN communiqué from October 1943 reiterated these points and blamed the 20-year Polish exterminatory policy for the situation. From the OUN perspective, the Polish underground promoted hostile attitudes toward Ukrainians and engaged in activities that sought to conquer Ukrainian territory, and therefore, neither the OUN nor the Ukrainian people could be held accountable for the massacres, since they were only fighting for their own survival. They viewed the Polish Polonization policy as a method of justifying their territorial acquisitions. If the population in an area regarded itself as Polish, then it followed to reason that

228 Lebed, *UPA*, 122.
229 Ibid, 122–123.

the territories of Polish settlement should become part of a Polish state. Thus, the OUN was focused on expelling Poles from Ukrainian territories, especially those colonists who had been settled there by the Polish State during the interwar period.

In the struggle for independence after World War I, the initial conflict between the two groups did not occur between the Ukrainians and the Polish Army, but rather with units that had been organized by local Poles. After the war, the Polish government increased colonization on the Ukrainian territory in order to increase its "Polishness" with the intent of Polonizing the land. The most extensive colonization had occurred in Volhynia, where many Polish war veterans had been settled. Ukrainians considered them to be a fifth column that had to be eradicated if independence was to be achieved. The OUN decided to reverse the Polish pre-war policy and Ukrainianize the territory by driving out the Poles. They claimed that Polish civilians were not to be attacked, but once the expulsion was initiated, violence inevitably followed. An article in an underground journal published in 1944 by O.S. Sadovy, "Where Are Poles Heading?" restated the Ukrainian position and added new observations. For example, the article asserts that the alarmed Polish leadership and clergy had aroused the Polish population to a struggle against Ukrainians, and that the historic Polish imperialism toward Ukrainians was the same as that of Moscow and Hitler's' Germany:

> "Polish imperialists: (1) do not acknowledge the right of the Ukrainian people to their own state and the Ukrainian people are destined to be enslaved by Polish and Russian imperialism; (2) do not recognize the right of Ukrainians to the territory of western Ukraine and consider it to be a permanent Polish territory."[230]

After examining the available sources, Ukrainian historian Volodymyr Viatrovych noted that "...the analysis of the documents gives no reason to suppose that the top leadership of the underground issued instructions to liquidate the Polish population in western Ukraine."[231] On the other hand, Polish sources blame the Ukrainian nationalists for arousing Ukrainians to kill Poles and seize their property. The attacks began at the end of 1942 and moved west, and all of Volhynia was engulfed by the end of 1943.[232] Regardless of whatever instructions were issued, once

---

230 See Shtendera and Potichnyj in Vol. 2 of *Litopys*, 49.
231 V'iatrovych, *Reydy UPA Terenamy Chekhoslovachchyny*, 95.
232 Szcześniak and Szota, *Droga*, 165.

a decision had been made to remove a population that refused to leave, violence was inevitable. This was especially true at a time of heightened ethnic animosity. Similar atrocities occurred after the war when the Polish army was deporting Ukrainians from Poland, although there is no indication that the army was instructed to kill civilians.

In the spring, as Ukrainian attacks increased on Polish settlements, the AK organized and guarded encampments where large numbers of Poles were better able to protect themselves. The civilians were not as defenseless as Polish sources frequently claim, since between the wars, paramilitary groups had been organized. Polish colonists, including large numbers of veterans, were issued arms and ammunition and most were still of combat age. Nevertheless, on July 30, 1943, the alarmed political arm of the Polish resistance appealed to Ukrainians to cease attacks, and expressed support for the Ukrainian independence with the caveat that mixed Polish-Ukrainian areas, such as western Ukraine, would remain in Poland. Such an arrangement was unacceptable to OUN, since western Ukraine formed a nucleus in their vision of an independent Ukrainian state, and the Polish appeal had the opposite effect than what had been intended.

> "Under the prevailing circumstances…[it had] the effect opposite to that intended: The killing of Poles increased, in order to clear out the Polish element in areas of mixed population and making them wholly Ukrainian."[233]

The growing conflict also led to an increase in Polish attacks on Ukrainian villages in the Lublin Province, west of the Bug River, especially by the more militant underground groups who advocated a more forceful approach toward Ukrainians, "…a peasant has to be treated brutally. You have to grab him by the snout because he does not understand gentle treatment."[234] The Polish extremists further advocated driving out Ukrainians beyond the Zbruch River, the traditional border between Galicia and eastern Ukraine. The sad and brutal episode was largely caused by the irreconcilable Polish and Ukrainian claims to western Ukraine.[235]

In June 1943, the increased chaos and the mass desertion of Ukrainian police prompted the Germans to organize a Polish police force and

---

233 Korbonski, 155.
234 Torzecki, *Kwesta*, 298.
235 Szcześniak and Szota, *Droga*, 164.

replace Ukrainians with Poles in the civil administration in Volhynia. The Polish underground reportedly advised the newly recruited Polish police not to participate in raids on Ukrainian villages,[236] but the advice was largely ignored and Poles who were controlled by the German authorities were likely to have had little choice in the matter. A Ukrainian underground document reports that in the Luts'k region, Germans had built a police force of approximately 2,500 men of which Poles comprised two-thirds, and the remainder were Germans, or other groups, including one Ukrainian unit of about 100 men.[237] Most Poles were not local men, but were individuals the Germans had brought from Silesia in the southwestern part of Poland or from L'viv. The enlargement of the Polish police force had the effect of intensifying the Polish-Ukrainian struggle since both sides by that time had armed contingents. The UPA began ordering Poles to leave the region in the spring of 1943 and an estimated 30,000 left for ethnic Polish territory in 1943–44,[238] while others migrated to towns for protection. Some Poles built fortified encampments and frequently received protection from Polish and Soviet partisans, and even Germans. Two such encampments, Ivanova Dolyna (Janowa Dolina)[239] and Huta Stepańska, were large and well-fortified, and although the fights over these towns are described in Polish and Ukrainian literature, the accounts differ radically.

A Polish source identifies Ivanova Dolyna as a Polish village with 600 people that was attacked by the UPA during the night of April 21–22, 1943, and the people were massacred.[240] A detailed Ukrainian account was also given by Roman Petrenko, who participated in the attack.[241] According to Petrenko, Ivanova Dolyna was a quarry with about 100 Polish workers, and it was not clear to UPA whether some had families at the quarry. The quarry had a large quantity of explosives that was guarded by a company of Lithuanians, and the UPA sought to purchase the explosives from the Lithuanians. The Lithuanians were willing to trade the explosives for tobacco and vodka and the Ukrainians agreed to

236 Torzecki, *Kwesta,* 297.
237 Shtendera and Potichnyj, eds. in Vol. 5 of *Litopys*, 25.
238 Szcześniak and Szota, *Droga,* 167.
239 This village had been part of the Polish state before World War II and named Janowa Dolina at that time.
240 Ibid, 166.
241 Petrenko, Roman. "Za Ukrainu, za ii Voliu" in Vol. 27 of *Litopys*, 132–35.

the arrangement; however, before the exchange took place, the Germans were informed and the Lithuanians backed out. Dubovyi, commander of the Zahrava Military District, was determined to acquire the much-needed explosives and as a result, he organized an attack on the quarry. Two railroad bridges from the town of Kostopil were dynamited in order to prevent quick German reinforcement during the attack. Two UPA sotnias participated in the operation. One was ordered to destroy the bunker that housed the German and Polish guards, and the second was ordered to destroy the administration building and sorting facilities. A 13-men squad including Petrenko headed for the storeroom that housed the explosives. Petrenko had worked at the quarry earlier and was familiar with the storage facility. While the fighting raged, over a ton of explosives with necessary detonation devices were removed and carted away in four wagons provided by the local OUN organization. The two companies met stiff resistance, especially from German machine guns in the bunker, and once the explosives were removed, the partisans broke off the attack.

Another mutually described event was the attack on Huta Stepańska. A Polish source reported that in July 1943, the village became a fortified camp sheltering several thousand civilians and was attacked by the UPA. After several days, the "heroic Polish defenders" broke out of the encirclement and were massacred by Ukrainians.[242] In the Ukrainian version of events, Huta Stepańska was a base for a Polish self-defense unit that had been armed by the Germans and had served as an auxiliary police unit, raiding Ukrainian villages either alone or with the Germans. As a result, UPA decided to destroy the village. According to the Ukrainian source, UPA had issued ample warning to Huta Stepańska's civilians. Several weeks before the attack people were ordered to leave, and most had left by the time of the attack. UPA assembled three battalions for the attack. A battalion normally had 400–500 men, and the large numbers were deemed necessary because a Polish partisan battalion and a Soviet partisan unit operated in the area and were expected to protect the village. UPA captured the village with unexpected ease, since the Polish partisan unit was no longer operational and the Red partisans, learning of

---

242 Szcześniak and Szota, *Droga,* 169.

a large UPA concentration, had left the village the previous evening.[243] After a brief fight, the remaining civilian population was fleeing the village when an incident occurred that epitomizes the struggle. A Ukrainian self-defense unit from a neighboring village that was guarding UPA's flank decided, contrary to orders, to settle some old scores with Poles by attacking and killing the fleeing civilians. The incident was reportedly investigated since Ukrainian sources claimed that UPA did not attack Polish villages unless they attacked neighboring Ukrainian villages. The two episodes indicate the nature of the conflict and the difficulty of determining reliable population losses and the circumstances surrounding these events.[244]

In the summer of 1943, the UPA Supreme Military Staff was established in Volhynia. The staff was headed by Dmytro Kliachkivs'kyi (codenamed "Okhrim," "Klym Savur"); Chief of Staff Col. Leonid Stupnyts'kyi ("Honcharenko"); Head of Operations, Col. Oleksandr Omeliusik; Head of Intelligence, Col. Ivan Lytvynenko, Head of Mobilization, Mykola Iarymchuk ("Oleh"); Adjutant and Head of Commissary, Roman Petrenko ("Iurko," "Omel'ko"); Director for Self-Defense Units, Col. N. Sovenko; Director for Training, Col. Fedir Polovyi ("Pol"); and the Head of the Ukrainian Red Cross, Khrystia Mostovych ("Verba").[245] The area was divided into four military districts which all had similar command structures. From west to east, the Turiv District included the present Volyn' Oblast and the Ukrainian districts in Brest and Kobryn, now in Belarus. To the east, the Zahrava District encompassed the central and northern portion of the Rivne Oblast and the Ukrainian area around Pinsk, now also in Belarus. To the south, the Bohun district comprised the southern portion of the Rivne Oblast and the northern part of Ternopil' Oblast, the Kremenets' area. The Ternopil' Oblast was part of Galicia and was the only Galician territory where the UPA operated openly at that time. The largest military district, Tiutiunnyk, included most of the Zhytomyr Oblast as well as the western part of the Kyiv Ob-

243 See Shtendera and Potichnyj, eds. in Vol. 5 of *Litopys*, 82–83.

244 A detailed description of the Polish-Ukrainian conflict in the east is beyond the scope of this study. This brief introduction describes only the origin of the conflict since it affected events that occurred west of the Bug River.

245 Petrenko in Vol. 27 of Shtendera and Potichnyj, eds., *Litopys*, 145–6. Throughout the insurgency the Ukrainian underground used pseudonyms to mask the identity of its members and protect their families from retributions by the authorities.

last. Little is known about the fifth district, called Pivden (meaning "south"), which was located in northeastern half of the Khmelnytsky Oblast and the northern part of the Vinnytsia Oblast. The Pivden district does not appear to have been operational and the UPA presence there had likely been limited. The districts were progressively subdivided into smaller units down to the village level, where a self-defense unit was usually formed. Sotnias and battalions usually operated in designated areas,[246] and each of the four operational military districts normally had several battalions.

Throughout 1943 and into the first half of 1944, the reorganized and enlarged UPA, totaling about 20,000 men at this time,[247] engaged in heavy fighting with Germans, Red Partisans, and Poles. At that time, the Germans were preoccupied with protecting supply lines to the front and requisitioning grain, cattle, horses, and young people for forced labor in Germany. Although the Germans had enjoyed Ukrainian support in western Ukraine at the beginning of the German invasion, the brutal policies of Reichskommissar Erich Koch had fundamentally changed that. By this point, UPA was driving Germans out of some small towns and holding them briefly, and attacked prisons in larger towns that were held by Germans, freeing the Ukrainian inmates.[248] The Germans' loss of control over the countryside meant that their requisitions could be conducted only by engaging in raids. Thus, throughout most of 1943, much of the UPA-German conflict revolved around the raids on Ukrainian villages and German efforts to farm plantations organized by the Soviets during their brief occupation. UPA partisans attempted to defend villages and destroy plantations where neighboring villagers were forced to work without pay. Comparatively small groups consisting of some Germans and auxiliary police, who were either Poles or former Soviet POWs, conducted the raids.

In addition to attacking prisons, the UPA also attacked German units and installations, especially if weapons and supplies could be captured. At the beginning of April, they captured an ammunition train and on May 2 1943, ambushed and killed General Viktor Lutze, a German

---

246 Sokhan and Shtendera, eds. in Vol. 2 (New Series) of *Litopys*), XLIV.

247 Petrenko in Vol. 27 of Shtendera and Potichnyj, eds., *Litopys*, 89.

248 Shtendera and Potichnyj, eds. in Vol. 2 of *Litopys*, 208 and 225.

police chief.[249] To suppress the growing UPA activity, Germans assembled a division-size force commanded by Gen. Erich von dem Bach-Zalewski, and launched an attack in August. The force consisted of two Hungarian regiments, a German regiment composed of SS units and police, a regiment of auxiliary police, as well as Uzbek and Cossack units.[250] The Germans used Soviet POWs for guard duties and organized them by nationality, with the term Cossack usually applying to Russians. In the ensuing three-day battle, both sides sustained heavy casualties, but the Ukrainians took the worst of it, which was evidenced by the fact that some large formations split into smaller units and blended into the countryside. Hungarians normally guarded railroad lines, were reluctant to participate in German pacification campaigns, and made secret mutual agreements with UPA not to attack each other.[251]

As the struggle continued, German control of the region diminished, and that of the Red Partisans increased. Throughout the war, the Red Partisans had mostly confined their presence to the swampy and wooded Prypiat River region, Polisia, and to the northeastern part of Ukraine, in the Chernihiv and Sumy Oblasts. The Ukrainian staff of the Movement was formed to increase and coordinate partisan activities from the Soviet held territory, with some accounts placing high-level party officials among them; including Nikita Khrushchev, the First Secretary of the Communist Party of Ukraine at the time and Dem"ian Korotchenko, the Second Secretary. The movement was coordinated by the Chief of Staff, Timofiy Strokach, a high-ranking NKVD officer, and was assisted mainly by other NKVD officers.[252] Weapons, supplies, and highly trained personnel were air dropped and, reportedly, some of the wounded were evacuated to Soviet-held territories for medical treatment. The major Red Partisan groups were located in the northern Ukrainian oblasts stretching from Sumy to Rivne.[253] In the summer of 1942, large Red units began coming down from Belarus to Polisia and Volhynia, but the more serious attacks began at the end of the year. Reportedly, Kovpak had a meeting

---

249 Ibid, 226

250 Shtendera and Potichnyj, eds. in Vol. 5 of *Litopys,* 21.

251 The agreements are discussed at length in Pahiria, Oleksandr. "Relations Between OUN and UPA and the Armed Forces of Hungary (1939–1945)." in *Litopys UPA*, Vol. 12.

252 Armstrong, *Ukrainian Nationalism*, 139–40.

253 Sokhan and Shtendera, eds. in Vol. 2 of *Litopys* (New Series), XXXIX.

with Stalin in August and was ordered to penetrate Ukrainian territory west of the Dnieper[254]. The operation began in October and the conflict with Ukrainians expanded throughout western Ukraine until the Soviet occupation in the spring of 1944. The Ukrainian National Self-Defense units remained dormant in Galicia, but Kovpak's raid had forced them to fight the Reds and Germans, and the self-defense units were mobilized and assembled into military type units as had been done in Volhynia. Further expansion of the UPA resulted in organizational change. Roman Shukhevych ("Taras Chuprynka") was appointed as Supreme UPA commander at the end of November, and the UPA was subsequently divided into three regional commands: UPA-North, UPA-West and UPA-South. UPA-North, commanded by Dmytro Kliachkivs'kyi, included Polisia and Volhynia; UPA-West encompassed Galicia under the command of Vasyl Sydor ("Shelest"); and UPA-South included an area to the southeast of Rivne Oblast and was headed by Omelian Hrabets ("Bat'ko"); the new organizational structure is provided in Chart 1.

254 Armstrong, *Ukrainian Nationalism*, 146.

Chart 1: Organization of UPA, 1944

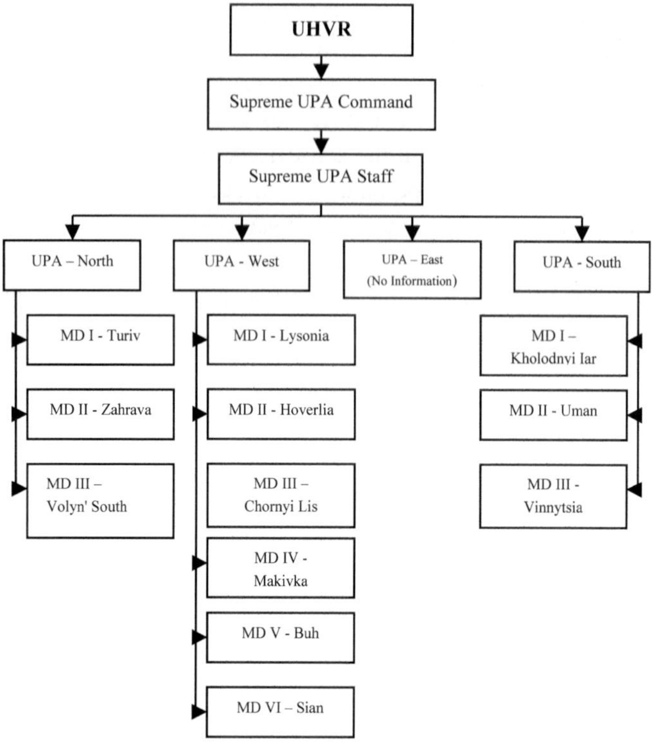

Source: Evhen Misylo, *Aktsiia "Visla"*, L'viv - New York, 1997, Appendix 12.
Notes: UHVR - Supreme Ukrainian Liberation Council; UPA - Ukrainian Insurgent Army; MD - Military District

As described in the 1943 UPA report for the Zahrava Military District, which covered events of the last half of September and the first half of October 1943, the Polish-Ukrainian conflict then took on several forms. Fights continued with the Polish units associated with the Germans, independent Polish partisans, and Poles in the Red partisan units. At the same time, Polish villages began forming small self-defense units, most of which were associated with the Polish partisans, forming de-facto reserves that received weapons from the Germans,[255] who now considered the Poles to be a useful counterweight against Ukrainians. Polish police who had replaced Ukrainian deserters supported the Polish self-

[255] Szcześniak and Szota, *Droga*, 172.

defense units. In the process, most atrocities seem to have been committed by Polish and Ukrainian self-defense units, and were largely related to village feuds. Large scale fighting between the UPA and various Polish partisan groups was limited until the fall of 1943, when the Home Army mobilized reserves for Operation "Tempest", and according to UPA documents, large numbers of Poles also joined the Red partisans at that time. The robust Polish participation is corroborated in a study by the Ukrainian Academy of Sciences, which estimates that Poles comprised about a quarter of the Red partisans in Ukraine.[256] Despite long standing Polish animosity toward the Soviets, UPA attacks had prompted the Poles to ally themselves with the Red partisans.

In the summer of 1943, dramatic changes on the eastern front intensified the partisan warfare in western Ukraine. After the debacle at Stalingrad in the winter of 1942–43, the Germans went on the offensive in the summer. The focal point of the attack was the Kursk salient located approximately 300 miles south of Moscow, where the Germans sought to envelope and destroy large concentrations of Soviet troops, and the offensive began on July 5th. The Soviets, having learned of the impending attack, prepared extensive defenses. The battle raged for a week, and the Germans were unable to penetrate the Soviet line. On July 12, after the Germans had exhausted themselves, the Red Army went on the offensive, relentlessly driving the Wehrmacht westward, and in early October, they crossed the Dnieper River near Kyiv, located about 330 miles west of Kursk. With the front in central Ukraine, large groups of Red partisans began moving west, especially along the Prypiat River. The Poles began organizing larger units in order to increase their presence and their claims to the territory before the Soviet occupation. As the hostilities escalated, a major UPA engagement with the Polish and Red Partisans took place in the autumn. A Red Partisan unit of several thousand men commanded by Petro Vershyhora entered the Volhynia Oblast from the north, and advanced south toward the *Sich*, an UPA encampment that had been used earlier as a training school for officers. During the advance, a large AK unit joined them and the combined force inflicted heavy casualties, capturing UPA supplies and driving the Ukrainians south. The battle was a

[256] Ibid, 180.

precursor to the larger scale Polish-Soviet operations conducted in the first half of 1944.

The Polish Warsaw Uprising of August 1944 has been well publicized, and the literature on the event is replete with accounts of the notorious behavior of the Red Army as it stopped at the outskirts of Warsaw and refused to aid the Polish underground, who were fighting Germans in the city. The uprising was not an isolated event; it was actually part of the general Polish insurrection (code-named "Tempest") against the Germans throughout Poland in the first half of 1944. In total, the AK lost over 72,000 men during the war, including 10,000 in the Warsaw uprising alone.[257] The Polish Government-in-Exile ordered its military arm, the Home Army, to mobilize and attack the Germans. The uprising was designed to occupy some areas and strengthen the exiled Government's claim to legitimacy and popular support at home. That legitimacy was challenged by the Communists who formed their own underground called the Peoples Guards, and by the Polish Peoples Army (*Ludowe Wojsko Polskie*), which was under the control of the Red Army. The 1944 insurrections took place primarily on the eastern territories, and included the Vilnius area, Belarus, and the Ukrainian territories of Polisia, Volhynia and the L'viv region. The 27th Division was first organized in Volhynia and had about 6,000 men, consisting of small Polish partisan groups and the Polish police who had deserted Germans, just as Ukrainians had done earlier. In Polisia, the 30th Infantry Division was formed and in the L'viv region, the 5th Infantry Division and the 14th regiment of Uhlans. The formations were assigned numerical designations based on the pre-war Polish Army units stationed in these areas.

The new formations began attacking German transportation facilities, fighting UPA, and at times, fought the Germans together with the Red Army—some Polish officers were even decorated by the front line Soviet commanders. The arrival of the NKVD troops changed these relations. Poles were ordered to either join the Polish Peoples Army or disarm, and officers were usually arrested. As the units rapidly disintegrated, some Poles joined the Polish Peoples Army, and others disarmed or moved west, crossing the Bug and San rivers.[258] Since the Soviet Union was planning to turn Poland into a satellite, the existence of patriotic

---

257 Korbonski, 58.

258 Ibid, 156–159.

units or insurgence in Warsaw had to be eliminated to ease the acquisition of Poland, and therefore, the Soviets had an interest in allowing the Germans to destroy Polish military units whenever possible.

Formation of the Supreme Ukrainian Liberation Council (UHVR)

When the Ukrainian partisan movement acquired wide support in western Ukraine, it became necessary to subordinate the military to a national organization rather than a single party. The impetus came from the UPA High Command during the winter of 1943–1944 and an Initiative Committee was formed to develop plans. The committee postulated the following concepts which the new organization was required to embrace: An unequivocal commitment to the establishment of the Ukrainian Sovereign State as the highest goal of the Ukrainian people; the recognition that an armed struggle was the appropriate method to secure independence; a declaration of the uncompromising struggle against the Russian and German occupiers; and the recognition that democracy was the appropriate form of government to install when the movement achieved victory.[259]

On July 11–15, 1944, as the Red Army rapidly advanced west, the First Great Assembly met in the Carpathian Mountains to form a new organization, the Supreme Ukrainian Liberation Council (*Ukrains'ka Holovna Vyzvol'na Rada*, UHVR) as the future Provisional Government of Ukraine. The Assembly, organized under the auspices of the Bandera wing of the OUN, was open to members of other political parties or private individuals who supported principles outlined by the Initiative Committee. The party affiliation of the delegates had not been published, but appears to have been fairly broad as some non-OUN members were elected to leading positions. In several days of work, the Assembly issued three documents outlining the structure and policies of the new organization: "The Provisional Structure of the UHVR"; "The Platform of the Supreme Ukrainian Liberation Council; and "The Universal of the Supreme Ukrainian Liberation Council." The UHVR provisional structure was skeletal in nature—the functions of the departments were not elaborated, and the document glossed over the details as it was written,

---

[259] Shtendera and Potichnyj, eds. in Vol. 8 of *Litopys*, 7–15

almost literally, within earshot of the advancing Red Army. Nevertheless, the Assembly became the highest organ in the Council and had the authority to appoint the Presidium and the heads of key departments.

The Presidium was to conduct daily UHVR affairs and included a president and three vice presidents. Kyrylo Osmak, a Kyivan Ukrainian who took an active part in the Ukrainian National Republic, was appointed as president. He remained in Ukraine after the second Soviet occupation, and was later arrested by the NKVD and subsequently died in prison. The First Vice President was Vasyl Mudry, who had been the leader of the UNDO and for a time Vice-Marshal of the interwar Polish Diet. In the fall of 1944, he fled to the West before the advancing Red Army, where he played an active role in émigré politics. The remaining members of the Presidium were mostly OUN members. The Presidium further appointed the members of the General Court, the Control Commission, Conference Commission, Information Bureau, and the General Secretariat. The UHVR chief executive was the General Secretary who supervised the departments for internal affairs, foreign affairs, military affairs, and finance, and the department heads were leading OUN members. The pivotal post of the General Secretary was given to Roman Shukhevych (whose principal *nom de guerre* was Taras Chuprynka). Shukhevych also served as both the head of military affairs and as an UPA Commander until his death in 1950 near L'viv.

The Presidium outlined basic goals, and its policies contrasted sharply with the narrower concept of the OUN integral nationalism. The more liberal and socialistic policies were influenced, in part, by bringing people of more diverse views into the movement and, as some have argued, especially eastern Ukrainians.[260] The main goal was the establishment of an independent Ukrainian State on all Ukrainian territories, defined (in the Ukrainian nationalist view) as the ethnic Ukrainian territories, which had, between the wars, been divided between the Soviet Union, Poland, Czechoslovakia, and Romania. The physical protection of Ukrainians and their leaders was the overriding task to which end the Council would work with the captive nations of Europe and Asia to foster friendly relations based on the mutual acceptance of independent states on the ethnic territory of each people.

---

260 Armstrong, *Ukrainian Nationalism*, 161.

In domestic matters, the goal of independent statehood would be attained through a broad range of social and economic measures, including the development of Ukrainian culture. All citizens of the new Ukrainian state would enjoy equal rights, freedom of thought and religion, and access to education. In economic matters, a largely socialist system was proposed, but private enterprises would be tolerated, private farming and trade would be promoted, but forest, water, and minerals, together with heavy industry and transport would be nationalized. The third document, the Universal that was addressed to the Ukrainian people, restated policies in the UHVR platform and urged ethnic Ukrainians to support it.

The formation of the UHVR did not alter the existing UPA structure nor did it diminish the role of the OUN-Bandera wing, and UPA continued to operate as an irregular army. UPA components in western territories that were eventually allocated to Poland remained subordinated to their superior organizations in Volhynia and Galicia.

As the war continued, the Ukrainian underground began expelling the Polish population from Volhynia, east of the Bug River, while at the same time, Poles began attacking Ukrainians west of the river in the Lublin Province. The Ukrainian actions, while brutal, had a clearly defined political purpose: to remove the fifth column as a necessary precondition for establishing a Ukrainian state. The Polish rationale for violence is less clear, although some of the more extreme elements did call for the removal of Ukrainians from the area. During the interwar period, the Chełm and Podlasie districts in the eastern portion of the Lublin Province had been targeted for Polonization since the Ukrainian identity in this area was weak. During the German occupation, the growth of Ukrainian nationalism increased and more people began calling themselves Ukrainians (instead of *Rusyns*), a name that Polish elites perceived as being linked with irredentism. In addition, many Poles perceived wartime Ukrainian cooperation with the Germans as Nazi collaboration. Their reaction to these phenomena was emotional and they sought to reverse the process by eliminating community leaders who in their opinion were at the forefront of the Ukrainian nationalist movement. The Ukrainian Central Committee compiled a list of 500 Ukrainian community activists killed in the region in 1942 and 1943. The enumeration includes only those individuals for whom church services were held, and the actual number killed was presumably much higher.[261] The selected killings cannot be attributed to random violence but must instead be understood as political assassinations.

Along with the rising Polish-Ukrainian hostilities, German colonization schemes during the war had escalated the conflict. At the beginning of the war, the Germans developed a grandiose plan to colonize much of Eastern Europe with the *Volksdeustche*, people of German ancestry, who were scattered throughout Eastern Europe. By November 1941, a plan was developed that called for the removal of 31 million non-German locals in order to establish German colonies in Poland, Ukraine and the Baltic regions with the expectation that the plan would be realized in about 30 years.[262] However, some resettlement of the Volksdeutsche was already in progress. From 1939 to 1941, about 30,000 Volksdeutsche—mostly from the Lublin Province—were moved to the territory of western Poland attached to the Reich, increasing German concentration in those areas.[263] Ukrainians requested permission for landless Ukrainian peasants or those who possessed little land be allowed to settle in the vacated Volksdeutsche homesteads. Approximately 6,000 people volunteered to be resettled, but because of opposition from local German officials, only 600 people were actually able to do so, and Poles settled the remaining farms.[264]

During 1941, SS General Odilo Globocnic developed a separate plan to establish a large German colony west of the Bug River with the approval of Heinrich Himmler, head of the SS. The plan called for settling Volksdeutsche from different regions of Eastern Europe in the Zamość, Hrubieszów and Biłgoraj counties and Ukrainians were to be settled in adjacent areas so as to form a security belt for the Germans.[265] The project was under SS control, but many German civilian administrators in the province opposed the plan, considering it too costly and noting that Poles would resist while Ukrainians were reluctant to participate. A German district official named Zorner reported that Ukrainians were uncertain and feared Polish reprisals and similarly, Kubijovyč claimed that

---

261 Isaevych et al., *Volyn'*, 493–508.

262 Madajczyk. *Generalna Gubernia w Planach Hitlerowskich: Studia*, 94–95.

263 Kubijovyč, *Ukraintsi*, 187.

264 Ibid, 189.

265 Motyka, *Tak Bylo*, 135–136.

Ukrainians were apprehensive and believed that the plan would not benefit them.[266] Despite the outcry, the SS began the operation on November 28, 1942. During the first phase (November 1942–March 1943) 116 Polish villages were affected, and in the second phase (June-August 1943), 293 settlements were deported either partially or completely.[267] As Poles were moved out, Germans began the process of settling some Ukrainians in vacated Polish homesteads on January 15, 1943. In view of their concerns, it is not clear whether Ukrainians volunteered, were forced to relocate, or it was a combination of both, although one Polish scholar claims that Ukrainians were also forcibly resettled.[268] In any case, the actual number of Ukrainians who were resettled into Polish villages appears to have been small, as Ukrainian leaders and the local population had been apprehensive about the settlement.

After the German reverses on the Eastern Front, the colonization scheme was abandoned, but had already had the effect of intensifying the Polish-Ukrainian conflict, since the German population transfers were conducted at the same time as Polish-Ukrainian hostilities were rising. Some writers attribute the increased violence to the Polish perception that Ukrainians had received comparatively greater privileges under the Germans.[269] Others more realistically claim that the increase of Ukrainian cultural and political activities threatened the future inclusion of the territory into a reconstituted Polish State.[270]

Massive Polish attacks on Ukrainian villages were possible because of the existence of a large Polish underground formed at the beginning of the war. In 1943, the various Polish partisan formations in the area totaled 50,000 and increased to 125,000 in 1944.[271] Large scale Polish attacks increased in 1943 as the Germans continued to deport Poles and resettle some Ukrainians.[272] The earlier selective assassinations had transformed into mass violence against Ukrainians. In May 1943, in Hrubieszów County alone, 52 villages were destroyed and 4,000 Ukrainians

266 Mankowski, *Miedzy Wisła a Bugem, 1939–1944*, 291–292.

267 Madajczyk, *Generalna Gubernia*, 113

268 Motyka, *Ukrainiska Parytzantka, 1942–1960*, 394.

269 Karpus, Zbigniew. "Chelmszczyna w latach okupacji niemieckiej." in *Polska Ukraina: Trudne Pytania*, t.10, *Karta*, 2006, 200.

270 Makar in Ibid, 216.

271 See Ibid, 219 citing Mankowski, *Miezdzy Wisła*, 179, 188, and 335.

272 See Motyka, *Tak Bylo*, 147 and Mankowski, *Miezdzy Wisła*, 318–319.

were killed in Polish attacks.[273] The Polish underground launched a large-scale attack against all Ukrainians, and these attacks were clearly not limited to Ukrainians who had been resettled on the evacuated Polish farms. In the spring of 1944, AK units were instructed that the "The lives of Ukrainians must be made difficult in the district, forcing them to move beyond the Bug or elsewhere."[274] In response, Ukrainians quickly expanded self-defense units and were reinforced by 11 UPA sotnias arriving from Volhynia.[275] Eventually a front line was established between the two groups, spanning approximately 100 miles along the Huczwa (Huchva) River and lasted until the arrival of the German-Soviet front in the summer of 1944.[276]

During the Communist period, little was written about Polish civilian losses in western Ukraine. However, after the collapse of Communism, numerous memoirs and monographs appeared and conferences were organized to discuss the matter, with wide-ranging estimates of the losses. American historian Timothy Snyder places Polish civilian losses in Volhynia for 1943 alone at 40,000 to 60,000, while Mikołaj Siwicki, who also surveyed the Polish literature, noted that estimates of Polish civilian losses ranged from 20,000 to a million,[277] and cited a number of publications with varying estimates. A Soviet source placed Polish civilian losses in Volhynia at 20,000, although Polish sources typically double that figure. Siwicki also published his own estimates, placing Polish losses in Volhynia at 20,000 and not more than 10,000 in Galicia.[278] Most publications do not indicate the sources of the data used to derive estimates and in view of the significant disparity, it is likely that unverifiable anecdotal information was used extensively. Throughout the intense fighting, the government in the countryside ceased to exist and could not possibly provide even approximate statistics. Furthermore, Polish estimates, as a rule, generally do not provide information on Ukrainian civilian losses, although one source notes that in late 1943, Ukrainian losses amounted to approximately 2,000 in Volhynia, com-

---

273 Makar, 223.
274 Siwicki, Mikołaj. *Dzieje Konfliktow Polsko-Ukrainskich*, 55.
275 Karpus, 201.
276 Motyka, *Tak Bylo*, 148.
277 See Snyder, *The Reconstruction,* 170 and Siwicki, *Dzieje Konfliktow*, Vol. II, 20.
278 Ibid, Siwicki, 28.

pared to Ukrainian statistics that placed their losses at 20,000–30,000.[279] Perhaps additional research and less bias could produce more reliable estimates, but estimates will always be questioned because reliable data on the casualties is not available. These shortcomings should not obscure the fact that thousands of civilians of both nationalities died in the conflict.

In the second half of 1944, the Polish-Ukrainian struggle that had been raging since 1941 had temporarily abated on the territory west of Bug and San rivers. The area was a war zone; at first the Germans attempted to thwart the Soviet crossing of rivers, and after the successful crossing, the Red Army prepared to cross the Vistula River further west. At that point, the Polish partisans had been largely eliminated, but a small number went underground and continued the resistance for the next several years. Most Ukrainian units at this time went east to avoid being trapped between the two armies.

The fate of the region, however, would not be determined by either Poles or Ukrainians, but by the three major allied powers. A general agreement was reached at the Teheran Conference, held from November 28 to December 1,1943, attended by Franklin Roosevelt, Josef Stalin, and Winston Churchill, with the three leaders reaching an agreement that the Curzon Line should form the basis for the Soviet-Polish border. The issue was revisited in greater detail at the Yalta Conference in Crimea, which was held from February 4 to February 11, 1945. Much had changed in the intervening year, since the German Army was no longer present on Soviet territory, having been driven back to Germany. By the time of the Yalta conference, much of the territory of present day Poland was occupied by the Red Army.

The Yalta conference dealt with many issues affecting Eastern Europe and the future of Germany, but no topic was more contentious than the Polish question. The Polish problems revolved around two major issues: the post-war borders and the nature of the Polish post-war government, the latter being the more contentious of the two issues by far. The United States and Great Britain agreed to the Curzon Line, but urged some modifications in the Polish favor. Roosevelt stated that the U.S. was willing to accept the Line, but urged Stalin to relinquish the city of L'viv, along with adjacent areas and the oil fields in the northern foothills

279 Bilinsky, Yaroslav in *The Ukrainian Quarterly*, No. 3–4, 2003, 243.

of the Carpathian Mountains, to Poland. Churchill also accepted the Curzon Line, despite the criticism that he received at home, but stated his view that the Soviet Union was entitled to the territory in view of the burden it had shouldered during the war. Nevertheless, he urged the Soviet Union to act magnanimously and cede L'viv to Poland. According to Churchill, Great Britain did not seek any gains; it was merely a question of honor. Stalin replied that the Polish question was not only a question of honor, but also a strategic concern since Poland had formed a corridor through which Germany had attacked Russia twice during the last thirty years. Invasions through the corridor occurred because Poland was weak and, therefore, Stalin stated that it was in the Soviet interest to establish a strong Polish state.[280] The Soviet Union, however, was not prepared to yield on the Curzon Line since, as Stalin pointed out, it had been proposed by Lord George Curzon and Georges Clemenceau during the First World War. "We could not return to Moscow and face the people who would say Stalin and Molotov have been less sure defenders of Russian interests than Curzon and Clemenceau."[281] Stalin then added that Poland could be compensated for the loss of territory in the east by acquiring additional lands in the west. He noted that during the visit of Prime Minister Stanisław Mikołajczyk in October 1944, the minister was delighted to hear Stalin's proposal that Polish western border be moved to the West Neisse River and agreed to the Curzon Line in the east. Stalin failed to mention that Mikolayczyk had also asked for the concession on L'viv and the oil fields. He then asked the western powers to support the Oder-Neisse line as the new Polish western border. The conference concluded with an agreement that the Curzon Line should form the Polish eastern boundary deviating in some areas from five to eight kilometers in the Polish favor, while at the same time, Poland should be compensated with substantial territorial concessions in the north and west. The allies decided that the final border in the two areas would be determined at a future peace conference.[282]

The relationship among the three allies became more strained following the Yalta Conference. As the Red Army advanced through East-

---

280 LaFeber, ed. *Eastern Europe and the Soviet Union,* Vol. II., part of Schlesinger, ed. *The Dynamics of World Power,* 49–50.

281 Ibid, 50.

282 Ibid, 63–64.

ern Europe, pro-Soviet regimes were installed in the occupied countries and the Polish problem, as earlier, took center stage. The Potsdam Conference, which was held outside Berlin from July 17 to August 1, 1945, was designed to settle post-war issues, but by that point, conditions had changed considerably. Roosevelt had died and Harry Truman took his place while Clement Attlee replaced Churchill. Stalin remained the only leader who had attended the previous conferences. More important than the change of leadership was the change of attitude among American officials when the Soviet methods and intentions became clear. W. Averell Harriman, the U.S. Ambassador to the Soviet Union, briefed President Truman before the conference on the recent Soviet policies, and communicated his opinion that the Soviet Union was pursuing a two track policy: cooperation with the U.S. and Britain while unilaterally extending Soviet control throughout Eastern Europe. American readiness to cooperate "...was being misinterpreted in Moscow...as an indication that the Soviet Government could do anything that it wished without having any trouble with the United States."[283] The Ambassador continued that a "barbarian invasion of Europe" was taking place, as the Soviet system of secret police and lack of individual freedom was being implemented in the neighboring countries. President Truman promised to be firm with Stalin at the upcoming conference and was confident that the United States would be able to have most of its demands satisfied.

At the conference, a fundamental difference emerged between the Soviet Union and the Western Allies over the Polish western border. After intense discussions, the Soviet proposal was accepted, and the Soviet Union received the city of Königsberg, now Kaliningrad, and the adjacent area. The Polish western border would be "east of a line running from the Baltic Sea west of Swinemünde, and thence along the Oder River to the confluence of the western Neisse River and along the western Neisse to the Czechoslovak frontier, including that portion of East Prussia not placed under the administration of the Union of Soviet Socialist Republics in accordance with the understanding reached at this conference and including the area of the former city of Danzig..."[284] The conference also indirectly sanctioned the earlier Soviet policy of driving out the Germans by agreeing to the mass deportations of ethnic Germans

283 Ibid, 74–75.
284 Ibid, 158.

from Poland, Czechoslovakia, and Hungary. The protocol stated that Germans from the three countries should be transferred in "a humane manner" and distributed among zones of occupation by the Allied Control Council of Germany. The three countries were not to expel Germans on their own authority since a large influx of Germans in the west might precipitate a famine.

The strongest disagreement at the conference centered on the political nature of the governments that would be formed in the post-war Eastern Europe. The Western Powers advocated broad-based democratic regimes that would not be hostile to the Soviet Union, while the Soviet Union was interested in forming pro-Soviet governments. The Polish problem was especially contentious since there were two groups claiming to represent Poland. The London-based Polish government-in-exile represented the legitimate interwar government of Poland that had been displaced by the Germans, and considering its extensive underground activities, it enjoyed more support than any other faction. As the war progressed, however, the Soviet Union was able to organize a communist group claiming to be the true representative of the Polish people. Despite all the persecutions in Moscow and the Soviet executions of the Polish prisoners of war, some Poles still supported Stalin and the Soviet system. On January 5, 1942, a small communist group met in Warsaw and reestablished the previously banned Polish Communist Party, renaming it the Polish Workers Party (*Polska Partia Robotnicza* or PPR).[285] The following year, Władysław Gomułka, a national communist who advocated communist ideology but eschewed Soviet methods, emerged as the PRP's first Secretary. The party made great strides under difficult conditions, expanding the network and organizing a partisan movement. Stalin did not rely solely on the new party, and formed a pro-Soviet faction out of Poles living in the Soviet Union. The formation of the Polish Peoples Army (*Ludowe Wojsko Polskie*) in the Soviet Union was under the nominal control of the Union of Polish Patriots headed by Wanda Wasilewska and another Soviet inspired organization, the Polish Committee of National Liberation (*Polski Komitet Wyzwolenia Narodowego,* PKWN), which was touted as a legitimate representative of the Polish people. After the Red Army captured the eastern Polish city of Lublin, the PKWN

---

285 Davies, *God's Playground*, Vol. II, 547.

(which was headquartered there) was recognized by the Soviet Union as being the de facto Polish provisional government. It was staffed largely by Moscow Poles,[286] including Edward Osóbka-Morawski and Marshal Michał Rola-Żymierski, as Stalin distrusted the more independent-minded members. As the Red Army occupied more cities, pro-Soviet elements were placed in pivotal positions and the influence of the London government gradually dwindled. At the conferences with the Allies, Stalin hence took the position that the refusal of the Lublin Committee, as it was now called, to accommodate members of the exiled government was an internal Polish matter.[287]

The collapse of the political order in Eastern Europe at the onset of World War II had provided Ukrainians with another opportunity to establish their own state. Poland had been eliminated and Russia, another traditional enemy, was expected to disintegrate under the impact of the German invasion. Finally, OUN leaders had believed that the West would defeat Germany in a repetition of the previous war. The Ukrainian task was to organize a credible military force, seize Ukrainian territory in a chaotic situation, and establish its own state. The Mel'nyk wing of OUN sought to organize such a force under German auspices, while the Bandera group, who were more distrustful of the Germans, chose to form a large independent partisan movement. At the same time, the German occupation provided western Ukrainians with the opportunity to participate in local governance, establish Ukrainian schools, and engage in political activities, all to a much greater extent than had been possible in interwar Poland. The German occupiers used Ukrainians as a counterweight against the Poles, though in the Generalgouvernement districts, principal German administrators clearly demonstrated pro-Ukrainian sympathies. These policies, coupled with OUN activities, enabled Ukrainians to gain regional advantages over Poles and served to intensify the mutual hostilities between the two groups. The situation in Volhynia had turned especially violent because of pre-war Polish colonization, rapid Polonization, and mutual small-scale attacks, evoking visceral hatred

---

286 The so-called "Moscow Poles" were representatives of the Polish Communist Party stationed in Moscow, i.e., delegates to the Communist International organization (Comintern).

287 LaFeber, *Eastern Europe*, 50.

in the local Ukrainian population toward their Polish neighbors. When the Bandera wing concluded that the Polish Government-in-Exile was determined to retain western Ukraine in the Polish State, a policy of ethnic cleansing was initiated. The draconian policy was undoubtedly influenced by the recent inhumane events in the region. The brief Soviet occupation of Baltic, Belorusian, and Ukrainian territories led to extensive deportations and executions, while Germans were exterminating Jews systematically. The OUN (b) policy of removing Poles seems to have stimulated violent Ukrainian civilian attacks on Poles as well, reminiscent of the violent eighteenth century peasant uprisings on the Dnieper. Thousands of people had perished by the time the Red Army occupied the region once again.

Chapter IV: Prelude to Expulsion, 1944–1945

Soon after the Red Army entered Poland in the summer of 1944, the Soviet Union and the Polish Committee of National Liberation signed border and population exchange agreements, setting the stage for three brutal years of partisan warfare in the Ukrainian ethnographic territories of southeastern Poland. Discussions at the meetings leading to the agreements are not available but were undoubtedly one-sided, since the Poles were not in a position to make demands. The PKWN, also known as the "Lublin Committee" after the city where it was formed, was organized under the auspices of the Soviet Union. Soviet support had made it possible for the organization to install itself as the head of a new Polish provisional government in lieu of reinstalling the prewar Polish Government-in-Exile. Although the signing of agreements was a perfunctory matter, the process of implementing provisions was much more complex, especially those related to the population resettlement. Polish partisan groups, which advocated the reconstitution of an independent Poland within the pre-war boundaries, were still sizeable despite the losses they had sustained fighting the Germans. At the same time, there was limited support for the Soviet proffered government. The new regime faced difficulty organizing loyal police and the army, and some units deserted and joined the partisans after receiving training and weapons. Due to the fact that they had Soviet support, the fledgling Polish communist government was never in danger of being overthrown, but fighting would be required to eliminate the opposition.

In addition to resistance among Poles, there was concerted opposition among Ukrainians, the people who were targeted in the agreements. Polish partisans and gangs as well as police and troops targeted them. After the arrival of the Red Army in the Transcurzon, Polish partisan attacks on Ukrainians had subsided but still continued for about a year. In addition to the organized groups, there were Polish village gangs who, while masquerading as patriots, robbed Ukrainian villages and killed civilians in the process. Finally, police and army units also committed comparable atrocities while under the guise of fighting the Ukrainian partisans. The Ukrainian underground had operated in the area during war and began re-organizing and expanding after the territory was assigned to Poland under the new border agreement. The underground sought to prevent the removal of the Ukrainian population and preserve the region as a historic Ukrainian land. The partisans had always enjoyed significant support among the Ukrainian population, but the support greatly increased when the deportations began as the partisans sought to thwart the removal of the population and to that end attempted to defend Ukrainian civilians from Polish attacks.

Establishment of the New Order

On July 20, 1944, just days after the Red Army entered Poland; Nikita Khrushchev wrote a letter to Josef Stalin urging him to incorporate the Ukrainian districts west of the Curzon Line into the Soviet Union. In Khrushchev's letter, he proposed the annexation of territory that had been part of the Russian Empire prior to World War I, part of the Lublin Province during the interwar years, and which had been the western edge of the historic Volhynian Principality (west of the Bug River). He stated that the territories proposed for annexation were "historic Ukrainian lands."[288] Just as the Tsarist government had established the *Kholm Guberniia* in 1912, Khrushchev suggested that the proposed territory would form the Kholm Oblast and encompass most of the same territory, including adjacent counties located along the old western border of medieval Rus's Galicia-Volhynia Principality. The proposed annexation encompassed a territory totaling 4,753 square miles (compared to the 2,066 square miles of the 1912 *guberniia.*) In addition to the former Volhynian lands, Khrushchev proposed that the western districts of Galicia, totaling 2,377 square miles, should be attached to the Drohobych Oblast[289]. The enlarged oblast would provide an additional buffer for the city of L'viv in case of a future war. As to the territories located south of the Carpathians on the Ukrainian border, the proposal called for adding Carpatho-Ukraine to the Soviet Union to form a Transcarpathian Oblast and adding parts of southern Bukovina to the Chernivtsi Oblast which borders Romania and

---

288 See Serhiichuk, *Trahediia Ukrayintsiv v Polshchi* (Ternopil', Vydavnytsvo "Ternopil'"), 1976. Note that the enumeration of counties for these territories can be found on pp. 67–70.

289 Drohobych was an oblast in the Ukrainian SSR at the time. It is currently part of the L'viv oblast.

Moldova. The proposed Transcarpathian Oblast would have an area of 8,448 square miles and the portion of southern Bukovina would have 2,584 square miles.

Although Stalin's immediate response to the proposal is unknown, it was not ultimately accepted although a similar plan was already being implemented. Unbeknownst to Khrushchev, Stalin and a few in his inner circle, including Soviet foreign minister Vyacheslav Molotov, were secretly putting their own plans into motion with respect to Poland's future. The fact that Khrushchev, head of the Ukrainian Communist Party, was unaware of the planned new borders of Ukraine indicates the extent to which Stalin had centralized Soviet decision-making.

As the Red Army crossed the lower San River in the late summer of 1944, chaos continued in the Transcurzon lands,[290] where Ukrainians comprised the demographic majority. Between July and early September, as the Red Army regrouped before heading west, only German army units remained in the area. The *Generalgouvernement* rapidly disintegrated as German civilian authorities fled. Some Ukrainians in German police units fled with them, but many deserted their posts to join the Ukrainian underground, which was able to recruit, operate, and train in comparative safety. Amidst the chaos, a question hung in the air: what would become of Poland's future, and where would its postwar frontiers be drawn? It was a question of utmost importance not only to the Polish government in exile, which aspired to reinstall itself to power, but also to Ukrainians living in southeastern Poland, where Polish repression and violence was a not-so-distant memory.

It soon became clear to all parties that Stalin had neither the intention of reconstituting the interwar frontiers of Poland, nor of reinstalling the Polish Government-in-Exile in any meaningful way. Within just days of the Red Army's arrival, the Soviets installed the Polish Committee of National Liberation as Poland's new provisional government. By installing a pro-Soviet government consisting of Moscow Poles who were Comintern members and who had arrived with the Red Army, local communists, socialists and other leftist groups, Stalin would be able to

---

290 "Transcurzon" (*Zakerzons'kyi krai*) was an OUN name given to Ukrainian districts in Poland after the 1944 boundary change. The name will be used in this study for brevity.

set Poland's future on a course more favorable to Soviet political interests.

One of the first orders of business was to secure Polish agreement on the disposition of new Polish-Soviet border. On July 27, 1944, Lublin Committee chairman Edward Osóbka-Morawski and Soviet foreign minister Vyacheslav Molotov signed a secret agreement in Moscow[291] that rendered a new Polish-Soviet border stretching from the Carpathian Mountains to the Baltic Sea. Article I of the agreement stipulated that Poland's eastern border would be based on the Curzon Line and adjusted in the Polish favor, specifying that "…territory east of the Curzon Line to the West Bug River and the River Sololkija south of Kryłów …" would be ceded to Poland. In Article IV, the Soviet Union further agreed that the Polish-German border should run west of the city of Swinemünde along the Oder and Neisse rivers, extending south to the Czechoslovakian border.[292] The terms of the agreement essentially shifted Poland's frontiers approximately 150 miles northwest, compensating for territories lost in the east by adding the former German territories of Pomerania, Prussia and Silesia, which would constitute Poland's new northern and western frontiers.

It is no coincidence that the Soviet-Polish border agreement was congruent with the so-called Curzon Line, a boundary that had been discussed at length between Stalin and the western allies at the Teheran Conference in 1943. In addition to its geostrategic advantages, the Curzon Line had additional historical and national significance for the Soviets, since these lands were part of historic Kyivan Rus', territories that Moscow had always sought to bring under its control. At Teheran, Stalin did not miss the opportunity to point out that the boundary was not a new idea invented by the Soviets—in fact, it had been first proposed in 1919 by British Foreign Secretary Lord Curzon as an armistice line marking the eastern frontier between Soviet Russia and the Second Polish Republic. The Curzon Line roughly traced the ethnographic divide between Poles and peoples of the Russian empire.[293] At Yalta, British Prime Min-

291 The agreement remained secret until August 16, 1945.

292 Eugeniusz Misilo, Ed. *Repatriacja czy Deportacja*; *Przesiedlenie Ukraincow Z Polski do USRR 1944–1946; Tom I Dokumenty 1944–1945* (Warszawa: Archiw Ukrainski, 1996), 17–18.

293 The Treaty of Riga is discussed in Chapter I.

ister Winston Churchill suggested that Stalin might make a magnanimous gesture by extending Poland's boundary further east to include the city of L'viv, which would at least partially placate Churchill's allies, the pre-war Polish government, which still remained in exile in London. Stalin maintained his position, reminding Churchill that his own countryman had proposed the boundary. An excerpt from a Soviet protocol from the conference reads as such:

> Stalin asked whether the Allies wanted the Soviet leaders to be less Russian than Curzon and Clemenceau...what would the Ukrainians say if they accepted the Allies' proposals? They might say that Stalin and Molotov had turned out to be less reliable defenders of the Russians and the Ukrainians than Curzon and Clemenceau. In what light would Stalin appear then on his return to Moscow?[294]

By 1945, the Red Army had occupied Poland and neither Churchill nor Roosevelt was in a position to make the Polish question a sticking point in the negotiations. Stalin's determination to create a Soviet-dominated Polish state, reinforced by Soviet control of the territory in question, eventually snuffed out the Allies' hopes of creating a free and independent Poland. In February, the western allies would make their formal acquiescence to the new eastern boundary, as well as accepting the Oder-Neisse line as the western frontier. They also sanctioned the forcible mass deportations of ethnic Germans from Poland, Czechoslovakia and Hungary. In doing so, the western powers—who had gone to war to liberate the whole of Europe from Hitler and his aspirations for a so-called Thousand Year Reich—acquiesced eastern Europe to Soviet control for decades to come.

The Population Exchange Agreement

On September 9, 1944, a few months after the Lublin Committee had signed the border agreement with the Soviet Union, they signed a population exchange agreement with three Soviet Socialist Republics: Lithuania, Belarus, and Ukraine. Nikita Khrushchev representing Ukraine and Edward Osóbka-Morawski for Poland signed the twenty-two-article instrument in Lublin. It was entitled, "Agreement Between the Polish National Liberation Committee and the Government of the

---

294 Plokhy, S.M., *Yalta*. p. 167. A detailed discussion of the political maneuverings between Stalin and the Allies can be found on pp. 152-180 of this book.

Ukrainian Soviet Socialist Republic on the Resettlement of the Ukrainian Population from the Territory of Poland to the USSR and Polish Citizens from the Territory of the USSR to Poland".[295] According to the terms of the agreement described in Article I, ethnic Ukrainians, Belarusians, and Ruthenians[296] on the Polish side of the border were all subject to resettlement in Soviet Ukraine. Likewise, ethnic Poles on the Soviet side were subject to "repatriation" within the new borders of Poland. Article I specified that the resettlements of Poles on the Soviet side were to be instituted only on the territory that had been part of the Polish State during the interwar period prior to September 17, 1939, the date of the Soviet attack on Poland. The agreement affected both Poles and Jews: all Poles were subject to resettlement, although some managed to remain, and the Jews were to be given an option of remaining or resettling in Poland.[297] The agreement emphasized the voluntary nature of the exchanges. People who were resettled to Ukraine were to be settled on collective farms or private farms, and those sent to Poland would be given plots of land based upon upcoming Polish land reforms.

According to Article II, the resettlement actions would begin on October 15, 1944 and end on February 1, 1945, and the period of September 15 to October 15 was to be used for preparation. The deadline could be extended by mutual agreement. Articles III, IV and VI outlined the financial aspects of the deportations, including the types of property that individuals could take with them. Such items included livestock, farm implements, or tools that were used in their occupation, as well as other moveable property. Items that were not permitted to be taken included gold, precious stones, works of art, money over 1,000 zlotys/rubles and motor vehicles. According to the agreement, owners would be compensated for the property left behind, including any un-harvested crops that remained. The agreement also stipulated that the re-settlers would be granted a five-year loan amounting to 5,000 rubles/zlotys after arriving at their new places of residence. Back taxes and pensions would be an-

295 Misiło, *Repatriacja*, Vol. I, 30–39. The term "deportation" is used in this text instead of "voluntary exchange" because the former describes the situation more accurately.

296 At that time, some people still referred to themselves as "Rusyns" or "Ruthenians" and had not yet adopted a Ukrainian national identity.

297 The agreement affected Poles, Jews, and other prewar Polish citizens: 787,000 people were removed, including 742,000 Poles, 33,000 Jews, and 12,000 people of other nationalities. See Jasiak in Ther and Siljak, *Redrawing Nations*, 181.

nulled when departing the country and transportation costs would be covered by Poland and the Soviet Union, with both countries handling the administrative aspects of the resettlements on their respective territories.

Articles VII through XI described the organizational structure and procedures for the deportations, including the designation of plenipotentiaries and their representatives by each country. In Poland, Zygmunt Rogalski and Józef Bednarz were the principal officials assigned to handle the deportation of Ukrainians. On the Ukrainian side, the Soviets informed Osóbka-Morawski that they had appointed Mykola Pidhornyi as the principal representative for the deportations.[298] The agreement stipulated that any differences or disputes between the two delegations would be mitigated and resolved by the governments of both countries. According to these articles, the commissions of the two countries were required to provide a list of individuals who were subject to deportations, were entrusted to control and supervise the process, and it was also incumbent upon them to provide any necessary assistance to the respective commissions.

The remaining articles, XII through XXII, specified the types of information that the resettlement commissions were to collect on each person, designated the deportation points, and laid out procedures for how deportees would be identified and scheduled for transport. The biographical information required for each individual included the individual's nationality and his or her relationship to other family members (a family was defined as blood relations and other members of a household.)[299] As to the physical location of the deportation commissions, the agreement identified a number of towns, many of which were county seats. It listed twenty on the Ukrainian side and eleven on the Polish side with the caveat that additional locations could be established as needed. Initially designated on the Polish side were the towns of Włodawa, Chełm, Hrubieszów, Tomaszów, Lubaczów, Jarosław, Przemyśl, Lesko, Zamość,

---

298 Pidhornyj was better known by the Russian version of his name, Nikolai Podgorny. He would later become the Chairman of the Presidium of the Supreme Soviet, holding that position from 1965–1977. He was replaced in Poland by Mykhailo Romashchenko at the beginning of 1946.

299 "Nationality" in this context applied to a person's ethnicity and their presumed nationalist loyalties, and the Polish citizenship of the designation deportees thus had no impact on their selection for deportation.

Krasnystaw, and Bilgoraj. In January 1945, after the Germans had been driven further west, an additional five locations were designated in the towns of Sanok, Krosno, Jasło, Gorlice, and Nowy Sącz. A number of exit points were established on the border through which the new settlers would be moved, and both countries stationed appointed representatives at the resettlement points. Older people, the disabled, and women with children were to be sent first.

Approximately a week after Poland and the Soviet Union signed the agreement; they issued detailed operational instructions that amplified its provisions.[300] The instructions restated certain points in the original agreement, but this time dwelled at length on enumerating properties that would be left behind by those who were resettled. The so-called "voluntary" nature of the exchange was also restated, along with further language indicating that individuals could request relocation either orally or in writing. The instructions further specified that oral requests were to be recorded by local organs and required relevant biographic information to be provided about applicants and their dependents. People who applied for resettlement to Ukraine were offered the option of settling either in towns or villages, and after that was decided, they had the further option of relocating to either collective farms or private plots. Families who chose collective farms were designated for resettlement in the eastern oblasts (regions) where collective farms had been formed in the 1930s, and would be provided with private subsidiary plots ranging from half an acre to over two acres of land. Those who chose private farms were to be settled in western Ukraine where collective farms had not yet been established. In the Galician oblasts in western Ukraine, individual farms would receive up to 17 acres of land. In the Volhynian oblast, approximately 37 acres per farm would be allotted since the soil was less productive. The Soviet Union also took on the responsibility of handling the resettlement of Poles in Ukraine and was responsible for providing the necessary transportation to Poland.

On September 20, 1944, the Soviets, who were determined to expedite the removal quickly, sent Population Exchange Commission members to Lublin. The membership consisted of a Principal Plenipotentiary

300 "Operational Instruction to the Agreement of September 9, 1944 Concluded Between PKWN and the USSR Concerning Resettlement of Ukrainians from Poland and Polish Citizens from the USSR," See Misiło, *Repatriacja,* Vol.I, 45–59.

and the supporting staffs. The Commission expanded rapidly during the deportation period (1944–1946) and ultimately some 375 people would serve.[301] On September 20, 1944, the first group of 25 members arrived in Poland. Initially the commissions were posted in eleven towns, but after Germans were driven out of the Cracow area in the fall of 1944, four towns were added in the Lemko region. Most commission members were in their 30's and 40's, two-thirds were Communist Party members, and there were 74 women among them. Of the ethnic distribution, Ukrainians totaled 287, Russians 77, Belarusians four, and there were seven individuals of other nationalities. These workers were among the officials targeted by the Ukrainian underground, and despite the protection of the Polish troops and Ministry of Internal Affairs (Russian acronym -- MVD units), ten were killed and nine wounded. Table 1 indicates the distribution of commissions by county and the size of their staffs. It should be noted that not all the counties had commissions—occasionally workers were sent to other counties to handle the increased volume of work (which accounts for the larger numbers in the second column.)

Table 1: Distribution of Soviet Deportation Personnel by Province and County

Province	County	Posted Staff	Staff employed
Lublin		161	222
	Biłgoraj	23	30
	Hrubieszów	23	44
	Chełm	23	33
	Krasnystaw	23	19
	Tomaszów	23	38
	Włodawa	23	38
	Zamość	23	20

301 Discussion in this section is based on the information in the final report written in February 1947 by Mychailo Romashchenko, the Soviet head of the Deportation Commission who replaced Mykola Pidhornyi at the beginning of 1946. The report is published in Serhiichuk, *Trahediia*, 219–286.

Rzeszow		163	281
	Gorlice	24	31
	Jarosław	23	33
	Jasło	24	20
	Lesko	23	52
	Lubaczów	23	42
	Przemyśl	23	48
	Sanok	23	55
Cracow		24	39
	Nowy Sącz	24	39

Source: Volodymyr Serhiichuk, *Trahedia Ukraintsiv V Polshchi,* pp. 227–8.

The commission placed great importance on personnel management and methods of work. The necessary instructions and statistical forms were issued to the local commissions and augmented by meetings. Undoubtedly, the most daunting task that faced the commission was the acquisition of the necessary means of transport, including rail and motorized vehicles as well as iron stoves to heat the boxcars. The report does not indicate whether the commission was successful in obtaining a sufficient number of stoves, but the transport situation was clearly dreadful since the shortage of railroad cars remained a major problem throughout the deportations. The most severe deficit occurred in February of 1946 when the commission requested some 3,300 cars and received only 97. This shortage resulted in deportees waiting at uncovered railroad stations for long periods of time, often running out of food and feed for their livestock. The longest wait occurred at the Uhnow (Uhniv) station, where 257 families waited from February 2nd to June 4th, 1945.[302] In addition to the lack of trains, there was the difficulty of transporting people to the rail stations since the Red Army had provided only 300 trucks. People came to the station either on foot or in their own wagons, but their own transportation was insufficient due to the shortage of wagons and draft animals. Occasionally, local Polish farmers transported people to the

[302] Serhiichuk, *Trahediia*, 256.

nearest station, and there were reports of Poles robbing the people while the accompanying troops neglected to interfere. The lack of material resources was also exacerbated by the lack of cooperation among local Polish officials.

In February of 1947, Mykhailo Romashchenko, the Soviet head of the deportation commission, issued a report that summarized the various aspects of the deportation process, wherein he described the difficulties encountered by the lack of support from the local administration as well as the problem of attacks by the Polish and Ukrainian undergrounds. The content in the report describes how the opposition of local officials was compounded by a shortage of qualified, politically reliable workers, a lack of resources, and violent opposition from the underground. Polish priests were also accused of complicating the deportation process by issuing false documents to Ukrainians, identifying them as Roman Catholics (therefore Poles) and rendering them legally ineligible for deportation. Reliable data on the number of converts are not available but these cases appear to have been few and confined largely to the Orthodox population in the Lublin Province.[303]

According to Romashchenko's report, Józef Bednarz, the Lubaczów County commissioner, had publicly stated that he disagreed with the policy of removing Ukrainians on the grounds that it would "depopulate Poland." To that end, Bednarz took overt measures to deny the commissions the necessary means of transport, claiming that there was a shortage of horses in the country. In the spring of 1945, he ordered the police to take cows and sows from the people at a railroad station, claiming that they were special breeding animals, but Soviet personnel thwarted the attempt. Romashchenko claimed that Bednarz personally visited Ukrainian villages, urging residents to convert to Roman Catholicism in order to avoid deportation. A similar claim was initiated against local administration officials in Krasnystaw County who allegedly resisted the deportations by withholding the transfer of wagons and neglecting to maintain the roads or provide protection for the people waiting at the stations. As a result, those tasks were left to the Red Army. In another county, a Polish communist declared that a Soviet system was to be introduced in the next several months, and this new reality obviated the need to remove the

[303] Ibid, 242.

Ukrainians.[304] Opposition to the deportations was evident in other counties as well, but with the exception of describing the actions of Bednarz, Romashchenko did not provide details about the nature of the opposition.

In addition to deporting the people, the commission was required to move livestock, grain, and farm equipment. In total, the 1944–1946 deportees took with them 238,487 head of livestock, with about half being milk cows, as well as 6,607 beehives. Livestock data indicate that an impoverished farming population comprised approximately 93.1 percent of the total number of deportees. Per family (excluding the urban component), this amounted to an average of 0.44 horses, 0.93 cattle, 0.38 sheep and goats, and 0.19 pigs. Additionally, people took with them 66,387 pieces of farm equipment, including 24,069 wagons, but left behind 666 million zloty worth of movable and immovable property and 461,317 hectares of un-harvested fields. Upon departure, the people turned over approximately 152,360 tons of grain, vegetable, and feed valued at 18 million zloty to the Red Army and the Polish government. Considering the impoverished state of the people and their hostility toward both the Red Army and the Polish Government, the "gift" had been either a requisition or goods that the deportees were unable to take with them. Romashchenko's report does not indicate the reason for leaving behind large quantities of agricultural products nor does it mention whether or not the people had been compensated. Additionally, people left behind unharvested grain and vegetables in their fields as the result of being forced to leave before the harvest seasons. To transport people, livestock and goods, 50 thousand cars were used, and an average of 2.2 families or 8.7 people were transported per boxcar at a cost of approximately 21 złoty per person.

In the beginning of 1945, as the Red Army moved west with the Soviet-German front, both the Polish and Ukrainian undergrounds increased their activities in eastern Poland. The Polish Underground attacked fledgling security forces, the local administration, and Ukrainian civilians in attempts to drive them out. The Polish partisans were extremely active in the Włodawa area during the first half of 1945, and at the beginning of March, a 120-man unit appeared in the area that was reinforced by a 350-man unit that had deserted the officer training school.

304 At that time, some members of the Polish and Ukrainian undergrounds believed that Poland would be incorporated into the Soviet Union as another republic.

The Armija Krajowa (AK) reportedly had five large groups totaling 850 men and enjoyed support from police and local officials. According to Romashchenko, they attacked and disarmed police, captured a railroad station and telephone equipment, and were threatening officials in the county seat of Włodawa. To the south in the Chełm region, a 440-man AK unit was terrorizing Ukrainians and by June, they had increased their numbers to 600. In the adjacent Krasnystaw County, the commission counted 240 bodies in the village of Wierzchowiny. The Polish underground was also operating freely in Hrubieszów, robbing and torturing Ukrainians. Local authorities and police, who made no attempts to stop them, occasionally joined.

On May 26, 36 policemen deserted and joined the Polish underground, bringing with them 38 rifles and two machine guns. They distributed leaflets urging the local Ukrainians to join them in the fight against the Soviet Union. Police in Dołhobyczów robbed Ukrainians as they were leaving, took their wagons and other goods, and even killed some people. Even a member of the Soviet commission was shot after showing his documents, then accused of being a Banderite and told that goods and property would not be allowed to leave Poland for the benefit of the bandits in the USSR.

Polish Resistance to the Communist Regime

Based on official Soviet reports and the reports of the Soviet Population Exchange Commission, the situation in the Transcurzon district was chaotic. Ukrainians opposed the communist authority, but more importantly, they were also opposed by a large segment of the Polish population. In a lengthy top-secret report of June 1945 to Stalin, Nikita Khrushchev wrote:

> As of June 1,1945 we have identified ten large AK bands totaling 3,300 operating along our (Soviet) border to the depth of 30 kilometers (approximately 19 miles.) A map indicating AK locations is included. Moreover, Polish nationalists use all legal means to organize their cadre. For example, a two-year old seminary in Lubaczów is preparing men for the AK. In these border districts there are examples of Polish nationalists using an organization of Peoples Militia to augment their numbers. Under the influence of AK agitation, draft-age youths in many places are declining to join the Polish Army, but instead join the Peoples Militia to obtain a weapon and then they join the partisans.[305]

He then offered some specific examples, noting that in April 1945, a unit of cadets from an officer school in Przemyśl had joined the Polish underground.[306] More importantly, a battalion of Polish troops (640 men) stationed in Lubaczów deserted to the AK on April 23, 1945 and were joined by the town's militia and some members of the security service.[307]

In his final report on the deportation, dated February 14, 1947, Head Commissioner Romashchenko included some observations and experiences that commission members had reported during the deportation in 1945, including the fact that the Polish police had arrested and beaten a commission member named Ivan Hulyy on April 7, 1945, for which he had been hospitalized. The note for April 28, 1945 states that nine partisan groups were operating in Hrubieszów County, and that AK controlled the northern portion of the county and UPA had the southern portion. On May 19, 1945, a 500-man AK group attacked the Ukrainian village of Warez and lawlessness prevailed in the area as local police and Polish communist party members had moved to the county seat of Hrubieszów for protection. Under the September 3, 1945 entry, Romashchenko noted the following:

> ...UPA groups remain in the southern portion of the Hrubieszów County. In the Warez area of the county on September 1, the car of the county head was destroyed on Warez-Belz road, near the village of Rusin, by a 300 men UPA unit. Three state security members were killed, (along with) a policeman, eight civilians and one was wounded. Among the dead was Kravchenko, deputy head of the regional security department. Evacuation of Ukrainians from that part of the county is absolutely impossible.[308]

---

305 Ibid., 154.
306 Ibid.,154.
307 Ibid.,155.
308 Ibid, 265. The other items are in Ibid, 263–264.

Ukrainian Reaction in the Transcurzon

As the new communist Polish government took shape, Ukrainian communities began organizing and demanding cultural and civil rights. Because the population transfers had been billed as voluntary, most Ukrainians expected to remain in Poland. Since the Red Army had occupied the Chełm region in July 1944, earlier than other Ukrainian districts in Transcurzon, Ukrainian villagers in that area immediately began petitioning the Soviets and the newly forming Polish government in attempts to improve their situation.[309] In July and August of 1944, Ukrainian residents submitted petitions to the Soviet government that focused on three types of requests: (1.) Requests that their territory be annexed to Soviet Ukraine, (2.) Demands for cultural rights, especially regarding the addition of Ukrainian schools (with Ukrainian as the language of instruction), and (3.) There were some requests for resettlement to Ukraine as a response to vicious Polish partisan attacks.

Of the first category, a total of ten letters signed by 2,227 people requested incorporation into Ukraine, and those letters were sent either to Stalin, Khrushchev, the Ukrainian Supreme Soviet, or to the Communist Party of Ukraine. In those letters, many of the petitioners expressed admiration for the Red Army and the Soviet Union and, as such, made an appeal to Soviet sympathies. They also enumerated atrocities committed against them by the Polish underground in 1943 and 1944. A letter to Khrushchev dated August 1, 1944 and signed by 85 people, includes the following appeal:

> ...In 1943 and 1944 about 193 villages were burned in the Chełm region and about 19,000 people were killed in various ways and their barbaric terror continues... we beg you to incorporate us into the Soviet Ukraine.[310]

A committee representing Ukrainians in Hrubieszów and Tomaszów counties sent a similar letter to Stalin in August 1944. The lengthy letter also catalogs Polish interwar oppressions including the destruction of 200 Orthodox churches. It alleges that during the war, many Polish nationalists who had registered themselves as Volksdeutsche became policemen and continued to abuse local Ukrainians, specifically mentioning a period in 1943 when Polish partisans, aided by the Volks-

---

309 The letters are published in Serhiichuk, *Trahediia,* 84–93.

310 Ibid., 84

deutsche policemen, began attacking Ukrainian villages.[311] According to the authors, the climax occurred in 1944, and during that two-year period, approximately 150 villages were burned and 15,000 people were killed. The authors goes on to enumerate seven villages that were attacked and reports the number of people killed in each village, ranging from 770 in Sagarin (Sahryn) to 35 for Teljatin (Teliatyn), and the number killed in the seven villages amounts to 1,828 people. The petition ends with a much more emotional plea than is found in the other letters.

> We humbly beg you on bended knee Our Father—Comrade Marshal Stalin—to liberate us from the new bondage and unite us and our Chełm Land, Ukrainian through the ages, with our Ukrainian Motherland in the USSR.[312]

In addition to enumerating wartime oppressions and atrocities committed by the Poles, the letters sent to the Soviets also catalogued oppressions that Ukrainians had suffered during the two decades of Polish rule in the interwar period. In one of the letters addressed to Stalin, 165 petitioners stated that during the period between the wars, Polish authorities had destroyed almost 200 Orthodox churches and had denied educational opportunities to Orthodox Ukrainians who had refused to convert to Roman Catholicism. The petitioners also claimed that after the brief Soviet occupation of the area of Poland in 1939, Poles had denounced anyone who had cooperated with the Red Army to the German authorities.[313]

The second group of letters asked the Polish administration to reopen Ukrainian schools, alleging that on August 24, 1944, the evolving Polish government had issued instructions to close schools that taught Ukrainian as the primary language of instruction. The Polish instructions did stipulate that if there were at least 40 Ukrainian children between the ages of 7–14, parents could petition authorities to organize Ukrainian schools, otherwise, pupils would be required to attend Polish schools and Ukrainian could be taught as a subject.[314] On August 27, 1944, the residents of the Hrubieszów County accordingly petitioned the government to open Ukrainian schools in the county, noting in their petition that there

---

311 People claiming to be *Volksdeutsche* were typically of mixed ancestral origins. Those of German-Polish ancestry sided with the Poles in the struggle.

312 Serhiichuk, *Trahediia*, 90–92.

313 Ibid., 92.

314 Misiło, *Repatriacja,* Vol. I, 19–21 and footnote l.

had been 165 elementary schools and three secondary schools earlier. In August 1944, delegates from the county made two trips to discuss the matter with education officials, but no concrete steps were taken. The second petition again requested that elementary and secondary schools be reopened and granted permission to hire qualified Ukrainians as teachers.[315] On September 5, the Polish Provisional Government's Department of Education issued new instructions permitting the existence of private and public Ukrainian schools, provided that qualified teaching personnel were available. Despite some nominal encouragement by the authorities, however, the schools were never actually established. In a letter from Lublin dated October 5, 1944, a Soviet repatriation official wrote to Dem"ian Korotchenko, Secretary of the Central Committee of the Ukrainian Communist Party, stating that no Ukrainian schools had been established in the area.[316]

In the third category of letters, two letters expressed interest in relocation to Ukraine. On August 1, 1944, villagers from Wasilow (Vasyliv) in the Chełm region submitted a petition of approximately 150 signatures requesting that their village be attached to Ukraine and if that was not possible, they expressed their desire to be relocated there. One man from Hrubieszów County, Volodymyr Ponahaibo, requested to be transferred to Ukraine with his family because of Polish atrocities. His letter explained that his village of Nowosiółki (Novosilky), which consisted of 226 households, was completely burned by Poles and 108 individuals had been killed, including his wife and four-month old child.[317]

In addition to individual villages and village councils that submitted petitions in the Chełm region, an organized committee was formed in Przemyśl and attempted to lobby the new Polish government for better treatment of Ukrainians. The earliest attempt to normalize relations was made on September 7, 1944, when the Ukrainian Citizens Committee of Przemyśl wrote to the county administrator requesting that Ukrainians be granted civil rights equal to those enjoyed by ethnic Poles.[318] Representatives of five counties in the Rzeszów Province made a more formal re-

---

315 Ibid., Document 3, 21–22.

316 Serhiichuk, *Trahediia*, 111.

317 Ibid., 85.

318 Misiło, *Repatriacja,* Vol. I, 26–27.

quest on July 7, 1945.[319] The petition, which included a 12-point memorandum, essentially restated the same demands made by Ukrainians during the interwar period: the indigenous Ukrainians desired to remain on their ancestral lands in Poland and demanded full civil rights. The memorandum also conveyed the committee's request for religious and educational reforms for the Ukrainian minority. They specifically asked that Ukrainians be permitted to openly practice the Greek Catholic faith and be granted equal access to government employment and educational opportunities, including the establishment of elementary and secondary Ukrainian schools, both academic and technical, as well as access to institutions of higher education throughout the country. On economic issues, the committee requested the establishment of a Ukrainian credit bank and full benefits for Ukrainians during the upcoming land reforms, suggesting that the land of Ukrainians who emigrated should be distributed among the remaining Ukrainians, and that restrictions on the sale of moveable property should be lifted. In the political sphere, Ukrainians requested political amnesty as well as the right to form a democratic party, a request that would require a drastic change from the hostile policies employed by some government organs toward Ukrainians.

A Polish government document dated July 20, 1945 reveals that the Polish government invited a Ukrainian delegation to Warsaw for a discussion in an effort to gain their support for the resettlements.[320] The delegation consisted of five signatories to the aforementioned petition, as well as an additional five members from the Cracow and Lublin Provinces. Two government officials named Zuniak and Grabowski represented the Polish side. The conference took place in Warsaw on July 24 and the discussions were recorded in a report,[321] although it is not certain whether the report is complete because three of the Ukrainian delegates are not recorded as having participated in the discussion. The report indicates that the Ukrainian delegation was divided on the subject of resettlement: while some expressed the view that the Ukrainian people were deeply attached to their land and did not wish to leave, delegates with leftist leanings supported the deportations. It is worthy to note that the leftist delegation present at the conference was disproportionately large

319 Ibid., 144–145.
320 Ibid., 143–44.
321 Ibid., 147–54.

considering that the area targeted for population resettlement had a negligible Communist following; however, it is unclear if this was the result of the government's hand-picked selection of Communist sympathizers or whether it legitimately resulted from a lack of non-Communist participants. Considering the fact that many Ukrainian community leaders had fled in 1944 before the advancing Red Army, it is plausible that those who remained may have been afraid to participate.

Dr. Jarosław Konstantynowycz, representing Ukrainians in Sanok County, opened the discussion by restating issues that arose in the earlier petition to which he was a signatory and elaborated on those points throughout the conference. He stated that the Ukrainians were deeply attached to the land, pointing out that some had even returned from America to farm, and the abundance of mixed Ukrainian-Polish families would complicate the resettlements. He also stated that the situation in Soviet Ukraine was unstable, and noted that Ukrainians and Poles had lived together for centuries. Further, Konstantynowycz argued that there were rumors circulating that the Polish eastern boundaries would be moved to the Zbruch River, sowing confusion amongst Ukrainians as to whether or not to move and therefore, he concluded, Ukrainians should be allowed to remain in Poland, Ukrainian schools should be re-opened, and political amnesty should be issued to Ukrainian citizens.

Piotr Dudka and Michał Donski represented the three western Lemko counties of Jasło, Gorlice, and Nowy Sącz. Dudka stated that no Polish-Ukrainian conflict existed in their area; many Lemkos had already left because of poverty, and those who remained wished to enjoy the same rights as Polish citizens. Donski stated that the population of the three counties considered itself Rusyn (Ruthenian), but with the arrival of Ukrainians from the east, people had begun to call themselves Ukrainians. He added that no ethnic conflicts existed in the area since most Ukrainians in Jasło County had already left for Ukraine, and the populations in Gorlice and Nowy Sącz largely remained and did not have the desire to emigrate. The remaining Ukrainian representatives supported resettlement to varying degrees with most of them hoping for relocation to the east, but some supported relocation to the former German territories in western Poland. Mikołaj Korolko, a communist party member, stated that about half of the Ukrainians had already left, many because of attacks by the National Armed Forces, a militant Polish partisan group.

The remainder wished to stay and enjoy civic and economic opportunities afforded to other citizens. As the conversations continued, Korolko's position changed, and he claimed that Ukrainians actually wanted to leave, alleging that only the nationalistic element wished to remain and was preventing others from leaving. He finally concluded that since Poland was planning to organize a national state for the Polish people, the Ukrainians should be made to leave. Wasyl Woytowicz and Jerzy Czolij, signatories of a 12-point memorandum advocating that the Ukrainians remain, also changed their positions during the conference, and expressed their support for the resettlement plans. Woytowicz claimed that 90 percent of the Ukrainians were peaceful people who wished to emigrate, but were prevented from doing so by the Ukrainian underground. To accomplish the transfer, Woytowicz suggested that a sufficient number of police and military troops would be required to deport supporters of the underground and to liquidate the underground itself. Czolij stated that only two percent of the underground was local and that the population would not work with them, but people were hesitant to move because of the upcoming harvest and the rumors circulating about the boundary changes.

As the war ended, most Ukrainians in the Transcurzon region interpreted the terms of the population exchange agreement literally, believing that the policy and process had a genuinely voluntary intent. To that end, ad hoc groups formed and began petitioning Polish authorities to establish Ukrainian language schools and provide other basic civil rights for Ukrainians. The authorities engaged these groups in limited dialogue but for an entirely different purpose, they hoped to use these groups to urge other Ukrainians to leave. The Ukrainian representatives were neither willing nor able to accommodate the Polish request. The people were much more in agreement with the rapidly expanding Ukrainian underground, which urged them to resist deportation at all costs.

Expansion of the Ukrainian Underground in the Transcurzon

The establishment of the new Polish-Soviet border physically divided the Ukrainian underground's organizational apparatus between Poland and Soviet Ukraine. During the war, both components had operated on the Ukrainian ethnographic territories west of the Curzon Line that OUN collectively termed the "Transcurzon Region" (*Zakerzonnia*) after the war. UPA was subordinated to superior organizations located further east in Ukraine. As the borders became fortified, however, it became increasingly more difficult for the western sectors to maintain communications with those in the east, and these conditions forced the underground's leadership to overhaul their administrative structure in Poland. In the spring of 1945, OUN established a new administrative structure called the Transcurzon Territorial Executive, which became the new hub for OUN activity in the Poland. It reported directly to the Supreme OUN Executive in Ukraine, but also had the authority to receive instructions directly from Munich where the OUN representatives, including much of the top leadership, were headquartered. Since the Executive was located outside the Soviet Union and able to operate more freely in Poland, it became an important link between units in Ukraine and the West.

As illustrated in Chart 2, the new Territorial Executive was divided into three operational regions headed by Iaroslav Starukh ("Stiah," "Iarlan," "1001," "h"); Vasyl Halasa ("Orlan," "Nazar," "Zenon," "Savchenko," "Dniprovsky," "Bis," "97," "1818") who also served as the first deputy in charge of propaganda and supervised OUN Region I. Region I administered the most strategically important counties in the Transcurzon region, comprising the Przemyśl area as well as Lesko and Sanok counties. It was divided into two districts: "Kholodny Iar," which had five sub-districts and "Beskid" which had six. When UPA activities extended to the western Lemko counties in the autumn of 1946, a special sub-district named *Verkhovyna* was established there, but was operationally subordinated to the Beskid district. Region II encompassed the northern portion of Przemyśl County as well as Jarosław and Hrubieszów counties, the one district ("Batiuryn") consisting of five sub-districts. Region III, which encompassed the Chełm area, had two districts: "Levada" with five sub-districts and "Lyman" with four. Polish intelligence estimated that 2,200 individuals served in all components of the OUN;[322] it should be noted, however, that Polish intelligence sources overestimated the size of both the OUN and the UPA.

322 Szcześniak and Szota, *Droga,* 242,

Chart 2: Organization of the OUN Territorial Executive

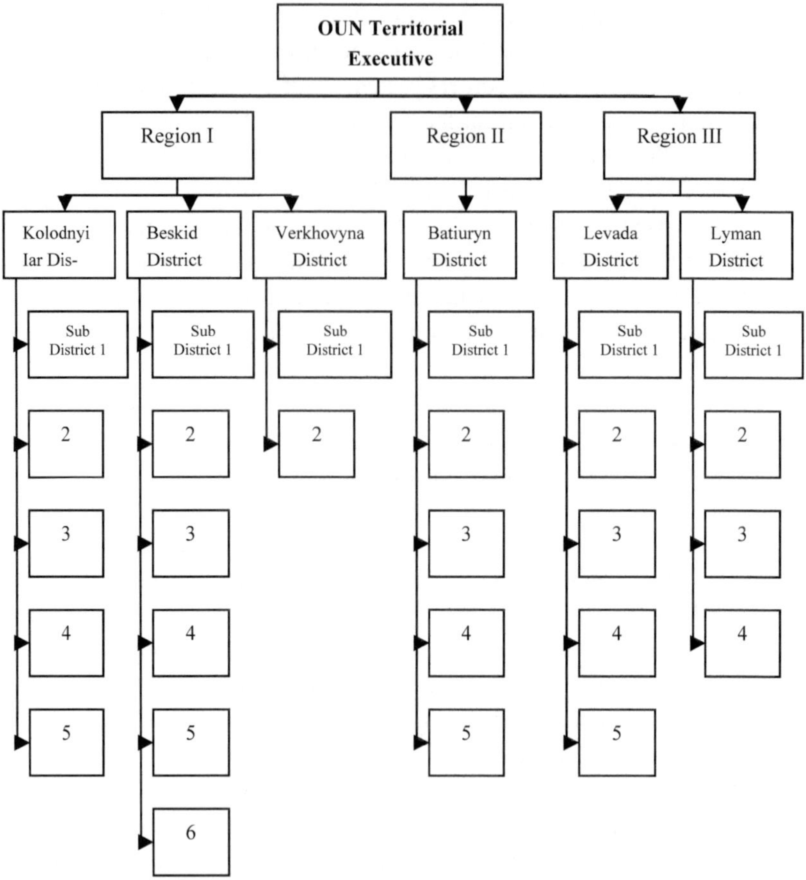

Source: Evhen Misylo, *Aktsiia "Visla"* (L'viv - New York, 1997), Appendix 14.

In addition to its regular civilian apparatus, OUN also had a quasi-military component called the *Sluzhba Bespeky* or SB, which was a security service and secret police organization. Petro Fedoriv ("Dalnych") directed intelligence and counter intelligence functions for the SB. SB also included administrative units (*Administratyvny Boivky* or AB), which performed police-type duties and maintained courier lines. The Security Service was subordinated directly to the OUN at all levels and had a similar administrative structure since it was organized by region, district, and sub-district. Region I was commanded by "Stary", Region II by "Shram" and Region III by "Zenon." The service was also divided into civilian and military sections.[323] The civilian section gathered intelligence, performed counter-intelligence tasks, and conducted investigations, while the military section consisted of armed squads of about a dozen men performing police work. The squads also provided security for the OUN network, although all OUN members were armed, made arrests, carried out executions, and fought Polish troops and police, either independently or in conjunction with the UPA units.

Communication was a crucial function in the underground's activities, since the OUN set the agenda for the entire underground and disseminated policies and views in numerous ways: by word of mouth, or through small brochures and leaflets among its own members as well as to UPA and the Ukrainian population at large. Since radio transmission technology was not well developed or trusted for fear of interception, contacts between different components was confined to word of mouth or through messages delivered by special couriers. The OUN's Transcurzon Territorial Executive maintained contact with foreign representatives in both Germany and Ukraine, but most of the effort was directed at keeping contact among its various organizations in Poland. The Courier Section ("Holodomor") was subordinated to the OUN and headed by "Letun"[324] until June 1946, and consisted of short and long communication lines.[325] The short lines transmitted messages among local self-defense units based in villages and the OUN sub-district organizations. The long distance lines transmitted information among districts and regions by the Courier Links of the Section, and the Links employed well-trained and armed couriers frequently using dead drops. The agreed upon spots where the communication was dropped provided additional security since the courier never made visual contact with the recipient. The principal OUN and UPA leaders resided in hideouts that served as headquarters, and only their immediate assistants knew the locations. They communicated with subordinates largely by dead drops and arranged personal meetings, which were infrequent. UPA also used the OUN communication network and both kept contact with superiors in Ukraine, although contacts became increasingly difficult since the Polish-Soviet border defenses were continuously strengthened. Couriers from Ukraine car-

---

323 Ibid., 262.

324 The real name of "Letun" does not appear in any of the available literature.

325 Ibid., 275.

ried messages to Poland, made contact with members of the Courier Section handed over their messages and carried communication from Transcurzon to Ukraine. The contact with the Foreign Section of the OUN in Germany seemed to have been well established and may have involved individuals in Czechoslovakia who aided the transmissions.

The OUN leadership clearly recognized the importance of communicating not only with underground members, but also to the general public in order to maintain morale and support for their cause. To that end, the underground press played a crucial role in the OUN from its inception, serving as a vehicle for disseminating the organization's policies, viewpoints, and relevant news (both domestic and international), initially in Ukraine and later expanding to the Transcurzon region. In the Transcurzon, the OUN was forced to quickly adapt its internal and external communications to address the rapidly changing political conditions; including regime changes, the redrawing of borders, and the deportation campaigns. Since underground leaders had access to foreign radio broadcasts and newspapers as well as the Polish press, they were well informed about events happening both in Poland and abroad, and sought to educate the Ukrainian people about the fluid current events as well as their own evolving views on the necessary objectives to reach the goal of Ukrainian independence. To that end, they established new publications that addressed the specific concerns that arose in the western districts.[326] The more theoretical publications placed the Ukrainian struggle for independence in a historical context and rationalized the underground's approach to achieving that goal. Other publications were more journalistic in nature, reporting current events in Poland and abroad, as well as the internal activities of the organization. Content in underground press publications included factual reports on local events as well as fictionalized stories or composite stories based on actual events. The fictionalized stories recounted common horrific events that Ukrainian civilians experienced on a daily basis in their attempts to avoid deportation or simply to survive. The prevalence of the genre points to the cathartic effect that it had on the frightened people.

The Informer was a theoretical journal ranging between 20 to 60 pages in length, with most of its content focused on current events. It re-

---

[326] The discussion is based on issues of five publications in Potichnyj, *Litopys UPA*, Vol. 16 (Toronto: Litopys UPA, 1997.)

ported on UPA engagements in the Soviet Union and Poland, and frequently compared the current struggle to earlier efforts to establish Ukrainian independence. It also contained analyses of political developments abroad, especially focusing on the growing tension between the Soviet Union and the western allies. The December 23, 1945 issue begins with an editorial that describes OUN's struggle since 1932, when two of its members were hanged by the Polish authorities. The author makes the assertion that through their own efforts, Ukrainians had managed to advance the struggle "...and now hundreds of thousands of revolutionaries and UPA soldiers, arms in hands, are fighting for independence!" The unsigned article urged its readers to continue the struggle for an independent Ukraine, proclaiming: "We are confidently looking to the future—victory is ours."[327] In the same issue, there is another article by Z. Savchenko entitled "International Relations." Savchenko's article describes the political events and trends that had occurred since the end of the war, noting that German and Japanese aggression had forced the USSR, the US, and England to form an alliance, but since the end of the war, there had been a growing split in the alliance which had produced conflict between the USSR and the western allies. Besides the disagreement between the two sides on many issues, the author noted the growing communist-inspired conflicts in China, Indo-China, Iran, Greece, and in other parts of the world. The author posited that the West had the choice of either countering these conflicts or becoming a member of the global USSR. Since western interests would not permit communist expansion, an anti-communist struggle would grow—a struggle in which Ukraine had an important role to play: "Imprisoned peoples of the USSR, including Ukrainians, have an important role in the worldwide anti-Bolshevik front. They are no less powerful within the USSR than the atomic bomb."[328]

The Weekly News was a pamphlet-length publication, and each of the two issues available in the West contains approximately six pages. The content was drawn mostly from foreign presses and radio broadcasts. The August 5, 1945 issue begins with an editorial entitled "What Are We Fighting For?" The title exemplified a recurring theme in the underground literature. It notes that although everyone was familiar with the

---

327 Potichnyj, *Litopys UPA,* Vol. 16, 91.

328 Savchenko, Z. "Do Kharakterystyky Mizhnarodnykh Vidnosyn." in Ibid., 98.

reasons for the underground's struggle, it was still necessary to clearly restate the OUN's main goal: to secure independence for the Ukrainian people. Achieving the goal, in the author's view, would enable Ukrainians to live in liberty and to be the masters of their own lands, but in order to make that happen, the people would need to rise above the numerous attempts that occupying powers had made, throughout history, to denationalize them. The author asserts:

> "The last war has revealed the bankrupt nature of Bolshevism. The Bolshevik leaders use Communist slogans to entice their slaves to fight German Fascism, but were eventually forced to reveal the true nature of Bolshevism. They played the Russian patriotic tune and in the process revealed their true imperialist Muscovite face, forever disillusioning those who, up until now, believed in their internationalist ideals…Today, the time has come to annihilate Muscovite imperialism. All subjugated peoples are joining the struggle and the Ukrainian people will have the honor of leading this mighty struggle because they were the first to fight Bolshevism".[329]

The pamphlet concludes with an "International Review of Political Events," an article devoted largely to the Potsdam Conference and the problems in the Balkans. The underground paid close attention to these matters in the hope that a third world war would develop between the western Allies and the Soviet Union. The proceedings of the conference are described without editorial comments, noting that the conference aimed to root out German militarism and National Socialism without subjugating the German people. It notes that the allies intended to deport ethnic Germans living in Poland, Czechoslovakia, and Hungary and resettle them within Germany's new borders, that the Polish western boundaries were to be finalized at a future conference but would run along the Oder and Neisse Rivers, and that Poland would also receive the free City of Danzig along with a portion of East Prussia. The conference had established a Council of Foreign Ministers from the ministers of England, the US, USSR, France, and China who were charged with concluding peace treaties with Italy, Romania, Bulgaria, Hungary, and Finland. Difficulties in the Balkans are described at length, especially communist attempts to seize the Greek government and Soviet attempts to establish bases on the Mediterranean. The author concludes that the conflicts were not likely to be resolved without war.[330]

---

329 Ibid.,193–194

330 Ibid., 196–197.

The Informational News, a magazine with issues averaging between 20 to 60 printed pages, reported on events in the Soviet Union. Its content was particularly focused on the growing tension between the Soviet Union and the western allies, and to that end, it reported or summarized foreign radio broadcasts and newspaper reports.[331] The November 25, 1946 issue begins with a lengthy editorial entitled "Political Review," which catalogs the differences between the USSR and the West and devotes considerable attention to the Paris Peace Conference. The Underground press always followed events in the Balkans very closely since it was an area of potential conflict between the former allies. Moreover, because of the region's proximity to Ukraine, any conflict that developed there would have an immediate impact on Ukraine. To that end, the editorial hones in on the dispute between the USSR and the western allies over the city of Trieste, and explains that the West advocated turning it into an international city and port, a scenario opposed by the Soviets. On this point, the British *Weekly Herald* is quoted directly, noting, "…it is not important whether Italy or Yugoslavia has the city, the crucial question is… whether or not Russia will have a base on the Adriatic Sea."[332] The editorial concludes that the wartime allies were unable to settle the German question and had tabled the matter for later consideration, and that no agreements had been reached during the five-week conference.

Forest Dweller, a humor magazine containing illustrations, was written specifically for the UPA and the local population in the Transcurzon. Its articles and illustrations delivered political messages through an entertaining medium of fictionalized stories; including satires of communists and foreign political figures and, ever so gently, the UPA itself.[333] The No. 7 issue contains a concluding portion of a poem about the fate of a fictitious character named Ivan Burdock (the term *burdock* in popular parlance means "useless weed.") After finding Ivan asleep in a hayloft, the Muscovites arrested him, tried his case according to the arbitrary legal norms, and subsequently sent him to Siberia where he died. The poem ends by admonishing everyone to fight, lest they meet the same fate as Ivan Burdock. The issue concludes "Adventures in Sleep (a

---

331 Ibid., 267–273.

332 Ibid,. 268

333 Ibid., 401–403 and 404–408. Two items are presented from issue number 7 dated August 1945,

Humorous Tale)," a fictional dark comedy piece about a dream of American President Harry Truman. In this story, the President dreams that he is kidnapped by a giant bird and taken to the Transcurzon region, where he is renamed "Ivan the Sufferer" and forced to endure the travails of the local people who were being driven off their land. Truman is deposited in the village of a farmer named Khoma, who suggests that for safety reasons, the President should disguise himself in peasant clothing and go barefooted. Khoma gives him cold potatoes for supper and the two men head for the woods to spend the night with the rest of the villagers. In the morning they join the others in returning to the village only to be attacked by Polish bandits. To save themselves, they quickly run to the barn. After moving the cow, Khoma lifts the floorboard on which the cow was standing and the two men descend into an underground compartment lined with boards and straw. During the night they emerge from their hiding place, run to a house where they meet Ukrainian partisans, and accompany them to another village. As they make their way through the woods, the president lights a cigarette, and one of the partisans tells him to extinguish it because it could cause them to be spotted by the Bolsheviks. The president refuses and the partisan responds by cutting a switch from a tree. He then lays out Truman over the stump of a tree and gives him twenty-five lashes. (About this aspect of the story, the author wrote, "…the (partisan) must be forgiven for this…because of (Truman's) peasant clothing, the man did not realize that he was a foreigner.") After additional travels, Truman comes across his wife and together, they go inside a house where a drunken Soviet soldier suddenly appears and attempts to rape his wife. At that point, the large bird reappears and whisks Truman and his wife away to the safety of the White House.

The Truman story, like many others that appeared in the magazine, was a fictional satire of actual events and situations that affected local people, and the stories were therefore relatable to the audience. Like the characters in the story, Ukrainians in the Transcurzon were constantly forced to evade deportation by the Polish army as well as enduring frequent attacks by Polish bandits, and those threats occasionally required them to flee to the woods. Because flight wasn't always possible, some built special hideouts in and around their homes, usually in attics or cellars. In some cases, people even constructed double walls to conceal themselves, or even resorted to climbing into wells. The introduction of the Soviet soldier in the story highlights a common problem experienced by Ukrainian women in the region. Although rape by Polish soldiers was not reported by the underground, the incidences of rape by former Soviet officers serving in the Polish army is well documented and appears to have been a pervasive threat.[334]

Only a single issue of the journal *Victory* is available. The issue was published in 1946, describes events that occurred in the Przemyśl area, and has a more aggressive tone compared to other publications. The issue begins with an article entitled "In the Footsteps of the November Milestone," which describes the November 1, 1918 Ukrainian conquest of L'viv under the command of Captain Dmytro Vitovs'kyi who later served as a colonel in the Ukrainian Galician Army. The author described the event as a turning point in Ukrainian political history, since it was the first time that the idea of regional autonomy within a foreign state had been replaced by the notion of engaging in a struggle for creating an independent state:

> …Our fathers were unable to retain independence but from that time until now, the Ukrainian people have not ceased their struggle for independence, and have not laid down their arms. Because they know and believe a deeply held truth—without a struggle there is no victory…The Ukrainian Insurgent Army, born of the people, has been carrying on this fight for five years, heroically defending property, honor, and the lives of our people.[335]

The accompanying story, entitled "Under the Ground," describes a desperate situation in a fourteen-bed underground hospital where seventeen sick men, most of them suffering from Typhus, were being cared for by only one doctor.[336] Because Polish troops were moving through the forest, the entrance to the hospital is sealed off. Eventually, rainwater drips through the roof and progresses into a deluge, and the infected soldiers begin to suffocate. They beg the doctor to open the entrance, but he hesitates, fearing that the Poles will discover them. After listening at the bunker's entrance, he finally determines that they are safe and opens the door, which allows fresh air to rush in, reviving the sick soldiers. The piece ends with a story moral that is typical of the underground literature: it is possible to overcome adversity if there is a will to persevere.

---

334 Ibid., 404v408.
335 Ibid, 527–528.
336 Ibid, 545–546.

Another story included in the publication is entitled "Letter from Prison." It was written by Vasyl Shchur, who was captured by the Poles while wounded and summarily sentenced to die. In the letter, Shchur asks his mother to visit him, if only by a prison wall, so that they could see each other again. He writes, "Mother, don't worry and cry. Be proud that you have a son who did not betray his people, nor did he bow his head in supplication. I was born only once and it is only once that I will have to die."[337] He sends greetings to his brothers and sisters and urges his mother to tell his friends to avenge his death and to never allow themselves to be caught alive.

Finally, an article in the issue entitled "We Do Not Know the Impossible" describes an UPA attack on the town of Dynów (Dyniv) on the night of November 16, 1946, when Baida's battalion attempted to secure medicine from the local apothecary. Polish police and local self-defense units defended the town, and casualties were light on both sides since the Polish defenders had fled to the other end of the town. The pharmacy was emptied and the owner was given some type of UPA promissory note for the goods, highlighting a typical measure that UPA used to compensate local Poles for goods or supplies that were taken for the Ukrainian cause.[338]

The underground's extensive publishing activities required printing facilities and a distribution network.[339] During the German occupation, printing facilities were usually placed in villages located in the mountains or in wooded areas. After the war, the increased pressure from the Polish military and the forcible deportations of entire villages required the establishment of more secure publishing centers. To adapt to the circumstances, UPA began building well-concealed underground bunkers in the forest, and a typical bunker consisted of three rooms: a dining area, a storage room and a printing area. Bunkers were dug either by the printers themselves or UPA units brought in during the night from distant areas that were unfamiliar with the area since secrecy was a major concern; if an individual familiar with the location was either captured or deserted, the bunker was promptly relocated in case the original location had been compromised during interrogations. Each publication had a publishing

---

337 Ibid, 549.

338 Ibid, 549–551.

339 The discussion is based on material in Potichnyj, Vol. 16 of *Litopys UPA*, 7–22.

unit that gathered and edited material as well as "technical links" who handled the printing. Administrators who were responsible for overseeing all aspects of the publication process headed the publishing units. The typical publishing staff included a radio technician who taped and edited foreign broadcasts and an editor who was responsible for the content, and who also wrote pieces and summarized relevant news from foreign presses. Other members included a technical editor responsible for printing, a supply manager, as well as typists and printers. The printing equipment was diverse: some was manufactured commercially and had been either purchased or captured during the German occupation, and the units built some equipment themselves. Since the acquisition of commercial equipment was no longer possible after the war ended, OUN technicians were forced to build equipment from available materials, including wood and rubber, and jokingly dubbed these handmade printing presses "Ukrainian Gutenbergs." An assessment of the available publications suggests that mimeographs were probably the most widely used equipment in the underground printing. In some cases, content was written on a typewriter or even handwritten, using carbon paper. Securing the required supplies for the extensive printing operation was a daunting task because in the years following the war, supplies acquired during the German occupation were either exhausted or had been destroyed by the enemy. Under the postwar conditions, the underground acquired basic supplies such as paper and ink by purchasing the items from workers in printing facilities, purchasing them on the black market, or by raiding Polish or Soviet facilities as a last resort.

Perhaps the most dangerous and potentially compromising task was distributing materials to UPA units and the population, which was usually accomplished by OUN couriers. Usually, OUN used official mail services to send OUN literature to foreign embassies and various institutions in the Soviet Union and Poland, but in some cases, female OUN couriers (who tended to attract less attention than males) were stationed in the cities of central Poland and assigned the task of distributing the material.[340] The underground hoped that employees at these institutions would read the materials and show them to their co-workers before turn-

---

[340] Most publications in this cited volume were discovered at the National Archives in Washington, D.C. by Professor Peter Potichnyj, who compiled them in the *Litopys UPA* multivolume series.

ing them over to the authorities, or that they would simply keep them and become at least passive supporters. Besides the domestic distribution, the underground placed great emphasis on informing the world—especially the West—of the Ukrainian struggle and viewed the Transcurzon region as a conduit to the West, since officials in the Transcurzon had better access to their counterparts in Munich, who in turn maintained contact with western intelligence services. This was a practical consideration since the underground was counting on eventually receiving support from the West and believed that disseminating information about a strong underground behind the Iron Curtain would encourage western support as tensions with the Soviet Union escalated. The content and selection of literature served to justify the struggle and to strengthen morale with the underlying notion that a major war between the Soviet Union and the western powers was imminent. They hoped that the war would provide an opportunity for the underground to establish powerful advocates among the western powers that would make Ukrainian independence possible. Although this view was self-serving, it should not be dismissed as mindless propaganda since many observers in the West held a similar opinion at the time. For this reason, as well as the geographical proximity to Ukraine, events in the Balkans, the communist insurgency in Greece, and the dispute over the city of Trieste were all given special attention in the underground literature. The OUN's point of view was that only a war between the Soviet Union and the western allies could save the underground from its otherwise inevitable annihilation. Furthermore, placing an emphasis on a third world war also served as a morale booster for both the underground and the Ukrainian population. The publications implied that if both could hold out a bit longer, the coming war would tip the circumstances in their favor. More curious, however, is the detached tone used in the more major publications, considering the fact that a life-and-death struggle raged around the publishers. The writers, who resided in isolated homesteads or inside underground bunkers, and who had lost many colleagues during the years of struggle, still managed to maintain a tone and style that is characteristic of scholarly literature, although some publications describing local events were less restrained. For example, the issue from the magazine *Victory*, which reported on events in the Przemyśl area, has a more biting tone than some of the larger publications.

While stories and articles contained in OUNs publications are generally based on actual events and are therefore not fictitious in nature, they are clearly selective and propagandistic. Although the literature extensively discussed military engagements and deportations, only successful engagements were reported and defeats were not mentioned. Heroic actions were extolled, heavily covered, and likely embellished, but desertions among the ranks were rarely reported. Civilian deaths at the hands of Polish troops, police, and bandits were typically reported in a cursory manner without editorial commentary unless the casualties were especially high or the event was unusually atrocious. In addition, internal issues such as medical care and treatment, provisioning, weapons acquisitions, and training received only scant attention since the publications were mainly focused on political issues, current events and combat operations. Nevertheless, these topics were crucial to the operations of the insurgency.

The ability to provide medical services was another vital need that posed a significant challenge to the insurgency. The OUN began organizing medical services at the same time that UPA was being organized.[341] The service was modeled on the Ukrainian Red Cross that had operated during 1918–1921, when the Ukrainian lands were divided among neighboring countries. The organization was unable to receive recognition or supplementary assistance from the International Red Cross, but endeavored to provide care wherever possible. During the brief German occupation of Ukraine, several branches were formed in major cities with the first branch organized in L'viv in June 1941, followed by branches in Rivne and Kyiv in September of that year. Care was provided mostly to Ukrainian political prisoners who had been freed from Soviet prisons, and to sick and wounded Soviet POWs. Although the German military never officially recognized the Red Cross, it was able to function until the military was replaced by a civilian administration that disbanded the organization and arrested its leaders. Most were released later, with the notable exception of Dr. Leonid Kurchaba, director of the L'viv branch, who died in a Cracow prison. During that period, organization members continued to provide some services unofficially, and those personnel later formed the core of the UPA Medical Service. In early 1943, UPA be-

[341] Ripeckyj, M., in *Litopys UPA*, Vol. 23, 7–19.

gan organizing in Volhynia and established control in part of its territory, during which time the Red Cross evolved into an important component of the underground and was subordinated to the OUN.

The Red Cross closely coordinated with medical units to administer medical aid to wounded combatants. Partisans wounded in the field received aid from medics attached to combat units who were armed, participated in battles, and were subordinated to the unit commander. The Red Cross also ran hospitals and provided long-term care for the sick and wounded. Hospitals were built in the remote villages and forests of Volhynia, although the training of the medical staff and the availability of medical supplies and equipment tended to be worse than what was available in facilities in Galicia, where the OUN was better organized. For this reason, some soldiers were transferred to Galicia where they could obtain better and more consistent medical treatment. Civilian physicians frequently treated the wounded, and some were executed by the Germans for aiding the UPA. The OUN aided the Medical Service by collecting and storing medicine, medical supplies, and instruments. Providing medical service after the war was much more difficult since the UPA was under constant attack and the Ukrainian civilian population was placed under greater surveillance. Consequently, medical facilities could no longer operate in villages and huts in the woods, and were forced to relocate to bunkers in the forests. The underground medical rooms were either hideouts or bunkers that typically consisted of a single room that contained fifteen to twenty beds. There was no significant difference between either types of facility except that the hideout version was smaller and better camouflaged, but more difficult to defend. Bunkers were dug either by the guards, or an UPA unit that was unfamiliar with the terrain and brought in during the night to construct the facility. Typical security procedures for bunkers usually consisted of placing a few armed partisans who, in the event of an attack, would be joined by partially recuperated patients who would help to defend the bunker while the severely ill or wounded were evacuated. The advantages of this strategy were negligible since smaller Polish units did not typically enter the forest looking for partisans; instead, they came in force with larger units and it was therefore unlikely that a few defenders could prevent the bunker's destruction. In the Lemko region, for example, one discovery by Polish troops resulted in the destruction of the bunker and all of its occupants. In addition to the constant danger of being discovered, the need to provide water, ventilation, heating, and lighting presented additional difficulties. During the winter, medical personnel frequently melted snow as a means for obtaining water, and used lanterns and candles for lighting.

The persistent shortage of medical personnel became more acute after the war, and the number of Ukrainian physicians was always small. Their numbers further dwindled as the Red Army advanced, prompting many to desert and flee to the west. To augment the physician corps that worked for the UPA, medical students who had not yet completed their studies served as doctors, and much of the supporting medical personnel received only 4–6 weeks of training. Many women served as nurses and caregivers in hospitals, but a great number of them lacked formal medical training.

In addition to serving as nurses and caregivers in hospitals, women played a major role in the leadership and operations of the organization. The first director of the Red Cross was Kateryna Zarytska who was later replaced by Halyna Didyk, who directed its operations until her arrest in 1950. Under the circumstances, the medical care that partisans received was quite rudimentary. Wounds could be dressed and some medications were provided; however, surgery and intensive care procedures and facilities were not available.

As OUN was organizing its administrative apparatus in the Transcurzon, UPA likewise formed a new military district that overlapped with the OUN organizations in Poland, and was subordinated to the regional UPA Command West in Ukraine. Military District VI (Sian) began its formation in 1944 and was fully formed by the end of 1945, making it the sixth military district of UPA. As illustrated in Chart 3, the Sian District was comprised of three tactical sectors commanded by Myroslav Onyshkevych ("Orest"): TS-26 (Lemko) with two battalions; TS-27 (Bastion) with one battalion; and TS-28 (Danyliv), which also had one battalion. Each tactical sector, including its respective battalions and sotnias, had nominal codenames as well as numerical designations in order to provide secrecy in communications

As the Red Army advanced westward across Ukraine, some civilians were fleeing west, no longer willing to live under Soviet communism. This was especially true in western Ukraine, which had been incorporated into the Soviet Union in September 1939. Prior to the German invasion in June 1941, the Soviet system was being introduced in the territory, a process that involved the nationalization of private property, collectivization, and most frighteningly, massive arrests and executions of people who were considered to be enemies of the Soviet regime. Typically, those arrested were sent to labor camps in Siberia, but when Germans advanced rapidly across the region, the retreating Soviet police executed prisoners held in local jails. In 1944, as the Red Army was approaching, hordes of people were fleeing westward from this area in fear of another "Red Terror." Many young men who were unwilling to leave Ukraine joined the rapidly expanding UPA. In the Transcurzon region, many UPA units were organized by former officers of the Ukrainian Auxiliary Police or by former factory guards (*Werkschutz*). Compared to the local boys, these men were better educated, had some military training, were committed nationalists, and many were OUN members. The most detailed information available on the organization of partisan units in the area is that of Tactical Sector 26 which comprised more than half of the partisan force in the Transcurzon. In the summer of 1944, a unit of factory guards stationed in the western Lemko region had learned of the German plan to transfer them to Slovakia and Yugoslavia to fight local partisans and as a result, decided to desert German ranks and join the Ukrainian underground, although doing so was risky at the time. German authorities learned of the plan and arrived at the barracks on the day before the planned escape. They arrested the guards and transferred them to Slovakia. Two guard officers managed to escape during the transfer, arriving later in the village of Wisłok Wielki (Vyslok Velykyi) in Sanok County where they made contact with the existing underground network.[342] Two UPA officers with the pseudonyms "Ievhen" and "Les" began organizing a sotnia. Ievhen became the commander and Les a warrant officer.[343] Lt. Vasyl Mizernyi ("Ren") who had been the commander of Ukrainian police in Sanok before his arrest by the Germans escaped from a prison in Cracow and later established contact with the under-

---

342 Wisłok Wielki, actually consisting of two separate villages, held historical importance for the partisans, since its residents had a comparatively more nationalistic orientation than other villages in the area. In December of 1918, after World War I, a so-called "Lemko Republic" had been formed in the village.

343 Warrant officers did not hold a command position but performed administrative functions for a unit.

ground in Wisłok Wielki on July 29, 1944.[344] As a senior officer, Mizernyi was urged to take command of the unit and organize other units since a growing number of young men continued to join; however, he initially declined the offer, claiming that he was too weak after his stint in prison. On August 4, 1944, Ievhen moved his sotnia east to the headwaters of the San River. To the north, in the Przemyśl area, two other sotnias were formed in a similar manner and moved south to the Lemko area under the command of "Lys" and "Burlaka." In that area, another sotnia was formed from an armed OUN unit and a squad of Ukrainian police commanded by "Bir" (Vasyl Shyshkanevych) a local police commander who had earlier fought Hungarians in Transcarpathia. On August 15, the four sotnias united to form a battalion under the command of the recovered Mizernyi, who subsequently moved the battalion deeper into the Carpathian Mountains where the men trained for a five-week period. After a great deal of internal discussion, a sotnia organized by the Mel'nyk wing of the OUN together with a small light artillery unit that had deserted from the Galicia Division were permitted to join Ren's battalion.

In an effort to legitimize his battalion as part of the UPA, Ren made repeated efforts to contact the UPA command in attempts to obtain formal approval for the formation of the new unit. In mid-September, several of Ren's officers finally made contact with senior UPA officers informing them that a new battalion had been formed in the Lemko region. The UPA officers were less than enthusiastic, since battalion-sized units had sustained heavy casualties in Volhynia after the Soviet occupation; however, they confirmed Ren as the new battalion commander and subordinated all UPA units to the UHVR. All sotnias in the region were formally attached to Ren's battalion and instructed to follow UHVR's policies concerning relations with other military and paramilitary groups; including the Germans, the Polish underground and the Hungarian Army. Relations with Germans had not changed—they were still considered an enemy and any contact with them was strictly forbidden. Because an understanding had been reached with the AK, attacks on the Polish underground were also forbidden unless they were conducted for purposes of

344 The discussion in this section is based on the information in Vol. 33 of Potichnyj and Lyko, *Litopys UPA*, 100–130. The 899-page volume provides documents and materials for the sector.

self-defense or in the defense of Ukrainian civilians. Since a similar truce had been arranged with the Hungarian Army, its officers were to be contacted in the event that hostilities should break out between the Hungarians and the UPA. All Jews were allowed to leave the UPA medical services after the Soviet occupation, and only those physicians who insisted on remaining in the UPA would be retained. A similar policy applied to Italians, Dutch, Belgians, and Slovaks, many of whom had escaped from German or Soviet prisons. The returning delegation passed on these instructions to Ren, who began preparations for the march east as the front was approaching.

In September of 1944, as the Soviet Red Army prepared to cross the upper San, Ren made plans to move east to avoid being trapped between the Red Army and the German Army. On September 25, he held a meeting with company commanders to discuss the impending march through the Carpathians, instructing them that the sotnias would move separately but were instructed to maintain contact with adjacent units while moving through the forest along creeks and ravines. At the time, more detailed tactical instruction was not possible because the front line was in flux. Regular horse-drawn wagons were disassembled into two-wheeled wooden carts for transporting supplies and ammunition. At this point, the battalion consisted of 11 sotnias, a light artillery unit, and small-armed OUN units, about 2,000 men in total.[345] The men had diverse backgrounds—most of the rank and file were young village boys who had no previous military experience. Others had served in the one or more of the following armies: Soviet, Polish, Czechoslovak (which had existed before the war), Hungarian, Romanian, or Slovak, and there were few who had served in the French Foreign Legion. Still others had served in Transcarpathian Sich, German auxiliary police units, the Ukrainian Legion, or were deserters from the Galicia Division. Additionally, there were even a few older officers who had participated in the struggle for independence after the First World War and had been trained by either the Austrian or Tsarist armies.

The battalion managed to cross the front line with minimal losses and had only three engagements. The first was a brief fight with the Soviet troops that UPA terminated quickly and units were ordered to avoid

---

[345] Ibid., 117.

fights. The second encounter occurred on October 2 when the partisans came under fire from the Hungarians, prompting the battalion to send a mounted unit under a white flag to the Hungarians; they identified themselves and were permitted to pass. Another encounter with Soviet troops proved more costly. A mounted platoon was sent on reconnaissance and was attacked by the Red Army. Part of the platoon returned, but fate of the remainder is unknown. Undoubtedly, some men were killed and others may have scattered among Ukrainian villages. Nevertheless, most of the contingent arrived safely behind the Soviet front line.

At the end of October 1944, Ren again made contact with the UPA command and was given a choice of going to Bukovyna, which had been part of Romania between the wars, or returning to the Lemko region. The option was presented to the battalion officers who chose the Lemko region since they were not familiar with Bukovyna. As the front moved west, Ren's four sotnias assumed the same names as their commanders' pseudonyms. "Nechai," "Veselyi" (Danylo Svistel), "Baida" (Petro Mykolenko), and "Burlaka" (Volodymyr Shchyhelsky) began a return march on October 27 and were to reassemble in the forest west of the San where they had trained months earlier. Veselyi and Nechai were ordered to move through the Carpathians, while Baida and Burlaka took a northern route through the foothills. Once again, sotnias on both routes were instructed to move independently while maintaining contact with each other. On the morning of November 18, Baida and Burlaka were attacked by the NKVD Border Guards and sustained heavy losses, and 17 men in Baida's sotnia were killed.[346] The two sotnias had been carting provisions, ammunition, and medical supplies that had impeded their movement and made them more visible, and the supplies were lost during the attack. Baida remained on the Soviet side of UPA operational territory, since he was a former Red Army lieutenant from the Poltava region, and his sotnia was made up largely of former Soviet soldiers from eastern Ukraine. The UPA command considered him to be more effective on the Soviet side because his soldiers were familiar with Soviet tactics. During nighttime attacks, they often employed the strategy of shouting in Russian in order to confuse the enemy.

346 The attack occurred west of the town of Boryslav. See Ibid.,122.

In the initial months, Ren traveled with Baida, but after the October NKVD attacks; he transferred to the Burlaka sotnia in order to cross the border. Burlaka's sotnia, along with Ren and his aides in tow, crossed the San River during the night of November 26–27 and headed for the designated forest. The other two sotnias apparently did not engage in serious fighting. The Veselyi sotnia reached their destination on the Polish side of the border in December; however, for an undocumented reason, Nechai's arrival was delayed until the spring of 1945. At that time, Soviet Border Guards who were quartered in nearby villages were steadily strengthening their border defenses. Patrols were sent out day and night, observation towers were built, areas fortified with bunkers and barbed wire, and strips of land plowed and harrowed along the border to detect crossings. The sotnias that had crossed the San spent the winter training self-defense units in some villages. On March 21, 1945, Soviet troops began a sweep in the Carpathians west of the San that lasted until the end of April. The heaviest fighting involved Veselyi's sotnia on March 21, lasting almost a day. The sotnia withdrew after sustaining heavy losses, 16 men were killed, including a platoon leader, and afterward Soviet troops and Polish police entered the nearby village of Strzebowiska (Strubovys'ka) and killed 45 civilians. Some days later, the sotnia was attacked again and sustained additional losses, including the death of Veselyi himself.[347] During the sweep, the Burlaka and Burii sotnias, which had replaced Nechai, crossed the Carpathians and entered into Transcarpathian Ukraine where they found that the situation was quiet and the climate more tolerable since the snow had melted.

Following the NKVD sweep, Ren broke up his battalion's sotnias into platoon size units and attached some to the village self-defense units. In October 1945, Dmytro Hrytsai ("Perebyinis") the UPA Chief-of-Staff, and "Taras," a member of the OUN Executive, arrived from Ukraine and were heading west. Critical of Ren's decision to break up the sotnias, Perebyinis ordered him to reconstitute the sotnias and expand them. Meanwhile, Taras met with local OUN leaders and made additional organizational changes. Both emphasized the importance of maintaining a strong UPA presence in the area as a means of facilitating contact with

---

[347] Following the death of Veselyi, the unit was put under the command of Iarych. He would later be replaced by Didyk who commanded the sotnia until the summer of 1946.

the west. In the autumn of 1945, UPA leadership placed all units in the area under the command of the Military District VI ("Sian"). After Perebyinis' inspection, UPA expanded rapidly and by the end of 1945, the two battalions had acquired the organizational structure that would remain in place until the summer of 1947.

Of the three tactical sectors, the largest was Sector 26, designated as *Lemko* and commanded by Ren. The territory of Tactical Sector 26 (TS-26) stretched north of the Carpathians and included Lesko and Sanok counties, and most but not all of Przemyśl County. This roughly coincided with OUN's Region I which also extended to the northern portion of Peremyshl' and encompassed the Kholodnyi Iar, Beskid and Verkhovyna districts. TS-26 units were given the codename "Attackers," and each of its two battalions usually had four sotnia units. The Lemko battalion, commanded by Ren, included three sotnias: "Bir," "Didyk"[348], and "Khrin" (Stepan Stebel'skyi). In addition, throughout the summer of 1946, two sotnias from Ukraine—"Karmeliuk" (Stepan Hnativ) and "Myron" (Volodymyr Horshko)—operated with the Lemko battalion. The Peremyshl' battalion had four sotnias named for their commanders' pseudonyms: the sotnias of "Hromenko" (Mykhailo Duda), "Burlaka" (Volodymyr Shchyhelskyi), "Krylach" (Iaroslav Kotsiolok) and "Lastivka" (Hryhorii Iankivskyi). This battalion was commanded by "Konyk" (Mykhailo Hal'o) until his death on January 6, 1946, when he was succeeded by "Baida" (Petro Mykolenko). Commanders of the Peremyshl' battalion also served as Ren's deputies for Tactical Sector 26.

The territorial zone of Tactical Sector 27 ("Bastion") began north of TS-26, basically coinciding with OUN's Region II (encompassing the OUN's Batiuryn District) and stretching across Jarosław, Lubaczów, and Tomaszów counties.[349] Its single battalion along with its subordinate units was nominally designated as the "Avengers." The commander was Ivan Shpontak ("Zalizniak") who was born in Transcarpathia and had worked as a teacher before joining the Carpathian Sich and participating in a struggle against the Hungarian occupation in 1938. Following his release from a Hungarian prison, he joined Col. Roman Sushko's unit in Slovakia, where he received military training. When Germany occupied

---

348 Didyk was replaced by Brodych in the summer of 1946.

349 See Potichnyj, *Litopys UPA,* Vol. 40. The volume provides 584 pages of documents and material on the Sector.

western Ukraine in 1941, he went to Rava Rus'ka in the L'viv oblast where he became an officer in the Ukrainian Auxiliary Police. On April 20, 1944, he deserted to UPA with 20 men in tow. As the front came through, the group took refuge in the woods and gradually expanded into a sotnia. Zalizniak went on to organize a battalion of four sotnias, to which a fifth independently organized sotnia led by Iaroslav Hamelia ("Bryl'") would occasionally cross the border from Ukraine and temporarily operate with the battalion.

From 1944–1945, sotnias were organized mainly from the local self-defense units and compared to TS-26, there was more turnover among sotnia commanders largely due to higher casualty rates. Nevertheless, the battalion was effective. Zalizniak rapidly gained a reputation as a capable and aggressive commander after his battalion attacked small and vulnerable police stations in 16 rural areas: "…during the night of March 27–28, 1945, the platoons in Zalizniak's battalion staged simultaneous attacks that destroyed all the police stations in Lubaczów and Jarosław counties."[350] Police at some rural stations that had not been attacked fled to the towns, effectively removing the official Polish presence in the countryside of the two counties for the duration of the insurgency. Among Zalizniak's sotnia commanders, Hryhoriy Mazur ("Kalynovych") emerged as the most capable. In 1944, he joined UPA as a rifleman, and despite a mere fourth grade education, had quickly risen through the ranks to become a sotnia commander two years later. The remaining commanders were Ivan Shumians'kyi ("Shum"), Mykola Taraban ("Tucha") and Hryhoriy Levko ("Kruk.") Shum joined UPA in the second half of 1945, became platoon leader and sotnia commander in September 1945, but was killed in September 1947. Kruk became a commander at the beginning of 1945, and Tucha at the end of the same year.

To the north, Tactical Sector 28 ("Danyliv") encompassed a large portion of Chełm and Podlasie, territories located on the western edge of historic Volhynia that roughly coincided with OUN Region III (the "Levada" and "Lyman" districts.) The sector's sotnias were designated as "Wolves" and had additional numerical designations. Prior to the establishment of the Transcurzon, this territory had been part of OUN's

---

350 Szcześniak and Szota, *Droga*, 281.

"Turiv" Military District headquartered east of the Bug River. UPA had formed there earlier than in the southern sectors as a response to Polish partisan attacks on Ukrainian villages, and self-defense units began organizing in Hrubieszów and Belz counties as early as 1942–43.[351] Anatol Sydoruk ("Iastrub") was among the first to organize a self-defense unit in Hrubieszów, and by the spring of 1943, "Karpo" (Pavlo Pylypchuk) formed another such unit. As attacks increased, local groups began forming larger units by recruiting and inducting local men, and reinforced them with units from the Turiv District. Compared to Sian's other two tactical sectors, Danyliv was smaller and weaker for a number of reasons. First, the OUN network in the Chełm-Podlasie area was weaker than it was in Galicia, where OUN had a better communications and support network (e.g. intelligence, materiel, provisioning, etc.). The Chełm and Podlasie regions had a more robust ethnic Polish population as compared to other sectors, and there was less support from the local Ukrainian population. Polish-Ukrainian enmity in the region was sharper vis-à-vis Galicia and had fomented violence. As a result, many local Ukrainians had fled to Ukraine after the arrival of the Red Army in the face of Polish attacks. In the interwar period, the region had been subjected to more aggressive Polonization tactics than other Ukrainian districts, as well as persistent attacks on the Orthodox Church. Prior to World War I, it had also been part of the Russian Empire where communism had gained some support among the local Ukrainian population, since many men in the sector had served in the Tsarist army and had been exposed to the same pervasive Communist propaganda that had ultimately led to the Bolshevik Revolution. Upon returning home from the service after World War I, some soldiers began disseminating communist propaganda and gained some followers, thus making the area more susceptible to the communist penetration. Ukrainian nationalist sentiments were relatively lower in the Danyliv sector compared to other sectors, and the underground's need for self-defense had taken on an urgency in light of the Polish attacks. As a result, some young men in Danyliv's territories had been conscripted to UPA, a condition that brought about higher desertion rates. The insufficient OUN network also stymied UPA's ability to signif-

351 See Potichnyj, *Litopys UPA*, Vol. 39, 7. This 1,043-page volume provides documents and material for the sector.

icantly strengthen the sector by its failure to motivate and mobilize the local population to provide greater support for the partisans.

In late 1944, Danyliv's battalion was encircled by NKVD troops and largely destroyed, with only one sotnia managing to break out of the encirclement. It was later discovered that Vasyl Levochko ("Iurchenko"), its commander at the time, was a Soviet agent who had likely led the battalion into a trap.[352] After that disastrous event, the battalion was reconstituted in March 1945, consisting of four sotnias that were comparatively smaller than those in other sectors. At that time, it was commanded by Marian Lukashevych ("Iahoda") who would be succeeded by Ievhen Shtendera ("Prirva") and Volodymyr Sorochak ("Berkut"). In 1947, the Wolves' four sotnias were led by Vasyl Iarmola ("Iar"), Ievhen Ianchuk ("Duda"), Semen Prystupa ("Davyd"), and Vasyl Kral' ("Chaus"). Chart 3 presents the UPA organizational scheme of the Sian District in 1947

352 Iurchenko deserted to the NKVD on December 12, 1944 with few of his aids. In August 1945, he was killed in an UPA ambush with some NKVD personnel. Captured documents listed the NKVD network in the area with over 160 people. See Ibid., 8, footnote 1

Chart 3: Organization of UPA in Poland, 1947

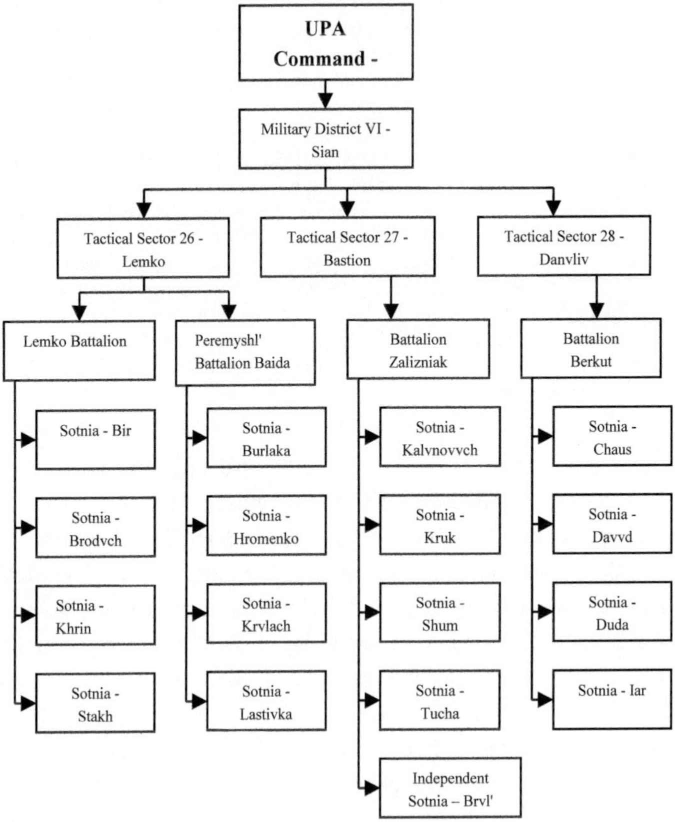

Source: Evhen Misylo, *Aksiia "Visla"*, L'viv-New York, 1997, Appendix 13.

Notes: UPA units had multiple designations that were used interchangeably in the underground literature. During the three-year period same units had different commanders and even changed numerical designation. Information in the table reflects the organizational structure towards the end of insurgency and identifications. Where numerical designations are not known, I have indicated "N/A" (not available.). Sotnias in the Tactical Sector 26 (Lemko) were called "Attackers" and were also assigned numerical designations: Bir -- Attacker 3 (96); Brodych -- Attacker 1 (94); Khrin -- Attacker 5 (95a); Stakh –N/A; Burlaka -- Attacker 4 (94a); Hromenko -- Attacker 2 (95); Krylach -- Attacker 6 (96a); Lastivka -- Attacker 7 (94b); Sotnia's in the Tactical Sector 27 (Bastion) were name "Avengers" and their numerical designations: Kalynovych -- Avenger 1 (97); Kruk -- Avenger 5 (97b); Shum -- Avenger 3 (97); Tucha -- Avenger 2 (98); Avenger 4 Operated briefly in early 1946 then was combined with Avenger 5. Sotnias in the Tactical Sector 28 (Danyliv) were called "Wolves" and with numerical designations: Chaus – N/A; Davyd -- Wolves 3, N/A; Duda -- Wolves 2, (100); Iar -- Wolves 1 (99). Source: Evhen Misylo, *Aksiia "Visla"*, L'viv-New York, 1997, Appendix 13.

Another important element of the UPA structure was its reserve force, which played a limited role in UPA operations. At the end of 1944, UPA began organizing Self-Defense Cluster Units (SKV) to protect the local population from Polish underground and civilian attacks. The SKV was to have perhaps 40 men that were divided into units called *Stanytsi*, which usually encompassed one or two villages. SKV members normally lived at home and were primarily engaged in civilian occupations, but also provided important aid to the UPA, and some even received UPA training. On the military side, SKV units patrolled the villages during the night to prevent attacks by Polish gangs, and detected and reported on the nighttime movement of Polish troops. They would occasionally join UPA for a specific operation and return to their home villages afterward. On paper, SKV may have looked as a massive organization but the reality was different: the quality and activities of the units was uneven and determined largely by local leadership. The TS-26 monthly operational reports for the first half of 1946 do not report any combat by the SKV. TS-27 reports do indicate some combat activity together with the regular UPA units, and the few available reports of TS-28 for the period do not indicate any activity. It is possible that some units engaged in combat without UPA, but if such activities were extensive, it is likely that they would have been documented in the underground literature. As the numbers of deported Ukrainians in the Transcurzon mounted, the size and activity of the SKV was reduced substantially. More so than military augmentation, perhaps the most important SKV service consisted of gathering food and clothing, providing shelter and intelligence, and caring for the sick and wounded.

UPA Tactics and Weapons

Most sotnias in the Transcurzon had approximately the same number of men and were equally armed with Soviet or German rifles. Some sotnias had Soviet submachine guns and squads typically had a light Soviet machinegun, while partisans also carried hand grenades. Sotnias frequently had additional machine guns and some had few light mortars, which were rarely used because they had to be carried. The performance of the sotnias varied depending on the ability and aggressiveness of the sotnia commander. Typically, a sotnia operated in a portion of a county, spanning perhaps fifteen to twenty villages, and only occasionally joined other battalion sotnias for a major operation. The commanders had to decide how actively to engage Polish troops and police when moving through rural areas, or consider attacking them at their encampments or police stations. The most celebrated commander in the Transcurzon was Stepan Stebels'kyi ("Khrin"), who came from the Przemyśl area with a small contingent of men. Khrin organized a sotnia in the eastern Lemko region that expanded to approximately 300 men, more than twice the number of most sotnias. The unit was sometimes called the "Lemko Sotnia" and between the fall of 1945 and May 1947, it had approximately a hundred engagements with the enemy, averaging more than one per week. Some engagements were defensive, but in many cases, Khrin sought out and attacked the enemy. His actions eventually earned him promotion to the rank of battalion commander and a Gold Cross, first class.[353]

The basic UPA tactics were ambush and surprised raids, especially at night. The objective was to inflict maximum casualties on the enemy while minimizing the unit's own losses by avoiding prolonged fights. For example, if Polish troops established a defensive position after the initial confusion of an ambush instead of scattering, the UPA unit would break off the fight. Encircling wooded areas where the partisans were suspected of being located was a frequent Polish tactic at the beginning of the in-

---

353 Potichnyj, *Litopys UPA,* Vol. 30, 21–22.

surgency. Because of good intelligence, the partisans usually vacated the threatened area; but if they were encircled, they would select a favorable position for a breakout, such as a wooded area or ravine, allow Polish troops to come close and then open fire. In such situations, the skirmish line would often be broken and the partisans would slip out. As the insurgency continued, the army largely abandoned the encirclement tactic. More direct attacks by UPA were used mostly in defense of Ukrainian villages.

While sotnias operated independently, they maintained contact with other units and reported to their superiors. The Sian Military District Commander Iaroslav Onyshkevych (his known pseudonyms were "Oleh," "Orest," and "Bilyi"') required all sotnias to submit monthly operational reports to their battalion commanders, who in turn used the information to prepare reports for him. Battalion reports were comprised of seven sections: (1.) Operations, which reported monthly engagements with the enemy, including schematic drawings of battles; (2.) Intelligence, which reported on the strength and movement of the enemy; (3.) Food and Supplies; (4.) Clothing; (5.) Weapons; (6.) Military and Political Training; and (7.) Commander's Observations and Requirements.[354] The reports did not indicate the numerical strength of the sotnias nor of the battalion and therefore, such vital operational information had likely been communicated by other means. Each sotnia's warrant officer was required to maintain a briefcase with the previous sotnia's reports and orders, expenditure journals, inventory of supplies, and records of other activities. The information was used to file each sotnia's monthly report. Furthermore, sotnias and battalions were required to establish archives for reports and other documents.

Through the monthly reports, the UPA command was able to exercise control over the widely dispersed units, and at the same time, an archiving system was designed and implemented to preserve the insurgency's documents for posterity. The latter goal was largely accomplished, although many documents were ultimately lost. Some were brought to the west and others were captured but preserved in Polish or Soviet archives. After the collapse of communism, many surviving documents became available to researchers in Poland and Ukraine. These sources and

---

354 Potichnyj and Lyko, *Litopys UPA*, Vol. 33, 11.

memoirs provide a fairly complete picture of the insurgency and their modus operandi. The documents reveal that provisioning was a serious challenge for UPA. Since UPA was a guerrilla force rather than a regular army, the partisans had to rely on the local population for much of their provisioning, especially food, through both an ad hoc basis as well as through an organized system. Frequently, UPA units emerged from the forests and entered the villages, where local civilian families provided them with food; however, most of their food was gathered systematically through the efforts of local activists and SKV members. Bread baking, for example, was usually organized in a designated village and passed to the UPA along with other produce. Food was stored in forest bunkers, and their locations were known only to individuals collecting food and by sotnia personnel in charge of provisioning. Such reserves were especially important in the event of increased troop movement. Available evidence suggests that the population was willing to share its meager food supply with the partisans who were generally viewed as defenders, but there was also social pressure to aid the cause of Ukrainian independence. OUN/UPA did not consider Polish villages to be sources of food and other provisioning, although this policy may have changed somewhat after the extensive deportations that occurred in the summer of 1946. Given the intense hostilities between Poles and Ukrainians, voluntary Polish contributions to the Ukrainian underground would have certainly been a rarity. A Polish source quotes Starukh's August 4, 1946 instruction for securing supplies from Poles by issuing promissory notes:

> …The underground is permitted to collect funds, and the donors must be given a printed document stamped and signed indicating the amount donated. Donations may also be requisitioned from those Poles who are able but unwilling to make a contribution, and the Polish underground must approve such requisitions. Robbing Ukrainians is strictly forbidden and subject to prosecution.[355]

Clothing was a more difficult resource to come by. While villagers could share their bread and potatoes, they were unable to provide UPA with clothing and footwear. As a result, the partisans wore German, Soviet, and Polish uniforms, frequently clad in parts of uniforms from different armies; however, as the resistance continued, most partisans were clad largely in Polish uniforms. Captured clothing was augmented with

---

[355] Szcześniak and Szota, *Droga*, 268–9.

purchases on the black market, an enterprise that flourished due to the chronic shortage of goods in regular stores. Some Ukrainians who had traded on the black market during the war began working for the underground and purchased supplies from their old Polish partners. It is unclear how the underground was able to finance their purchases, since both Polish and Ukrainians civilians were strapped for cash and neither Polish nor Ukrainian sources report bank robberies. A Polish source, cited earlier, reports that Starukh received 200,000 rubles from the OUN Executive, but the amount could not have been sufficient to cover purchases of clothing, footwear, medicine, printing supplies, and the other material needs of his unit. It is likely that some funds were obtained from black market trading; a Polish Army report states that their soldiers were selling stolen livestock on the black market, which suggests that the Ukrainian underground might have been in the market as well, selling captured Polish Army horses and livestock confiscated from Polish civilians. Partisan raids on apothecaries and other facilities that contained the necessary supplies supplemented black market purchases; however, neither Ukrainian nor Polish sources provide any indication that the underground received foreign aid. Support for the partisans, to a varying degree, was common and widespread in most Ukrainian districts and arguably enabled UPA to survive more than three years against overwhelming odds.

In "A History of the Ren Battalion," Dr. Modest Ripetsky, an UPA physician stationed in the upper San valley in the eastern Lemko region during the winter of 1945 as the Polish and Soviet forces swept area, stated the following:

> UPA was able to survive attacks by special NKVD units in the area due to the tenacity of the UPA soldiers and, above all, the astonishing support of these Lemko villages. The complete support of the whole population, from small children to the elderly, saved UPA units from perishing. The local population considered UPA sotnias and self-defense units as their own army, strongly supporting them by providing food, intelligence, and hiding and caring for the sick and wounded in their own homes.[356]

Battles in the Transcurzon, Continued Mayhem

In addition to fighting the communist forces, the Ukrainian and Polish undergrounds continued to fight each other. As the Red Army

---

356 Ibid, 125–126.

continued to occupy western Ukraine, however, both sides became interested in eliminating their mutual hostilities and cooperating in order to meet a common threat. Talks between UPA and AK began during the summer of 1943, and on February 10, 1944, a "Protocol" was signed that established a truce and laid the foundation for cooperation. Both parties agreed to recognize the right of the two peoples to establish independent states; declared the Soviet Union a common enemy; designated territories on which each underground would operate; exchanged information; and proposed contact between the Ukrainian representatives abroad and the Polish government-in-exile in London.[357] The agreement represented a monumental shift of the Polish underground on the Ukrainian question. The Polish government-in-exile, which was committed to the establishment of the prewar Polish eastern boundary, refused to approve the "Protocol" and instead moved forward with "Operation Tempest." The operation on the Ukrainian territory was concentrated largely in Volhynia, but also extended to the Ukrainian districts west of Bug River. While the Polish partisan presence was sharply reduced to the east of Curzon Line after the Soviet occupation, it remained strong in the west and the fighting between Poles and Ukrainians continued, especially in the Lublin Province. Both sides eventually acknowledged that the Soviet occupation of Poland was detrimental to their objectives, a condition that changed the relationship between the two undergrounds.

In the early months of 1945, both sides in Transcurzon made attempts to reach an understanding, although concrete measures were not taken until Zalizniak, on one night at the end of March, simultaneously attacked police stations in two counties.[358] Rumors and panic spread in the Polish underground that a large UPA force had arrived from Ukraine, prompting the Poles to resume contact with the Ukrainians. The negotiations did not aim for a comprehensive agreement between the two sides as had been done earlier, but were instead conducted at local levels. The first agreement was signed at the end of April between the Lemko Tactical Sector and the local Polish leaders, but it was never implemented. At the end of May, more fruitful negotiations were undertaken in the Hrubieszów area with both sides agreeing to a truce and promising to operate on their own ethnic territory, as well as agreeing to exchange intelligence

357 Shtendera, "In Search", 1980, p.274
358 Ibid, 278.

and publications, and to cease attacks on civilians. The agreement had the effect of calming hostilities and contributed to the reduction of attacks on the civilian population, although some Polish groups that were not affiliated with AK continued attacks on the Ukrainian population, and not all AK units observed the truce. At that point, UPA was better able to concentrate on preventing the deportation of Ukrainian civilians, and although additional meetings were scheduled for the near future, they never materialized. AK was undergoing a drastic reorganization after having lost 50,000 members who had accepted government amnesty, and it was renamed *Wolność i Niezawisłość* (-WiN, "Freedom and Independence") on September 15, 1945. Additional meetings took place in Tomaszów and Biała Podlaska where the agreements, similar to those in Hrubieszów, calmed the region. The height of cooperation was reached in May of 1946 when AK-WiN and UPA jointly attacked a garrison in the county seat of Hrubieszów.[359] AK-WiN attacked a Polish police station and freed its prisoners while UPA leveled a Soviet Internal Troop compound by using captured handheld Katyusha rockets and destroying other valuable installations. The local agreements were mutually beneficial; however, the Polish government-in-exile in London continued to discourage WiN from cooperating with the Ukrainians and eventually demobilized the organization in the winter of 1946–47. After the demobilization, only a skeletal underground network structure and small-armed groups remained. Some informal cooperation between the two undergrounds continued until the final destruction of UPA in 1947, especially in missions that involved obtaining supplies on the black market. The mutual agreement was not always observed by all AK units and had no effect on other Polish partisan groups, especially civilian gangs that continued attack and rob Ukrainians throughout the deportation period.

After the Red Army had moved west of the Transcurzon, Polish partisan attacks resumed on Ukrainian civilians, although they were not as numerous as earlier and appear to have been conducted largely by bandits rather than organized partisan groups. Based on the Soviet Population Exchange Commission's reports for 1945, Ukrainian civilians were attacked by Polish partisans, bandits, and Polish police. Robberies were widespread throughout the region but were more frequent in the Lublin

359 Ibid, 291.

Province. By the end of May 1945, 135,000 people had left the Transcurzon, of which 113,000 were from the Lublin Province where people had been subjected to Polish partisan attacks for several years.[360] A man from the Krasnostav County, after boarding the train, noted: "We can laugh for the first time in five years."[361] In Hrubieszów County, the report for February 23, 1945 describes what appears to have been a fairly common occurrence:

> Under the orders of AK, daily robberies are perpetrated against the Ukrainian population emigrating to the Soviet Ukraine. Local authorities and Polish soldiers are participating in the robberies. Robbers take livestock, farm equipment, and kill those who offer resistance. In the villages of Khozhovtsi and Bohutych 32 families were robbed, the bandits took 38 horses, 25 cows, 17 pigs and 20 wagons.[362]

Although Soviet reports attribute the attacks to the AK, their principal opponent, it is far more likely that these events can be attributed to banditry, in which AK did not typically engage, and other Polish partisan groups. Robberies by local police were apparently not uncommon either, and such occurrences were reported in the spring of 1945 in both Hrubieszów and Lubaczów counties.[363] The report further notes that in the spring of 1945, people in Sanok County were being driven out of some villages and forced to emigrate. In the village of Lubno, for example, 100 Ukrainians were killed and the remaining villagers fled to Sanok and asked to be sent to the Soviet Union.[364] Another Commission reported:

> ...On June 6, 1945, AK commanded by "Sokol" attacked the village of Wierzchowiny, Krasnystaw County. During the attack Ukrainian population was brutally killed, including women, children and the elderly, and their goods taken. The Commission went to investigate and counted 240 mutilated bodies. In the Jarosław County, National Armed Forces group commanded by "Mewa" (Jan Toth) and "Radwan" (Bronisław Gliniak) attack three Ukrainian villages... killed over 1,000 Ukrainians, among them infants and elderly people.[365]

As the deportations continued throughout 1945, Ukrainians were buffeted from all sides by Polish partisans and by Polish and Soviet troops. The Polish underground was especially active during the first half

360 See Misiło, *Repatriacja czy Deportacja, Tom 2/Vol. II*, Appendix No. 5.
361 Serhiichuk, *Trahediia*, 136.
362 Ibid, 261.
363 Ibid, 263, 280.
364 Ibid, 273. There was no Lubno village in the county. This is apparently a reference to Lubne, a village in the adjacent Lesko County.
365 Ibid, 246–247.

of 1945, and in a number of incidents, they inflicted horrendous casualties on Ukrainians. A majority of the attacks took place in the northern portion of the Transcurzon, where the ethnic fighting in Volhynia had spilled over to the west of the Bug River. There, the Polish population was more numerous than elsewhere in the region. The attacks were exacerbated by German colonization and continued afterward, with both sides motivated by ethnic hatred and the desire to drive out the other. A Soviet report notes that in early 1945, the Polish underground had killed approximately 1,000 Ukrainians, robbed approximately 2,500 households, and burned 700 farmsteads in the Lubaczów area, and further north, the casualties were much higher.[366] The mayhem, however, was not limited to the north but affected all districts in the Transcurzon. On March 3, 1945, an AK unit commanded by Lt. Josef Biss attacked the Ukrainian village of Pawłokoma (Pavlokoma) in the Przemyśl area, aided by men from neighboring Polish villages. The villagers were led to the church where 365 were shot, their bodies subsequently dumped into pits dug in the cemetery. In retaliation for the atrocities, a local Ukrainian self-defense unit burned the Polish village of Borownice, and later in the year, the UPA sotnias of Hromenko and Burlaka destroyed the remaining Polish villages that had participated in the attack: Dylągowa, Bartkowe, Łączki, Sielnice, and Pawłokoma which had since been resettled by Poles.[367]

On April 17, 1945, the village of Piskorowice (Pyskorovychi) was attacked by a unit of armed men of the nationalistic National Military Organization, who were commanded by Jan Toth ("Mewa") and Josef Zadzierski ("Wolyniak") whom AK regarded as a "bandit." Similar to the Pawlokoma massacre, a large group of residents was herded to the schoolhouse on the pretext of discussing resettlement. Upon their arrival, 358 were machine-gunned. Many more people were killed in other parts of the village and adjacent settlements, which brought the overall total to 1,344.[368] Another attack was carried out on June 6, 1945 by units of the same organization in the village of Wierchowina (Verkhovyna) in Krasnystaw County. Unlike most other attacks of this type, the Wierchowina massacre was investigated by the Polish authorities most likely because the inquiry had been requested by a communist party official and

---

366 Ibid, 245.

367 Misiło, *Repatriacja,* Vol. I, 86–87

368 Ibid, 108–110.

countersigned by the General Secretary, Władysław Gomułka. The investigation concluded that 197 people had been killed, including sixty-five children under eleven years of age, and also noted that the villagers had been robbed of clothing, footwear, household items, and livestock including cows, pigs, and horses.

Attitudes and Views on the Deportations

The deportations that began in 1944 were presented as voluntary resettlements by the Polish government, and indeed, many of the Ukrainians who left their property were not technically removed by the direct use of force. Some who had left did so voluntarily but most fled to escape attacks by the Polish underground and civilian gangs. However, in the second half of 1945, the situation would become more intense as the government introduced the practice of forceful expulsions in earnest. The first part of this process involved various administrative measures, such as raising taxes to a point that was cost prohibitive for landowners. Finally, the Polish Army was deployed to expedite the deportation. The resettlement program was interpreted differently by the various parties involved, according to their agendas. The Soviet view was expressed concisely by Khrushchev in a top-secret report to Stalin in June 1945:

> ...The Ukraino-German nationalists abroad (in the Transcurzon) are conducting strong agitations against resettling the Ukrainian population on the territory of the USSR. They engage in terror against those who wish to resettle in the Soviet Union.[369]

During the war, the Soviets developed the tactic of equating Ukrainian opposition to Soviet authority as "German-Ukrainian Fascism," and used this rhetoric for the remainder of the Soviet period.[370] The initial Ukrainian cooperation with the Germans was used as an effective propaganda tool; all German atrocities were attributed to the Ukrainian opposition, and the Soviets labeled them as "fascists" or "Nazis" accordingly. More interestingly, this view was accepted at the highest levels of the Soviet leadership. Khrushchev's views on many Ukrainians wanting to resettle may have been strengthened by Soviet reports from the Transcurzon, which conveyed that Ukrainians were well disposed to resettlement

---

369 Serhiichuk, *Trahediia,* 155.

370 See Weiner, *Making Sense of War*, 165.

in the Soviet Union. The head of the political department of the First Ukrainian Front, Lt. Gen. Lev Shatilov, wrote a top secret report to Khrushchev, telling him that the Ukrainian population in the Lublin province in the northwest had a positive attitude toward relocation, but, thus far, had not taken any concrete steps. The willingness to move was confined mostly to areas where the Polish underground had been robbing and terrorizing villages. He noted that many people had stated: '"All the same we have to leave. Once the Red Army leaves, we cannot live here.'"[371]

In a report from Tymofiy Kal'nenko, Pidhornyi's deputy, to Dem"ian Korotchenko, the Ukrainian party chief, Kal'nenko wrote that although the Ukrainians were willing to relocate, they were being restrained by the OUN and the clergy which were both agitating against relocation. He noted that OUN, under the slogan "Not A Step From Our Land"[372] was spreading propaganda against leaving and frightening people with famine in Ukraine and deportations to Siberia. He further stated that the Archbishop of Przemyśl had instructed priests to urge their parishioners to resist resettlement and specifically described how Victor Kuchmylo, a priest in the village of Lukovo and also a graduate of L'viv University with a degree in philosophy, had criticized the Soviet Union during his sermon and urged his parishioners not to leave. He further noted: "Of the twelve individuals from Przemyśl County who declared their intentions to leave, seven had revoked their applications."[373]

In a letter dated February 19, 1945, Gen. Col. Lev. Mekhlis of the Fourth Ukrainian Front informed Khrushchev that 70,000 Ukrainians (Ruthenians) of Gorlice County were ready to leave. Having been economically exploited by the Poles, the general noted, the local population was ready to relocate as soon as the Red Army arrived. The population held meetings and passed resolutions to inform the Red Army of their desire to emigrate to the Soviet Union.[374]

---

371 Serhiichuk, *Trahediia,* 129.

372 Ibid, 142. Publicizing the famine was not a propaganda ploy but a reality, and many people starved in postwar Ukraine. See also I.O. Voronov, and I.H. Pyliavets, *Holod 1946–1947r.* (Kyiv: Znannia, 1991.) The famine is mentioned in isolated areas but figures are not provided.

373 Serhiichuk, 1997, 142.

374 Ibid, 147

Despite evidence to the contrary, Soviet reports maintained the party line that Ukrainian civilians wished to relocate, but were being prevented from doing so by the Ukrainian underground. Most of the Soviet reported information concerning Ukrainian attitudes toward resettlement was gathered through public meetings, which had the tone of political lectures rather than open discussion forums where attendees might feel free to disagree with the lecturer without consequence. Under the circumstances, many people may have outwardly agreed with the speaker and later ignored him, which could have confused Soviet officials. Nevertheless, the Soviet regime had excellent intelligence services that would have been aware of the popular reluctance to leave although high party and government officials chose to maintain the party line, even amongst themselves.

The Poles, on the other hand, held a more realistic view. The Governor of the Lublin Province, whose jurisdiction encompassed the northwestern Ukrainian territory where Polish-Ukrainian strife was most brutal, wrote a secret letter to the Polish government that portrayed Ukrainians as being antagonistic and expressed his view that removing them would require forcible measures. He noted that during the German occupation, the Ukrainians had shown no loyalty to the Polish people or to the Soviet Union; on the contrary, they had supported anti-Polish and anti-Soviet policies. He claimed that based on five years of occupation, it was evident that some Ukrainians had worked with the Poles, but the majority were nationalistic, chauvinistic, and hostile toward the Polish and Soviet governments. He asserted that Ukrainians were attempting to infiltrate newly formed police and government organs and many people were changing their nationality to avoid deportation. He concluded that voluntary resettlement was therefore unrealistic and deportation would be required.[375]

A number of Polish officials reported a similar pattern in the western Lemko counties, where prior to the war, most people had called themselves *Rusyni* (Ruthenians). During the German occupation, Ukrainians had enjoyed more cultural rights and had established Ukrainian language schools and other cultural organizations in the region. This had prompted many younger people to identify themselves as Ukrainians, a

---

375 Misiło, *Repatriacja*, Vol. I, 67–69.

phenomenon that many local Polish officials found disturbing. With respect to resettlement, some Lemkos left voluntarily but most, as in other areas of the Transcurzon, demonstrated no desire to leave. The Nowy Targ County administrator asserted that although some identified themselves as Ruthenians, most should be viewed as enemies of Poland and the Red Army.[376] Similarly, the Jasło County administrator also discussed the nationalist sentiments among Lemkos, but noted that because the war had devastated the area, some areas contained land mines that prevented many Lemkos from returning to their native villages, and they were consequently disposed to relocation.[377] In Gorlice County, where General Mekhlis had claimed to have found 70,000 people willing to resettle, the deputy county administrator reported that people were not willing to leave their land under any circumstances.[378]

The Polish portrayal of Ukrainians, as shown in these letters and reports, is colored by ethnic animosities and therefore must be viewed with reservation, but Polish assessments of Ukrainian reluctance to leave cannot be doubted. Reports by both the Polish and Soviet governments tended to blame ethnic animosities on the Germans, and indeed, wartime German colonization schemes west of the Bug River had provoked mutual violence. In reality, however, anti-Polish sentiments had been strong prior to the war due to the repressive policies of the interwar Polish government. Given the relative tolerance of the German administration toward the Ukrainian minority in Poland, Ukrainians had a greater opportunity to promote their native language and culture through increased educational access and the proliferation of cultural organizations. These factors had the effect of strengthening Ukrainian national identity and increasing Polish animosity toward Ukrainians.

Compared to the Polish and Soviet reports, those of the Ukrainian underground provide a vastly different perspective on the disposition of the population concerning resettlement to Soviet Ukraine. The underground's reports describe only the methods of avoiding deportation, and indicate that the OUN/UPA took as a given that the Ukrainian population in the Transcurzon was opposed to resettlement. A Spring 1945 OUN report from the Przemyśl area notes the reactions of people from several

---

376 Ibid, 124.

377 Misiło, *Repatriacja*, Vol. I., 129.

378 Ibid, 172.

villages at meetings organized by the resettlement commission. In response to the suggestion that Ukrainians should move to Ukraine, a woman in the village of Stefkowa (Stefkova) declared that they already lived in Ukraine. People of Wańkowa (Van'kova) left the meeting when the topic of relocation was broached, and three individuals who signed the agreement took back the forms. In Paszowa (Pashova), a woman declared that they would not move in order to avoid dying of hunger.[379] Women at the meetings were more outspoken than men as they were less likely to be beaten or arrested.

A fall 1945 report classifies the Ukrainian population's attitudes toward the deportations into three categories. The first category described residents who lived in villages where forced deportation policies had not yet been applied (Sanok and Lesko counties). The reports noted that the people supported the underground, followed their instructions, and were prepared to resist, but feared that if deportations were conducted during the winter, they might not be able to hold out. In the second category were villagers who had managed to evade deportations by fleeing to other villages where the local population had already been deported. Although that group had lost most of their own belongings, most had managed to gather foodstuffs left behind by their deported neighbors. This group was likewise supportive of the underground, but feared another wave of deportations during the winter. Consequently, some were changing their nationality by obtaining falsified documents from local officials and Polish priests. The third category listed in the report described people who had been subjected to harsh treatment such as food being withheld from them, for example, but who had still refused to relocate. They managed to flee to the forests or neighboring villages during resettlement actions. The report noted that those people believed that war was imminent and that only another war could save them.[380]

Despite the occasional disagreements between the members of the Soviet Population Exchange Commission and the Polish government, they worked in tandem to deport the Ukrainians. The Soviet effort was confined largely to registration, providing transportation, and conducting propaganda meetings that extolled the virtues of resettlement and en-

379 Ibid, 120.
380 Serhiichuk, *Trahediia*, 181–2.

couraged villagers who favored relocation to speak out. The number of such village participants was small, since those who wanted to relocate and agitated for relocation would have run afoul of the underground. To encourage more people to volunteer, the Soviet Commission placed articles in the Polish press that advocated resettlement and printed propagandistic testimonial-type letters of those who had left, which never failed to indicate the favorable conditions that the author was experiencing as the result of the resettlement location.

The Polish government played a more active role in the resettlement program, since it was charged with bringing Ukrainians to the railroad stations. The government initially encouraged the formation of Ukrainian committees, hoping that the strategy would encourage more volunteers. They soon abandoned this approach when they became convinced that the committees were against resettlement. The Ukrainian underground, on the other hand, viewed committee members as communists who favored deportation. In actuality, both sides were partially correct since the views among committee members varied, but the majority of the members were against deportation. The Polish Government eventually concluded that Ukrainians could not be enticed to relocate solely through propaganda and it would be necessary, therefore, to employ forcible measures. On October 20, 1945, Józef Bednarz, Poland's Chief Representative for Evacuation, wrote to provincial leaders in Cracow, Rzeszów, and Lublin, asking them to apply the 1937 law permitting the evacuation of unreliable populations located along the state borders.[381] In his view, enforcing this law would accomplish two goals: first, to remove the Ukrainian population, and second, to eliminate the Ukrainian underground. How thoroughly the law was invoked throughout the provinces remains uncertain, but a leaflet issued September 25, 1945 by Józef Labuz, county administrator of Nowy Sącz, ordered the population to leave. The leaflet contained the following instructions:

> All residents of Ukrainian and Ruthenian (Lemko) nationalities in the Nowy Sacz County are required to evacuate the border area within 14 days, starting from the day following this announcement, for security reasons and defense of border. If the inhabitants do not leave the border area (county) within specified period, they will be removed by force.[382]

---

381 See Ibid, 255 and Misiło, *Repatriacja,* Vol. I., 255

382 A photocopy of the leaflet is reprinted in Misiło, *Repatriacja,* Vol. I, 233.

The threat was never enforced since the government did not have physical control of the area. Nevertheless, by the autumn of 1945, the government committed itself to using force; however, the reluctance of the people to move and the increasing UPA activities made the task daunting. The Soviets made preparations for the deportation of Ukrainians in 1944, shortly after the Red Army entered the current boundary of Poland with the end of war in Europe still half a year away. The Soviet haste was motivated by the desire to present to the West, at the post-war conference, a clearly delineated ethnic boundary that coincided with their proposed Polish eastern border. This policy did not anticipate the numerous obstacles that the authorities would face when attempting to remove people who refused to abandon their native land. The refusal was compounded by Polish resistance to the newly proffered Polish communist regime, which would be instrumental in deporting the people. Finally, the rapid growth of the Ukrainian underground, which was determined to prevent the removal of the Ukrainian population, was another major obstacle. During this period, a small number of people did emigrate voluntarily and a larger share left, especially from the Lublin Province, because of Polish partisan attacks. The bulk of the population, however, was removed only after the war, when a large portion of the Polish army and police could be deployed to remove the people by force.

Photographs

Photo 1: Deportation of the village of Ustrzyki Gorne during Operation Vistula in April 1947
(Public Domain)

Photo 2: Women and children from Wola Piotrowa (Sanok County) in Sunday dress (cultural clothing) shortly before World War II.
(© Pelagia Volian'ska Tzin'kalo, Corinna Caudill)

Photo 3: Stepan Goliash "Mar" (2nd from left, top row) and his men pose with a Lemko family, circa 1946.
(© copyright 2005-2010 by *Litopys UPA*. Photo from *Litopys Ukrains'koii Povstans'koii Armii (UPA) Annual Calender* published by Litopys UPA Toronto-L'viv, 2008)

Photo 4: Officers of the Peremyshl' battalion as they prepare an attack on the town of Bircza, January 4, 1946. Third from the left is Mykhailo Hal'o ("Konyk") who was killed two days later on January 6th during the engagement.
(© copyright 2005-2010 by *Litopys UPA*. Photo from *Litopys Ukrains'koii Povstans'koii Armii (UPA) Annual Calender* published by Litopys UPA Toronto-L'viv, 2006)

Photo 5: Teodor Bulas "Balai" Sotnia. Photo taken in early 1946.
(© copyright 2005-2010 by *Litopys UPA.* Photo from *Litopys Ukrains'koii Povstans'koii Armii (UPA) Annual Calender* published by Litopys UPA Toronto-L'viv, 2010)

Photo 6: Members of the Underground Printing Press, Lesko area in the Lemko region. From left to right: Nadia Goliash "Marika" (sister of Stepan Goliash "Mar"), "Novyi" (Director of the Technical Link), "Dora" (Typist), "Step" (Rifleman)
(© copyright 2005-2010 by *Litopys UPA.* Photo from *Litopys Ukrains'koii Povstans'koii Armii (UPA) Annual Calender* published by Litopys UPA Toronto-L'viv, 2007)

Photo 7: Minister of Defense Michał Rola-Żymierski and General Stefan Mossor, Commander of Operation Vistula.
(Source: Szcześniak and Szota, *Droga do nikąd*, 403)

Photo 8: The last inspection of General Karol Świerczewski, Lesko area
(Source: Szcześniak and Szota, *Droga do nikąd*, 425.)

Photo 9: Members of the OUN Beskid District heading west in the summer of 1947. The third man from the left (wearing the civilian hat) is Modest Ripet'skyi ("Horyslav,") the Battalion physician.

Photo 10: Easter celebration by OUN members, Lemko region, 1946.

Photo 11: Sotnia of Volodymyr Shchehels'kyi "Burlaka" in the Przemyśl area, Winter 1946.

(© copyright 2005-2010 by *Litopys UPA*. Photo from *Litopys Ukrains'koii Povstans'koii Armii (UPA) Annual Calender* published by Litopys UPA Toronto-L'viv, 2005)

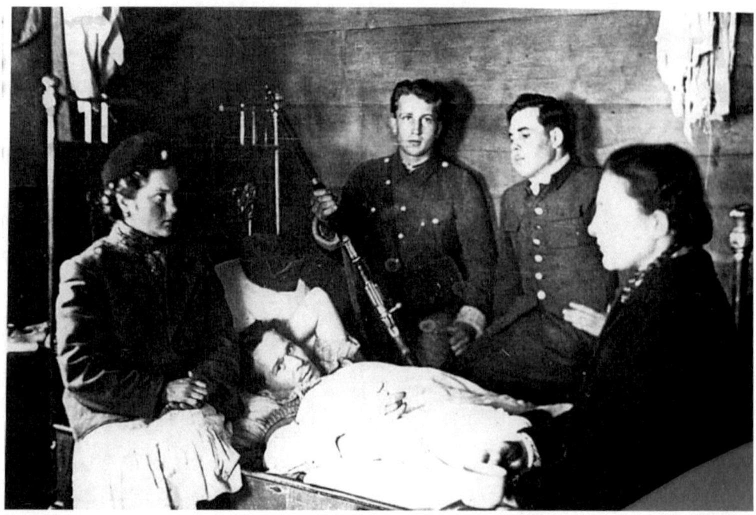

Photo 12: Hospital in an Underground Bunker. Jarosław region, 1946.

(© copyright 2005-2010 by *Litopys UPA*. Photo from *Litopys Ukrains'koii Povstans'koii Armii (UPA) Annual Calender* published by Litopys UPA Toronto-L'viv, 2006)

Chapter V:
Expulsion to the East: Operation Rzeszów

By the end of the war, the various Polish partisan formations that had organized during the war were still operational, with the exception of the communist People's Guards that became part of the provisional government. Despite their reduced strength, these groups continued to stage occasional attacks on Ukrainian villages. The reduced level of violence did not bring any respite to Ukrainians as the Polish Army and police commenced the deportations after the war by resorting to force. A September 1945 -WiN report for the Przemyśl area describes the new approach to deportation. The document notes that at the end of the August, the deportations began with the arrival of the Polish Army (commanded by Soviet officers.) These units were often manned by Poles from western Ukraine who were hostile toward Ukrainians. The report notes that Polish army units, sometimes reinforced by NKVD units, swept through the villages, robbing and committing atrocities against the people. Some Ukrainians engaged in armed resistance and many of them joined UPA.[383]

The attacks by the army and police actually began in the spring of 1945, as evidenced by an April 6, 1945 report of an attack on four villages in the Lubaczów County.[384] A battalion of Polish Internal Troops attacked the villages, reporting that they had killed about 400 Ukrainian partisans without sustaining any losses. Such a scenario was highly unlikely since that figure represented the size of the Zalizniak's battalion, which continued to operate in the Lubaczów area until 1947. Since UPA reports do not indicate a major engagement in the area, it is more likely that this incident was part of the Polish army's common practice of routinely killing civilian men and reporting them as Ukrainian partisans. The battalion reported capturing a number of German and Soviet rifles and confiscating 40 cows, 14 horses, 100 sheep, two pigs, and two horse-drawn wagons, apparently used for carting stolen goods.[385] In the operational reports issued during the deportations, Polish commanders report-

---

383 Misiło, *Repatriacja,* Vol. I, 211.
384 Ibid., 104.
385 Ibid., 104–105.

ed to their superiors how many partisans had been killed in specific villages, the number of livestock taken, and often reported the number of wagons taken. The Polish military leadership was aware of the approximate size of the Ukrainian underground and must have realized that if their troops were killing partisans by the hundreds in numerous villages, the Ukrainian underground would have been destroyed in a matter of months. Written instructions by senior civilian and military officials authorizing troops to kill Ukrainian civilians and seize their property has not been found and probably was never issued; nevertheless, the authorities clearly condoned this behavior for several years in order to facilitate the expulsion of the Ukrainian population.

On September 21, an attack was carried out on against the villagers of Stare Brusno in Lubaczów County, where Polish troops burned the village and killed 120 Ukrainian civilians, wounded 93, and took six horses and two wagons.[386] By the autumn of 1945, the new policy of forcible deportation began with Polish army units routinely burning and robbing villages and killing civilians, a state-sanctioned terroristic system that would become standard practice for the next two years.

At the beginning of September of 1945, the Polish Army deployed three army divisions, the 3rd, 8th and the 9th, to the Ukrainian-inhabited districts, an incident that marks the beginning of the Polish government's systematic forcible expulsion of Ukrainians.[387] The deployment of the divisions sent alarms through the underground and all UPA units and OUN personnel were ordered to prepare for what was anticipated to be a decisive struggle. The underground assumed that Polish authorities would adopt Soviet tactics since numerous Soviet divisions had swept across the countryside and forests of western Ukraine earlier that year, where they had inflicted heavy losses on UPA units. Partisans operating in Poland were vulnerable to such sweeps since they had been operating on a narrow strip of land along the eastern border. Only the Lemko region provided an exception with its densely forested terrain that stretched along the Carpathians approximately 95 miles from the Soviet border toward Cracow. Although UPA units could have crossed into ethnic

---

386 Ibid., 228–229. In this incident, the troops were ambushed by the partisans near the village and sustained some losses. Afterward, they retaliated against the nearby village.

387 Ibid., 12. See also Szcześniak and Szota, *Droga,* 361.

Polish territory, such moves would have been dangerous since there would have been a greater chance that their presence would be monitored and reported by local Poles.

OUN and UPA directives reflected the political mood and proposed a plan of action against the new threat. On September 13, Dmytro Dzioba ("Stal'"), head of OUN Region II, issued a directive to his subordinates stating that the enemy would begin their offensive immediately, and ordered that units that did not receive detailed instructions should take appropriate action at their own discretion.[388] The underground was ordered to free deportees who were waiting for transport at the railroad stations and to burn abandoned Ukrainian villages to deprive Poles from confiscating anything of value, a tactic that would make it difficult for the government to resettle Poles in those villages. In September 1945, Sian Military District Commander Onyshkevych issued the following instruction to all UPA units:

> The communists have begun the forceful deportations and those who are conducting the deportations must be attacked, including members of the exchange commission. Deported villages must be stripped of any useful material, including food and construction material, which should then be burned. All food must be secured and stored in the forest or inside concealed bunkers. Sick soldiers and some others may be sent east with deported families. If contact with superiors is impossible, commanders must take independent action based on the situation at hand. If units are unable to survive in their usual locale, they must move to another area, even if it is located on Polish territory, remembering that this is a dangerous undertaking. Officers and political instructors must conduct meetings with the partisans, steeling them for action against our own land (a scorched earth policy) ...we will not abandon our native land without a fight, like slaves with bowed heads. Let everything burn behind us, let no one profit from our labor, and let the enemy know that we will not perish without a fight.[389]

Throughout the deportation campaigns, UPA burned numerous abandoned Ukrainian villages, an arson that Polish literature occasionally suggests were Polish villages. In the Transcurzon, partisans attacked Polish villages only in retaliation for their attacks on the neighboring Ukrainians. There were two reasons for burning former Ukrainian villages: emotional and practical. The underground wanted to prevent the Poles from benefitting from the Ukrainian tragedy by carting off whatever was left behind. Second, and most importantly, to prevent Poles who had

388 Misiło, *Repatriacja,* Vol. I., 206–208.
389 Ibid., 200–201.

been deported from the east from settling in the former Ukrainian villages, a practice that the underground viewed as tantamount to seizing and colonizing Ukrainian land. On the practical side, allowing the government to settle a hostile Polish population in the area would undoubtedly provide a more favorable operational environment for Polish troops (including access to lodging) and would therefore make the area less secure for the partisans. Although the scorched earth policy made things difficult for Ukrainians who managed to return to their destroyed villages, the underground leadership rationalized that they would find some way to survive—perhaps through the assistance and support of neighbors. The directive further ordered the destruction of communication lines and transportation facilities in attempts to thwart the deportations; including telephone and telegraph lines, railroad lines and bridges, and road bridges.

In their counterattacks on Polish raids and deportation roundups, UPA personnel were obliged to inform the Polish police that the attacks were retaliations and to urge them to surrender by explaining that the underground's principal mission and focus was to fight communism, not to fight Poles as the result of ethnic animosities. In some cases, leaflets were distributed by hand in Polish villages.[390] The leaflets contained information informing the Polish troops that if they surrendered, UPA would take only their weapons and clothing and leave them alive; however, if they refused, appropriate actions would be necessary. While there is no evidence that Polish troops or police at any time voluntarily surrendered, it is clear that some were taken prisoner. It is also important to note that many of the UPA instructions and directives suggest that there were protocols in place for the treatment of prisoners and civilians. Some of the documentation contains explicit rules of conduct, such as forbidding the burning of Polish villages unless it was unavoidable, and violence against civilians was forbidden under any circumstances, especially violence against women and children."[391]

The execution of Dzioba's directive was demonstrated in two engagements in Lubaczów County that occurred in the fall of that year. UPA units were instructed to kill members of the exchange commission and conduct retaliatory raids on police in the town of Nowa Grobla (No-

390 Misiło, *Repatriacja,* Vol. II., 318

391 Misiło, *Repatriacja,* Vol. I, 207.

va Hreblia), which had a railroad station that served as a main shipping point for Ukrainian deportees from Lubaczów and Jarosław counties. On September 15, a sotnia from the Zalizniak battalion attacked the stations at Nowa Grobla and Oleszyce, killing four soldiers, wounding 15, and destroying the stations and railroad tracks. On October 7, they attacked the Grobla station for a second time. Another OUN unit issued similar instructions concentrating on specific problems.[392] The instructions note that the forcible deportation had begun, ordered all underground members to remain at their posts collecting food, instructed civilians to thresh grain quickly and hide it, and advised them to flee with their goods and livestock in the event that Polish troops approached their villages. In addition, the instructions required the activation of SKV units, which were assigned the task of enforcing military discipline among the people, noting that "anarchists" (presumably Ukrainians who were amenable to relocation) should be punished:

> Do not allow the deportations to happen. Advise the people that those who have decided to leave are sitting in the railroad stations starving. Troops who are forcing people to leave should be attacked without regard to casualties…concealed bunkers should be built, and if the village houses are burned, people should build huts in the forest…all the people should be engaged in the struggle.[393]

While it is difficult to ascertain the extent to which the underground's directives had an effect on Ukrainian civilians, it is likely that many decided on their own accord to resist the deportations regardless of the underground's advice. Whether deciding to do so on their own or by following instructions, numerous sources document a widespread and robust resistance effort among civilians. There are numerous anecdotal accounts of people building hideouts, hiding their grain and other goods, and frequently disassembling wagons and scattering their parts to prevent confiscation.

Other than Polish and Soviet claims, there is no clear evidence to suggest that the underground engaged in terror against Ukrainian civilians, although the underground literature does report some beatings. Considering the realities on the ground, large scale harassment would have proven both difficult to initiate and counterproductive to the underground's goals and objectives. SKV members were usually village boys

---

392 Ibid., 191–192.

393 Misiło, *Repatriacja,* Vol. I, 192.

who were related to many local families, and enforcing draconian measures against their relatives would have been impossible. UPA units were more diverse, but local men usually made up a majority and would have been equally reluctant to use force against their own people. Finally, OUN and UPA depended on the population for food, occasional shelter, and intelligence, and if they would have engaged in mass terror tactics, it seems likely that the local civilians would have withdrawn their support for the cause. However, some reports do indicate that forceful measures were used in certain circumstances. In a September 1945 report, sotnia commander Burlaka stated that some people in the village of Jankowce (Yankivtsi) had fled to the woods at the approach of the Polish troops, but others had remained and converted to Roman Catholicism. The SB reportedly beat the converts with canes.[394] Although there are anecdotal accounts of similar incidences of UPA reprisals against Ukrainians who were considered disloyal to the cause, these types of stories are not widely reported in either UPA literature or in information gleaned from memoirs and interviews with people who eventually emigrated to the west. It is therefore reasonable to consider that such incidences were outliers to the general relations between UPA and the local population.

During the final months of 1945, Polish authorities intensified their deportation efforts, although a large-scale Soviet style operation against UPA would not materialize until two years later. To counter the new threat, the underground developed a multi-pronged approach that focused on reducing conflict with the Polish underground: encouraging Ukrainians to resist deportation, attacking Polish troops and police, attacking exchange commission offices and personnel, and destroying transportation and communication lines.

To reduce tensions between Poles and Ukrainians, the underground conducted propaganda campaigns and issued warnings to both the Polish population and troops. Although conflicts with Polish civilians continued to be a problem, this abated to a degree due to UPA's cooperation with the major Polish underground group (-WiN). Nevertheless, Polish gangs still occasionally robbed neighboring Ukrainian villages, and Polish self-defense units continued to accompany Polish army troops and police on

394 Ibid., 236–238.

village raids. Because they were not subject to the command structure of the Polish underground or the regular army, members of Polish self-defense units were more likely to rob civilians and were occasionally recognized by villagers and reported to the UPA, who sometimes staged retaliatory raids on the villages of the offenders. Two documents described below, a warning letter and a leaflet, provide examples of how UPA would typically address such problems.[395] One warning was addressed to the mayor of the Polish village of Poraż in Sanok County, an official UPA suspected of working with Polish bandits who were robbing Ukrainians. In the letter, the partisans claimed to know the names of the robbers and ordered the mayor to cease and desist with aiding them before it was too late. The warning ends with a slogan: "Long Live Friendship and Cooperation Between Ukrainian and Polish Peoples in Their Struggle Against Moscow's Imperialism." The leaflet was addressed to the Polish population and began with a salutation: "Freedom for Nations and Individuals and Death to Kremlin and Its Hirelings". It was signed "The Ukrainian Insurgents." It noted that in the preceding months, there had been cooperation between the Polish and Ukrainian underground organizations and that UPA expected Polish cooperation against the Soviets, whom they regarded as a mutual enemy. They warned that traitors to the cause, or those who would attack Ukrainians, would be met with reprisals. The letter reminded the Polish people that the UPA was fighting only the Kremlin and the Polish traitors who were serving Red Moscow, noting that the Kremlin hirelings included Polish troops and some civilians who had robbed Ukrainians. The Poles were warned to cease their activities or face severe punishment, and assured that those who were innocent would not be harmed. It further proclaimed that the UPA would be aided by the "honorable Polish people and their underground."

In addition to communications with the Polish population, there were a number of leaflets dated between September-October 1945 that were addressed to Polish troops. They enumerate points stated in other leaflets. One leaflet begins with the salutation "Freedom for the Individual, Death to Tyranny!" The leaflets, which were also signed by "The Ukrainian Insurgents," contain a message of cooperation in the spirit of common interests. One document states:

---

[395] Ibid., 197–199.

> Polish Soldier! We are turning to you because we realize that not all of you have become a blind tool of the Muscovite hirelings and we believe that there are many sincere Polish patriots among you and not false Stalinist democrats…Remember where your place is, is it among those who serve in the interest of Moscow or among those who bravely struggle against Moscow and its imperialism? …Don't listen to the Muscovite hirelings who are ordering you to terrorize civilians and with your own hands, creating greater enmity between our peoples. Follow your human instincts and patriotism that demands a common unity in a common struggle for freedom…We Ukrainian Insurgents are not fighting the Polish people, we are only fighting Bolshevik invaders.[396]

Considering the numerous atrocities that were committed against Ukrainians in 1945 and in the years that followed, the leaflets seemed to have had little effect on the behavior of Polish soldiers or civilian self-defense units. The deportations continued throughout the fall of 1945, and the situation became more intense as OUN and UPA became more organized and shifted their focus to disrupting the deportations. To bolster the resolve of the people against leaving, the OUN leadership in the Przemyśl area instructed its members to organize a campaign that would emphasize the hardships endured by the deportees and provide practical advice on how Ukrainians could protect themselves and their property. The documents stressed the importance of thwarting the deportations:

> The people must be made aware that the deportations have been initiated by Moscow, and that the Poles are being used as a tool. They must be convinced that this is their struggle, and OUN and UPA are only providing assistance. A 'whispering' campaign must be instituted, but carefully planned agents may pose as former deportees who fled Ukraine and describe the difficulties that deportees are facing there. Others may pose as anti-communist Poles who are critical of the deportations and attended hardships, but must, of course, speak Polish. Reliable village leaders must be sought out and informed about the anti-deportation campaign, and they must be convinced to agitate against leaving. OUN members must occasionally visit them to raise their spirits. Civilians living in the woods must be visited, reassured, and encouraged to build bunkers for themselves, as well as shelters and storage facilities. The underground must know the locations of civilian storage bunkers with contents that may be valuable should the people abandon them. The current struggle must be presented as an effort to protect what is Ukrainian, not as an effort to attack Poles. Stress that our objective is to protect Ukrainians from perishing rather than denying Poles a piece of Ukrainian territory. The burning of abandoned villages must be presented as an effort to cripple deportation rather than as an anti-Polish act—if we must abandon this land, we will leave only ashes behind us. Efforts must be made to minimize panic among the people by reassuring them that the enemy is not strong enough to deport everybody. People must be instructed to base their refusals to leave on official decrees which state that resettlement is voluntary. A defeatist attitude is spreading among the people that everything is lost and that further efforts and sacri-

---

396 Ibid., 235.

> fices are pointless. This attitude must not be tolerated among the people or the UPA. The Polish terror and the heroic resistance of the Ukrainian people must be documented and photographed as much as possible.[397]

Whether it was due to directives or to native ingenuity, many Ukrainians adopted the underground's suggested practices by constructing concealed bunkers to hide both their goods and themselves, especially in villages along major roads frequently traversed by Polish troops. On the approach of troops, many people hid in ravines behind villages or fled to the forests, a scene reminiscent of earlier centuries when people had fled Tatar raids to avoid captivity. In addition to evasive actions, some attempted to change their legal status by acquiring Polish passports or converting to Roman Catholicism. Many attempted to take advantage of a law enacted during the Austrian period that allowed individuals to apply to the county government to change their confessional status from Greek Catholicism to Roman Catholicism. During the Austrian period, such requests had been viewed favorably by Polish officials as a first step toward Polonization and were usually granted automatically. The tactic, however, did not go unnoticed by Polish officials. The Chief of Staff of the 9th Infantry Division, Colonel Gierasimienko, complained that Ukrainians in the village of Stary Dzików (Staryi Dykiv) in Lubaczów County had been issued documents indicating Polish nationality and that the county administrator had even issued papers to a Ukrainian priest, a policy that "... was impeding the deportations."[398] Similarly, the deputy administrator of Nowy Sącz County asked for clarification to the law related to changing of religion, claiming that it was an old law that was being used to avoid deportation rather than specifically for religious purposes.[399] The Ministry of Public Administration in Warsaw responded that changes in religious status should be granted, but instructed county administrations not to grant changes to nationality status.[400]

Requests to change religion in the western Lemko region underscored the desperation of the people since the Lemko people were religiously conservative. Before the war, some had even converted to Orthodoxy as the result of feeling alienated by the "Romanization" of the

---

397 Ibid., 214–219.

398 Ibid., 131.

399 Ibid., 230–231

400 Ibid., 247.

Greek Catholic Church. In addition to the problem of religious conversion, deportees who managed to return to their farmsteads presented additional difficulties when they recounted their experiences in the resettlement process to their neighbors. Reportedly, ten families returned to Nowy Sącz and Nowy Targ counties in the western Lemko region, and their descriptions of their horrifying ordeal convinced many residents to remain. In some cases, the returnees found that their farmsteads had already been settled by Poles—a situation that provoked conflicts.[401] Ukrainian men who had been conscripted into the Red Army in 1944 and 1945 faced a similar situation after being discharged and returning to their villages.[402] In Nowy Sącz County, 179 demobilized Red Army conscripts whose families had gone east returned to their homes after the war and wished to remain in their native villages. Central authorities advised local officials that because these men had served in the Red Army, they had forfeited Polish citizenship and should be deported as any foreigner who entered Poland illegally.[403] The Polish authorities, determined to remove all Ukrainians, resorted to force and subverted the law to achieve their aim.

The underground's anti-deportation campaign was supplemented by the its scorched earth policy which included the destruction of abandoned Ukrainians villages, as well as communication and transportation lines and other infrastructure that could be useful to the enemy. As Ukrainians abandoned their villages, the Polish authorities sought to resettle the villages with Polish deportees from the east as well as local Polish people.[404] Even unsettled villages provided valuable materials for local Poles since the Ukrainian deportees were unable to take everything, including items such as farm implements, utensils, and construction materials. In order to deny resources to the resettling Poles or to local foragers, UPA partisans took what was useful for their purposes and burned the remainder. They also staged attacks in Ukrainian villages where Polish newcomers attempted to resettle. One such incident occurred in the village of Nowosielce (Novosil'tsi) in Sanok County, which had been comprised of

---

401 Ibid., 258, 270–280.

402 When the Red Army occupied Ukrainian districts in the fall of 1944, many young men were conscripted to the army and sent to the front with little training.

403 Ibid., 305–306.

404 Ibid., 232–234.

about 250 abandoned Ukrainian households and was subsequently resettled by Poles who had been deported from Galicia (western Ukraine) in late 1944 and early 1945. The new settlers were armed and could count on reinforcements from two neighboring Polish villages as well as an army garrison in Sanok. On December 30, 1945, two sotnias attacked the village at midnight, destroying the railroad station and driving out the Poles who were informed by the UPA that, "...we are burning our (Ukrainian) houses." The partisans permitted them to leave with their cattle and other belongings. Although an organized battle did not materialize during the attack, some households did attempt to defend themselves, an action that resulted in about 15 civilian deaths.[405] Because of the threat of violence and the destruction that had occurred during the war, very few Polish deportees were actually settled in the vacated Ukrainian territory; instead, most were directed to the newly acquired (formerly German) territories in the north and west of Poland which included the historic German territories of Silesia, Pomerania and East Prussia.

UPA's attacks on population exchange commission personnel and the railroads proved to be their most effective method for disrupting the deportations. Due to the threat posed by UPA, Polish officials needed police or military escorts to enter villages and conduct their affairs, which usually involved resettlement meetings with local Ukrainians. The commissions followed the Soviet practice of obtaining voluntary agreements (even if under duress) by having the villagers sign forms agreeing to the resettlement. In some cases, people were beaten or threatened as a form of encouragement. In Lesko County, for example, troops distributed the resettlement forms and pointed pistols at those who refused to sign.[406] The constant fear of partisan attacks during that period clearly hampered the commission's efforts to such an extent that even some of the villagers who had been forced to sign were still able to avoid deportation since UPA was staging raids on railroad stations and freeing people who were waiting for trains. In the November 15, 1945 raid on a railroad station in Oleszyce, UPA reportedly freed several thousand people.[407] Although many railroads were attacked throughout the Transcurzon, most of the available underground literature for this time focuses on attacks in

405 Ibid., 304.
406 Ibid., 251–252.
407 Ibid., 208–209.

Lubaczów County, which may have been more severe compared to other areas. Józef Bednarz, the Chief Representative of the Polish Population Exchange Commission, reported on the disruptions:

> Since October 10 (two weeks ago), two loaded transports are waiting to leave but because of attacks every night, and the destruction of railroad lines and bridges by Ukrainian bands, there are no connections between Lubaczów, Jarosław, and Rawa Ruska, and therefore the trains cannot leave…Because of the attacks, evacuations from the Lubaczów area have been halted.[408]

As 1945 drew to a close, Polish and Soviet efforts during the year failed to achieve the objectives of the Population Exchange Agreement. By the end of that year, which was approximately a year-and-a-half after the deportations had begun, only about one-half of the total Ukrainian population had been removed from Poland. Of those, a small number had truly left voluntarily, but most had done so in response to coercive measures, Polish partisan attacks or through forcible deportation. Those who remained were generally located in less accessible areas, and as time went on, they grew more determined to remain. At the same time, the underground's expansion during that year gradually became more entrenched, a factor that largely removed the Polish government presence in the countryside and confined Poles to the towns. As the year progressed, both sides—the Polish authorities and the UPA—developed strategies that they would employ for the next two years. By the year's end, Polish authorities no longer relied on propaganda to effect "voluntary" resettlements; instead, the army and police were directly given the power to forcibly remove Ukrainians, actions that UPA countered by attacking transportation and communication networks, significantly retarding the deportations and forcing Polish and Soviet agents to extend the deportation deadline.

On December 14, 1945, Poland and the Ukrainian SSR signed an updated protocol that extended the deportations to June 15, 1946, and the Polish government began planning a more energetic campaign to meet the new deadline.[409] On January 23, 1946, the General Staff of the Polish Army issued an operational document entitled "Ending the Fight with

---

408 See Szcześniak and Szota, *Droga,* 227. Citation of the letter to the governor of Rzeszów Province.

409 Misiło, *Repatriacja*, Vol. II, 6.

Banditry."[410] The document contains an analysis of the army's past operations against the UPA and concludes that the underground survived because of a combination of excellent concealment tactics and the support of the local Ukrainian population. Ukrainians, therefore, were to be deported and the area would subsequently be populated with Poles who would be resettled from the Soviet Union. The document notes that the Polish army's effort to liquidate the UPA had been ineffective because of poor intelligence, indecisive operations, poor deployment and mobility, as well as the failed strategy of assigning small units to fight partisans who were more adept and experienced at maneuvering in the forested terrain. The document further notes that shortages of materiel compounded the problem since Polish troops had lacked adequate transport and clothing. It also cited specific problems, including a statistic that some forty percent of troops operating in the Cracow Military District had not been provided with adequate footwear.[411] More fundamentally, the document contains an acknowledgement of the Polish Army's failure to meet its two main objectives—to remove the Ukrainian population and to destroy the UPA; however, the wrong tactics had been chosen and the number of troops committed had been clearly inadequate for both tasks. Troops who were stationed in towns often made periodic forays to the countryside in platoon or company size strength, and these units usually headed for a village on foot without sending a patrol ahead or putting out flankers, an oversight that invited UPA ambushes. If a unit managed to avoid an ambush, it would generally arrive in a village and begin searching for partisans, a process that typically included pilfering the personal belongings of the Ukrainian villagers (usually portable items such as clothing and watches, but they occasionally took livestock, especially horses.) During these raids, the army frequently burned houses and killed some civilian men, and afterward the unit returned to town and reported the number of "partisans" killed. This approach was evidently designed to induce the population to sign the necessary repatriation documents, giving the appearance of voluntary departure as had been specified in the population exchange agreement. The insistence upon a legal fiction had the effect of increasing atrocities—people first had to be terrorized into submission instead of simply being taken to the railroad station and sent east.

---

410 Szcześniak and Szota, *Droga*, 392.

411 Ibid., 392

The 1944–1945 campaign had been poorly coordinated as well, as the 8th and 9th Polish infantry divisions, which were the most heavily involved in the deportations and campaigns against UPA, had not been subordinated to the Cracow Military District that encompassed the area; instead, they were directly subordinated to the General Staff which would have been less familiar with the local conditions. The 3rd Division had been detached from the Lublin Military District, was sent to the Rzeszów Province, and operated independently without coordinating with the other two divisions. In addition to the poor communication structure between the army units, the fledgling Communist regime had adopted a Soviet system of multiple armed formations: police, internal security forces, border guards, railroad guards and the regular army, all of which were engaged in assisting the deportation efforts and fighting UPA. The numerous units reported to different ministries that were poorly coordinated in terms of communication and transportation functions and were therefore incapable of quickly responding to partisan hit-and-run tactics. To rectify the problem, the General Staff proposed transferring the Cracow Staff to Rzeszów, to coordinate the campaigns of 8th and 9th divisions, to demobilize the 17th division in Cracow and assign its trucks to the other two divisions and allocating one or two trucks to each battalion. The 3rd Division was instructed to return to the Lublin Province to conduct deportations there and to fight the UPA, and in all divisions, troops not currently participating in the campaign were to receive additional training.

The General Staff's proposal was largely implemented and on April 5, 1946, Operational Group Rzeszów (*Grupa Operacyjna "Rzeszów" -- GOR)* was formed to conduct the campaign.[412] Most of the Ukrainian population as well as three of the four UPA battalions were located in the Rzeszów Province, but despite its name, the Rzeszów campaign was extended to the Lublin Province in the north, which covered seven Ukrainian counties, and two western Lemko counties were subordinated to the Cracow Province. To this new campaign, Operation Rzeszów, the army committed three divisions—the 3rd, 8th, and 9th divisions; as well as two regiments—the 14th and 18th infantry regiments, all of which amounted to a full one-quarter of its total army strength. Although the units were

412 The operation was to end officially on October 31, 1946. See Misiło, *Repatriacja,* Vol. II.,7

considerably undermanned, totaling only 11,700 men, they were augmented by men from the Border Guards, Internal Troops, and police.[413] At the same time, the UPA was at its maximum strength with over 2,000 men serving in sotnias and were supported by OUN and SKV units. The new campaign unfolded with more Polish troops raiding villages, and thus the burning, looting, and killing increased with more civilians being taken to deportation points where they were forced to sign the necessary relocation documents.

The 8th Division operated in Sanok and Lesko counties, reinforced by the 18th Regiment, whereas the 9th division covered the Przemyśl area, and 3rd division, reinforced by the 14th Regiment, and was deployed in the Lublin Province. Some of the most vicious attacks took place in the Sanok-Lesko area, where many regiments were commanded by the former Soviet officers. Soviet officers of Polish ancestry were employed extensively in the Polish Army and at times, some engaged in criminal behavior. On January 2, 1946, Tadeusz Pawłusiewicz, Head of Lesko County, sent a secret letter to the governor of Rzeszów. The letter was signed by twelve county officials, including the police chief and his deputy.[414] They accused Lt. Colonel Mikołaj Kiryluk, the commander of the 36th regiment, of incompetence and criminal behavior and included allegations that Kiryluk's troops had engaged in robbery, seized and vandalized buildings and furniture in the towns and had raped and killed Ukrainian civilians, with these actions having led to retaliations from UPA. The document reports that Kiryluk had been robbing people at the market place, had taken 25,000 zloty from the village of Postołów (Postoliv), and had forced women to have sex with him at gunpoint. The letter continues that because he was inept at fighting UPA and deporting the Ukrainians, the partisans had moved to the forest and were not being pursued. They roamed the countryside ambushing troops and destroying police stations, and had managed to disarm a 12-man station in Wołkowyja. Therefore, any travel outside the town was dangerous. Kiryluk's troops burned several Ukrainian villages, and UPA retaliated by burning Polish villages and killing Poles. Two soldiers were killed and Kiryluk attacked Mchawa (Mkhava), burning 40 Ukrainian houses

---

413 See Misiło, *Repatriacja,* Vol. II, 7, and Szcześniak and Szota, *Droga,* 381.

414 Misiło, *Repatriacja,* Vol. II, 10–14.

and 14 Polish houses, killing 5 Poles.[415] The Colonel was planning to deport the Ukrainians without adequate strength to protect the Polish population, oil fields, and bridges; and the letter asserted that if he pursued his plan, a catastrophic situation would ensue in the county.

The Colonel presented his side to the division commander, and although the full text of the report is not available, it ended with this sentence: "I carry out my assignment not out of fear, but according to my conscience and honor as an officer and my affection for my beloved fatherland, the Soviet Union."[416] With respect to the Mchawa incident, Colonel Jan Rutkowski sent a top secret report to the Minister of Defense, Marshal Michał Rola-Żymierski [417] According to this version of the story, a Captain Pielinski of the Border Guards had sent three Guardsmen to Mchawa to secure some wagons for his trip. While there, the men were having a meal in a Polish home when Ukrainian partisans surprised them, and in the ensuing fight, two soldiers were killed and one was wounded. In response, the Guards sent a 130-man unit that burned forty-one houses—31 Ukrainian and 10 Polish—killing six people in the process and wounding two.[418] Colonel Rutkowski noted that the matter was still under investigation. Information is not available on the final disposition of the two cases nor can accusations be verified, although it is documented that Lt. Colonel Kiryluk returned to the Soviet Union on April 2, 1946. Incidents of this nature were reported frequently during Operation Rzeszów and followed a similar pattern. Civilian officials would accuse the military of some transgression and the army would investigate and issue a report, claiming that the accusation was either false or exaggerated and nothing further was pursued about the matter.

Some of the most vicious attacks were conducted by the 34th regiment stationed in Sanok and commanded by another Soviet officer of Polish extraction, Lt. Colonel Stanisław Pluto. Throughout January, his troops attacked numerous villages throughout Sanok County, burning houses and killing civilians in each village raid. The troops did not search for partisans nor did they order the villagers to leave. Instead, the cam-

---

415 In the attack on Mchawa, a mixed Polish-Ukrainian village, it is likely that some Ukrainians were also killed, but the letter does not provide information on Ukrainian casualties.

416 Ibid., 14, Footnote 1.

417 Ibid., 17–18.

418 The nationality of the victims was not specified.

paign was designed to terrorize the people as a prelude to the so-called "voluntary" emigration. The most atrocious attacks by Pluto's regiment were carried out in the villages of Karlików (Karlykiv) and Zawadka Morochowska (Zavadka Morokhivs'ka). On January 24, 1946, the troops stationed in the Polish village of Bukowsko raided Karlików twice, and during the day several men were arrested and found dead outside the village after the troops had left. During the night, approximately 100 soldiers attacked Karlików again and within the span of approximately one hour, they burned about a dozen houses and killed fifteen civilians, including a 72-year-old Ukrainian priest named Oleksiy Malarchyk as well as the priest's wife, daughter and granddaughter. A soldier bayoneted the granddaughter, who was only four years old. The remaining victims were all men. A few were killed at home but most were led to the center of the village and shot. Reportedly they were sprayed with automatic weapons then each man was shot individually in the head. Dmytro Syvyi was shot in the arm and fell in the snow, where he apparently fainted. He was then shot in the head, but the bullet only grazed his head. Later, he awoke in the snow among the dead bodies, including that of his brother, Seman, and not seeing any soldiers, he made his way home along the creek. His wife hid him in the closet for fear that the soldiers would see him again and kill him. Afterward, he was taken to an UPA doctor who bandaged him, and it turned out that he had not been seriously wounded. After most troops had left, a unit of Didyk's sotnia arrived in the village, driving out remaining troops and capturing two. During the same day, Khrin's sotnia engaged a 120-man unit that was pillaging the nearby village of Zawadka Morochowska and killing civilians. In that incident, two platoons of the sotnia that were augmented by an SB unit (SB units were comprised of approximately a dozen men) had been stationed in the woods outside the village when Pluto's troops began advancing on the village. The civilian men fled to the woods—a typical scenario since by that time, it was becoming standard practice for Polish troops to kill Ukrainian men caught in village raids. Shortly after the arrival of Pluto's unit in Zawadka, wailing was heard in the village as troops attacked the villagers who remained. In response, Khrin's sotnia launched an attack that precipitated a fierce three-hour battle. Pluto's unit was driven out, leaving behind two 82mm mortars, some small arms, ammunition and other supplies. Ren's battalion report for January puts Polish losses at five killed and nine severely wounded.[419]

The following morning, on January 25, 1946, five companies of Polish troops, including two trucks of NKVD troops and self-defense units from the Polish village of Niebieszczany, approached Zawadka again. Some troops surrounded the woods to prevent a possible partisan attack, while others attacked the villagers killing seventy people, including men, women and children. Many others received various injuries but data for this group was not reported. An OUN report, based on information provided by family members, enumerated fifty-six victims by name and frequently reported their ages and method of execution. The atrocities were more horrific than usual—not because of the number killed, which was not unusual, but due to the extremely brutal methods used to kill these people. Most victims were either shot or bayonetted, but seven people were burned alive and four had their eyes gouged out and noses and tongues cut out. Among the seventy killed were number of small children; the youngest was Kateryna Izdebska, a six-month old infant who had her throat slit. Besides killing people, the troops burned twenty-seven houses and took seventeen horses, thirty cows, poultry, grain, and other items. After returning to their base, the regiment claimed to have killed eighty Ukrainian partisans in the village.

After this episode, some people left the village and camped in the forest, while others chose to remain in the village and were subjected to additional raids over the next few months. When the village was raided again on March 28, some people managed to flee to the forest and those who were caught were attacked and beaten, and 11 men were killed. On April 13, the troops arrived again. They killed four men and told the people to leave in three days or they all would be killed. Finally, on April 30, troops again surrounded the village and took the remaining 78 people, which by that point included only four men, to the nearby town of Zagorz which had a railroad station for the deportation to the east.

The case of Zawadka Morochowska is unique in the sense that a large-scale massacre was committed by the Polish Army rather than by partisans or bandits, and the terror was carried out systematically, with at least three separate attacks occurring over a three-month period. In nu-

---

419 See Misiło, *Repatriacja,* Vol. II, 24, 121. and Potichnyj and Lyko, *Litopys UPA,* Vol. 33, 260.

merous Ukrainian villages, there were virtually complete slaughters of the inhabitants, but these acts were usually perpetrated by the Polish partisans rather than the Polish army and were especially prevalent in the Lublin Province in 1943–44. Documentation indicating the reasons for the attacks on Zawadka Morochowska has not been located, nor is there a readily plausible explanation. The village had been destroyed by the Germans in 1944 and was only partially re-built by 1946 and could not have provided food or shelter for the partisans. When troops were attacked in a village, it would occasionally provoke retaliation, but retaliations were usually neither frequent nor systematic. Just days after the attack on Zawadka, Pluto received the *Virtuti Militari,* the highest Polish medal for bravery in combat and on February 23 was awarded the "Silver Service Cross." On June 1, he was relieved of command and transferred to the personnel department. He returned to the Soviet Union in August 1946.[420]

After the war, the Polish Army had many Soviet officers in command positions. In April and May of 1940, NKVD troops executed the Polish officer corps in Katyn forest and in other camps in the Soviet Union. When the Soviet Union began organizing the Polish Peoples Army, Polish officers were few and politically suspect, necessitating the use of Soviet officers, most of them of Polish ancestry. Eventually, Soviet Field Marshal Konstantin Rokossovsky, an officer of Polish extraction, was appointed as Minister of Defense of Poland in 1949. More unusual was the appointment of at least two Ukrainians: the notorious Kiryluk and Major General Ostap Stetsa, who had an unusual biography. Stetsa was born in the village of Komańcza in Sanok County and had joined the Sich Riflemen, which later became a part of the Ukrainian Galician Army. By 1920, he joined the Red Army and later completed his studies at

---

420 For each attack on the village, OUN described the event in a separate document published in *Litopys UPA,* Vol. 34, pp. 342–351. After the deportations, the documents were translated into Polish and published as a brochure with the title "On the Bloody Path of Stalinist Democracy: The New Lidice," and additional information was added about the Karlików attack. The brochure is reprinted in Misiło, 279–287. Discussion in the text is based on these documents. With respect to Zawadka Morochowska, the underground published a pamphlet, "The New Lidice" in Polish, listing names of individuals killed during the three raids. The name "Lidice" is a reference to the Czech town destroyed by Germans in 1942 as retaliation for the Czech underground killing Reinhard Heydrich, a high-ranking Nazi official in Hitler's inner circle.

the Frunze Military Academy in Moscow. In 1944, he was transferred to the Polish Army and eventually served as the head of the Operational Department of the General Staff. After de-Stalinization, he returned to the Soviet Union.[421]

During the deportation period, the Polish army instituted a disastrous practice of having *Ochotnica Rezerwa Milicji Obywatelskiej* (Volunteer Reserve of the People's Militia or ORMO) of the neighboring Polish villages accompany Polish army units that were attacking Ukrainian villages. The militia appears to have committed more atrocities than regular troops and was more prone to robbing and looting. Members were frequently recognized by Ukrainian villagers and reported to the UPA, who occasionally retaliated against their villages.

Despite the terror tactics, many Ukrainians still refused to leave. Major Borys Lancman, another Soviet officer and a Chief-of-Staff of the 36th Regiment, called a conference of local officials to plan additional deportations. The conference concluded that village mayors and priests would need to be assembled and instructed them to inform the Ukrainians to either leave or be declared terrorists. On January 15, they held a meeting with people who were targeted for removal, including 269 from the town of Lesko and the village of Huzele (Huzelia) who agreed to leave, but the total who consented was a much lower number than had been anticipated. The people were to be transported by train to Khyriv, located in the L'viv oblast on the Soviet side, a distance of approximately 37 miles. When UPA attempted to occupy the village, which was approximately two miles from Lesko, they were repelled and pushed back on the 17th. Nevertheless, they destroyed the railroad station at Łukawica (Lukavytsia), cutting the tracks to Lesko.[422]

In addition to frightening and intimidating the people, more direct measures were taken as well. The village of Manasterzec (Manastyrets') in Lesko County, for example, was surrounded by troops. People were loaded into nine railroad cars and shipped to the deportation point, but the Soviet side refused to accept the deportees because their documents were not in order. A January 1946 OUN Beskid report described the deportation methods for this period and recorded that the forceful removal began in December. According to the report, Polish troops would typical-

---

421 Misylo, ed. *Aktsiia "Visla": Dokumenty*, 63, Footnote 1.
422 Misiło, *Repatriacja,* Vol. II, 20–21.

ly enter a village and tell people to clear out in a day or two and then return to escort them to the railroad station where the required documentation was completed. During this phase, the villages of Dąbrówka Ruska (Dubrivka Rus'ka), Storoze Wielke (Strozhi Velyky), Stroze Male (Storozhi Mali), and Zablotce (Zabolotsi) were almost completely deported while other villages were only partially deported. In exchange for permission to remain in their villages until spring, the people in Dąbrówka Ruska gave troops 70,000 zloty and Zablotce gave 17,000 zloty.[423] Nevertheless, both villages were deported the next day.[424]

The amount of resistance offered to the deportation varied by village. In general, people in more remote wooded areas with access to forests and greater partisan protection were less likely to leave. By January 20, the army's tactics had changed, and troops began operating in larger units of about 120 men, beating, killing, and robbing people. In Sanok County, three houses were burned in Płonna (Polonna) and the people were beaten. Likewise, people were beaten and robbed in the nearby villages of Mokre, Morochów (Morokhiv), Zboiska (Zbois'ka), Wola Sękowa (Volia Sen'kova), Wola Jaworowa (Volia Iavorova) and Tokarnia. In Tokarnia, the priest and the village mayor were severely beaten and forced to stand in the snow for several hours lightly clad. Robberies, beatings, and murders occurred in Belchova, Ratnawica (Ratnavytsia), and, of course, in Karlików and Zawadka Morochowska. The report notes that the Ukrainians were blaming UPA for not providing protection, leaving them no choice but to move,[425] and other villages responded by petitioning military and civilian officials. The mayors of five villages in Sanok County sent a letter to Marshal Rola-Żymierski protesting the deportations, noting, "Resettlement is voluntary, and those who wished to resettle had left the previous year. Moreover, Ukrainians are not colonists but have been living on their ancestral lands for generations."[426] Another petition followed from 12 villages in the Komańcza area in Sanok County addressed to the President of the Council of Ministers, which was subordinated to the Prime Minister of Poland. The authors stressed that local Ukrainians had served in the Polish Army in 1939 and

---

423 At the time, an American dollar sold for about 800 zloty on the black market.
424 Misiło, *Repatriacja,* Vol. II, 17
425 Ibid., 37–41.
426 Ibid., 46

from 1944 to 1945, and that some had even given their lives for Poland. The signatories were either former servicemen or family members who had lost their sons in the war. The petition further noted that resettlement was supposed to be voluntary and the removal of the population would result in economic losses for Poland. Still another petition from eight villages in Szczawne (Shchavne) area signed by war veterans and orphans demanded a halt to the forceful deportation. Despite these attempts, all of the petitions were ignored.[427]

In the western counties of the Lemko region, the deportations had also intensified. In the counties of Gorlice, Nowy Sącz and Nowy Targ, the underground presence was comparatively lighter, mainly consisting of a platoon size OUN unit and smaller SKV units. Consequently, those western units were unable to significantly impede the deportations, but severe fighting in the east and the destruction of railroad bridges did hinder the removal of people in those counties. On February 1, 1946, a conference was held in Gorlice to deal with the perennial problem of deported Lemkos who were illegally returning from the Soviet Union.[428] The conference concluded that adequate transportation should be provided and returning Lemkos should be quickly assembled, no later than February 10, at four locations: Rychwald/Owczary (Rykhvald), Rozdziele (Rozdill'ia), Bodnarka (Bodnarivka), and Gładyszów (Hladyshiv). The county police were permitted to establish additional deportation points if necessary. Nevertheless, the policy was applied to all Ukrainians and a deportation schedule was published for different sections of the county. All Lemkos were to be deported between March 1 and April 15, 1946, and it was specified that people were allowed to take livestock and two tons of goods.[429] In Nowy Sącz County, 6,000 people were readied for deportation as a result of the policy, although many of them claimed Polish nationality in attempts to avoid being removed. It is important to note that national relations were less strained in the western Lemko counties compared to places in the east since the size of the Ukrainian population was smaller and more importantly, nationalist sentiment was less widespread.

---

427 When the Red Army began conscripting young men in 1944, some joined the Polish Army. See Ibid., 45–49 and 52–53.

428 Ibid., 36–37.

429 Ibid., 50.

In Krosno County, a lengthy letter was written by several thoughtful Poles to Władysław Gomułka, a native of the town of Krosno, decrying the deportations of Ukrainians from the area. The letter notes that the region was being depopulated and had begun to resemble a huge cemetery. Economic activities were depressed, and Poles who were unaccustomed to the demanding life in the mountains were not likely to settle the land. Over two-thirds of the Lemkos had left "voluntarily," and the remainder wished to till the land as before and live in peace with Poles. The letter alleged that the real enemy was Polish reactionism, asserting that people should not be deported because of their nationality, language, or religion. It cautioned that if the young worker-peasant republic embraced racist views akin to those of Hitler and resorted to terror to drive out people who wished to remain, it would place a black spot on the history of the young republic.

> To place ourselves over someone, to attack him at night, to rob and imprison him because through generations he acclimated himself to the barren land and wishes to remain here, because he was our loyal brother giving his last suit to a Polish soldier escaping the Germans; during the partisan period his doors were always open to the Polish fighter, sharing with them his last piece of bread. To punish him severely for all of that would be an unheard of lawlessness.[430]

The letter concludes with a request for Gomułka to treat the remaining Lemkos humanely, to protect them from attacks, and to allow them to till the land in the spring to prevent hunger. Gomułka responded by writing to Władysław Wolski, the Vice Minister of Public Order, an agency responsible for Secret Polish, Intelligence and Counterespionage. Gomułka asked Wolski to order the State Department for Repatriation to cease the forcible deportations of Lemkos and to reach a similar understanding with the Ukrainian repatriation officials on the Soviet side. He further requested that General Władysław Korczyc issue appropriate instructions to the units in the area concerning the change of policy and similarly informed appropriate organs in the Rzeszów Province about the

---

430 Ibid., 77. At the time, Władysław Gomułka was Vice Minister and General Secretary of the Central Committee of the Polish Workers. A few references in the letter require clarification: first, as the Polish Army was disintegrating in 1939, some soldiers traded uniforms for civilian clothing and blended with the population. Second, during the war, there was a small leftist Lemko partisan group who worked with the pro-Moscow Polish partisans. A description of this group is provided in Horbal, *Lemko Studies*, 413–416.

change.[431] Although no response to Gomułka's requests has been found, his letter clearly had no effect since the deportations continued unabated. In any case, the decision had already been made in Moscow and Gomułka could not have changed it even if he had wished to do so.

At the beginning of 1946, warfare between the Ukrainian underground and the Polish army further intensified and continued throughout the summer until the deportations to the east had been concluded. A detailed enumeration of battles that occurred during the first half of 1946 is presented in Appendix II, which reveals the nature and intensity of the struggle that occurred during Operation Rzeszów. The appendix includes information on actual UPA engagements with Polish troops by Tactical Sector 26 during the time period of January–July 1946. Attempted ambushes by UPA and contacts with troops that did not result in actual combat (e.g., firing at each other at a distance) are excluded.

The year 1946 began with increased Polish attacks on Ukrainian villages in the southern counties of the Rzeszów Province. Based on a January 1946 report of Tactical Sector 26, 58 locales in four counties were affected; Brzozów (Boroziv)—six villages; Lesko (Lis'ko)—21, Przemyśl (Peremyshl')—6, and Sanok (Sianik)—24.[432] UPA placed Polish strength at about 10,000 men; in the Przemyśl area—3,000–3,600 troops and 240 police; to the south—5,200 troops, 283 police, 802 Border Guards and 169 men in small units guarding bridges, railroad and oil fields. The Poles were opposed by seven sotnias from the Peremyshl' and Lemko battalions as well as two independent sotnias sent from Ukraine, totaling approximately 1,400 men. The strength of each sotnia was not reported in the monthly report, and SB units had perhaps 60–70 men. Ren's reports, which cover an eight-month period, do not mention SKV units that were either participating in battles with sotnias or operating alone. The units provided some protection against Polish gangs, but were far too small to oppose the larger Polish units. Even if they were successful, it is likely that the troops would have returned in force and massa-

---

431 Ibid., 103–104.

432 An abbreviated version of the report is given in Misiło, *Repatriacja,* Vol. II, 28–31; and the full version is available in Potichnyj and Lyko, *Litopys UPA*, Vol. 33, 227–428. Ren's reports follow a slightly modified format compared to earlier descriptions. Operations of the UPA units in TS-26 are based on Ren's eight monthly reports dated between December 1945 and July 1946.

cred the village. Polish troops staged 13 attacks and the partisans staged 20, and UPA also responded to several attacks on Ukrainian villages.

UPA attacks on Polish villages fell into two categories: conducting reprisals for attacking neighboring Ukrainian villages and burning former Ukrainian villages resettled by deported Poles from the east. On January 1, 1946, Hromenko's sotnia of the Peremyshl' battalion attacked the Polish villages of Dylągowa and Sielnica for the second time due to reports that the residents were robbing and harassing neighboring Ukrainian villages. The two villages were burned completely with no casualties sustained on either side; however, 12 head of cattle and four horses were taken. The Polish residents fled west of San River and it is not clear whether or not they ever returned. On January 11, UPA burned three Polish villages whose residents were accused of terrorizing Ukrainians. Two villages, Lipowiec (Lipovets) and Królik Wołoski (Korolyk Vols'kyi) were formerly Ukrainian and were subsequently resettled by Polish deportees. A third village, Korolyk Pol's'kyi (Królik Polski) was a Polish village where 30 Ukrainian families had been expelled.[433] The underground frequently reported Polish civilian attacks on Ukrainian villages; however, similar Ukrainian civilian attacks on Polish villages were not reported either by the underground or by Polish sources. There was considerable animosity among neighboring Ukrainian and Polish villages and it is therefore likely that Ukrainians would have staged some attacks.

The town of Bircza (Bircha), located 50 miles west of Przemyśl, was attacked several times by UPA because it served as a staging area for raids on Ukrainian villages, which were followed by extensive deportations. Polish troops were also quartering in the abandoned Ukrainian villages and extending their control over the countryside. The Peremyshl' battalion, commanded by Konyk at the time and reinforced by a battalion from Ukraine commanded by Pavlo Vatsyk ("Prut"), attacked the town on October 22, 1945. Prut staged a surprise attack and captured the town, destroying 40 buildings, army barracks, a court building, a post office, and a jail where they freed the prisoners. Seven Polish soldiers were captured in the process, and it was reported that Polish losses included 150 dead and almost 200 wounded.[434] The size of the battalion was not reported nor is Prut mentioned again in the underground literature, since he

433 Potichnyj and Lyko, *Litopys UPA*, Vol. 33, 250.
434 Ibid., 701.

returned to Ukraine. During the same night, Konyk along with two sotnias drove Poles out of the abandoned Ukrainian villages, while the two remaining sotnias attacked villages in other areas. Troops returned to the town and during the night of November 29–30, Konyk, with his four sotnias, executed another attack on Bircza and its adjacent villages. The troops were driven out of villages and fled to the town, alerting the garrison, which was well prepared. When the sotnias approached the town from different directions supported by an 82mm mortar; the Poles repelled the attack. Casualties for that engagement were not reported. Konyk, still determined to capture Bircza, staged another attack on January 6, Ukrainian Christmas Eve, presumably because the Poles were not likely to expect an attack on a revered Christmas holiday in the Ukrainian church. The attack was scheduled for one o'clock a.m. on January 7, and the battalion was divided for a two-pronged attack: Burlaka and Lastivka were to strike from the east, and "Ors'kyi" (replacing the wounded Hromenko) and Krylach were to advance from the west. Konyk traveled with Ors'kyi. Konyk's group arrived an hour later than planned because of a long march over difficult snowy terrain, and therefore, a simultaneous attack from two directions did not take place. At the same time, there was an estimated 1,200 troops and police in town armed with mortars, light artillery. They had prepared trenches and bunkers, and the attacking partisan units were illuminated with searchlights. The attack was successfully repelled and Ren's monthly report placed Polish losses at about 70 killed with many wounded, and the UPA had 23 killed, including Konyk and Ors'kyi, and 22 were wounded, some severely.[435] It was an unusual UPA attack since the partisans normally had excellent intelligence and never attacked fortified towns, especially those that were defended by a large body of troops. The command of the battalion was immediately taken over by Baida, and it was less active for about two weeks following the unsuccessful attack as it regrouped. Later that month, it resumed its hit-and-run tactics and the destruction of bridges. During that time, a unit of Lastivka's sotnia destroyed three bridges, burning two of them, including a railroad bridge near Sanok that according to Polish engineers required a month to rebuild.[436] A week later, near Lesko, Burlaka destroyed a railroad station, a warehouse, some build-

---

435 Ibid., 254.
436 Ibid., 263

ings, and a 36-car train loaded with wood. His sotnia dynamited tracks at the station in three places, causing traffic on the line to be halted for several weeks.[437]

While Konyk chose to attack troops in towns, putting them on the defensive to reduce raids on villages and impede the deportation process, Ren's Lemko battalion in the south concentrated on destroying transportation and communication lines. The battalion launched swift attacks, usually in the middle of the night, and conducted ambushes to achieve the same objectives. On January 6, the Didyk and Khrin sotnias burned the former Ukrainian villages of Dezhno (Doshno) and Woltuszowa (Voltushova), which by then had been resettled by deported Poles who were, according to an UPA report, "...harassing neighboring Ukrainian villages."[438]

Throughout the campaign, the underground burned abandoned Ukrainian villages to prevent resettlement by hostile Poles from the east who would have created difficulties for them, and thus their movements were observed and reported. In addition to rational considerations, there was a vengeful, emotional side to partisan activities. UPA units sought to prevent the neighboring Poles from carting useful materials from abandoned villages so as to prevent them from benefitting from the Ukrainian tragedy, stating that "Only ashes would be left where Ukrainians had once lived."

On January 10, Myron, the commander of an independent sotnia, unsuccessfully attempted to take the police station in Cisna (Tisna), but returned a few days later and destroyed the station.[439] Bir's sotnia demolished a bridge near Baligród and destroyed three miles of telephone line. A week later, they burned five wooden bridges in the same area using straw and kerosene, and destroyed another telephone line.[440] Myron divided his sotnia and with a characteristic burst of activity, burned 35 bridges in the Lesko-Baligród area between January 21 and 28 in a hilly territory where there were many small wooden bridges that spanned numerous creeks. The month ended with a large-scale Polish attack on Didyk's camp near the Czechoslovakian border. The previous autumn,

---

437 Ibid., 258
438 Ibid., 248
439 Ibid., 263
440 Ibid., 255

the sotnia had moved from the Baligród area and built underground bunkers in the forest between the villages of Przybyszów (Prybyshiv) and Wislok Wielki, an unusual arrangement since most sotnias did not keep permanent camps. Elements of the three Polish regiments, the 34th, 46th and the 37th, totaled about 1,000 men. They moved on the camp from several directions. Some were transported by trucks and supported by mortars and artillery stationed in Karlików. Several days prior to the attack, Didyk's sotnia left for the town of Rymanów (Rymaniv) where 350 troops were garrisoned and rendezvoused with Khrin's unit in the village of Puławy (Pulavy). The units stayed in the village for two days awaiting intelligence reports on the situation in the town when a courier finally arrived from Ren with orders not to attack. As the sotnia was returning to the bivouacs, an attack was underway on their camp. Inside the camp was a squad including some cooks, a doctor, and four medics. When the shooting started, the squad leader, codenamed "Oslavytsia," ordered everyone to abandon the camp and head for another complex of forests. Their march brought them in contact with a Polish skirmish line that was advancing on the forest. Employing a typical UPA tactic, the squad permitted the line to advance very close and then opened fire. The line broke and the squad escaped with only Oslavytsia wounded. Two partisans on the lookout separated from the others and hid in tall fir trees where they observed the destruction of their camp. Ren reported that the Polish troops had captured a German anti-tank weapon along with 1,600 rounds of rifle ammunition. The Polish side had one machine gunner killed and several soldiers were wounded. In addition, he reported that many supplies had also been captured, including 450 pounds of potatoes, 66 pounds of meat; 100 pounds of beans, salt, kitchen utensils, and underclothing.[441] As the troops positioned for an attack, many people from neighboring villages, especially Przybyszów, fled to the forest with their livestock and some were killed during the shelling. A Polish source described the attack as a success, claiming that 23 partisans had been killed, two were captured, and 20 huts were destroyed.[442]

In February, a high level of activity continued on both sides, and the two partisan battalions engaged in 21 operations. UPA destroyed more bridges, staged attacks and ambushes on troops, and conducted meetings

441 Ibid., 250.
442 Szcześniak and Szota, *Droga*, 391.

with villagers, urging them not to leave.[443] Myron's sotnia burned 15 bridges in the Lesko-Baligród area and destroyed a telephone line. "Brodych" (Roman Hrobelsky), replacing an ill Karmeliuk, burned a bridge, cut a telephone line, staged an attack on a police station, and blew up a railroad bridge. Khrin's sotnia burned the abandoned village of Stroze (Storozhi) and attacked a 20-man unit they caught taking hay from abandoned houses in Zahutyń, killing two people and capturing 10 horses in the process. The Poles responded, but the 150-men relief unit was ambushed and suffered severe casualties: 24 killed, 35 wounded, and six captured. Khrin then destroyed a railroad station in Mokre and drove out 30 defenders, killing two and capturing weapons and ammunition. The following day, the sotnia ambushed 100 soldiers near Bukowsko, killing four and capturing seven, including Lt. Bronisław Kuzma, a Soviet officer born in Stalingrad. Kuzma was the company commander in the 34th regiment that had committed atrocities in Karlików and Zawadka Morochowska, activities in which he had personally participated. To the north, Lastivka's sotnia ambushed troops, killing 20 and wounding 6, but also suffered losses. The Polish units then resumed with raiding more villages, especially during the night, usually entering from the direction of the woods to cut off any possibilities of escape. Using Bircza as a base, the troops made forays into about a dozen villages, arresting men and even posing as UPA partisans. An UPA deserter who traveled with the troops aided their efforts by identifying partisan haunts.

In the south, the fighting intensified. The 8th division, headquartered in Krosno, sent two infantry regiments and an artillery regiment to Sanok and Lesko Counties. The regiments formed maneuvering units comprised of approximately 150–300 men and engaged largely in attacking Ukrainian villages. The troops also engaged in repairing destroyed bridges and a telephone line in the Baligród area. Ren's monthly report notes that the status of the two battalions had not changed: clothing, weapons, ammunition, and food were judged to be satisfactory and the healthcare situation had also improved. As in his previous report, every sotnia was engaging in military and political training and delivering political lectures to the population. People were instructed on methods of

443 The description is based on an abbreviated February report in Misiło, *Repatriacja,* Vol. II, 54–55 and in Ren's report provided in Potichnyj and Lyko, *Litopys UPA*, Vol. 33, 273–289.

concealment, strategies to avoid deportation, international relations, UPA's mission, etc. At the end of the report, the commander noted a lack of suitable reading material for the men, particularly materials pertaining to the struggle for Ukrainian independence that had occurred between 1917–1921.

During the first months of 1946, the fighting was concentrated in the south, but clashes and deportations occurred in the north as well. In Zalizniak's battalion, sotnia commander Shum reported a Polish attack on the village of Lubliniec (Liublynets). Many residents had fled, but some had been captured, a few were shot, and some others were arrested. During that time, Polish troops were not very active in TS-27. In March, however, hostilities increased, with Polish strength estimated at 3,220. Most operations were small and battalion units were occasionally reinforced by SKV units. UPA placed its own losses at 100 killed, 45 wounded, and one captured. Enemy casualties were reported as 1,027 killed and 720 wounded.[444] Polish losses reported by TS-27 were much larger compared to other sectors and in some cases clearly improbable. Warfare increased in TS-28 as well during the first few months of the year, but the available information for that sector is less complete. At the end of February, the partisans were attacked in the forest by a large NKVD unit and had 30 men killed.[445] Based on reports from the local population, Soviet losses ranged from 50 to 143,[446] and for the period of the insurgency, reports of Soviet forces operating in the Lublin Province are more frequent than for other areas in the Transcurzon. A March 1, 1946 OUN Region III report from the Chełm area notes that during the 1946 census, many Ukrainians declared themselves as Poles to avoid deportation while others, on the advice of Polish priests, had converted to Roman Catholicism.[447] In at least one case, Ukrainian partisans beat a new convert and burned his house. The report further noted that the people were not defending themselves vigorously, claiming it was useless to fight the Soviets

On March 9, 1946, Shum's sotnia, reinforced by a platoon from Chaus' sotnia and a local SKV unit (197 men in total), destroyed a bridge

---

444 Potichnyj, *Litopys UPA*, Vol. 40, 84.

445 *Narodnyy Komitet Vnutrenykh Del*: National Committee for Internal Affairs

446 Potichnyj, *Litopys UPA*, Vol. 39, 170.

447 Misiło, *Repatriacja,* Vol. II, 60

and attacked a railroad station in Lubycz (Liubych). They destroyed railroad cars, buildings, office equipment, telephones, and killed seven individuals including members of the exchange commission. Ukrainians who had been awaiting deportation at the station went home.[448] A TS-28 report notes heavy fighting with Soviet forces. On March 25, the 6th Division's 14th regiment arrived in Lubaczów from Cracow and the following day the regimental commander, Lt. Colonel Szeliga, organized a conference with local officials and a Soviet representative. The discussion centered on expeditions to Ułazów (Ulaziv) since the residents there had agreed to leave the previous autumn. They decided that if they encountered difficulties, the deportations would shift to deporting people in Lubaczów along with its adjacent villages.

In March 1946, clashes increased in TS-26. During that month, the partisans had 32 engagements, more than they had in any other month, with transportation and communication lines being the major targets in their attempts to impede the deportations.[449] At the beginning of March, Lastivka's sotnia destroyed three wooden bridges in the Przemyśl region, and a few days later, one of his platoons ambushed Polish troops, killing three of them. On March 3, Polish troops attacked the village of Turzańsk (Turyns'ke) in the Lemko region and burned 10 houses before they were driven out by a platoon from Didyk's sotnia. A more serious engagement took place on March 9th near the village of Wola Matiaszowa (Volia Matiyashova) in Lesko County, where Bir and Brodych attacked a Polish unit of about 300 men. According to Polish statements, 18 soldiers were killed and the number of wounded was not reported. UPA had one killed and one missing in action. A few days later, Khrin's sotnia destroyed two bridges near Bukowsko, destroyed approximately three miles of telephone line, and cut telephone poles. Around the same time, the sotnia destroyed three railroad bridges, tore up almost a mile of track, and threw the rails into the Osława River. On March 11, in the Przemyśl area, Lastivka's sotnia ambushed a Polish unit and captured two officers who were carrying valuable classified documents. The following day, his sotnia collaborated with Burlaka's in destroying some nearby oil wells.

---

448 Misiło, *Repatriacja,* Vol. II, 61–62

449 Description for March is based on the information in Misiło, *Repatriacja,* Vol. II, 84–87 and Potichnyj and Lyko, Vol. 33, 290–318.

In addition to focusing on the destruction of transportation and communication lines, UPA began staging ambushes on roads used by Polish troops. In one incident in March, Myron and Lastivka ambushed a wagon carrying six soldiers, killing one and capturing five. Later in the month, Myron destroyed seven bridges and set up an ambush killing a Polish lieutenant. Didyk's sotnia was also quite active during March. On the 15th, he ambushed a unit of Polish troops at night, although their losses could not be determined due to darkness. He also destroyed a bridge over the Osława as well as a sawmill, since UPA had begun targeting sawmills to deny troops the necessary materials for rebuilding wooden bridges.

On March 19, the population exchange commission arrived in Mokre and Morochów, protected by 160 soldiers and two armored trains. Polish troops began rounding up Ukrainian civilians for deportation. Didyk, supported by two small OUN units, attacked the troops at midnight. Polish losses were estimated at five killed and many wounded, and the underground had one killed and four wounded. On March 20, Didyk, Khrin, and Myron attacked a large group of Border Guards in Jasiel (Iasel'), killing 24, wounding six, and capturing 79. The partisans had two wounded, but managed to capture many weapons, ammunition, and supplies. UPA reported that the unit killed nine people in Polany Surowiczne (Poliany Surovychni) and five in Wisłok Dolny (Vyslok Dolishnyi) and burned 32 houses. Polish historian Grzegorz Motyka writes that about 20 soldiers were released and remainder were apparently executed.[450] A few days later, Didyk struck the railroad station in Komańcza destroying 40 cars, buildings, and a bridge, although the Poles escaped with an engine car with two wagons and fled to Łupków (Lupkiv) located on the Slovak border. A few days later, he attacked the station in Łupków, which was protected by border Guards, and destroyed the station and barracks. Although Polish losses could not be estimated, UPA had six wounded. Khrin, reinforced by Myron, attacked the town of Bukowsko. The town was a staging point for Polish troops, and a Polish gang in the town was robbing Ukrainian villages. Two days later, he attacked troops near Szczawne killing 31, wounding 40 and capturing nine, without any losses. On the 30th, Bir, Khrin, and Myron attacked troops

---

450 See Potichnyj and Lyko, *Litopys UPA*, Vol. 33, 294–295. Comparable Polish losses are reported in Motyka, *Tak Bylo,* 313.

in Średnie Wielkie (Serednie Velyky) where Polish troops were engaged in deporting Ukrainians. The Poles had 106 killed, 15 wounded, and eight captured. Burlaka and Hromenko, on the last day of the month, burned abandoned villages in the Przemyśl area. In his monthly report, Ren noted that clothing in the two battalions was unsatisfactory, armaments were adequate, and there was an ongoing shortage of medical supplies and trained personnel. He further noted that to alleviate the shortage, 26 partisans received medical training and 24 had satisfactorily completed the training. During that month, 18 men received medical treatment for wounds, two returned to their units, and the rest were still hospitalized. Additionally, 10 riflemen received treatment for illnesses that were not combat-related, five were discharged, and the rest were still receiving care. He also noted that a deserter from Bir's sotnia had been caught and received a death sentence, which had been commuted to six months of rehabilitation, although the nature of the rehabilitation was not specified.

Due to the heavy fighting, military training had virtually ceased and political discussions were heavily curtailed. The talks were confined to the partisans and centered on the life and works of Ukrainian poet Taras Shevchenko, born March 9, 1814, whose personal struggle and triumph served as inspiration for the underground.[451] The lectures emphasized Shevchenko's achievements in the face of extreme difficulties and implied that the underground could achieve similar victory, if there existed the will to persevere.

After three months of heavy fighting, the Polish government fell short of achieving its goal: less than 23,000 Ukrainians had been deported; including 4,000 from the Lublin Province, almost 19,000 from Rzeszów, none from Cracow, and 177 from other parts of Poland. Their failure was mostly due to ineffective tactics, since the army vastly outnumbered the partisans. According to a Polish source, the UPA was stronger than ever and had forced the army on the defensive.[452] The army initiated few offensive operations other than raiding villages, but re-

451 Shevchenko, an orphaned serf, became a spokesman for his people through his poetry. He is still revered by Ukrainians of all political persuasions.

452 The description of the Polish operations and tactics is based on the accounts in Szcześniak and Szota *Droga*, 388–390. The authors had access to the Polish army archives.

sponded mostly to UPA attacks, an ineffective tactic since the partisans had usually disappeared long before the troops arrived. Operations against suspected UPA locations usually entailed positioning troops in strategic locations near forests, and the artillery commenced firing at designated times. Troops typically formed a skirmish line and advanced into the forest. Their light artillery fire was ineffective against the partisans' small units, which were on the move in the expansive forested areas. Skirmish lines were typically very thin—the distance between soldiers ranged from only a few meters to dozens of meters. If encircled partisans were unable to escape before the ring closed, they usually positioned themselves in a ravine or in a wooded area leading out of the forest, allowed the skirmish line to advance very close and then opened fire, and then breached the line to make their escape. In some cases, they even turned around and attacked the line from the rear.

In addition to sweeps on suspected areas, the army tried other tactics as well. The 36th regiment broke out into seven companies in order to sweep through the countryside in search of partisans. These units operated independently of each other, but had difficulty locating the partisans. Other companies set up ambushes along roads used by UPA, were equally unsuccessful, and many officers did not believe in ambushes. Because the civilians were fearful of being deported (and men feared being shot), they typically fled to the woods at the approach of the Polish troops, thereby inadvertently alerting the partisans. In addition to their lack of success on the offensive, the army also underestimated its opponent and failed to provide adequate defense for its garrisons, resulting in attacks on the 8th, 28th, and 30th regiments. The situation moved the commander of the 3rd division to comment on the defense of the 30th regiment:

> The defense of the regiment existed only on map and paper. In reality, there was no defense. Fire points at the garrison were not maintained. Ability to patrol neighboring villages was inadequate. There was no communication among battalions during the attack.[453]

Over the next few months, the deportation efforts intensified as the Polish army began preparing to meet the deadline. Colonel Rutkowski sent a report to the Army Chief of Staff, General Korczyc, concerning in-

---

453 Szcześniak and Szota, *Droga,* 390.

structions for the 8th and 9th divisions.[454] The March 2 meeting with senior officers was conducted by General Adam Daszkiewicz, Chief of Staff of the Fifth Military District (Cracow), at the 8th Division's headquarters. Regimental commanders and commanders of independent units were assigned specific operational areas and given oral instructions on fighting the partisans and deporting the Ukrainians. Daskiewicz ordered the establishment of a curfew and issued rules for maintaining order with Ukrainian civilians, which included shooting them if they failed to comply. All Ukrainian males were to be considered partisans and a few were to be shot in public in order to terrorize the population and deter resistance. Some officers objected to the draconian order, claiming that all Ukrainians did not support the underground, but their objections were ignored. Among the objecting officers was Lt. Colonel Julius Hübner, commander of the 32nd regiment, 8th Division, who related his objections to a Capt. Kniaziew. The order, in his view, would drive Ukrainians into the arms of the underground and worsen relations with the Soviet Union. Hübner claimed that he had been instructed to kill between 50–70 civilians or burn a village for every 1–5 soldiers killed, but stated that he had not implemented the policy. Instead, he proposed that the Ukrainians should be removed quickly and their villages burned, forcing UPA to live in the forest. Hübner's proposal was rejected, his regiment was accused of failing to execute assignments, and Colonel Berezowski was given some type of supervisory role over the regiment. Hübner complained about the order to the Cracow District and was later transferred. In the margins of the report, Korczyc requested that General Stefan Mossor, Deputy Chief of Staff, investigate the matter. Mossor replied that Daszkiewicz had been personally advised to conduct a vigorous campaign, but had done so within the limits of the law. He deemed Rutkowski's report as having been grossly exaggerated.

Mossor's comments followed a pattern that had been well-established by that time. When complaints of atrocities were lodged with the army, the investigating officer would dismiss the allegations as distorted or exaggerated. It should be noted that many Soviet officers in the Polish Army were of Polish extraction born in eastern Belarus or central Ukraine and were typically more brutal than officers raised in Poland.

---

454 Misiło, *Repatriacja,* Vol. II, 93–95.

Regardless of what Daszkiewicz actually said, the type of policy he advocated had been followed since the beginning of the deportations, although until this point, it had not been systematic. Civilian males were routinely shot and then reported as partisans, a practice that reached ludicrous proportions at times since the reported UPA losses were higher than the partisans' actual numbers. The Polish intelligence service had a reasonably accurate estimate of the total UPA strength and the high command must have been aware of the exaggerated partisan casualties, and therefore, the atrocities being committed against Ukrainian civilians. The army was required to remove Ukrainians who were adamantly opposed to the deportations and so they relied on terror tactics, while the political leadership continued to insist that the exchanges were voluntary.

The actual losses of the two combatants are difficult to determine—Polish figures of the UPA losses are unreliable since civilians were included in their estimates, and their own losses have not been fully published thus far. The UPA reports appear to give fairly accurate figures for their own losses, but Polish casualties were usually estimated and clearly overstated in many cases. Polish losses were based on UPA estimates by commanders in the battle who, in most cases, could not accurately count the enemy's dead, and estimates were also based on secondhand reports by Ukrainian civilians.

With respect to the actual deportations, another meeting was held in Przemyśl to devise a plan for the city and the county. Identification papers were to be verified, people subject to deportation would be required to register for removal, and those who refused to leave would be removed by force within a period of three days. The 6th Infantry Division was expected to arrive from Cracow to conduct deportations in the county. A more comprehensive plan was developed by the security committee in Rzeszów for April, May, and June, and was signed by General Daszkiewicz.[455] The plan designated an area of operation for five regiments, all of the 9th Division, and an independent 14th regiment; the regiments were required to remove all of the Ukrainians and to clear the area of partisans. The 14th and 30th regiments were assigned to Lubaczów County. The 26th regiment operated in Jarosław County east of the San River with the 40th regiment operating in the same county, but assigned

455 Ibid., 99–100.

to the west of the river. The 28th Regiment and the 6th Division were responsible for the Przemyśl area. Troops were ordered to accomplish their assignments in April and May by removing the population from the border region and along the transportation routes. All forms of transportation, including railroads, trucks, wagons and carts, were to be utilized and villagers were to be removed within two to three days. Colonel Witold Popko, commander of the 9th Division, wrote to Daszkiewicz in Russian, relaying that the 26th, 30th, and 14th regiments were deporting people in Jarosław and Lubaczów counties, while the 28th Regiment was removing Ukrainians from the city of Przemyśl with the aid of police. Comparable information for the 8th division's operations in the Carpathians has not been found, but on April 26, General Mossor issued a deportation schedule, in Russian, for counties in the three provinces inhabited by Ukrainians.[456] Commanders were required to submit their comments on the plan to the General Staff by May 1st.

The Final Drive to the East

In the spring, as the deportations intensified, the residents of many villages fled to the forest since the snow had mostly melted and the partisan attacks had increased. Due to their tightening schedule and the recalcitrant population, Polish troops dispensed with the formality of forcing people to sign voluntary resettlement forms, and simply proceeded with driving people to the deportation points. A local official in Lubaczów who was supervising the removal wrote to Bednarz concerning the violation of the rules and asked for his advice. The letter notes that Colonel Berezowski, another Soviet officer of Polish extraction, ordered troops in the Lubaczów area to drive all Ukrainians, including mixed families, to the railroad stations for immediate deportation.[457] The colonel would determine who was eligible to leave regardless of the documents issued by other government agencies. The official wrote that by deporting mixed families, a practice that was prohibited by the population exchange agreement, there would be Poles among the people sent to the Soviet Union. The outcome of the disagreement is not indicated, but there were

---

456 Ibid., 106
457 Ibid., 109.

complaints of false documents obtained by Ukrainians and the fact that the colonel had decided to take the matter into his own hands.

In addition to conducting forcible removals, the Polish Army modified its tactics by operating in larger numbers, setting up ambushes along partisan routes, entering forests, and occupying villages until all the people were expelled. In one operation, troops ambushed a squad from Lastivka's sotnia, killing nine and capturing two. The pace of the deportations escalated throughout April. Thirteen villages in the TS-26 area alone were deported during the period of April 23–25. (It was a rare occasion that troops would manage to deport an entire village, since there were usually at least a few families who remained by fleeing to the neighboring villages or the forest.) The Polish Army also increased its sweeps for partisans, including the forests where UPA was known to be hiding. Further south, about 2,000 troops swept through the forest in the Komańcza area destroying two bunkers and killing a wounded partisan, and the Polish side had one killed and five wounded.[458] Two battalions swept through the forest around Bukowsko and entered Tokarnia, killing several civilian men.

In April, Bir, Karmeliuk, and Myron, whose sotnias operated in Baligród-Lesko area, were ordered to enter Slovakia and disseminate information about UPA and the Ukrainian struggle for independence with the hope that the western press would report the UPA's incursions. Detaching three sotnias for propaganda missions to Czechoslovakia during the height of the deportation was unusual; it is therefore likely that the OUN leadership in Munich ordered the missions to strengthen their hand in dealing with the American and British intelligence services. OUN strove to inform the West about the Ukrainian insurgency both in the Soviet Union and in Poland. Each unit spent about two weeks in northeast Slovakia and covered wide swaths of territory on the Polish-Czechoslovakian border, where much of the territory was settled by a southern branch of Lemkos who considered themselves to be either Ruthenians or Ukrainians.

Information about UPA and its program was spread orally and through literature. Bir took 485 leaflets with him—most were printed in Slovak although a few were in Ukrainian—and distributed them among

---

458 Description is based on Ren's April report in Ibid., 110–14 and Potichnyj and Lyko, *Litopys UPA*, Vol. 33, 319–336.

the population, organizations, military units, and police. The goodwill mission required the partisans to be on their best behavior, but the need for food provisions presented a delicate problem. The men could not take two weeks of provisions along with them and had to rely on the local population without resorting to force. Partisans from the previous raid advised others not to ask for food directly, but to simply talk to the people and they would offer food.

In an earlier foray in Czechoslovakia, which had occurred in September of 1945, an incident with Myron's unit had left a bad impression on the local population. To preclude a similar occurrence in 1946, he excluded some partisans who were inclined to misbehave, although Bir and Karmeliuk did not report similar selections. Sotnias avoided hostile contact with local police and troops and were aided by local agents who apprised them of the troop movement and helped to distribute literature. In his reports, Myron did not indicate that any fights had occurred, although Bir reported an ambush without giving details, and also noted that three men had separated from the rest and had not rejoined the unit. Slovak forces showed little inclination to pursue the partisans, but the Czech units were more aggressive and it was therefore important to avoid them. Myron stayed for Ukrainian Easter in Slovakia, attending a church service in a Ruthenian village. His men joined the parishioners in singing the traditional Easter song "Christ Is Risen," and after the service, they were invited for the traditional Easter breakfast with 2–3 UPA men in each house. After returning home, both commanders along with the political instructor in Bir's sotnia wrote detailed reports and emphasized that more literature should be taken in the future.[459] In general, the mission was considered a success. The partisans had made a positive impression on the local population, and were praised for their exemplary behavior.

In April, UPA increased their attacks on the transportation network in Poland, on Polish troops, and on villages and towns suspected of raiding Ukrainian villages or serving as staging points for troops.[460] In retaliation for the destruction of Ukrainian villages, Didyk burned two Polish villages: Nadolany (Nadoliany) and Nowotaniec (Novotanets). Khrin burned Bukowsko, having warned the town at the end of March to cease

459 Ibid., 592v627.

460 Information for the 26th Sector is based on Ren's report for April, in Potichnyj and Lyko, *Litopys UPA,* Vol. 33, 319–336.

robbing Ukrainians. His sotnia reportedly destroyed some 500 buildings and took 15 horses and 25 cows. Soon afterward, he attacked the Polish villages of Czaszyn and Tarnawa for carting Ukrainians to the deportation points, destroying all wagons in the lower part of Czaszyn and 150 wagons in Tarnawa. Burlaka and Lastivka ambushed troops near Bircza, killing 32 soldiers and wounding 10. A platoon of Didyk's sotnia attacked troops in Mikow (Mykiv), where they reportedly killed about 25 and had 9 men killed and two wounded and destroyed a railroad bridge between Łupków and Komańcza. Didyk was relieved of his command on April 22, reportedly for health reasons. His real name was not reported in the underground literature, although he is described as an older man who had served as an officer in the Austrian Army. He walked with a cane but reportedly had no difficulty keeping up with the younger men. He perished during an attempt to reach the West in 1947. Brodych took command of Didyk's sotnia, as earlier he had commanded Karmeliuk's sotnia during the latter's prolonged illness.

In April of 1946, heavy fighting continued in TS-27 and to a lesser extent in TS-28, and bridges and railroad stations were designated as UPA's primary targets. An unspecified sotnia from the Zalizniak battalion attacked a railroad station in Uhnow (Uhniv) destroying train cars, killing 30 soldiers, and capturing heavy weapons, and the Ukrainians at the station fled. The Jarosław-Rava Rus'ka Line was cut, an engine and three boxcars were destroyed, and numerous railroad and road bridges were blown up. UPA placed enemy strength in TS-27 at about 4,000; half of those were army troops, special Soviet units were estimated at 500, and the remainder consisted of Border Guards, Internal Troops, and police. At that point, Ukrainian villages were under increasing attacks; some were terroristic in nature designed to frighten people enough to leave, and in other raids, civilians were simply driven to deportation points. Besides attacks by the government forces, some Polish partisans continued to attack villages. On May 28, Volyniak's group, supplemented by local Polish civilians attacked the village of Dobcza (Dibcha), killing 18 people and burning 45 houses before being driven off by the UPA.[461] Despite the UPA attacks, the deportation accelerated in the spring and some local officials issued false documents to Ukrainians identifying

461 Potichnyj, *Litopys UPA*, Vol. 40, 377.

them as Poles. The head of Jarosław County advised village mayors to urge Ukrainians to declare themselves Poles in order to obtain the necessary documents.

To the north, TS-28 also experienced numerous fights with both Polish and Soviet units. Two sotnias attacked an NKVD barrack in Hrubieszów, and on May 28th, the building was damaged with rockets although enemy losses could not be estimated. Later in the month, two police stations were destroyed in the town of Warez; Polish losses were placed at 45 killed, and the partisans reported only two wounded. The population was constantly harassed by troops and Polish civilian gangs, and the thinly stretched UPA forces in the area were unable to provide much protection. Most engagements were not large-scale, although there were exceptions—a partisan unit of 65 men ambushed a truck convoy killing 43 soldiers and destroying 19 trucks. In another attack, three bridges were destroyed near Hrubieszów. The UPA losses reported minimal losses in the various fights, but in an attack on a bunker, the partisans reported that 10 of their own had been killed and 2 were captured.[462]

On May 10, 1946, the State Security Commission met in Warsaw to discuss security matters and make plans for the deportations. The meeting was attended by Marshal Rola-Żymierski, Minister of Public Security, along with Radkiewicz and some senior army officers. The report of the discussion noted that there were still 31,182 Ukrainians who had to be removed before the deadline.[463] The Polish-Ukrainian Population Commission worked out the removal details and the army was ordered to secure the roads and railroad lines in order to prevent attacks by hostile bands. Governor W. Rozga from the Lublin Province issued yet another appeal to Ukrainians urging them to leave, writing that the people should not listen to the propaganda of the "fascist band" about the difficulties of life in Ukraine. Pleading that both peoples needed peace and the population exchange was necessary to achieve the peace, he wrote, "Go to your Fatherland –Ukraine."[464] The Ukrainians ignored Rozga's letter and similar appeals, since most believed that they already lived in their Fatherland. Furthermore, the information concerning the difficulties in Ukraine were widespread by that point, having been communicated not only by

462 Potichnyj, *Litopys UPA*, Vol. 39, 175–177.
463 Misiło, *Repatriacja,* Vol. II, 133–135.
464 Ibid., 178–179.

the underground but also by deportees who had returned after having been resettled there.

Since Polish appeals for voluntary resettlement had proven ineffective, the Polish government had to resort to force to meet the deadline. A Polish deportation commission official from Tomaszów County wrote a letter dated May 22 in which he noted that the population in the county had been removed by May 10. The letter stated that troops were guarding the Belz-Rava Rus'ka railroad line that would be transporting the Ukrainians and further noted that troops had stripped the metal roofs from several buildings and carted them to an undisclosed location.[465] On May 22, soldiers had rounded up people in two villages, Kniazie (Kniazi) and Wereszyca (Vereshchytsya), without bothering to ascertain their nationality. During the roundup, the people were robbed of cattle, horses, sewing machines and other belongings. Eventually, some were permitted to return, presumably Poles and mixed families. The writer noted that reports of similar incidents had been received, but not on the same scale.

In the Sanok area, where heavy fighting continued throughout May, the underground resistance threatened to disrupt the government's deportation plans for the county. In order to handle the situation, General Korczyc issued a top-secret report to General Rotkiewicz, head of Operation Rzeszów, instructing him to introduce a "wartime method" in the county. "The method should be introduced as necessary, not publicized, and can be rescinded only by the government..."[466] It is not clear what the method entailed or why it was necessary to keep it a secret. The contention between the civilian and the military authorities usually centered on the army failing to obtain an agreement to leave before removing people from a village. The general presumably wanted to dispense with the formality and simply bring the people to the deportation points. Another letter from the Ministry of Defense instructed the troops not to deport oil workers from Sanok and Lesko counties. Those counties were covered by the 8th Division and the high command was not satisfied with the performance of the division. Rotkiewicz notified the division commander, Colonel Stanisław Hrabowski, that he was not meeting his quota; instead of deporting 500 families daily he had deported somewhere between 250–270 families. He also noted that the deportation data had been falsi-

465 Ibid., 147–148

466 Ibid., 144.

fied, singling out the reports of Divisional Chief of Staff, Lt. Colonel Roszkowski, who had reported that 1,000 families were awaiting deportation at the station in Łukawica (Lukavytsia), and 200 in Rymanów. In reality, there were 200 families in Łukawica and 40 in Rymanów, and the number of railroad cars that had departed for the Soviet Union had also been exaggerated. Hrabowski was ordered to meet the quota, to ensure accurate reporting, and to confine Roszkowski to three days of house arrest.[467] The reasons for the eighth division's poor performance cannot necessarily be attributed to incompetence—operating in the Carpathians posed a number of additional challenges that were not present in other sectors. The mountainous terrain was covered with large forests—not only was this ideal for the UPA units that were active in the region, but the forests also provided excellent hiding places for civilians who wished to avoid deportation. Ren's May report for TS-26 noted that the army had adjusted its tactics to expedite the deportations. Troops who were garrisoned in towns began raiding villages at night, advancing from the direction of the forest to cut off escape routes. Anyone who was captured was typically beaten and robbed.

As the deportation deadline grew closer, the Polish government began to take more aggressive steps toward removing Ukrainians from the western counties of the Lemko region. To that end, a conference was organized on May 7 in Cracow to plan the deportations in two counties, Nowy Targ and Nowy Sącz, which were administratively subordinated to the province. Attendance at the conference included the commissioners of the two counties, local officials, a Soviet representative, and Colonel Michał Chilinski, a former Soviet officer of Polish extraction.[468] Skibinski, Nowy Targ's commissioner, reported that 112 deportees had returned from Ukraine, and in addition, there were 49 demobilized Red Army men, and 38 people returned from work in Germany. At the time, the Ukrainian underground presence in this area was minimal, consisting of some village self-defense units and small OUN groups. Josef Labuz, the Head of Nowy Sącz County, noted that 17,753 people had been removed, 7,652 still remain in the county, and 2,200 had been designated for deportation. He noted that people were evading deportation and stated that force and motorized transport were required since "using 100 wagons

467 Ibid., 148–149.
468 Ibid., 129–132.

daily panics the population" and finally, he recommended that the deportations should be concluded by May 20. Józef Lib, the head of the political department in the province, reminded the conference participants that the use of force was forbidden by the population exchange agreement between the two countries. County commissioners then asked for lengthening the deportation period, but Colonel Chilinski countered that the current instructions called for the removal to be completed by the 20th. The conference was moved to the office of the governor who stated that in consultation with the Ministry of Public Security, people who claimed to be Poles and were loyal to the state should be allowed to remain. Colonel Chilinski agreed with the decision, asked for a list of people subject to removal, and promised to provide trucks for the Nowy Targ deportations. The conference concluded that people in the county should be deported between May 13–15, and May 17–25 in Nowy Sącz. Meeting the deportation deadlines proved to be more difficult than what had been anticipated at the conference. Writing to the political department in Cracow, Skibinski stated that the Lemkos who had returned and those who had served in the Red Army were to be deported by force in the Szczawnica (Shchavnytsia) gmina. Of the 376 individuals subject to removal, some went to the newly acquired territory in the west, while others had fled to the forest. The authorities were able to send 43 persons to the Nowy Sącz station, but the Soviet Commission accepted only seven and released the rest.[469]

At another conference on May 26, officials discussed the difficulties associated with removing people from the two counties.[470] Captain Sokolowski, a representative of the Cracow Military District, claimed that some local officials had been bribed to interfere with the army's removal effort. The Army brought 1,040 people to the station; of those, the police released 15 families and more were released at the station due to the lack of food or fodder for the livestock. The chairman of the County People's Council, Antoniszczak, noted that 4,600 hectors of land had not been sown, and what had been sown would not be harvested because of deportation.[471] Captain Wlodzimierz Wec, another participant, noted that the population's mood toward the resettlement had changed, and people

---

469 Ibid., 163.
470 Ibid., 156–162.
471 Ibid., 159.

were avoiding deportation and fleeing to the mountains after they had been warned by returning Lemkos who described the difficult life on collective farms. In the Szczawnica Gmina, approximately 50 percent of the population had fled to the forests. According to official statistics, over 20,000 people had been deported between April 1945 and May 1946, and by June 1, 1946, 5,436 still remained.[472] Further east, the methods of deportation in Gorlice County in the Rzeszów Province were described by inspector Wacław Wójcik in a July 4th report to Bednarz.[473] An Operational Battalion of the 14th regiment had arrived in the county to remove people by force. Deputy County Commissioner Siewerski appealed to Lt. Adler, a former Soviet officer, insisting that troops should treat the Lemkos humanely because unlike Ukrainians in other counties, they were not likely to offer armed resistance. In the ensuing discussion, it was determined that the deportations would be based on a list of people subject to removal, excluding American citizens, mixed families, and other designated people.[474] During the chaotic removals, however, the list was ignored, everyone was forced to leave, and the troops engaged in criminal behavior. Army troops began robbing people, killing some, and taking goods and livestock—even a Polish maintenance man doing road work, who was not subject to deportation, had his bicycle taken. Police in Gorlice returned the bicycle to the man, but the thieving officer went to the office of the county head demanding the bike. When he did not find the official, the officer began cursing him.[475] The police were also able to recover some livestock sold to Polish civilians; additional documents were submitted that alleged that Lt. Adler had raped some women during the removal. Although the supplementary documents are not included in the Misiło's collection, they have been described in a footnote.[476] Mikhailo Romashchenko, a chief Soviet representative, also wrote to Bednarz concerning the unlawful deportations in Nowy Sącz and Gorlice counties, urging him to prevent similar occurrences in the future.

---

472 Ibid., 152.

473 Ibid., 189–192.

474 At the turn of the 20th century, many Lemkos immigrated to the United States and were employed in the coal mines and steel mills of western Pennsylvania. After World War I, some returned with American-born children who were U.S. citizens.

475 Misiło, *Repatriacja,* Vol. II, 189–192

476 Ibid., 192, Footnote 2.

Two OUN reports provide additional information on the 1946 deportations in western Lemko region.[477] The first describes an ambush of a Population Exchange Commission that included two Soviet representatives, a Polish representative, a police chief, and a policeman. The commission was enumerating people for removal, and in the early evening, the members were traveling in a wagon along the road. A local OUN group halted the wagon. Most of the occupants surrendered immediately, but when one Soviet representative attempted to flee, he was seriously wounded in the legs and then shot. Another Soviet representative was questioned and "liquidated" because of his determined effort to remove Ukrainians. Both of these men had typical Ukrainian surnames. The two policemen were freed and the fate of the Polish representative was not indicated in the reports. The second report describes the general situation, noting that the local Polish population had recently become more hostile toward the Ukrainians and were spreading propaganda indicating that sooner or later, the Ukrainians must leave. According to the report, local Poles were taking whatever they could during the deportation actions, which included disassembling the better houses and hauling them away. In areas where the deportations had been completed, the remaining Ukrainians were told to accept Roman Catholicism if they wished to remain. On May 15, the deportation actions in Nowy Sącz and Gorlice counties began, although in Krosno and Jasło counties where a few Ukrainians remained, the additional deportation actions occurred later. Troops raided the villages during the night, removing people within a few hours' time. Many people had fled to the forest, including the Polish informants. Adults in several villages fled to the forest, and the troops took anyone who remained (including women and children) to the station in Gorlice. Some people fled to the forests from the railroad stations without their belongings, while others collected items such as eggs and wheat to bribe soldiers and police, hoping that they would be allowed to remain. The draconian deportation actions eventually prompted some to flee to Czechoslovakia.

The protracted UPA insurgency in western Ukraine and Poland brought about cooperation among three neighboring countries to fight the underground: the U.S.S.R., Poland, and Czechoslovakia. The Polish-

---

[477] Ibid., 41, 153–154.

Soviet cooperation had begun before the war ended. The Soviet Union sealed their border with Poland and NKVD units frequently aided Polish forces fighting the UPA in Poland. Czechoslovakia was brought into the fray immediately after the war when several partisan units entered northeastern Slovakia. In the summer of 1945, an UPA battalion consisting of three sotnias, commanded by Pavlo Vatsyk, "Prut", crossed the Soviet-Polish border in small groups and re-grouped on the Polish side in the Carpathians. These units, totaling perhaps 500 men, entered northeastern Slovakia in August. It was territory populated by eastern Slavs who identified themselves as either Ruthenians or Ukrainians.[478] There, units spent several weeks getting acquainted with the local population and informing them of their political aims. Their presence was reported by the Slovak press, and the information presumably made its way to the West. The incursion prompted Czechoslovakia to form a 2,500 men border guard unit on December 13, 1945 and to sign an agreement with the Soviet Union on January 1, 1946, which provided for joint protection for their border.[479]

Cooperation was initiated between the Czechoslovakian and Polish governments after Bir, Myron, and Karmeliuk's sotnias crossed from Poland into Slovakia in April of 1946. The raid had received broad coverage in Czechoslovakia and eventually throughout the world. In response, Czechoslovakia formed Operational Group *Ocel*, commanded by Colonel Jan Herman, which reached an agreement with Poland on May 6, 1946. The two sides agreed to exchange information and to allow pursuits across their borders, and they appointed exchange officers to coordinate the effort. The new protocol was soon tested when a large group of Ukrainians fled to Czechoslovakia to avoid deportation. On May 14, Rotkiewicz telegraphed Chief of Staff Korczyc, telling him that 2,500 Ukrainians and Poles had fled to Slovakia and advised Colonel Herman to return the Poles and send the Ukrainians to Transcarpathia.[480] The telegraph contained two critical errors. First, a large number of Ukrainians had camped near the Slovak border, but did not cross en masse until approximately the 20th. Second, given the hostility between the two

---

478 V'iatrovych, *Reydy UPA*, 66

479 Szchesniak and Szota, *Droga*, 420 and Viatrovych, *Reydy UPA*, 78

480 Misiło, *Repatriacja,* Vol. II, 138–139.

groups, there is no evidence nor is it probable that Poles would have traveled with Ukrainians to Slovakia.

How Ukrainians were enticed to cross the border is not clear, although an anecdotal account provided by Peter Szpynda of Karlików appears to be plausible. He maintained that his family and others had camped in the forest south of Przybyszów. After an UPA-Polish fight, a partisan told them to leave the area since the Poles were expected to return in force.[481] This apparently was a reference to a three-hour fight that occurred on May 17 between Khrin's sotnia and a Polish contingent of about 500 men.[482] The civilians were located about seven miles north of the Slovak border and had temporarily moved south until a suitable location could be found to make camp. Soon after, Czechoslovak troops arrived at the camp. The informed the people that they had crossed the border but would be permitted to resettle in Czechoslovakia. Based on the sparse information available, it is not clear if the offer represented an official Czechoslovak ploy or was merely an ad hoc suggestion by an officer. UPA reported that Ukrainians had been promised resettlement in the deported Hungarian villages of Slovakia, although some believed that they would be resettled in the Sudetenland. The latter location, which was on the German border, had a special appeal—if the resettlement did not prove satisfactory, escaping to Germany was a possibility. According to Szpynda, his father had consulted with others since many lived in the forest at the time, and they concluded that the offer was genuine.[483] The word of Czechoslovak resettlement spread rapidly throughout the mountains and was readily accepted by the desperate people. Believing the offer to be a ploy, Khrin's sotnia held several meetings in the forest with the different groups, urging them not to leave.[484] The Ukrainians could not be dissuaded, since the situation at home was unbearable—many had their houses burned and family members killed and lost much of the livestock and meager possessions with no end in sight. At the same time, many had great faith in the Slovaks and Czechs as a civilized people. During the interwar period, Czechoslovakia had been a stable democratic

481 This information was obtained in a personal conversation with Peter Szpynda by this author in Astoria, New York circa 2000.

482 See Potichnyj and Lyko, *Litopys UPA*, Vol. 33, 350–351

483 Conversation with Peter Szpynda, Astoria, NY, c. 2000.

484 Potichnyj and Lyko, *Litopys UPA*, Vol. 33, 350

state where Ukrainians living there had been treated much better compared to those living in Poland. Soon after making the decision, many returned from the forest to their villages. They quickly assembled their wagons, removed goods from concealed bunkers, hitched horses, cows, or both to wagons and headed for Slovakia over the mountains, usually called the Low Carpathians in this area.

By May 20, a large group of Ukrainians crossed the border over a period of a few days. Czechoslovakian reports estimated the numbers at over 3,000 people. Wagons traveling over the dirt roads were able to cross with a considerable amount of effort, but it was a difficult trek through mountainous territory. In the areas where hills rose sharply, animals were able to pull wagons up a hill for a while with people pushing from behind, and occasionally, the travelers would stop to rest and place stones behind the wheels to keep the wagons from drifting downhill. After the collapse of Communism, a letter was found in Prague, believed to have been written by a Ukrainian priest who had witnessed the event and wrote that the people had come from seven villages:[485]

> Wagon after wagon came, some pulled by a horse, others by two horses, by a cow, by a cow and a horse, one man did not have a horse or perhaps the horse perished on the road. He hitched himself to the wagon and hunched over and pulled, assisted by his wife. Almost every wagon has small children bunched together like wet pigeons (it rained that day), knotted three here, four there. Women and men walk along the wagons barefooted, ragged, and hungry. They lead their livestock—cows, sheep, and goats—faces darkened because of severe suffering and fear of an uncertain future. Others are pulling two-wheeled carts or children's wagons. A disturbed girl, her mental state caused by the tragedy, is sitting on a wagon talking to herself and waving her hands, while a woman sitting next to her is crying and calming the girl. Human wailing blends with cows' mooing, sheep bleating and wagons clanking…it is an unusually mournful, five-to-six kilometers long funeral procession beginning at 1:45 and ending at 4:45.[486]

Some time after the people had encamped on a mountain, they were surrounded by Czechoslovakian troops. Shortly afterward, a meeting was held and an officer declared that all Ukrainians, from the youngest to the oldest, were Banderites and would be sent back to Poland where Polish troops awaited them at the border. Around that same time, Khrin's sotnia

---

485 The seven villages were Wisłok Wielki (Vyslok Velykyi), Przybyszów (Prybyshiv), Karlików (Karlykiv), Radoszyce (Radoshytsi), Dolzyca (Dolzhytsia), Osławica (Oslavytsia), and Płonna (Polonna).

486 Mushynka, Mykola. "Trahediia Lemkiv Pol'shchi" *Suchanist*, May 1991, 65.

had advanced to the border and was mistaken for Polish troops—an easy mistake since by then, most partisans were outfitted in Polish uniforms. The Czechoslovaks unwittingly initiated talks with the sotnia, telling the partisans that people were being sent back and wanted to photograph the occasion of the two armies meeting. Khrin refused to be photographed, and informed the stunned interlocutors that he was a Ukrainian partisan, and that UPA was fighting Bolshevism and considered Czechs and Slovaks to be friends. He also warned them not to mistreat the Ukrainian people.[487]

On May 21, Rotkiewicz informed the General Staff that over 2,000 Ukrainians had been sent from Slovakia to the village of Jasiel on the Polish side, and requested transport. People actually were sent further east to Łupków, and therefore, it's possible that the presence of the partisans may have changed the plan. The Czechoslovak Army took the people from Kalyniv on the Slovak side to Łupków just inside the Polish border, some Czechoslovak trucks were provided, especially for transporting children and the elderly. The trucks were met there by about a dozen Polish soldiers who waited for a while, but as the evening approached they got into their truck and left. The caravan arrived during the night and the next morning, it began the long trek to the nearest functioning railroad station, located some 12 miles to the north in Szczawne. A few Czechoslovak vehicles were seen on the road to the railroad station but there were no Polish troops in sight, indicating that it was not a well-coordinated operation. On the way to Szczawne, some Ukrainians managed to flee to the mountains once again, but most went to the station.[488] The villagers were ardent UPA supporters and had adamantly resisted deportation for two years, but for most of them, the latest episode seemed to have broken their will to resist further.

The extended schedule required the deportations to be completed by June 15, but they actually extended through July. Toward the end of May, the 53rd Regiment arrived in Włodawa (Voldova) in the Chełm region, and began deporting people from the town and surrounding villages. According to an OUN report from April–May, 1946, troops would

487 Potichnyj and Lyko, "Zustrych Vidilu UPA z Czechoslovatskoho Armiyu." In *Litopys UPA*, Vol. 33, 627–629.

488 Rapawy, Stephen. "War Comes to Karlykiv." *Lemkivshchyna Magazine*, Spring, Vol. 2, 2000, 14.

surround a village at dawn and allow people two hours to pack and leave. Those who refused to leave were taken to the station immediately without any belongings. People were permitted to take one cow and some belongings to the station, where they were required to sign forms indicating their voluntary agreement to leave. Those who refused were denied food, and if a family member escaped, the family was deported immediately.[489] Following the deportation, a commission consisting of several officers arrived in Włodawa to investigate the behavior of troops not only toward the Ukrainians, but also toward the local authorities and Poles as well. They determined that several soldiers had taken 12 kilograms of sugar from a man named Dymitruk, a communist with a Ukrainian name, and that they had beaten him and told him to go to the Soviet Union because "communist rule had ended" in the area. Local police had been disarmed because of the excessive number of Ukrainians, a charge that the commission denied. The deportation was forceful and "brutal," and in some villages, people were allowed only 10–20 minutes to leave. The commission reported that UPA was not active in the area, but intelligence indicated that young people were fleeing to the forest, opposition was growing, and an UPA unit had arrived from the Hrubieszów area.[490] Later, the Włodawa County Commissioner instructed local officials to urge Ukrainians to leave, allowing them to take up to two tons of goods, further advising that those who refused to leave were to be deported by force.[491]

Further south, in Lubaczów County, the Polish government continued the deportation campaign with a considerably greater degree of difficulty on account of UPA's activities in the area. On May 28, the sotnia commander Shum from TS-27 reported that his sotnia destroyed two railroad bridges on Belz-Rava Rus'ka line and had on the following day ambushed a truck carrying approximately 30 soldiers, killing about 10 and wounding several more. About 50 soldiers were escorting a convoy of Ukrainians to a deportation point when the sotnia opened fire on the troops, and both civilians and soldiers fled during the fight.[492] A June 21 secret army report summarized the deportation effort in the area over a

489 Misiło, *Repatriacja,* Vol. II, 184–185.
490 Ibid., 198–200.
491 Ibid., 200–201.
492 Ibid., 194–195.

two-year period.[493] The most recent round of deportations had begun on March 1946 and was conducted by the 3rd and 5th divisions and supplemented by the 53rd regiment. Between October 1944 and June 20, 1946, approximately 128,367 people were removed from Tomaszów, Hrubieszów, and Włodawa counties. The report noted that between 1944–1945, 58,073 people had left Chełm, Zamość, Biłgoraj (Bilohrai), and Krasnystaw without the aid of the army. As noted earlier, a large number of people had fled the area because of vicious attacks by the Polish underground and were frequently aided by local authorities and police. As they had done elsewhere during the deportations, UPA attacked troops, railroad stations, bridges, and communication lines, forcing the troops to defend themselves and the infrastructure, and aid in evacuation. The UPA continued to be active after the deportation, mainly by burning abandoned villages and preventing Poles from settling them. The report concluded with an unrealistic proposal that the security of the region should be transferred to local police and better-armed ORMO units, even though the army had been unable to break up the UPA.

In the Rzeszów Province, where most Ukrainians lived, the deportations continued apace. Łańcut (Lantsut) County was a largely Polonized area with a small number of Ukrainians; out of reportedly 111 Ukrainians who lived there, 41 had been removed. In Brzozów (Bereziv) County in the Przemyśl area, the 32nd Regiment was ordered to remove three villages—Ulucz (Uliuch), Hoczew (Hochiv), and Jablonica Ruska (Iablonytsia Rus'ka) and to report the results. The Border Guards reported that some Ukrainians were fleeing from the nearby villages to their relatives in Przemyśl. In Krosno County in the Carpathians, approximately 12,196 Ukrainians had resided in the fall of 1944, but by May 31, 1946, 11,815 had been removed from the town itself and from 12 of the nearby villages. Of approximately 381 people who remained, 94 were Ukrainians and 287 were of mixed ancestry.[494] As the deportations were ending, the army issued a July 12 report that described the difficulties they had encountered as well as the accomplishments they had achieved during the Operation Rzeszów.[495] The report noted that UPA had destroyed bridges, railroads, attacked troops, especially smaller units, and then went on to

---

493 Ibid., 217–220.
494 Ibid., 206–207.
495 Ibid., 153–159.

describe the operations of the 8th and 9th divisions since July 24, 1945. The 8th Division was deployed mostly in the Lemko territory that extended from Gorlice County in the west to Lesko County in the east. At the beginning of May 1946, most troops and Border Guards were stationed in Sanok and Lesko counties where the majority of the Lemkos lived, and where UPA was comparatively more active than in other areas of the Transcurzon. The division faced constant attacks and their operations were hampered by the lack of passable roads and means of transport in the hilly, wooded terrain. The situation improved in April when soldiers who had fought in the war were demobilized and replaced by fresh troops. The 9th Division operated in Przemyśl, Jarosław and Łańcut counties while the 3rd Division covered Lubaczów, which was part of the Rzeszów Province. Deportation actions in the Przemyśl area were completed by May 14, 1946, by May 18 in Jarosław, and by June 4 in Lubaczów. The division faced the usual difficulties due to the lack of information from the local authorities concerning the number of people who were subject to deportation and the problem of enumerating those of mixed ancestry. The report stated that most Ukrainians did not wish to leave and had either acquired false documents or fled to the forest, and also noted that local authorities had failed to provide adequate support, occasionally releasing people from the deportation points. The report published a table, claiming that 273,810 people were subject to deportation and by July 13, only 9,449 had remained in the province. More complete deportation data for the Rzeszów Province by county can be found in Table 3.

Similar reports were issued for the Lublin and Cracow provinces.[496] The Lublin report, dated July 29, provided information for seven counties where most Ukrainians in the province resided. It noted that between 1944 and 1945, 137,313 people had left for the Soviet Union without the involvement of the army. The army began deportations there on September 6, 1945 when elements of the 3rd Division arrived in Lubaczów, Tomaszów, and Hrubieszów counties. The division operated largely in Hrubieszów County until April 1946 and deported 17,954 people. Subsequently, the main effort shifted to Tomaszów County and by July 13, the

---

496 Ibid., 266–276.

deportation actions in the province had concluded.[497] The division had faced strong resistance from the UPA who attacked communication and transportation lines as well as attacks on the troops. After the conclusion of the deportations, 72 Polish soldiers were decorated for bravery in combat and awarded 74,005 zloty, a token compensation awarded largely for capturing weapons.

The July 23 report from the Cracow Province covered four counties—Nowy Sącz, Nowy Targ, Gorlice, and Jasło, with the latter two being part of the Rzeszów Province. The authorities in that area faced a less daunting task since the OUN/UPA presence was light and any form of resistance came mostly from the civilian population hiding in the mountains. In April 1945, the Population Exchange Commission arrived in Nowy Sącz. The initial evacuation was largely voluntary since many people in the area held pro-Russian sympathies and were willing to leave. Many others left for economic reasons, since the area was poor and had suffered considerable destruction in the autumn of 1944 when a major battle was fought around Dukla Pass in the Carpathians south of Krosno. While some did leave voluntarily, most chose to remain and their resolve was strengthened when Lemkos who were previously deported returned to the region and described the difficult living conditions they had experienced in Ukraine. Interestingly, Polish reports on the returning Ukrainians were confined exclusively to Lemkos, but it is likely that other Ukrainians must have returned as well. In the spring of 1946, troops began removing people by the use of terror, including atrocities, even though resistance was virtually nonexistent. Much of the population was able to avoid deportation by fleeing to the forest and to other villages where removal had already been completed. A Cracow Military District report stated that by the beginning of July, approximately 95.7 percent of the eligible population had been removed from Nowy Sącz and 95.4 percent from Nowy Targ.[498] Despite the encouraging figures, it would become evident the following year that the Polish statistics for the Operation Rzeszów deportations were grossly overstated because data for the 1947 Operation Vistula campaign reveals that in fact, about one-third of the total population of Ukrainians had managed to evade deportation to Ukraine.

---

497 Ibid.

498 Ibid., 270.

Ren's June 1946 report catalogues both UPA attacks and Polish deportation efforts in TS-26, and reports 28 engagements with Polish troops.[499] The Peremyshl' battalion's sotnias engaged troops and police throughout the month: Krylach destroyed five kilometers of telephone line and a week later, his sotnia attacked troops killing 17 and seriously wounding four, while Burlaka captured 23 soldiers cutting hay and later released them after taking their weapons and uniforms.[500] Hromenko and Burlaka attacked an exchange commission, killing four Poles. At the end of the month, Burlaka attacked army troops, killing four. In addition to the major engagements, sotnias frequently clashed with troops and police in smaller skirmishes and staged a number of unsuccessful ambushes because the troops either did not arrive or had taken different routes than the underground had expected.

The fighting was more intense in the Lemko region. In Sanok County, Khrin's sotnia attacked troops who were rebuilding a railroad station. During this incident, seven soldiers died in the burning houses and 12 wounded men who managed to escape were mistaken for AK and were ambushed and killed by other Polish troops. At that time, troops in the Lesko-Baligród area had begun moving by trucks, which for them was a mixed blessing since trucks increased mobility but made the troops more susceptible to costly ambushes. On June 8, Myron's sotnia ambushed troops on the road to Baligród, destroying a truck, killing 16 and wounding four without sustaining any losses. Another sotnia's platoon mined another road in two separate sections; in one section, two wagons that were carrying Ukrainians to a deportation point were destroyed, killing people and horses, and in the second section, a road and drainage ditches were mined and an ambush was set.[501] When a Polish convoy of 12 trucks arrived, three were destroyed with mines and small arms fire, and many soldiers were killed in the ditches by the exploding mines. In that incident, a total of 28 soldiers were killed and 30 were wounded without any UPA losses. In another instance, Bir and Karmeliuk mined a road near Baligród in two places. When a convoy of trucks arrived in one

499 Events for June are reported in Ibid., 236–238 and Potichnyj and Lyko, *Litopys UPA*, Vol. 33, 369–394. The table for the Polish losses during the first half of 1946 (Ibid., 387–92) was labeled erroneously as it covers only the first three months.

500 Throughout the Ukrainian districts, Polish troops used scythes to cut grass for hay to feed their horses and occasionally harvested grain.

501 Potichnyj and Lyko, *Litopys UPA*, Vol. 33, 378

area, 40 soldiers were killed and about 20 were wounded. Although Polish losses cannot be verified independently, there can be little doubt that soldiers traveling in trucks were more vulnerable than soldiers on foot. Major roads in the area were dirt roads covered with gravel and had drainage ditches on both sides. Troops on foot, if ambushed, could take cover quickly in the ditches, while those packed in trucks could be killed by mines or small arms fire, or when exiting the trucks.[502] The report also noted that Polish activities were minimal, confined mostly to reconnaissance. Troops modified their earlier tactics by spending nights in the forest near selected villages, then entering at dawn.

As they had done in previous months, most UPA sotnias continued their military and political training. During the month of June, Bir provided 200 hours of military training for 50 partisans, equivalent to approximately 25 eight-hour days, and it is not clear whether the men had any previous military training. In addition to raising military efficiency and political awareness, the training kept the men busy when they were not on the march. Compared to earlier months, the physical condition of the partisans had worsened, and the commander's reports noted that their clothing was unsatisfactory and their medical problems had become much more severe. A June 1946 report for TS-26 noted a shortage of medical supplies, especially bandages, as well as an outbreak of typhus in several sotnias that had afflicted 13 men in both battalions. Weapons and ammunition were adequate since UPA units had added to their arsenals after successful attacks on Polish troops. Several tables are appended to the monthly report indicating the losses of both combatants for the first six months of the year as well as an inventory of captured equipment, an important source of supplies for the UPA. According to the report, the Polish side had 469 men killed, 202 wounded, and 129 captured. During the same period, the two UPA battalions had 31 men killed, 16 wounded, and four who had been severely wounded in the battle and had shot themselves to avoid capture. In terms of equipment, the report noted that UPA had captured three 82mm mortars, three 54 mm. mortars, 22 light machine guns, 80 submachine guns, ammunition, 154 rifles, clothing, and food. Major clothing items included 112 pairs of shoes, 147 overcoats, 26 jackets, and large quantities of food. The report noted that

---

502 UPA used abandoned mines from the war, but most seem to have been produced by the underground using mortar and artillery ammunition.

weapons, ammunition, food and clothing were captured from the enemy, but did not indicate whether or not the items had been taken from Polish civilians or from military stores. The partisans lost five light machineguns, 31 rifles and small quantities of other weapons and ammunition.

Ren's report for July, the last one available, described more intense clashes by both sides and, despite the official conclusion of the deportation campaign, also cited an increase in Polish atrocities against Ukrainian civilians compared to the previous month. [503] At the beginning of July, after the deportation deadline had already passed, troops arrived in the village of Terka in the upper San valley. They rounded up the remaining people (many had already been sent to the east, and took them to the neighboring Polish village of Wołkowyja. There the people were placed in a barbed wire enclosure and confined there for two days. Afterward, they were taken back to their village, locked in a deserted house and the house was set on fire. Twenty-eight people were burned alive.[504] During the night of July 17, Bir staged a retaliatory raid on the village of Wołkowyja where Border Guards Troops also kept their headquarters. The five-hour fight resulted in 30 Guardsmen killed and 25 wounded and the village self-defense unit (ORMO) had 45 killed. UPA reported two killed and five wounded.[505] At that point, UPA was no longer attacking transportation and communication lines, but instead focused on attacking buildings in Polish and Ukrainian villages where troops were quartering. The report noted that the two battalions had an adequate supply of weapons, ammunition, and food; the latter was obtained from both the Ukrainian population and the "enemy." On the other hand, medical supplies were still unsatisfactory and eight men in Khrin's sotnia had contracted dysentery and required medical treatment.

During the month of July, the deportations in the countryside had been largely completed, but people at the railroad stations were still being sent east. The troops, nevertheless, continued to terrorize the remaining Ukrainians, burning villages to deny UPA lodging, but promising to

503 Ibid., 395–428.

504 See Vaida, Iaroslav. "Trahediia sela Terka," in *Lemkivshchyna Magazine*, Fall, 2001, 22. During the raid on Terka, thirty-five people lost their lives and their names and ages are given on page 24 of the article.

505 Potichnyj and Lyko, *Litopys UPA,* Vol. 33, 399–400.

spare those who would inform on the UPA. In his monthly battalion report for July 1946, Ren noted that during this period, Polish efforts were directed solely against the partisans, and the army deployed larger units that frequently entered the forests in attempts to destroy them. Finally, in addition to the larger engagements, the report also indicates that there had been several minor clashes; however, losses were not recorded for either side.

As Operation Rzeszów came to a conclusion, the Polish military issued a number of reports outlining plans for the final elimination of the UPA, although Ukrainian villages were still being raided.[506] The General Staff issued a July 15 report claiming that during the operation, UPA had sustained considerable losses in men and materiel in the Lublin and Rzeszów provinces. It contended that larger UPA units had been broken up and the partisans had taken to operating in small groups of 10–30 men, similar to the Polish underground. To buttress the contention, the report noted that attacks had decreased on the transportation system and came to the erroneous conclusion that UPA had been significantly weakened. In fact, the decrease in UPA attacks was actually the result of a change in tactics. After the 1946 deportation campaigns concluded, the underground no longer considered communication and transportation infrastructure to be their primary targets. Although the sotnias had sustained some losses in combat and through desertions, they were still capable of engaging the enemy despite their reduced size.

To eliminate the underground completely, General Wojciech Bewziuk, a former Soviet officer commanding the Lublin Military District, deployed three regiments to the Hrubieszów area where Zalizniak's Battalion operated. The general informed the General Staff that UPA forces in the area would be liquidated by July, and General Jan Rotkiewicz was similarly optimistic, declaring that UPA would be destroyed in the Rzeszów Province within a month's time. To accomplish the task, the 8th and 9th divisions were to remain in place because the Staff had determined that the Internal Security Troops and Public Security Troops had been ineffective. Adequate funding was required to establish reliable intelligence and the remaining Ukrainians were to be deported since they were viewed as being responsible for aiding the underground. The report

---

[506] Misiło, *Repatriacja,* Vol. II, 261–262.

concluded with a number of recommendations for eliminating UPA within a one-month period. First, they specified that troops had to be issued the necessary field rations, clothing, footwear, radio equipment and additional gasoline was to be issued to the Eight Division. Second, the remaining Ukrainians were to be assembled at several points and deported by police and security forces without indicating where were they would be taken. Finally, UPA was to be informed that their struggle was futile.

Two days later, the army issued a report concerning security matters for the upcoming parliamentary election scheduled for January 17, 1947, and included a section on the struggle with the UPA.[507] It stated that the destruction of the UPA had been largely successful and that the insurgency's elimination was to be concluded by August 15. Like other reports, it restated that responsibility for eliminating UPA had been placed on the army since the previous performance of police and security forces had been unsatisfactory, largely because they had been unable to recruit Ukrainian informants without whom UPA would not be overcome. It also noted that the role of the police and security forces was to deport the remaining Ukrainians with the cooperation of the Soviet Union, and to that end, they were directed to establish garrisons on Ukrainian territory. ORMO would also be expanded to provide additional protection for the local Polish population. Finally, troops were charged with protecting and helping Poles to harvest their lands and were also directed to organize harvests in the Ukrainian districts.

On August 20, the State Security committee, whose membership included Marshal Rola-Żymierski and several senior generals, convened a conference in Warsaw to discuss security measures for the upcoming elections and to further discuss the continued struggle with the Polish and Ukrainian undergrounds.[508] The protocol of the conference summarized the major items considered, including the need to increase discipline in army ranks and eliminate undesirable elements among them. The attention to this matter was likely due to a recent report that troops were behaving badly toward Polish civilians. According to the report, troops were entering villages under the pretext of looking for Polish partisans and weapons, abusing the residents, and stealing goods and livestock which they were shipping to the newly acquired German territories in the

[507] Ibid., 263–264.
[508] Ibid., 299–301 and 265–266.

west. The protocol did not provide additional information on how the livestock were being transported, but shipping animals across Poland would have certainly required a well-organized network capable of handling large volumes in order to make the enterprise profitable. Most likely, the livestock and valuables came from Ukrainian villages where troops routinely seized valuables and livestock, especially horses, while similar behavior in Polish villages would have been the exception, since troops were less likely to enter Polish villages and rob their own people. The soldiers apparently sold most of their stolen property on the black market, which had become a thriving institution in post-war Poland.

With respect to UPA, the protocol indicated that the Polish army had initiated a new approach in an attempt to fill the intelligence gap. In July of 1946, 49 units of Polish troops dressed as Ukrainian partisans began a special undercover mission in the Ukrainian territory. The units, which ranged in size from 20 to 100 men, were formed on July 19, 1946 from troops of the 8th and 9th divisions. Their goal was to sniff out UPA supporters in the villages, but the changing of uniforms did not bring much success toward realizing the goal. The September 1, 1946 OUN report for the western Lemko region noted that the units attacked not only partisans, but they also attempted to uncover UPA supporters and sympathizers, arresting anyone whom they considered to be suspicious. The ploy was poorly conceived since partisan units typically operated within a defined area of a county and were by then recognizable to the local civilians. The appearance of a strange unit would have aroused immediate suspicion and the troops would have had to be fluent in Ukrainian to make such an impersonation plausible. Since neither Polish nor Ukrainian sources provide additional information about the units, it is likely that the experiment was unsuccessful and quickly abandoned.

The protocol further discussed the situation with both undergrounds and made recommendations. It noted that the Polish underground units that were operating in Cracow, Katowice, Lublin, and Gdańsk provinces had staged 246 attacks in the first half of 1946. The UPA continued to operate, though at reduced strength, but had not been decimated after the deportation as previously thought. The protocol failed to mention that the 1946 deportation campaign was not as thorough as Polish reports indicated. In fact, approximately 200,000 Ukrainians still remained, a sufficient number to provide food, shelter, intelligence, and even some recruits. The protocol did acknowledge, however, that the underground was receiving some support from the remaining Ukrainians and mixed population; however, they did not believe that the partisans would be able to replenish their ranks with new recruits and therefore expected them to be destroyed under the relentless attacks.

Operation Rzeszów officially ended on October 31, 1946. The Polish army's tactics during the operation are described in a Polish source that is based on army reports.[509] Although all Ukrainians were to have been deported and UPA destroyed, the army failed at both tasks to a considerable extent. The command had direct control of only two of the divisions, the 8th and 9th, and through the Provincial Security Committee, they had to coordinate operations with Internal Security Forces, police, and Border Guards. The troops were required to attack quickly and destroy the partisans, but without adequate motor transportation, radio communication, and telephones, a rapid response was impossible. Moreover, the troops were required to be on the move, engage in nighttime operations, and improve their intelligence; but none of the orders had been meaningfully implemented. The old tactics of one-day forays into the countryside continued, and nighttime attacks and ambushes were rarely employed. Furthermore, two-thirds of the troops were assigned to the deportation operations and only a few regiments were allocated to protect the railroad lines and fight partisans, the troop strength was clearly insufficient for the task. Overloaded with numerous assignments, the two divisions were able to mount only 15 operations against the UPA in the month of June. In July, many units were reassigned to harvest grain and hay. After the referendum, the 9th Division, with a detachment of Internal Troops, was assigned to destroy the Zalizniak and Baida battalions. The 8th Division, after detaching 30 percent of its troops for guard duties, was directed to work with the 18th Regiment to destroy the larger Ren Battalion. During the 20-day period in July, the division initiated 44 actions; four were conducted by platoon-sized units, 25 by companies, and the remainder employed at least two companies or a battalion. Operations that lasted two days or longer tended to be more effective; however, most operations, 38 in total, lasted only about one day. Those lasting two days or longer were more effective, and the division claimed to

509 Szcześniak and Szota, *Droga*, 399–408.

have killed 51 partisans during this period. The 9th Division conducted 65 operations during the same period. Of those, 47 were battalion size, stayed in the field longer, and reportedly killed 34 partisans. In total, Polish troops initiated 101 actions in September, but the number dropped by half in October. In the Rzeszów operation, the military claimed to have killed 910 partisans, but this was an unrealistically high figure compared to the size and strength of UPA after the operation's conclusion. They also reportedly arrested over 1,000 supporters or suspicious individuals.

Following the deportations, General Rotkiewicz, head of the Operation Rzeszów Group, concluded that the UPA was now on the defensive. Rather than developing and executing offensive attacks against the army and exchange commissions, he believed that the partisans were focused on gathering food, clothing, money, attacking Polish civilians, eliminating Ukrainian informers, and catching deserters. However, the underground still remained a problem, and support from the remaining Ukrainians had complicated the task of destroying UPA. As a result, Rotkiewicz proposed that the remaining Ukrainians must be relocated either to the Soviet Ukraine or western Poland.[510] Energetic steps to eliminate UPA were to be undertaken immediately, but several regiments had been sent into ethnic Polish territories to subdue the Polish underground. In order to consolidate force strength, the remaining units of the 8th division were attached to the 9th Division, and in the months that followed, a more systematic approach would be undertaken to defeat the UPA. The two divisions were instructed to attack the partisans relentlessly. The police were assigned to protect oil fields, the Railroad Security Service was to guard the railroads, and the Border Guards brigade and the 8th Division were issued snow suits and skis to traverse the snowy terrain. The new plan called for Lt. Colonel Zwolinski, who commanded several regiments and a Border Guard unit, to destroy Zalizniak's battalion. Lt. Colonel Wygnowski, who commanded a comparable number of troops, was assigned to attack Baida's battalion. Commanding a larger force, Colonel Bielecki was assigned to eliminate Ren's battalion, and the Border Guards were to destroy "Lys's" sotnia in Gorlice area ("Lys" was another

510 Misiło, *Repatriacja,* Vol. II, 308–309.

pseudonym for Smyrny's large OUN unit.)[511] Polish troops were to operate in larger units than they had earlier, with the average unit comprised of about 150 men and 15 officers. Several officers from the internal troops and police were also attached to each unit, presumably to provide better intelligence. The operation was hampered by the upcoming parliamentary elections, during which time three-fourths of the troops in both divisions had been reassigned to provide security.

On the Ukrainian side, Starukh, the head of OUN in Poland, issued instructions to Ukrainians urging them to boycott elections since it was an internal Polish matter. Instead, he urged the underground to gather food and supplies for the winter, continue training, expand the intelligence network, and increase the revolutionary élan. During the second half of 1946, the fighting in the two northern sectors subsided despite extensive Polish sweeps through the countryside. Most engagements that occurred at this point were small, but the partisans did mount few large operations: Elements of the Zalizniak battalion raided the town of Tarnogród (Tarnohorod), securing four wagons of medical supplies, and units from the Danyliv Battalion attacked Polish troops in Waręż (Variazh). It is clear that the partisan units in the three tactical sectors remained intact after Operation Rzeszów. Ren's battalion experienced a substantial reduction of activity, in part because Myron and Karmeliuk had returned to their home base in Ukraine. The absence of Myron was especially noticeable since he had been an aggressive commander who initiated numerous successful attacks. At the same time, a new sotnia was organized in the battalion, eventually commanded by Stakh. The sotnia was formed officially on June 1 and consisted of two platoons transferred from Khrin's sotnia, who had at one time commanded about 300 men, and this core group was augmented by new recruits with some key positions filled by men transferred from other sotnias. The new sotnia trained for two weeks, the new recruits receiving additional training, and then went into active operation in close proximity to Khrin.

By the fall of 1946, Ren's battalion consisted of Bir, Khrin, Stakh, and Brodych, with the latter relocated many miles away in the west. In autumn of 1946, the Brodych sotnia was transferred to the western Lemko region where only small OUN units had operated thus far. The sotnia

---

511 Szcześniak and Szota, *Droga*, 409–410.

was originally organized in the east and had entered the eastern Lemko region in the winter of 1945, where it sustained heavy losses in the upper San valley during the Soviet sweep through the region, including the death of Veselyi, who had been the commander at that time. The reconstituted unit was replenished with local recruits, mostly Lemkos, and then sent west.[512] The reason for the transfer of the sotnia was not reported, although Khrin had been complaining that too many sotnias had been concentrated in the Sanok and Lesko areas and urged the UPA Command to relocate some to the west. In any case, it is likely that the reduction of the Ukrainian population in the east was a significant factor in the transfer. The actual process of relocating the Brodych sotnia was a precarious task, since the Germans had mined the approaches to the Dukla Pass. On the eastern side, the mined fields stretched from the Krosno region to the Carpathians, a distance of about 20 miles. Earlier that summer, a special UPA unit worked to clear a path through the minefields, and in the fall, Brodych's sotnia (approximately 120 men) walked single file through the cleared area without incident[513]. After arriving in the west, the sotnia was aided by an OUN network headed by "Smirnyi"/"Chernyk" (Mykhailo Fedak) who commanded a sizeable unit and organized self-defense units in villages with pro-Ukrainian views. Unlike the situation in the eastern Lemko region, where support for the underground was strong, there were mixed sentiments in the west. Many villages provided food, shelter and information, but others were clearly hostile and informed on the partisans. As a result, Brodych's sotnia was more vulnerable than those in the east, where UPA was able to control the countryside to a considerable extent, forcing Polish troops to proceed cautiously. In the west, the sotnia operated alone and the Poles were better informed of its movement, forcing the partisans to constantly remain on the defensive. The underground literature does not indicate the sotnia's objectives and there is no evidence of any tangible accomplishments. The unit was constantly on the run, sustained heavier casualties than those in the east, did not offer much protection to the local population, nor was there a noticeable increase in national awareness among the local population

---

512 Reportedly, Lemkos comprised about 90 percent of the Khrin and Stach sotnias. See Potichnyj, Peter. "The Lemkos in the Ukrainian National Movement During and After World War II." in Best and Moklak, Eds., *The Lemko Region*, 154.

513 Dmytryk, Ivan. *Zapysky Ukrainskoho Povstantsia v Lisakh Lemkivshchyny*, 118.

Despite the official conclusion of Operation Rzeszów and the reports that the underground had been significantly weakened, the deportations and Polish terror against Ukrainians continued. Several OUN reports provide additional information about events in the Transcurzon during the second half of the year. An OUN report for the Włodawa (Voldova) region in the north described incidents that occurred in the village of Krzywowierba (Kryvoverby) in July after the Soviet personnel handling deportation left for the USSR. The troops arrived, forced people to sign necessary the documents for deportation, and then vacated the village without removing the residents. A few days later, the troops returned to the village, rounded up the villagers, and told them to pray because they were about to be shot. After the prayer, the soldiers beat them and told them again to leave. "Such terror remained throughout July" in the area.[514] During this period, the residents of 27 villages left for Ukraine, either partially or completely. In other villages, some converted from Orthodox religion to Roman Catholicism to avoid deportation, with the conversions were done secretly due to fears of retaliation by the underground.

Troops in the Przemyśl area attacked Wola Wołodzka (Volia Voldovs'ka), burned 28 remaining houses, robbed the residents, and captured a female operative named "Ofilia" who worked with the underground. She was tortured and subsequently sent to Sanok. According to the local Poles, the attack was done in retaliation for the UPA raid on Olchowce (Vilkhivtsi) where Polish troops were regularly stationed. The report concluded that the remaining Ukrainians were being terrorized by Polish bandits.[515] Another report noted that local authorities had informed Ukrainians about the extension of the deportation deadline in several counties, but only 500 people had been deported during the extended period.[516]

The August OUN report for the eastern Lemko region stated that the Polish Army had disseminated leaflets to Ukrainians families, urging those with sons in the UPA to report them to the authorities. Those who failed to comply would be sent to concentration camps and their property would be confiscated. At the same time that the leaflets were being dis-

---

514 Misiło, *Repatriacja,* Vol. II, 319.

515 Ibid., 311–312

516 Ibid., 336–337, 340, and 342–343.

tributed, the authorities were recruiting Ukrainians in villages close to towns for leftist parties. Prospective recruits were promised aid through the United Nations Relief and Rehabilitation Administration (UNRRA) if they cooperated, and as an added inducement, were given the guarantee that troops and police would not harass them. The report also noted that the general attitude of the people toward the UPA was positive, but young men were avoiding joining UPA and there were cases where some preferred serving in the Polish Army.[517] This appears to be the only report of Ukrainians joining the Polish army and it does not indicate the number of men who joined, nor does it describe the specific circumstances associated with their enlistment. The report also does not reflect the significant change in conditions, since by that autumn, two-thirds of Ukrainians had been deported and the remainder had been impoverished as the result of burning and looting, severely limiting their ability to support the underground. At the same time, the smaller population base had naturally reduced the number of potential recruits, and those who had been interested in joining UPA would likely have joined earlier. The October report stated that the Poles were spreading propaganda that the underground had been defeated and that there would be no war, and warned the remaining Ukrainian civilians that those who supported the partisans would be severely punished, even entire villages. Another report indicated that some young people had left for German territories were encouraging others to come through correspondence. Among the arrested, some were told during interrogations that they would be released only after signing documents for relocation to the west.

A July OUN report for Verkhovyna in the western Lemko region noted that the mood of the people in that area had turned more pessimistic due to lowered expectations that a third world war would happen, and the declining possibility of the underground achieving success. This resulted in a decline in popular support for the underground. The report captured information from the period of June–July 1946 and noted that during that period, the underground had initiated four attacks—some people had approved and others disapproved, fearing that the Poles would retaliate. The November report for the region notes that the situation was rapidly deteriorating, people were being beaten and arrested,

---

517 Ibid., 310.

and the number of informants had increased. It described the Ukrainians as being firm in their refusal to relocate to the east because of the horrific letters they were receiving from relatives in the Soviet Union. Some people had changed their attitudes toward UPA after coming into contact with the well-organized and well-armed Brodych sotnia that had arrived from the east, but many still remained fearful:

> Successful attacks on the Polish troops produced a colossal change of attitude among Ukrainians who previously viewed the partisans as bandits, but now consider them to be credible defenders...Despite the increased support for the underground, many are fearful of being reported to authorities, and in Rusyn villages that do not considered themselves Ukrainian, reporting on partisan activities is considered an obligation and is done openly.[518]

Romashchenko's report provided additional information on the activities of UPA during the deportation, although his estimate of the partisan strength is inflated. He noted that in the autumn of 1945, UPA units totaling about 500 men were operating in the Włodawa area in the Lublin Province. They had attacked a police station and conducted propaganda activities against the deportations. He estimated that further south in the Biłgoraj area, there were 2,000 partisans who had closed down the railroad in Lubaczów. In Tomaszów, the UPA attacked commission workers and cut the railroad line to the Soviet Union. UPA was especially strong in southern Hrubieszów, where 300 partisans had halted the deportations. In the Przemyśl area, UPA took control of the territory between the San River and the Soviet border, where approximately 31,680 Ukrainians were living. There the partisans recruited and trained their men. In the Sanok-Lesko area, UPA reportedly increased its strength from about 400 men in the spring of 1945 to 2,000 men in early 1946, and set about demolishing bridges and railroads. A railroad bridge and 100 cars were destroyed in Zagórz, requiring 15 days to repair the bridge. The UPA strength that Romashchenko and the commission estimated was clearly overstated, and the Polish intelligence service may have double or triple counted some of the same units that ranged over large areas. The assessment was further complicated because sotnias were frequently broken into platoons that operated independently, and partisans from the same sotnia could appear in several different places, making it seem as though UPA had more units than was actually the case. To thwart the deporta-

---

518 Ibid., 341–342.

tion, UPA attacked transport and communication lines. Romashchenko reported that 11 railroad stations and 29 bridges were destroyed, in addition to 50 road bridges, 3 locomotives, 193 railroad cars, and 53 kilometers of railroad line. Some lines were repaired, but in the Carpathians, one line (comprised of several miles of track) remained inoperative throughout the deportations. During the two-year period, Romashchenko reports that 482,880 people had been removed. Table 2 shows deportation data from a Polish source that reflects a slightly higher number. The largest number of people, 62,655, were deported in June, 1946 as Operation Rzeszów was ending.

Table 2. Deportation of Ukrainians from Poland to the USSR, 1944–1946, By Province

Deported	**By**		**Lublin**	**Rzeszów**	**Cracow**	**Other**	**Total**
November	15th	1944	N/A	N/A	N/A	N/A	3,505
December	10th	1944	16,449	3,450	N/A	N/A	19,899
January	1st	1945	N/A	N/A	N/A	N/A	39,864
March	1st	1945	N/A	N/A	N/A	N/A	81,323
April	25th	1945	94,971	38,561	N/A	N/A	133,532
June	1st	1945	112,722	58,980	2,967	1,039	175,708
July	1st	1945	119,201	61,722	2,967	1,047	184,937
August	1st	1945	125,381	72,182	2,967	1,230	201,760
September	1st	1945	125,464	84,748	18,157	1,316	229,685
October	1st	1945	127,599	107,496	18,157	1,359	254,611
November	1st	1945	128,400	136,535	19,049	1,428	285,412
December	1st	1945	130,480	154,006	19,610	1,461	305,557
January	1st	1946	131,261	158,931	19,812	1,487	311,491
February	1st	1946	131,570	171,051	19,829	1,506	323,956
March	1st	1946	131,587	172,966	19,829	1,615	325,997
April	1st	1946	135,610	189,594	19,829	1,683	346,716
May	1st	1946	146,191	210,041	20,185	1,683	378,100
May	15th	1946	157,636	227,097	20,185	1,683	406,601
July	1st	1946	190,734	267,795	19,599	2,169	480,305
August	1st	1946	193,420	267,380	20,093	2,915	483,808

*N/A – Not Available

Source: Eugeniusz Misiło, *Repatriacja Czy Deportacja,* Vol. 2. (Warszawa: Archiwum Ukrainskie,1999), Appendix 6.

Romashchenko disaggregated his figures by nationality: Ukrainians totaled 439,903; Russians 23,848, Ruthenians 18,759; Belarusians 126, and others 244. The Russians would have come from the eastern portion of the Lublin Province, an area that had been part of the Russian Empire until the First World War. Based on the prewar censuses and population studies, their numbers had been grossly overstated. For whatever reason, some deportees must have identified themselves as Russians. Ruthenians came from the western Lemko region where the term was used widely, but some also used the designation in the eastern counties in the hope of avoiding deportation. Women comprised 53.7 percent of the deportees, children 13 years and younger amounted to 29.4 percent, the 14 to 55 age group, 59.8 percent, and those 56 and older amounted to 10.7 percent. Figures by province and county are presented in Table 3. The last two columns indicate the eligible population deported, which was a gross overestimation as will be described later.

Table 3. Number Deported by Province and County, 1944–1946

Province and County	Deported		Percent of Total	
	Families	Persons	Families	Persons
Total	***122,622***	***482,880***	***97.4***	***97.0***
Lublin Province	**53,015**	**193,420**	**N/A**	**N/A**
Biłgoraj	4,277	16,523	88.7	91.6
Hrubieszów	18,653	68,658	98.2	98.1
Chełm	8,965	33,195	96.3	96.3
Krasnystaw	874	2,707	81.5	77.0
Liubart	227	811	100.0	100.0
Radynsk	83	274	100.0	100.0
Tomaszów	11,097	40,742	99.6	99.6
Włodawa	7,296	25,030	95.7	93.0
Zamość	1,543	5,480	93.6	93.7

Rzeszów Province	**64,531**	**267,380**	**N/A**	**N/A**
Gorlice	3,620	15,058	90.7	87.0
Jarosław	9,292	36,666	98.2	99.0
Jasło	1,780	7,270	92.0	94.7
Lesko	8,764	39,505	97.5	99.3
Lubaczów	9,951	43,172	97.6	98.0
Przemyśl	16,494	64,831	98.7	99.0
Sanok	14,630	60,878	97.2	96.3
Cracow Province	**4,554**	**20,093**	**N/A**	**N/A**
Nowy Sącz	4,554	20,093	95.8	90.9
Other Areas	**522**	**1,987**	**N/A**	**N/A**

*N/A – Not Available
Source: Volodymyr Serhiichuk, *Trahedia Ukraintsiv v Polshchi* Ternopil, 1997, p. 233.

The years of violence inflicted heavy losses on Ukrainians, tens of thousands died, but it is difficult to precisely estimate the losses because available data are fragmented and cannot be verified. The information is based on eyewitness accounts, reports of the Soviet delegation in Poland in charge of the population exchange, and the OUN reports. Statistics for the Lublin Province are based on eyewitness letters and confined to locales where the massacres were unusually high. As noted in Chapter IV, Ukrainians from the Lublin counties had written to Soviet leaders when the Red Army arrived in 1944, asking to have their territory incorporated into the Soviet Ukraine. This area sustained much heavier casualties than any other Ukrainian region in Transcurzon because of systematic Polish partisan attacks in 1943 and 1944. Letters asking for incorporation into Ukraine were typically signed by large numbers of people and enumerated civilians who had been killed in their areas. An August 1, 1944 letter, signed by 85 villagers, was sent to Nikita Khrushchev. The villagers claim that about 193 villages had been attacked, killing approximately 19,000 people in the process. [519] An ad-hoc committee representing Hrubieszów and Tomaszów counties wrote to Stalin in August, claiming that

[519] Serhiichuk, *Trahediia*, 84.

over 150 villages were burned in their area and about 15,000 people had been killed. The letter then lists seven villages giving number of people killed in each village, with the numbers ranging from 35 to 770 people. In his final report on the deportation of Ukrainians from Poland, Romashchenko accepts the figure of 15,000 killed in the Lublin Province and notes that based on the "far from complete data" of his office, an additional 4,370 Ukrainians had been killed during the deportations.[520] Finally, there are some OUN reports about villages where large numbers of people had been killed. Despite all these shortcomings, it is reasonable to assume that about twenty to twenty-five thousand Ukrainians were killed between 1942 and 1946. During this period the Polish population losses are placed at 599 people despite UPA attacks on Polish villages.[521]

After nearly two years, the deportations to the east, which had been implemented in several phases, had finally ended. Initially the resettlements had been effected on a voluntary basis, but in the Lublin Province, many Ukrainians had fled because of Polish partisan attacks. After the war, with small share of Ukrainians already removed, the Polish authorities increasingly relied on force. Several divisions were moved to the Ukrainian districts, augmented by police and special military formations, Border Guards, Internal Troops, etc. The military faced an enlarged and aggressive UPA force that was determined to prevent the deportations. To thwart the removal of the Ukrainian population, the partisans attacked troops, population exchange commissions, and most importantly transportation and communication networks. The Polish military deployed an insufficient number of troops to forcibly remove the recalcitrant population and simultaneously fight partisans, and when the year ended, less than one-third of the population had been removed. In the spring, a new campaign commenced, Operation Rzeszów, an operation that was essentially similar to that of the previous year, but had been assigned a larger force. The fighting with the UPA intensified, and again, the partisans concentrated on destroying bridges, railroads, and cutting telephone lines, the principal method of communication. Because the weather was warm at that time, many civilians fled to the forest, especially in the Carpathians, and some crossed the border to Slovakia. During this phase,

520 Ibid., 243.

521 Szcześniak and Szota, *Droga*, 529

about 150,000 people had been removed and authorities erroneously concluded that most Ukrainians had been removed.

Chapter VI:
Expulsion to the West: Operation Vistula

At the conclusion of Operation Rzeszów in 1946, Polish authorities erroneously concluded that most of the Ukrainians west of the Curzon line had been deported. They estimated that perhaps 14,000 to 20,000 still remained, and that the Ukrainian underground had been largely destroyed. For the Poles, it was a gross misreading of the situation, considering the fact that close to 200,000 Ukrainian civilians had actually managed to evade the deportations, and the Ukrainian underground remained a viable force to be reckoned with. Although the UPA had sustained losses during the heavy fighting in the first half of the year and their units were slightly smaller, the UPA units had nevertheless remained operational. Approximately 200,000 Ukrainian civilians who remained were able to provide the underground with recruits, intelligence, and provisions; however, it was at significantly reduced levels since some two-thirds of the pre-war population had already been deported to the east. There was a reduction of combat in the region during the last months of the year, as Polish troops confined themselves mostly to small-scale operations against the partisans and UPA had largely curtailed offensive operations after half a year of heavy fighting.

Despite the official government assessment, many high-ranking Polish officers were skeptical that the underground had indeed been decimated and continued to insist upon the total expulsion of Poland's Ukrainian minority. As the eastward deportations ended, the only remaining option was to relocate the remaining Ukrainian population to the newly acquired German territories in the west, where they could be thinly scattered among ethnic Poles with the aim of rapid assimilation.

At the beginning of 1947, the Polish army deployed more troops to the Ukrainian districts, concentrating them in the southern portion of the Rzeszów Province. Przemyśl, Sanok and Lesko counties were partisan territory, where two of the four UPA battalions operated and offered formidable resistance to the army. The conflict steadily escalated in January and February of that year, but the situation changed drastically in late March.

On March 28, 1947, General Karol Świerczewski, Second Vice Minister of Defense, was ambushed and killed while conducting inspections of troops near Baligród while en route to the village of Cisna. The ambush provided the government with a pretext to activate a secret operation that had been in the works since 1946: the so-called "Operation Vistula" (Akcja "Wisła"[522]) which would deport the remaining Ukrainians to the former German territories that Poland had acquired from the Yalta Agreement. The deployed troops now had two missions: to destroy UPA and to remove the Ukrainians who had managed to avoid the prior deportations. After accomplishing much of their mission in the south, most units were to be shifted to other counties in the province as well as to the Lublin and Cracow provinces. Based on official records, about 140,000 Ukrainians were deported to former portions of Prussia, Pomerania, and Silesia and, as in the previous year, the removal was chaotic and people suffered similar deprivations. By autumn of 1947, the underground was largely destroyed. Most sotnias were reduced to a fraction of their former strength, but most remained in tact during deportation. With the population deported, UPA's rationale for fighting in Transcurzon had been eliminated, and without the support of the local people, the insurgency was simply unable to function. Accordingly, some units crossed the border to fight in Ukraine, and others were ordered to head for the American Zone in Germany. Many were killed or captured by the Czechoslovaks, and the captives were transferred to either Polish or Soviet authorities. Despite the difficulties of traversing Czechoslovakia, hundreds still managed to reach the west.

Preparations for Operation Vistula

In the fall of 1946, a relative calm prevailed in the area. Polish troops reduced their harassment of Ukrainian civilians and people resumed peaceful pursuits. Army attacks on the partisans was scaled down, and the underground turned its attention to winter preparations, primarily the task of securing grain and foodstuffs. During the spring, the Ukrainians had sowed and planted; however, most had been deported before the harvest season. As a result, those who remained, including the under-

522 To conduct the deportations, a special military formation was organized—Grupa Operacyjna "Wisła " (GOW), Operational Group "Wisła".

ground and local Poles, harvested the crops. Because of the reduced population base, the UPA could no longer count on the local population to provide food to the extent that they had earlier, and the partisans were forced to provide for themselves. Despite the sizeable loss of the population, the underground was preparing to continue the insurgency in Transcurzon.

The Polish military was keenly aware that the difficulties with the underground had not been resolved, and in their view, the complete removal of Ukrainians was a necessary first step in eliminating the underground. In his report dated September 10, 1946, General Jan Rotkiewicz, commander of Operation Rzeszów, recommended that the Ukrainians who had not been deported by the expiration date of the agreement should henceforth be deported to the newly acquired territories in the west.[523] After a hiatus of several months in the autumn of 1946, the Polish army resumed operations against UPA in the Przemyśl-Sanok-Lesko area and began gathering data on the remaining Ukrainians. The Operational Staff of the Ninth Division in Przemyśl issued a lengthy report concerning operations that were to be conducted in the first half of February 1947.[524] The report noted that UPA was in a grave situation and offered several reasons to support the assumption. Among the reasons cited, the report noted that UPA units were avoiding contact with Polish troops; they operated in small groups, and were attempting to survive the winter and waiting for more favorable conditions in the spring. It further noted that a morale crisis among the insurgency was indicated by desertions and increased robberies, and observed that a crisis was further indicated by UPA's failure to disrupt the January 19, 1947 parliamentary elections

In reality, the report was based on dubious assumptions, and the Polish army had grossly underestimated the strength of the underground. First, the corresponding underground literature does not indicate specific orders to operate in smaller units, although it was standard practice for sotnia commanders to allow platoons and even squads to operate independently. Such tactics provided junior officers the experience of operating independently, confused the enemy as to the size and location of the partisans, and eased provisioning. Second, while it is likely that UPA in-

523 Misiło, *Repatriacja,* Vol. II, 309.

524 Misiło, *Repatriacja,* Vol. II, 41–42.

creased its raids on Polish villages. This can be attributed to the need for provisioning as the result of the deportation of the Ukrainian population. Third, although desertion may have increased around that time, the underground literature for that period does not indicate a rise in desertion rates. Finally, the underground had never involved itself in elections, considering them to be an internal Polish matter.

In February 1947, the Ninth Division's immediate assignment was to destroy Baida's battalion in the Przemyśl area, which consisted of four sotnias. The division had two regiments and was augmented by a light artillery unit, 12 anti-tank units and a unit from the Internal Security Corps.[525] Although the use of artillery had proven to be ineffective during Operation Rzeszów the previous summer, the army nevertheless deployed it again. Since UPA did not have tanks, it's likely that the anti-tank weapons were deployed for the purpose of destroying bunkers. Col. Ignacy Wieliczko, commander of the division, served simultaneously as head of the Rzeszów Security Commission and in that capacity, all army units, security forces and police in the province were subordinated to him. On January 31, 1947, he ordered all units to report on the number of Ukrainians in the province.

The increased presence of Polish troops resulted in more frequent contact with the UPA. At the beginning of January, the partisans suffered high casualties in two fights near Przemyśl that resulted in 19 men killed, and near Lesko, seven men were killed and four were captured.[526] Based on information provided by the captives, an UPA hospital was destroyed near Lesko later that month. About a dozen members of the staff and guards were killed and one guard was captured, although the total number of patients who died was not indicated.

At the beginning of 1947, UPA had a total of four battalions, which were divided into 17 sotnias and totaled about 1,400 men. At that time, the average size of a sotnia was approximately 80 men, although the strength of individual sotnias varied. The overall strength of UPA was approximately two-thirds of what it had been a year earlier, at its maximum strength. The reduction had resulted from two independent sotnias returning to Ukraine as well as attrition resulting from men killed in

---

525 The Internal Security Corps had about 32,000 men although the size of the unit attached to the division was not reported.

526 Misiło, ed. *Aksiia "Visla,"* 44, Footnote 2.

combat, the severely wounded who could no longer serve, those who had been captured, and deserters. Although the partisans had managed to partially replenish their ranks since the conclusion of Operation Rzeszów, their recruiting base had been reduced with the partial loss of the Ukrainian population. It became more difficult to find willing recruits since most young men who had wished to join UPA had done so earlier.

While the Polish army was conducting its anti-partisan operations, the General Staff developed a new deportation plan in the autumn of 1946 and early 1947,[527] General Stefan Mossor, the future commander of Operation Vistula, was a vociferous proponent of the deportation. In a top-secret report to Minister of Defense Marshal Michał Rola-Żymierski, dated February 20, 1947, he noted that the remaining Ukrainians "create a base for the UPA and a possibility for an irredentist movement in the future."[528] Although the Polish pre-war boundary had been moved west, Polish officials feared that the boundary might be adjusted again in the future and Ukrainian areas could be attached to Ukraine. To forestall that possibility, Mossor urged the minister to organize an energetic operation in the spring, with the goal of deporting all Ukrainians to the Recovered Territories and dispersing them among Poles where they would be quickly assimilated. He appended a table to the report indicating that 20,306 Ukrainians still remained in 12 counties.[529]

Despite the considerable resources committed over several years by the Polish State to remove Ukrainians and destroy the underground, Polish authorities had never accurately enumerated the Ukrainians in Poland. The task would not have been exceedingly difficult because interwar censuses and specialized population studies existed that would have better informed them about the Ukrainian population. Five days later, at the Rzeszów State Security Commission meeting, Mossor repeated his earlier proposal and stated that the matter had been discussed with Rzeszów's governor, who would in turn contact the central authorities with the proposal to deport the remaining Ukrainians. On March 27, one day before the Świerczewski ambush, he presented the finalized deportation plan to the State Security Committee and declared that the deportation of the remaining Ukrainians was an urgent matter. Mossor was not

---

527 Motyka, *Tak Bylo*, 405.

528 Misiło, ed. *Aksiia "Visla"*, 57.

529 Ibid, 57–58.

alone in his fervor, since other officers also demanded similar action. The commander of the Cracow Military District, Mikołaj Prus-Więckowski, noted that approximately 2,000 Lemkos live in Nowy Sącz, claimed that they were supporting UPA, and called for their deportation to the west. The Chief of Staff, Colonel Nikodim Kunderewicz of the Lublin Military District, reported on a dispatch sent on February 17, 1947 by Władysław Wolski, the Chief Plenipotentiary of the Ministry for Recovered Territories. The dispatch stated that the Polish government would begin a deportation campaign that would extend to October 3, 1947. [530] On March 27, the General Staff reported that UPA was having difficulties, lacked adequate support from the local Ukrainian population, and faced obstacles in obtaining food and clothing.

It was within this context, in the early months of 1947, that the Polish government took preliminary steps toward the deportation campaign that would come to be called Operation Vistula (Akcja "Wisła.") Army units were ordered to enumerate Ukrainians who were subject to deportation. At that time, Polish authorities claimed that the new round of deportations was a reprisal for the recent ambush of General Świerczewski. However, instructions to the Internal Security Corps, which were issued at the beginning of March 1947, outlined the procedure for the upcoming Operation "R", the earlier name for Akcja Wisła that included the removal of the Ukrainian population.[531]

On March 28, 1947, while conducting an inspection tour of army units in southeastern Poland, General Świerczewski was ambushed and killed by an UPA unit near Baligród. A commission was formed to investigate the ambush, and several weeks later, they issued a report on the general's itinerary and the ambush.[532] According to the report, the general had flown to Cracow on March 23 to inspect troops of the Fifth Military District. During the next several days, he and General Mikołaj Prus-Więckowski, commander of the district, inspected troops in Cracow, Rzeszów, Jarosław, and Przemyśl. On the evening of March 27, they arrived in Krosno from Przemyśl to inspect troops of the Eighth Division

---

530 Ibid, 63.

531 Shapoval, Iurii. *OUN i UPA na Tereni Polshchi (1944–1947 rr.)* (Kyiv: NAN Ukrainy, 2000), 189–196.

532 The following description is based on a report of April 17, 1947 issued by a commission charged with investigating the ambush ads published in Misylo, ed. *Aktsiia "Visla,"* 118–127.

in Sanok. At noon that day, through an unsecured phone line from Jarosław, the Division was informed that the general would arrive the following day from Krosno and was asked to provide a vehicle and security detail for the two generals. Colonel Jan Bielecki, the division's commander, called the staff to inform them of the impending inspection. Col. R. Ilnicki, the division's Chief of Staff, relayed the information through an unsecured phone line to Lt. Colonel Gerhard, commander of the 34th regiment in Lesko, who in turn informed a battalion commander in Baligród through an unsecured line, speaking in French for added security. In the evening, the two generals reached Sanok, where they were greeted by military and civilian authorities. They inspected the honor guards while an orchestra played. At 11 p.m. that night, General Świerczewski held a meeting with Colonel Bielecki and other senior officers of the division, questioning them on the political situation in the area and the political training of the troops. At the end of the meeting, the general decided that he would inspect the 34th Infantry Regiment in Lesko the following morning, and also expressed his desire to inspect the Border Guard troops. Bielecki named several locations where Border Guard units were stationed, including the village of Cisna, but the general made no decision at the time, stating only that he wished to leave for Lesko at 6:30 in the morning.

At 6:30 the next morning, the two generals and Colonel Bielecki, along with other senior officers, left for Lesko in a two-truck convoy. Troops were posted at strategic locations along the route and a well-armed 22-man security force in two Dodge trucks accompanied the generals.[533] Upon arriving, the general inspected an NCO school of the 34th Regiment and afterward, immediately departed for Baligród where the convoy arrived at 8:00 a.m. During that segment of the trip, an additional truck with 31 men was added to the convoy, but there were no troops posted along the route. After inspecting troops in Baligród, Świerczewski decided to inspect the Border Guard unit in Cisna despite the fact that Colonel Bielecki and Captain Karczewski, a Border Guard battalion commander, advised the general that the road between Baligród and Cisna was dangerous. Świerczewski ignored their advice and stated that

533 Under the Lend-Lease program during World War II, the U.S provided the Soviet Union with equipment and supplies, including trucks. After the war, some of these items were transferred to the Polish Army.

trucks that had returned to Lesko should turn around and head for Cisna. He then asked if there was a telephone line between Baligród and Cisna, and after being advised that there was, he stated: "Don't telephone them that I am coming. We will surprise them." However, an unidentified person using an unsecured line telephoned Cisna at about 9:00 a.m., advising the Border Guards of the general's visit.

At about the same time, the three trucks left for Cisna. The first, a Dodge, carried the two colonels and an 18-men guard unit armed with two machineguns, automatic weapons, rifles, and grenades. General Świerczewski and General Więckowski, along with several senior officers and four soldiers with two machine guns, were in the second truck, also a Dodge. The third truck, a Soviet ZiS, carried the officers and 19 men from the NCO school in Lesko who were armed with rifles and one machine gun. The three-truck convoy had a total of 49 men and was much better armed than a typical army unit. When the convoy arrived outside Baligród, the first truck developed engine trouble. Świerczewski ordered Lt. Colonel Gerhard to transfer to his truck, and ordered his driver to pass the stalled vehicle. The convoy now consisted of two trucks carrying 33 men: Świerczewski, Gerhard and six others were in the lead truck and the 25-man security detail was traveling in the second truck behind them. At about 9:30 a.m., a few miles south of Baligród, the convoy came under fire from a wooded hill on the right side of the road that was approximately 1,000 feet high. Świerczewski ordered his driver to increase the truck's speed, but after traveling approximately 130 feet beyond a small bridge, he ordered the driver to stop the truck and ordered the others in the vehicle to take cover in a ditch on the right side of the road. At that point, the second truck containing the security detail arrived at the bridge, and the partisans attempted to encircle the convoy. The general ordered the troops to stop and exit the vehicles, and to take cover in the ditch on the left side of the road along the stream, where they were to shoot upward and protect the flanks. He positioned himself in a gully by the stream and upon raising himself upright, he received a bullet in the stomach, yelling , "I have been wounded!" Two officers and several soldiers rushed to his side but as they headed toward the stream, the general received another bullet in his left shoulder blade. Soon afterward, he was helped to a secure place and bandaged, but died shortly afterward, as the stalled third truck arrived and the partisans broke off the attack. According to one report, three people in Świerczewski's convoy had been killed: the general, his driver, and a junior lieutenant. The autopsy revealed that the general had actually received three wounds: two in the stomach and one in the shoulder. Under the circumstances, the Polish losses were light. The trucks had apparently arrived as the partisans were deploying. A subsequent investigation revealed, based on shell casings, that the ambush had stretched approximately 1,600 to 1,900 feet along the road. Investigators concluded that the partisans had at least eight machine guns and had used prepared machine gun nests during the attack.[534]

The commission reached a number of conclusions about the ambush, some erroneous, and subsequently made recommendations. It concluded the ambush was carried out by Bir's sotnia, which was normally operating in the area, and had ambushed a Border Guard unit in the same spot four days later, killing 32 soldiers. Moreover, partisans from the Bir sotnia later boasted to villagers of accidentally killing Świerczewski and having learned later about his death. The partisans seemed to have been attributing the action to UPA in general and not their sotnia, specifically. (In any event, the ambush was actually carried out by Khrin's sotnia, one of four sotnias in the Ren Battalion, with men from both Khrin's and Stakh's sotnias.) The report continued, alleging that the partisans had shouted, "Urrah!" a Soviet Army battle cry that had also been used earlier by the Tsarist Army, although the Ukrainian nationalists never used a Russian battle cry. The report was very critical of the security measures that had been provided for the general and the poor preparation of the unit. It noted the inadequate security protocols, including the transmission of uncoded military information by phone that had informed other units and civilian authorities, including a Ukrainian priest, of the general's itinerary.[535] Although the Eight Division had provided adequate security between Sanok and Lesko, the protection had been poor in the Baligród-Cisna section. The investigation revealed that no officer had been designated to command the security of the convoy, no special unit had been assigned to protect the general, the number of troops assigned

534 Misylo, ed. *Aktsiia "Visla"*, 122.

535 As noted earlier, an unidentified individual phoned Cisna from Baligród concerning general's visit. The phone was apparently at priest's residence, and was probably the only phone in the village. The priest, Ostafy Kharkhalis, was arrested and spent a year-and-a-half in Jaworzno prison without being charged.

to the security detail had been insufficient, and no deployment plan had been developed in case of an attack. The report does point out that the general had made a last-minute decision to travel to Cisna against the advice of his officers, who were familiar with the local situation, and further noted that Świerczewski believed that the UPA danger had been exaggerated. Although it wasn't indicated in the report, it is possible that the general had based his opinion on earlier military reports that claimed that UPA had ceased their attacks and was in disarray. The commission proposed a continuation of the investigation, with a particular focus on examining the connection between the Ukrainian and Polish undergrounds, implying that UPA may have been informed of the general's travels by Polish partisans.

On the date of the Świerczewski ambush, Lt. Colonel Wacław Kossowski of the General Staff was ordered to investigate the matter and arrived at the scene of the ambush on the following day to carry out his work. Two weeks later, in early April, he filed two reports that in many respects were similar to the later commission's report, but also included additional information.[536] The Kossowski reports emphasized the inadequacy of the anti-partisan operation that had been conducted over the last eight months, and he was highly critical of the Eighth Division that operated in the area. Kossowski wrote that since the conclusion of Operation Rzeszów, operations against UPA had been passive, limited to occasional forays to the countryside with limited results and if an occasional contact was made, troops did not pursue and destroy the partisans. The recent reduced partisan activities had been caused by severe winter conditions, and with the coming spring, UPA had become more aggressive. Moreover, more Ukrainians remained than Polish army had previously believed and the division had taken too little interest in the civilians who were supporting the underground. He noted that southeast of Cisna, an UPA stronghold, no soldier had set foot there in the last half a year.

To underscore the inaptitude of the troops in the division, Kossowski also relayed an incident that took place upon his arrival at the scene of the ambush on March 29th. He had arrived with a 30-man security detachment that included Lt. Colonel Gerhard, the commander of the 32nd Regiment in Lesko, who was in the ambushed party. As the colonel

536 Ibid, 87–92.

was describing the ambush, security men with rifles and machine guns on their shoulders were milling about, and no patrols were sent nor were any guards posted. At that point, friendly fire broke out between army troops and the Border Guard unit, each occupying a separate hill overlooking the road. The security group along with their officers scattered although bullets were flying about 300 feet above the road. Kossowski was especially critical of the unit's use of uncoded telephone conversations to transmit military information and used the example of the telephone line between Baligród and Cisna. He noted that the partisans controlled the area, but the line had not been destroyed because, in his opinion, the underground had found it useful. Contrary to the commission's finding, and basing his opinion on the phone call to Cisna and Świerczewski's meetings with local civilian officials, Kossowski concluded that the ambush had not been coincidental and that the underground must have placed an inside agent in the general's entourage.

Because of the timing of the events, Kossowski's conclusion seems improbable. Świerczewski left Sanok at 6:30 and was ambushed at 9:30 a.m. In the intervening three hours, he had visited Lesko and Baligród and, at the last minute, had decided to visit Cisna. Therefore, UPA could have learned of his movement only if their agent had been in the general's entourage and he had communicated with them by radio. Others, including General Mossor, who actually praised the division, did not share Kossowski's evaluation. Additionally, there was no actual evidence of UPA infiltration, an unlikely scenario since the UPA did not use radio communications, but instead communicated by couriers using coded language and dead drops. With respect to the Cisna call, even if the underground had planted an agent in the village, there would have been insufficient time to locate Khrin in the forest, and in turn, it is unlikely that Khrin could have organized an ambush within a half-an-hour period. Nevertheless, the investigation of the ambush continued, and in April 1948, a trial was held in Warsaw for 22 captured UPA men, most of them from the Khrin and Stakh sotnias. Of the condemned men, 10 were executed and 12 received long-term sentences.[537] Among other evidence, the trial sought to find a Polish link, but none was found. Despite the

---

537 Ibid, 127, Footnote 10.

show-trial theatrics, later Polish assessments concluded that the general had died in a random ambush.

The underground literature provides little information on the ambush. Khrin wrote two pieces on his underground experience that made their way to the West, but information describing his activities in the Transcurzon region is missing. A brief discussion of the event is given by a platoon leader in Khrin's sotnia, Oleksa Konopads'kyi ("Ostroverkh"), who had not personally participated in the ambush.[538] Ostroverkh reported that Khrin had slept little during the night and smoked constantly, and speculated that he had received some information. According to Ostroverkh, on the morning of the ambush, Khrin left two platoons in camp that were exhausted by the previous days of fighting. He left the camp with the remainder, as well as with units from Stakh's sotnia. Upon returning, he removed a political calendar (presumably Polish) from his bag, thumbed through it, came across a bald headed general and said to Ostroverkh, "We zapped this character." Realizing that a general had been killed, Khrin had ordered his partisans to break camp and leave the area.

Stepan Dzhula ("Dovbush") is the only Ukrainian who participated in the ambush and wrote about it when he reached the West. He wrote that Khrin awoke the cooks at about 4:00 a.m. to prepare breakfast for the sotnia at 6:00, and that the men had left at 7:00. The partisans arrived at the ambush site with three platoons from Khrin's sotnia and two from Stakh's, although he did not indicate the total strength of the ambush group. Dzhula's platoon commanded by "Hran" was sent some distance to the north from the main body. The trucks arrived as Hran was deploying his squads and the partisans, who were not yet ready, opened fire. As the fight continued, the partisan "Oslava", lying next to Dzhula, noticed a bald headed man in a white overcoat, waving his hands as though he was giving orders. Dzhula noted that Oslava fired twice at the man with his Soviet carbine; however, there is no way of knowing whose bullet actually killed the general.[539]

Immediately after the ambush, a telegram was sent to Col. General Władysław Korczyc, Chief of the General Staff, informing him of Świerczewski's death. The telegram noted that the convoy had been attacked

538 Potichnyj, ed. *Litopys UPA*, Vol. 30, 318–319.

539 Dzhula-Dovbush, Stepan. *Neperedbachyna Dolia*: *Spomyny*, 167–170.

by about 150 men, and the fight had lasted about two and a-half hours. It notes that in addition to the general, an officer and two soldiers were killed and three had been wounded. The general's body was transported to Sanok and the following day, General Zawadzki was scheduled to fly from Krosno to Warsaw with the remains. Colonel Dmytro Voznesens'kyi requested that the general's family, totaling three persons, would be flown from Moscow to attend the funeral.[540]

The news of the general's death spread quickly throughout the country by press and radio, and the Politburo met the following day to consider the event and to prepare future plans. The protocol of the meeting indicates that the funeral was discussed and the general was awarded "Virtuti Militari," First Class, Poland's highest decoration for military valor. More importantly, the Politburo decreed that all Ukrainians and mixed families supporting the underground must be deported to the western territories, settled no closer than 60 miles from state borders, and scattered among the Polish population. The deportation campaign was to be coordinated with the USSR and Czechoslovakia, and the final deportation plans were to be prepared within one week.[541] The same day, the Council of Ministers also held a meeting where they made a number of decisions, noting that the general had commanded the Second Army and had fought in Spain. They decided that the government would finance a state funeral, and two monuments would be built to memorialize the general, one at the location of the ambush and another in the cemetery of the Second Army on the River Nysa (Neisse). Further, his widow and young children would be provided with a pension.

In 1897, Karol Świerczewski was born in Warsaw, which was then part of the Russian Empire. He moved to Russia in 1915 and joined the Red Army in November 1917. After the Russian Civil War, he received advance training at the Frunze Military Academy in Moscow. He fought in the Spanish Civil War under the pseudonym "Walter", commanding the 14th Brigade and later the 36th International Division. At some point, he commanded the American Brigade and addressed their reunion in 1946. After returning to the Soviet Union, Świerczewski held various posts and at the beginning of World War II, he commanded the 248th Ri-

540 Voznesens'kyi, apparently a Ukrainian, was Świerczewski's son-in-law and a Soviet adviser to the Polish security forces. See Misylo, ed. *Aktsiia "Visla,"* 70, Footnote 5.

541 Ibid, 71.

fle Division. In August 1943, he was transferred to the newly forming Polish Peoples Army, where he served as the deputy commander of the First Corps and subsequently commanded the First and Second Armies, participating in the Prague and Berlin operations as commander of the Second Army. After the war, he was assigned to command the Third Military District (Poznań area) and was appointed as the Second Vice Minister of Defense on February 14, 1946.[542]

Świerczewski's death energized Polish efforts to destroy UPA and deport Ukrainians, and the military, governmental and political departments quickly developed plans to accomplish both objectives. On March 30, two days after the ambush, the Military Security Committee held a meeting in Rzeszów, chaired by Colonel Wieliczko and attended by senior officers. After a four-hour discussion, they issued a plan to realize those objectives.[543] The current strength of the Polish Army was viewed as insufficient to destroy the UPA, and the Committee issued a new plan that assigned the fight with the Polish underground to police and security forces, while reinforced army units supported by security forces and the Border Guards would operate against the Ukrainians. The task required the following measures to be taken: deport Ukrainians and mixed families as well as Poles who were aiding UPA; establish concentration camps for Ukrainians caught with arms; establish a military field court to adjudicate armed captives; and destroy the property of the deportees so as to prevent its use by the Ukrainian underground. The deportation campaign would be administered by the Provincial Security Commission, civilian authorities would settle Poles in former Ukrainian areas, security would be provided by police and ORMO, and special forces would be organized to guard oil fields and bridges to relieve the army and police of the responsibility. In addition to the Eighth and Ninth Divisions, additional troops would be moved into the area and the strength of Internal Security Troops would be increased from 3,000 to 7,000. The Eighth Division would be reinforced by battalions from the Fifth, Seventh and Tenth Divisions of the former Second Army and two regiments that had been detached earlier and sent to Łódź would be returned to the division. Ground units were to be supplemented by airplanes, which would be used for communications, patrolling, and the bombardment of partisan

542 Ibid, 69–70, Footnote 2.
543 Ibid, 75–77.

camps. The operation would be aided by lightly armed vehicles, communications units to intercept partisan radio communication, and police dogs. In addition, the Committee determined that an agreement should be reached with Czechoslovakia in order to prevent UPA from entering that country.

Two days after Wieliczko's proposal, Marshal Michał Rola-Żymierski, Minister of Defense, and General Radkiewicz, Minister of Public Safety, issued an order that was similar to the proposal.[544] The order noted that UPA had become more active in the Sanok and Lesko areas, where they had recently ambushed troops and a Border Guard unit (a clear reference to Bir's ambush). The reason for the increased aggression was not indicated in the order, but it's likely that the warm weather and the change in army tactics were factors. During the winter, Polish troops usually remained in their garrisons, making only the occasional foray to the countryside, but by spring, they were actively seeking out the partisans. The operation against UPA was set to commence on April 10, headed by the Eighth Division and additional units from other formations. At the time, the division had two regiments that were to be reinforced by a maneuvering battalion of a 1,000-man Internal Security Corps unit from Rzeszów, a 360-man maneuvering battalion of the Internal Security Troops from Cracow and Lublin, four armored vehicles, and a 200-man maneuvering unit from the Cracow Military District. Additionally, the Eighth Division would receive communications equipment, transport, and adequate supply of gasoline, food, and ammunition.

As preparations were being made for the destruction of the UPA, the military sought to seal Poland's borders with the Soviet Union and Czechoslovakia. The Soviet border had always been well guarded and difficult to cross, although UPA units and couriers frequently managed to slip through. The Czechoslovakian border, however, was porous and complicated by the topography. The Lemko region on the Polish side stretches over 95 air miles, but the border meanders along the crest of the Carpathian Mountains, totaling perhaps 125 miles on densely forested ground, a condition that would have required a massive amount of troops to completely seal the border. On April 8, the Polish Chief of Counterintelligence, Juliy Burgin, informed the Vice Minister of Internal Security,

---

544 Ibid, 83–84.

Roman Romkovski, that the Czech General Staff had ordered General Jan Herman in eastern Slovakia to seal the border and establish cooperation with a Polish operational group stationed near the Dukla Pass. In another note written two days later, the chief stated that the Polish request had been granted and the border had been sealed since April 5.[545] Finally, on April 14, Marshal Rola-Żymierski sent correspondence to the Czechoslovak Minister of Defense, General Ludvik Svoboda, and Soviet Marshal Nikolay Bulganin, requesting that the borders be sealed.[546] On April 17, the Polish Embassy in Prague raised concerns about the border issue, and on the following day, the Czechoslovak Ministry of Foreign Affairs reassured the Embassy that the appropriate institutions had been notified. Several days later, Svoboda informed the Ambassador that only a portion of the border had been closed since April 5 and that on April 19, he had issued an order to the army to close the entire border with the Lemko region. The Poles, anxious to receive a firm commitment from Czechoslovakia, held another meeting at the border on May 8. General Mossor, who was accompanied by five senior officers, represented the Polish side and the Czechoslovak side sent three generals and four staff officers.[547] The Czechoslovak side agreed to protect the border, but stated that the total length could not be adequately guarded due to distance, terrain and the lack of troops. Therefore, they requested that the Polish side notify them three to four days in advance of an attack, providing the location, further specified that the request to block the border should not exceed four to five kilometers.

For the Polish side, this proposal was less than ideal. The Ukrainian partisans were constantly on the move and their clashes with troops tended to be quick and unpredictable, and under such conditions, advanced notice was impossible. The parties agreed to hold additional meetings on May 12 and May 15 that would determine the dates, times and places requiring a guarded border. They reached an agreement to communicate by phone and radio. The Poles set up their station on the Czechoslovakian side and the Czechoslovaks did likewise in Sanok, which is located over 25 miles from the border. The two sides agreed to permit their troops to cross each other's border in pursuit of the partisans. On May 28, Czecho-

545 Ibid, 85.

546 Ibid, 98–99.

547 Ibid, 255–257.

slovakian Premier Klement Gottwald and General Svoboda signed an agreement designating special Czechoslovakian and Polish units to pursue the partisans across the border until the UPA was destroyed. The Polish units were further allowed to operate on the Slovak side, subordinate to the local commander. The Charge d'Affairs of the Embassy in Prague notified Warsaw about the agreement.[548] With respect to the Soviet Union, the available information indicates that both sides agreed to communicate and cooperate to prevent border crossings.

During the month of April, a large number of troops were deployed in the southeastern portion of the Rzeszów Province. Minister of Defense Marshal Rola-Żymierski and Minster of Public Safety Gen. Radkiewicz issued a directive for Operation "East," earlier noted as Operation "R" and subsequently renamed Operation Vistula (*Akcja Wisła)*. The operation was to be commanded initially from Sanok and later shifted to Rzeszów, and army units, security troops, and police were subordinated to the command. The operational area was divided into four regions: S--Sanok; R--Rzeszów; L--Lublin; and G--Gorlice. On the following day, April 17, the two ministers issued another order outlining the procedure for combating the underground and deporting the Ukrainians. Supplementing the order are numerous appendices that provided detailed information and also outline several major objectives. The first objective was the destruction of the UPA in the Sanok, Przemyśl and Lubaczów areas, an operation that was to continue until the underground was completely eradicated, with a special focus placed on destroying their command structure. Second, the military was instructed to work closely with the *Polski Urzad Repatriacyjny* (PUR, State Administration for Repatriation) to deport all Ukrainians to the northwest (former German territories) and disperse them among Poles. Third, all Ukrainians were subject to deportation, including mixed Polish-Ukrainian families working with the UPA. Finally, the order specified that the deportation operations to the southeast of Baligród were to be comprehensive (it was not clear whether some Poles would be deported as well.)[549]

Major General Stefan Mossor, Deputy Chief of the General Staff, was appointed to command the military operation. He was assisted by representatives from the ministries of security and public administration,

---

548 Ibid, 389.

549 Ibid, 102–104 and 108–111.

as well as the director of the PUR. The deportations were scheduled to begin around April 24, but were ultimately delayed until April 28 because the necessary transportation had not yet been assembled. The directive gave Mossor broad powers over other agencies on the affected territory. All security forces and police were subordinated to him and he had the right to issue orders to the commanders of the Fifth and Seventh military districts related to the operation. Working through the civilian representatives attached to the command, he also had the authority to issue orders to civilian agencies, including post and telegraph agencies. Table 4 lists the army units and a division of Internal Security Troops totaling 17,500 men, specifying their areas of deployment. All army regiments were classified as "select", meaning that they were composed of more elite units.[550]

Table 4. List of Units of the Operational Group "Wisła"

Headquarters and Location	Unit and Location	Number of Soldiers
Grand Total		*17,350*
Command of the Operational Group "Wisła"		150
6th Division	6th Regiment, Osławica	800
Komańcza	2nd Regiment, Hurne (sic)[551]	800
7th Division	7th Regiment, Manasterzec	800
	10th Regiment, Jawornik	
Tyriava	Ruski	800
Voloska	11th Regiment, Trzcianiec	800
8th Division	1st Regiment, Bukowsko	1,200
Lesko	8th Regiment, Lesko	800

550 Motyka places army and Internal Security Troops at 19,335. When other security units are added, excluding Border Guards, it totals about 21,000. See Motyka, *Tak Bylo*, 406–407.

551 This is a typographical error. No such location exists, as stated in the text.

9th Division	9th Regiment, Bircza	1,000
Przemyśl	5th Regiment, Przemyśl	800
	3rd Regiment, Lubaczów	800
	14th Regiment, Jarosław	800
Corps for Internal Security		
Baligród	3 Brigades	4,500
Total Directly Engaged in Deportation		**14,050**
	Supporting Elements	
Border Guards	4th regiment, Dukla	800
Reserve	12th Regiment, Sanok	800
Police		700
Transport	1st Motor Regiment, Ol-chowce	500
Sappers	5th Sapper Regiment, Zagórz	500
Total		**3,300**

Source: Evhen Mysylo, ed., *Aktsiia* "Visla." (L'viv - New York, 1997), p.112.

At the time, Polish units were comparatively much smaller than those of other contemporary armies, with a typical Polish division being equivalent to a regiment or a brigade. The force was directed against two UPA battalions in Tactical Sector 26 (*Lemko*), which consisted of seven sotnias and totaled approximately 700 men. Mossor ordered that one division, comprised of about 3,000 men, should be assigned to pursue each sotnia. In his April 20 directive to the troops, he stated that the UPA force totaled "…almost 2,000 wonderfully armed men with iron discipline"[552] The partisans had more machine guns and automatic weapons compared to Polish units of comparable strength. The 17,500-man force was directed against the Baida and Ren battalions. Archival documents reported by Szcześniak and Szota place UPA strength in the Transcurzon

552 Misylo, ed. *Aktsiia "Visla",* 144.

in spring of 1947 at 1,330, noting that they were supplemented by OUN units that totaled several hundred men, as well as some SKV groups who were relatively inactive during the operation.[553]

The initial operation was directed against UPA's Tactical Sector 26. This included the Baida Battalion in the Przemyśl area, which had approximately 412 men across its four sotnias; and the Ren Battalion in the Lemko region, whose three sotnias totaled about 300 men. These two battalions were known for having aggressive commanders and being well armed with machine guns, rifles, and automatic weapons. Most automatic weapons at that time were Soviet machine pistols using pistol size ammunition and had either a magazine of 36 rounds or a drum of 71 rounds. Both types could be fired in semi-automatic or automatic mode. Baida's battalion included the sotnias of Burlaka (120 men with 12 machine guns along with other weapons), Hromenko (120 men armed with 12 machine guns and 16 automatic weapons, with the remainder carrying rifles), Lastivka (91 men with 8 machine guns), and Krylach with 81 men. Ren's Battalion formally consisted of four sotnias totaling 420 men: Bir (100 men with 15 machine guns and 22 automatic weapons), Brodych (120 men who at the time were operating 60 miles west in the Lemko region), Khrin (120 men with 15 machine guns and 25 automatic weapons) and Stakh (80 men, many of whom were new recruits, armed with 8 machine guns). Khrin's sotnia, comprised of 120 men divided into four platoons, was particularly aggressive and well-armed. One platoon would occasionally pose as a Polish unit (dressed completely in Polish uniforms), confusing Polish civilians and authorities. The platoon occasionally engaged in firefights with Soviet units and border guards, prompting Soviet authorities to complain about Polish attacks on their men. As discussed in the previous chapter, it was the typical tactic of Khrin, as a sotnia commander, to seek out Polish army convoys and set up ambushes.

The Rola-Żymierski-Radkiewicz directive covered many aspects of the operation, including political indoctrination of the troops. The Polish army was patterned on the Soviet model: its units had political officers who were required to explain the current party line, a crucial function since the communist party enjoyed only limited support in Poland. The

---

553 Szcześniak and Szota, Droga, 428–429.

directive identified key points to be covered during the indoctrination, including the requirement to inform troops about the importance of deportation as a crucial step in eliminating opposition to the government. Toward the end of April, the Political Department issued a document entitled "Hitler's Heirs," which enumerated points that were to be stressed in political lectures with the troops. Following the Soviet approach, it demonized the UPA by associating the underground with Nazi atrocities against civilians. According to the document, the lectures should emphasize that almost three years earlier, Hitler's Germany, the heart of Fascism in Europe, had been destroyed; however, not all Fascist elements had been liquidated. It noted that the UPA consisted of soldiers from the SS Galician Division who had participated in suppressing the Warsaw Uprising, as well as some men who had later joined Vlasov's Army. To tear up the roots of "Ukrainian Fascism," it was the soldiers' duty to deport Ukrainians who support UPA. Finally, the troops were urged to avenge Świerczewski's death.[554]

The document clearly distorted historical events for propaganda purposes. The UPA burned Ukrainian villages almost exclusively to prevent Poles from resettling and therefore benefitting from the Ukrainian tragedy. Attacks on Polish villages were rare, and when they did occur, they were usually tied to some form of retaliation. With respect to the Galician Division, the number of men in UPA ranks had always been small, although several divisions' officers did hold key positions. Contrary to the claim in the document, the Division had not participated in the suppression of the Warsaw Uprising. At the time, it was widely known that units of General Andrii Vlasov's Army (the Russian Liberation Army which consisted mainly of Red Army veterans) and the Kaminski Brigade (Russian National Liberation Army) that had actually participated in the fighting. Both had been subordinated to the German high command. Several other documents characterized UPA in a similar way, restating the same arguments. One document in particular asserted that the defeat of UPA was necessary for the stability of the region and its eventual resettlement by Poles in the Ukrainian districts by military colonists.

---

[554] Misylo, ed. *Aktsiia "Visla",* 188–191.

[555] Such language was reminiscent of the interwar Polonization policies in Volhynia.

In addition to demonizing the UPA, Polish propaganda sought to impress upon the troops the necessity of treating the deportees humanely, explained the reasons for the deportation, and placed an emphasis on urging the Ukrainian partisans to surrender.[556] During the deportations, troops were instructed to treat the Ukrainians as normal Polish citizens, and allow them to take property and livestock to the resettlement locations. They warned that violence was forbidden and would be severely punished, since mistreatment would only aid the partisans' attempts to paint Polish troops as the enemy of the people, and therefore increase resistance. A Polish leaflet to the population described the disruptive UPA activities and their support by the people. To eliminate UPA's support base, all Ukrainians were to be deported from the border zone, based on the 1936 law, and their removal would enable them to lead peaceful lives in another part of Poland.[557] Another leaflet directed at the "Fooled Members of the UPA Bands," accused them of working for former SS division members and policemen. The leaflet described the partisans as hungry, raggedy, constantly on the run, living like wild animals, filthy, cold, and covered with lice because they had no means for basic hygiene. It reminded the partisans that their leaders were keeping them in the forests by telling them that a third world war was imminent, a nonsense that no one seriously believed. Toward the end of the leaflet was a subheading: "Whoever surrenders voluntarily, arms in hand, will live." The leaflet then noted that during the last month, a great deal had been learned about the Ukrainian underground, the authorities knew who they were, and their total destruction was imminent.

> "Operating in smaller units, changing territory or fleeing abroad will not save you… allied troops are waiting for you at the border."…Abandon your life of crime and surrender to pursue normal, peaceful lives."[558]

---

555 Ibid, 190

556 Ibid, 192–194.

557 The 1927 law, as amended in 1936, permitted local officials to remove people from a two kilometer border zone temporarily or permanently for security reasons. During *Akcja Wisła*, the law was applied in the western Lemko region regardless of the distance from the border. In 1950, the law was again applied to remove a small number of Ukrainian families from four villages in the Nowy Targ County. See Ibid, 60–61.

558 Misylo, ed. *Aktsiia "Visla"*, 193.

There is no evidence that the Polish propaganda efforts produced the desired results of intimidating the partisans to surrender en masse. Nevertheless, the policy of torturing and executing captive UPA soldiers proved to be stronger deterrents for effecting surrender.

Although the Vistula deportation campaign was ultimately less violent than Operation Rzeszów had been, some violence did occur. By 1947, the process of mass deportation was better organized, the army was more disciplined, and there was no charade about it being a "voluntary" resettlement. People no longer had to be beaten and terrorized to sign a meaningless piece of paper; they were simply rounded up, brought to railroad stations, and shipped to the west as quickly as possible. There is also no indication that the Ukrainian population blamed UPA or had reconciled themselves to their fate. Instead, their anger and outrage was directed toward the Soviets and the Poles. With respect to the partisans, a genuine amnesty with humane treatment would have stimulated desertion and presented UPA with more serious problems vis-à-vis the local Ukrainian population, especially in the later stages, and could arguably have provided the Polish side with badly needed intelligence. However, the Polish Communist regime, with its Stalinist policies, was not interested in simply defeating the opponent, but insisted on their total extermination. During the three years of fighting, captives were tortured in order to obtain information, and then either shot or sentenced to long prison terms. Under such circumstances, the tactic of dropping leaflets on the forests was not likely to produce surrender.

The military and civilian preparations for Operation Vistula continued in tandem during the month of April. On April 11, the Politburo noted that Władysław Wolski, Vice Minister of Public Order at the time, would submit a deportation plan within a week and stated that the deportations would commence in two weeks' time. The Politburo also appointed Gen. Mossor to command the military side of the operation, Col. Grzegorz Korczyński would command the Ministry of Public Security Forces, and Col. Juliusz Hübner would oversee the troops of the Internal Security Corps. On April 14, the deportation directive was issued to the appropriate departments of public administration, resettlement agencies, and PUR. In four sections, it outlined the procedures for removing the population.[559] The authorities were instructed to provide adequate transportation to enable people to take as much property as possible; including livestock, farm implements, grain, potatoes, and other edibles. The policy was initiated to ease food demands on the government and provide the necessary tools for farming in the west. Additionally, care was to be taken that property left behind would not be destroyed, and any violations were to be reported to the military authorities, the Ministry of Public Safety and the Political Department. As the military herded the people to designated assembly points, they were required to provide security, medical care, and to gather information about the deportees to include the size of their farms in hectares (including arable land) and the types of buildings left behind. Personal data was required to be disaggregated for each person by village, gmina, and county. The information was to accompany each person and be turned over to PUR personnel at the railroad station who were responsible for managing the people in transit and tasked with determining their final resettlement destinations. All family members were to be placed in a single boxcar together with their property, and later sorted for urban or rural placement. Each train was required to have about 20 guards and a convoy commander, who would maintain the list of the people in the convoy, and then provide the list to the PUR representative for determining the final destination. At the last station, people were to be unloaded and provided with food, lodging and transportation to the final destination. At that point, the deportees became wards of the resettlement authorities, who were provided with lists of available domiciles by local authorities. The PUR was required to bring the deportees to an appropriate village, and if no dwellings were available, the village mayor was required to provide them with temporary lodging. In such cases, a number of families could be lodged in a larger farmstead until adequate housing could be provided.

Later in the month, the Ministry for Reclaimed Territories and PUR each issued virtually identical instructions, paralleling Wolski's plan, but providing additional details.[560] Documents enumerating the deportees and their property had to be sent either to the County Resettlement Department in Szczecinek (West Prussia) or to the Provincial Resettlement Department in Olsztyn (East Prussia). At the initial assembly point (rail-

---

559 Ibid, 86 and 96–97.

560 Ibid, 134–142.

road station), the PUR representative was to work closely with the military representative, and people awaiting departure were to have medical care, ensured adequate sanitary conditions, and provided with three meals per day. At the time of loading, the requisite information for Ukrainians was recorded on pink paper, and Poles settling in the west were recorded on blue paper. Although the two groups did not travel on the same trains, the color designation was apparently designed to avoid confusion at the final destination. Two sealed envelopes were issued for each family designating their initial rail stop as either Oświęcim (Auschwitz) or Lublin, and a final rail destination such as Szczecinek or Olsztyn. Oświęcim was a major railroad junction northwest of Cracow, but because it was associated with the German death camp, the name was crossed out and "Katowice," a large city in the same area, was written in by hand; the trains, however, continued to arrive at the Oświęcim station. Based on information contained in the documents, trains from Katowice or Lublin were directed either to Olsztyn or Szczecinek. The Ministry's document indicates that initially 5,000 families were to be sent to rural areas and 1,500 to urban areas in the Olsztyn Province, regardless of their previous place of dwelling. The Szczecin Province was required to settle 7,500 families in rural areas and 2,000 in urban areas, although virtually all Ukrainians came from villages. A family considered to be "suspicious" was required to be settled in a village without any other Ukrainians, while other families could be settled in larger numbers. Once unloaded, the trains were required to return immediately to the designated stations in the Ukrainian districts.

As the operation against UPA and the deportation preparations continued, more partisans were captured and suspicious people were arrested. This required new procedures and facilities to adjudicate and house the captives. Ukrainian partisans were tried by local military courts. On May 2, a rumor spread among railroad and police personnel that UPA had attacked a rail transport near Jasło and that the attack had been repelled, but subsequently, some civilians who were being transported shot and killed five soldiers. The following day, the Politburo issued an order extending the use of repressive measures against civilians. Although the rumor proved to be false within a week's time, the order was not rescinded. Thus, the new repressive policy was justified by a hoax, just as Świerczewski's assassination was used to rationalize the Vistula campaign.[561] The order established a military court for partisans and designated the concentration camp Jaworzno as a place to imprison civilians suspected of supporting the underground. After the war, Poland seized German camps and interned captured German soldiers, the Volksdeutsche, and others they considered hostile to the new regime. Jaworzno was a satellite camp of Auschwitz where 5,910 individuals had died between 1945 and 1946.[562] In the spring of 1947, part of the facility was designated as a place to exclusively intern Ukrainians. On April 24, two orders were issued providing for the arrest and imprisonment of 194 people in 16 villages of the Sanok County.[563] From the Sanok-Lesko area, the first transport of Ukrainians arrived at Jaworzno on May 9 and the second transport arrived on May 14, totaling 307 people, including 49 women. The prisoners were marched five miles from the railroad station to the camp, guarded by troops of the Internal Security Corps. They beat the prisoners during the march and encouraged Polish civilians to participate, claiming that these people were responsible for Świerczewski's death.[564] The camp had 14 barracks guarded by more than 300 Internal Security troops, and 12 watchtowers with machine guns and searchlights. One side of the camp had a sixteen-foot high brick wall, and the other sides were enclosed with barbed wire fences. As the deportations continued, there were reports of some Ukrainians illegally leaving the resettlement territories and returning to their villages to harvest grain. On July 16, Mossor issued a secret order to troops and security forces to arrest the individuals and send them to Jaworzno.[565] By March 1949, 3,873 Ukrainians were imprisoned in the camp, including 707 women, dozens of children, 27 priests (including the priest from Cisna who had received a telephone call about Świerczewski's visit), along with much of the Ukrainian intelligentsia. Because of hunger, illness, and beatings, 162 people died and were buried in nearby woods in unmarked graves.[566] How many people were actually guilty of supporting the underground is uncertain and to a considerable extent depended upon how "support" was defined. Throughout the insurgency, most Ukrainians had provided food, occa-

---

561 Ibid, 235–236 and 257–258.
562 Ibid, 171, footnote 1.
563 Ibid, 185–186.
564 Ibid, 291, footnote 2.
565 Ibid, 369–370.
566 Ibid, 172.

sional lodging, and information on troop movement when partisans arrived in their villages, and in that sense, almost all Ukrainians were guilty. Far fewer in number were the activists who had regular contact with the underground collecting food and intelligence, and in many cases those individuals operated clandestinely. Eventually, most prisoners were released from Jaworzno because the prison authorities, despite the numerous interrogations and beatings, could not find any evidence to keep them in prison.

The operation against the underground and the coinciding deportation campaign were carried out in three phases. The first phase was conducted in the Przemyśl-Sanok-Lesko area and the Lublin Province, where people were to be removed by the middle of May. The second phase began in June, when the operation shifted to northern Przemyśl County, Lubaczów County and counties in the western Lemko region. At the end of June, additional troops were sent to the Lublin Province to remove people from the large swampy and wooded areas which were only sparsely populated by Ukrainians at the time. The third phase commenced in July, when special units were formed to comb the countryside where the deportations had been completed, destroying what remained of the underground and removing civilians who had thus far evaded deportation.[567] The new strategy differed sharply from earlier efforts where the both the deportation activities and the pursuit of partisans were conducted simultaneously along the 300-mile eastern border. At that point, the enlarged, better trained, and better armed units were directed to the heart of the insurgency in the southeastern counties, which was the operational territory of Tactical Sector 26. The change in strategy enabled the Poles to achieve overwhelming numerical superiority. Some 3,000 troops would pursue a sotnia of 100 men or less. As a result, the UPA was overwhelmed and the civilians could no longer evade deportation in areas that were saturated with troops. The troops initially concentrated on deporting people instead of fighting the underground until May 2, when General Mossor issued an order reversing the emphasis, making the vigorous pursuit of the partisans their top priority.[568]

Another directive described civilian support for the partisans and the difficulty of fighting the underground in hilly and wooded terrain,

---

567 Ibid, 30–31.
568 Ibid, 228.

and also outlined tactics to be used henceforth. The directive accurately described the UPA organizational structure and correctly concluded that UPA was being supported by an OUN civilian apparatus. It further noted the following points: (1.) UPA was largely armed with automatic weapons and machine guns and had ample supply of ammunition and hand grenades; (2.) The partisans wore the uniforms of various armies, including Russian, Polish, and German, and stated that almost all of them had UNRRA overcoats (i.e., U.S. Army coats), a gross exaggeration; (3.) There was a network of hospitals in underground bunkers located in inaccessible areas and well camouflaged, virtually impossible to locate. (4.) The partisans used bunkers to store food, ammunition, and supplies; and (5.) The partisans moved at night and their tactics were based on surprise-ambushes and quick raids. They frequently attacked small units as well as civil administration and bridges. After the attacks, the partisans would disperse and return to their villages and live as civilians. [569]

From more than the three years of fighting, the Polish army had learned a great deal about the underground, but still did not fully understand their methods of operation. The UPA was a standing army and not an ad hoc formation of armed civilians. When a young man joined the UPA, it was for the duration of the struggle, however long that would take. Many men served in units operating far from their native villages, and if their unit operated in the area and passed through their villages, it provided them with opportunities to visit their families, which could be a rare event since UPA did not issue furloughs. The village self-defense units were always a marginal force in Transcurzon region and were seriously weakened by the deportations to the east. By the spring of 1947, the SKV had virtually ceased to exist. When troops approached a village, the local men usually fled to avoid execution while the women and children remained. It's likely that the absence of men that led the Poles to conclude that all village men were partisans. During Operation Vistula, troops were directed to change tactics, operate very cautiously, use flankers during marches, and to guard encampments. If contact was made with the enemy, they were instructed to form an encirclement to prevent the partisans from escaping. In the event of an escape, the partisans were to be pursued and destroyed. Emphasis was placed on capturing partisans as

---

[569] Ibid, 157–159.

a means of gaining intelligence. Any contact with the partisans was required to be reported immediately to other divisions specified in the order. Curfews were to be established between 11:00 a.m. and 4:00 p.m., and check points were placed at bridges, railroad stations and exits from villages. Although Polish authorities were tasked with constantly checking identification papers, few people actually had papers and of those who did possess them, most papers would have been issued during the German occupation era. People, especially men, avoided contact with the authorities for fear of being deported or arrested and did not attempt to acquire new Polish documents. Troops were required to arrest suspicious persons and after questioning them, were required to turn them over to the Public Safety Administration for transfer to Sanok. Greek Catholic priests were thoroughly scrutinized since the authorities believed that they formed an important component of the underground, which was another erroneous assumption.

As the preparations continued, a flurry of new orders was issued which assessed UPA's strength and activities and proposed new tactics. The orders were largely repetitious, but most provided some additional information and new methods of operation. Stationed in the village of Kulaszne (Kuliashne) in the Sanok region, the Seventh Division issued a special order on April 24 that outlined the current operation against the partisans. Troops were instructed to pursue UPA units and work with the PUR to remove the Ukrainian population. The order targeted three UPA sotnias that were stationed in Sanok and Lesko counties, those of Bir, Khrin, and Stakh, but their actual locations were unknown. The order included speculation that the units might have left the area: Bir to Czechoslovakia, and Khrin to the Przemyśl area. The division, consisting of two regiments and working with security forces and police, was ordered to locate and destroy Stakh's unit. It was instructed to coordinate the offensive with other divisions in the area, including the Sixth Division in Komańcza, the First Division of the Internal Troops Corps in Baligród, and the Eighth Division in Lesko. On the eve of the deportation, four divisions, along with security forces and police, operated in the two counties where they believed the underground to be encamped.

A few days into the deportation, Mossor issued another order outlining the deportation plan and criticizing the performance of the troops.[570] After ten days of action, he noted, the army had not learned anything new and had accomplished little; instead, the partisans were attacking troops and stealing cattle under their noses. He acknowledged a few small accomplishments, noting that a handful of partisans had been killed or captured and the Eighth Division had located a bunker containing valuable documents. The troops were to concentrate on the primary objective —destroying the underground rather than removing Ukrainians civilians. "Sweeps" were abandoned since they had been deemed ineffective. Special well-armed units were organized to gather intelligence and larger units were formed and required to respond rapidly if partisans were located. At the beginning of May, Polish troops made several contacts with UPA and uncovered six bunkers, four of which were empty and two containing partisans who had opened fire on the troops. One bunker had two men—one committed suicide and another was captured. The second captured bunker contained five men, all of whom were either killed or had shot themselves to avoid capture, but valuable documents were found (probably those mentioned by Mossor earlier) and Polish casualties were not reported. The troops began to uncover the better-camouflaged bunkers, and the higher success rate can be attributed to the increasing number of captives, some of whom revealed additional bunker locations. By May 2, Minister Rola-Żymierski reported that the Polish side had lost five men, killed 28 partisans, had arrested and captured 1,582 suspicious people, and troops had captured some weapons and ammunition.[571]

Another directive described the changing UPA tactics and proposed new methods of fighting. At that time, the partisans attacked in small units for the purpose of obtaining food and then disappeared. If necessary, they entered Polish districts, but not for the purpose of seeking revenge. By that point, most Ukrainian villages had already been deported or were guarded by troops, and many bunkers had been destroyed. Polish villages would have been the only remaining source of food. During the blockades, the directive continued, the partisans were moving to the rear of the troops, spreading propaganda and leaflets among Poles and terrorizing security personnel and police in villages. It alleged that UPA commanders directed sotnias from well-concealed bunkers in forests, ravines,

---

570 Ibid, 227–230.
571 Ibid, 238–240.

and even from cellars and wells in the villages, with the goal of avoiding capture. The description provided in the directive is largely inaccurate and based on faulty intelligence, since the high underground command typically exercised minimal control over operational units due to primitive communication networks and the rapidly changing nature of partisan warfare. Communications were naturally reduced during intense campaigns against them. In reality, sotnia commanders were always operating on the ground with their men and had to fend for themselves. The partisans did not tend to hide in wells and cellars, however, civilians did so to avoid capture and execution. In some cases, false walls were built in the cellars. The directive advised the army that when contact was made, units should surround the partisans and leave some reserves in case of a breakout from the encirclement. Since the partisans typically moved at night over frequently traveled paths, ambushes were to be made in these areas and, if necessary, might last for several days. In such situations, the directive advised army units to set up two ambushes about 125–150 feet apart so that the enemy could be hit at both ends, and mandating them to pursue and capture any partisans who attempted to flee. Toward the middle of May, most people had been removed from the three counties and thus, some divisions shifted to other areas, but special units were formed to pursue the partisans until their complete elimination.

Deportation to the West

Throughout the month of April, military and civilian departments issued numerous directives that explained the necessity for deportation, detailed their operations against UPA, and issued additional procedures for removing Ukrainian civilians. These documents provide insight into how the 1947 operation was conducted. The directives of each department concentrated on their assigned tasks, but there was considerable repetition among the documents. On April 20, General Mossor issued a synthesized version of the directives that outlined methods for fighting the underground and deporting the remaining Ukrainians.[572] According to Mossor's directive, the removal was to be completed in no longer than four weeks, ostensibly to provide enough time for people to sow and

572 Ibid, 144–149.

plant in the resettlement areas. He noted that the area southeast of Baligród was lightly populated and most villages had been burned; however, the zone between the Dukla pass and Krosno, as well as and the area southwest of Przemyśl along the San River were densely settled by Ukrainians who were hostile toward the government. Other districts in the southeastern Rzeszów Province were settled largely by Poles whose loyalties were questionable. According to Mossor's assessment, the territory located southeast of Jarosław was settled mostly by Poles and the UPA rarely entered the area. Further north, Lubaczów County had a mixed population, and Mossor therefore anticipated that fighting partisans in both counties would be relatively easier than it would be in the Rzeszów province. He noted that the information obtained on the underground and Ukrainian settlements was tentative, and anticipated that the true situation would emerge during the operation and would thus require the Polish Army to adapt. Mossor noted that although the Polish-Soviet border was tightly guarded along the Soviet side, the Czechoslovak border left much to be desired, and he promised to visit the border and issue instructions to enhance security. Arriving units were ordered to pursue the enemy while the deportation plans were finalized. Phase I would begin in the San valley south of Przemyśl and troops would be concentrated in Lesko and Sanok counties, with the urban population removed first. Operations were scheduled to begin on or around April 25 or 26 and would commence simultaneously in the designated areas. Mossor anticipated that the removal in that zone would be completed in two weeks, and afterward, the bulk of the troops would be shifted north to the area between Sanok and Lubaczów.

After Phase I, the two divisions would remain in the Lesko and Sanok areas to pursue the partisans while three divisions would be moved north to Przemyśl and Lubaczów counties. Mossor believed that gathering intelligence on the underground was of critical importance, and assigned his deputy commander for intelligence to coordinate the intelligence gathering effort. Information gathered by the various departments would be forwarded immediately to the deputy. Special emphasis was placed on uncovering the activities of Greek Catholic priests and intelligentsia who (Mossor believed) were the driving force behind the underground's activities, asserting that these groups had contact with the Polish intelligentsia and Polish clergy who had issued false documents to

Ukrainians. Mossor's assertion is neither corroborated by the Polish archival documents nor the Ukrainian underground literature. In actuality, relations between Polish and Ukrainian civilians were hostile and there was little cooperation between them. The general's directive went on to enumerate the locations of stores to feed troops and horses and the locations of fuel depots. It also outlined a number of difficulties that he predicted were likely to occur during the operation. First, the Polish authorities lacked reliable information on the nationality of the people, and therefore, determining who was subject to deportation would be difficult. Second, the sparse railroad network would impede the removal process, and they would need to transport some people in trucks to distant railroad stations. Third, the terrain lacked sufficient hay and oats to feed the animals of the deportees, a condition that would require feed to be imported from other districts.

On April 23, the Operational Group Vistula Headquarters issued final instructions concerning procedures for removing the Ukrainians.[573] Polish units were required to surround the targeted villages at dawn and to guard all roads leading out of those villages, especially roads and paths leading to adjacent forests. They were also required to hold meetings with the people of each village to inform the villagers that the removal was for their own good and that those individuals and families who remained illegally would be henceforth treated as partisans. Mossor's directive mandated that troops should evacuate each village in less than five hours, and charged clerks with the responsibility for recording the number of people leaving and cataloguing their belongings, including livestock. The deportees would allowed to take the maximum amount of property possible; including clothing, farm implements, grain, and root crops. The directive additionally required the religion and nationality of each individual to be documented and verified through prewar passports, school reports, military service papers, and other relevant documentation. Individuals and families with infectious diseases were required to be separated from the rest of the population. The data collected on villagers would be used by authorities at regimental (main) assembly points to determine the allocation of transports. The directive advised that a typical deportation scenario should take place at about eleven in the morning;

---

573 Ibid, 173–175.

the convoy would proceed under guard to the assembly point, and the troops would approach the village. The troops would need to take the necessary security precautions in the case of partisan attacks intended to free civilians, a scenario that they had frequently encountered in previous years. When appropriate and feasible, empty wagons would be permitted to return to the village to retrieve the remaining goods and property of the deportees.

The directive also clearly specified that soldiers who engaged in "trading" with the deportees, (a euphemism for robbing) would be court marshaled. In addition to logistical requirements, PUR ordered the formation of medical units that would be sufficiently staffed and come equipped with the necessary medical supplies to provide primary care at assembly points supported by the Polish Red Cross. It also stated that medical facilities should be established in Szczecin and Olsztyn to provide a full range of medical care for the new arrivals. A post deportation report noted that the recommended care was largely non-existent and the same was true of many of the other services outlined in Mossor's directive and related documents.[574] On April 23, the Operational Group "Wisła" (Operacyjna Grupa "Wisła" OGW) issued another directive that regulated the procedure for efficient operation of the assembly points and loading of the population.[575] According to the directive, PUR representatives were required to provide amenities at the railroad station, including barracks for people awaiting trains, a parking area for wagons, a field kitchen, and medical services. Each train was required to have a designated military commander to be responsible for security.

Both PUR and military officials were instructed to work closely with the Security Administration, railroad officials, and railroad troops. Security was required for the transit to the west; on average, a few dozen soldiers would be needed to staff each train. They were required to jump off the train before it came to a full stop in order to prevent any possible escapes. Based on enumerations of individuals from each village that arrived at the deportation point, a report was given to the commander at the assembly point, who would in turn check the list of names against documents provided by other agencies that listed suspicious individuals. The officer would work closely with his political officer, as well as PUR and

574 Chojnowska, "Operacyja "W," 48.
575 Misylo, ed. *Aktsiia "Visla,"* 179–181

security officials, to ferret out dangerous individuals. Based on the information contained in the directive, suspected individuals were divided into three categories: (A.) People on the list of the Security Administration; (B.) Individuals on the list of military intelligence; and (C.) People who were deemed suspicious based on information gathered from other deportees.[576] There were undoubtedly informants among the deportees, but it is likely that some people became intimidated during the interrogations and reported anything they considered to be unusual about their neighbors. Few allegations were based on substantive information; most consisted of rumors and innuendos, and individuals suspected on these grounds were eventually released. Suspected individuals were separated and shipped to Jaworzno concentration camp, and in some instances, people in any of the three categories were settled separately from other Ukrainians in the west. As the deportation date approached, the police were placed on a 12-hour work schedule and required to submit daily activity reports. No individual could leave the police station without permission. The Seventh Division issued detailed instructions to its two regiments, the Seventh and Eleventh, at the assembly points (usually railroad stations), appointed officers in charge, and enumerated villages assigned to each assembly point. The directive identified seven assembly points and approximately 80 villages subject to deportation on April 28.[577]

At the designated time, the deportation actions commenced in the four counties. Four villages were removed in the northern county of Lubaczów, although the main effort was concentrated in the southeast: Przemyśl, Sanok, and Lesko counties. The deportations proceeded as planned and troops flooded the area, with some surrounding the villages while others pursued the partisans. The Polish strategy was effective, placing the UPA under siege. Heavily outnumbered and constantly on the run, the partisans could not demolish bridges, attack railroad stations and troops, nor could they provide security for the people in the forest as they had done the previous year. Unable to flee and heavily guarded by troops, the surrounded villagers packed their belongings, formed columns, and headed for assembly points. Many families were without

576 Ibid, 158. Most people did not appear on any list and were therefore not provided with a designation.

577 Ibid, 199–201.

horses and therefore unable to take many belongings with them since the army had not provided enough trucks for this purpose. As more people were herded to the assembly points, the shortage of trains became a serious problem. The authorities had underestimated the number of Ukrainians by a factor of ten. During the first day, 13 villages in the Bircza area were removed. Further east in Przemyśl County, 10 villages comprised of 487 families were deported, including both Ukrainian and mixed families. In another part of the county, nine villages comprised of about 250 families were herded to the assembly points. Families with horses were taken first, and at the assembly points, wagons were unloaded and sent back to move families without horses. Seven villages, comprised of 1,252 people, were evacuated in Sanok County. The Seventh Division's report states that some kissed the ground saying "goodbye Ukrainian land".[578] Most were sent to the railroad station in Szczawne, with another 228 people taken to the assembly point in Bukowsko, a Polish village without a railroad station. The village had been largely destroyed the previous year by partisans as a reprisal for robbing the neighboring Ukrainian villages. When the Ukrainian deportees arrived, Polish civilians and ORMO began robbing the people, claiming it was stolen goods that belonged to them. Although troops had orders to protect the deportees and prevent robberies, the army failed to take preventive measures since many were hostile toward Ukrainians. On April 29th, the first transport, "R-10," left the Szczawne-Kulaszne station with 268 people and 150 head of livestock. An April 30 report described the coinciding operation against the UPA and the deportation of the population,[579] noting that more than a 1,000 people had been gathered at assembly points in the Przemyśl County as well as about 2,000 in Sanok County. It also reported that six transports were leaving daily from 11 stations in Lesko and Sanok counties. Because rumors had spread in the Przemyśl area that people were being sent to Siberia, military and political personnel tried to calm the people and convince them that rumors were false and contrary to instructions.[580]

In addition to the deported Ukrainians, some Poles were preparing to leave as well, although they were not subject to deportation. The re-

578 Ibid, 265.
579 Ibid, 223–224.
580 Ibid, 225.

port derisively notes that a Franciscan priest at the Sunday sermon expressed sympathy for the "Ukrainian brothers." A county commissioner reported that people were leaving grain, potatoes, and farm implements due to the lack of draft animals. Reportedly, one truck was allocated per every two families without horses. There were also reports of frightened people being given only 20 minutes to leave, which prevented them from taking their property.

Despite the fact that the Operation Vistula deportations were better organized and less violent than operations from the previous year, violence and excesses did occur. The Communist Party complained of the brutal behavior of Polish troops toward deportees in the village of Krywcza (Kryvcha) in Przemyśl County, where a number of people had been severely beaten for no apparent reason. At the Party's insistence, an investigation was conducted, during which time General Mossor wrote to Minister Rola-Żymierski that the people who were beaten were "...crooks working with the UPA..."[581] The Krywcza affair was not an isolated incident, but part of a much more widespread pattern of behavior. "Soldiers of all units participating in Operation Vistula engaged in robberies, beatings, and devastation."[582] The number of people who were killed or injured has not been reported.

On May 16, the Minister of Public Safety, General Radkiewicz, issued a report that summarized army activities between May 11th and May 16th. By May 10th, 43,003 people from 240 locations had been deported, and just five days later, the number increased to 49,894, filling 150 train transports. In the process, 159 individuals were removed from the transports for working with the underground and 277 informants were distributed among 62 trains. Areas under the control of First, Fourth and Seventh divisions had been cleared and 560 persons were captured during the operation, 475 by troops and the remainder by police.[583] On May 20th, the State Security Commission reviewed Phase I of the operation, and personnel involved in the process presented their reports.[584] Mossor started the proceedings by describing the operation against the underground and the deportations. He claimed that the UPA had disbanded in-

581 Ibid, 277–278, Footnote 2.

582 Chojnowska, 51.

583 Misylo, ed. *Aktsiia "Visla"*, 289–291

584 Ibid, 297–301. Summary of Mossor's one and a half page report.

to small groups, evaded Polish blockades, and had not engaged in combat. He stated that the civilian network of the underground had been destroyed, along with bunkers used for hiding or storing supplies and archives, and contact points had been located. He also mentioned that the deportations initially presented some problems as too many people were herded to the assembly points, some had not been allowed to take all their belongings, and some officers had behaved brutally toward the people. Measures were taken to secure the territory after the population was removed, and three battalions of the Internal Security Troops would remain in the towns of Baligród, Bircza, and Lubaczów. The Eighth Division would remain in the Sanok-Lesko area until September and one regiment of the division would potentially remain until the spring of 1948. Mossor required police stations to be established in each Polish village; estimating that about 500 total policemen would be required and recommended that the ORMO system should be strengthened as a reliable defense against the partisans.

Other speakers at the conference were military men and their remarks were focused mainly on the continued operation against the UPA. Vice Minister Wolski, a civilian, was an exception. He commented on the problems encountered during the removal of the population, noting that the transportation system was so inadequate that many people were unable to take large quantities of goods with them, even cattle. The Minister did not elaborate on the matter, but cattle in all villages were walked to the nearby railroad station. Any cows left behind could not be attributed to the lack of transport, but rather, to the lack of time the villagers were given to vacate their premises. Some villagers were driven out very quickly, without being given enough time to collect their goods and cattle. Wolski further indicated that a large quantity of grain and root crops had been left behind and suggested that measures should be taken to secure the foodstuffs for the state.

For Phase II of the operation, which was being implemented after May 8, Mossor ordered the redeployment of troops from the southeast to the west and north. The Sixth Division stationed in Komańcza was transferred to the Gorlice area and ordered to destroy the partisans. The Seventh Division was shifted from the Sanok area and assigned to destroy the Zalizniak Battalion and to begin deportations in Jarosław County and in the southern part of Lubaczów County. The Third Division, reinforced by three regiments, received orders to operate in the northern part of Lubaczów County, and was tasked with destroying UPA, deporting the local population, and clearing the southern counties of the Lublin Province. Two divisions remained in the Sanok-Lesko area; the Eighth Division and a division of the Internal Security Troops, while the Ninth Division remained in the Przemyśl area. All three groups were instructed to continue pursuing the partisans and to deport the remaining Ukrainians.[585] On May 18, OGW's Headquarters was transferred from Sanok to Rzeszów for the second phase of the operation. Deportation actions in the Lublin Province were then conducted in June and July. A Communist Party report states that despite the fact that some people were fleeing to the forests, almost 500 families had been removed from Włodawa County by June 15.[586] Soon after, officials made preparations to deport Ukrainians from other areas in the province and assembled trains in Tomaszów County for the removal. The planned deportation of approximately 800 families in Biłgoraj County was postponed until August, which allowed people there to harvest and thresh grain. Deportations in the western Lemko counties of Nowy Sącz and Gorlice were conducted mostly in June, and a request had been made to assemble trains at the end of May to handle the removal from the Gorlice area and Nowy Sącz. The State Security Commission reported that at the beginning of July, a total of 123,500 Ukrainians had been removed. The deportations were scheduled to be concluded by July 15, allowing officials an additional seven days to verify that all of the targeted people had been deported.[587] Table 5 presents the deportation data by county and province.

---

585 Ibid, 258–263.

586 Misylo, ed. *Aktsiia "Visla,"* 319.

587 Misiło published data on the number of people deported by date, village county, number of trains used, disaggregated by the number of people and livestock on each train, and their settlement in the north and west by province. See Ibid, 366, 437–489.

Table 5. Enumeration of Ukrainians Deported During Operation Vistula, by Province and County

County	Number of Localities	Number deported	Number subject to deportation
Grand Total	***795***	***119,367***	***6,871***
	Cracow Province		
Nowy Sącz	21	8,439	422
Nowy Targ	4	821	N/A
Total	**25**	**9,260**	**422**
	Rzeszów Province		
Brzozów	12	2,043	N/A
Gorlice	51	11,329	1,118
Jarosław	119	14,122	102
Jasło	16	533	77
Krosno	13	755	253
Lesko	82	24,647	882
Lubaczów	75	10,083	588
Przemyśl	137	20,797	1,889
Rzeszów	1	62	N/A
Sanok	68	11,582	901
Total	**587**	**95,953**	**5,810**
	Lublin Province		
Chełm	1	N/A	17
Hrubieszów	128	7,635	580
Krasnostav	2	8	N/A
Tomaszów	52	6,504	39
Zamość	1	7	3
Total	**183**	**14,154**	**639**

*N/A – Not Available

Source: Evhen Misylo, *Aktsiia "Visla"*, (L'viv - New York, 1997), 462

The military emphasized extreme vigilance due to the fact that some people were escaping and returning to their villages. Escapees were arrested and turned over to the police. Another report states that assembly points were flooded with partisans traveling with civilians and planning to continue the insurgency in the west. As a result, personnel at the stations were required to closely monitor the people waiting for transport and to arrest suspicious elements and turn them over to the police, especially those who were armed.[588] Although the report claims that the information was quite accurate, the underground literature from that time indicates that OUN/UPA had no plans to continue the fight in the west, a struggle that would have been pointless and impossible given the lack of a contiguous support base in the western resettlement regions. Because the troops reported seeing a larger number of men in the Ukrainian population than they had seen in the past, the authorities erroneously concluded that the partisans were traveling west. The men were actually civilians who had remained with their families and did not flee as they had done earlier. However, some members of the lower echelon of the underground network remained at home rather than fleeing and were ultimately deported with their families. Table 6 summarizes a three-month period of the 1947 Vistula campaign, showing both people and livestock that required a total of 548 trains.

Table 6 Number of People and Livestock Deported, April 29–July 30, 1947

Area and train Designation	**Number of Trains**	**Dates**	**Persons**	**Horses**	**Cows**	**Sheep and Goats**
Total	***548***	***4/29-7/30***	***139,479***	***20,458***	***45,729***	***49,297***
Sanok R10-R164	155	4/29-6/4	46,454	4,410	10,812	8,904
Gorlice, R201-R254	54	5/28-6/30	14,096	1,455	6,131	5,109

588 Misylo, ed. *Aktsiia "Visla",* 316

Rzeszów, R301-R355	55	5/1-6/25	21,916	3,656	6,241	1,169
Lublin, R417-R440	24	6/4-7/27	6,543	2,367	3,583	7,902
Lublin, R395-R509	115	6/19-8/8	8,886	2,033	2,421	4,781
Lublin, R361-R416	56	5/2-8/12	16,900	2,336	4,354	2,875
Nowy Sącz, R255-R297	43	6/28-7/22	10,510	687	5,904	3,640
Rzeszów, R356-R361	6	7/9-7/19	1,775	296	533	288
Lublin, R450-R479	30	6/28-7/21	9,266	2,566	4,526	12,420
Chełm, R480-R489	10	7/8-7/30	3,133	652	1,224	2,209

Source: Evhen Misylo, Aktsiia "Visla" (L'viv - New York, 1997), 465–82

The deportations in Lesko and Sanok counties were largely completed in the first week of May, but continued until the end of the month. People in the Lemko region were taken to the local stations and transported directly to the western provinces. In territories north of Sanok and Lesko, trains were leaving from only two or three stations in each area. Much of Przemyśl County (designated as Rzeszów in the table) was also cleared in the first week of May. People from Przemyśl and many from Jarosław County were sent to the railroad station at Przeworsk, located approximately 25 miles from Przemyśl. Przeworsk, a town that had been thoroughly Polonized by World War II, was a significant distance from the Ukrainian population centers. People from the rural areas were forced to walk the distance, usually without being permitted to stop and rest periodically. At the end of May, the deportation operations shifted to the western Lemko counties: Jasło, Krosno, and Gorlice (all three counties are included in the "Gorlice" designation in the table.) People were deported from stations in their county seats with the exception of the town of Zagorzany (located north of Gorlice in the Nowy Sącz area), which was deported mostly in the month of July. Information for the Lublin Province is incomplete, but it is clear that most people were deported in July. Table 7 presents deportation data by county and province; the figures, however, are not complete, especially for the Lublin Province. A 1950 study by agencies of the affected counties concluded that Ukrainians lived in 1,738 localities and not just the 795 specified in the table.[589] The tables account for most of the Ukrainian population, but do not account for demographically mixed villages or villages where Ukrainians were a minority. An August 1 document of the State Security Commission to the Cracow and Lublin Military Districts notes that some Ukrainians who remained in Krasnostav, Zamość, and Biłgoraj counties in the Lublin Province were required to be deported regardless of loyalty or party affiliation.[590] Exceptions were made only with the approval of either the Minister of Defense or the Minister of Internal Affairs. People who cooperated with the authorities (the nature of the cooperation is unclear) were given special consideration—they were sometimes allowed to remain until the completion of the harvest season, and permitted to take additional property. Immediate families of Ukrainian officers in the Polish Army and individuals in the security forces were permitted to remain only with the permission of the respective ministries. Ukrainians who were demobilized from the Polish Army or those who had fought in the Polish Communist underground (*Gwardia Ludowa*, GL) were required to be deported, but were to be sent in separate trains to Silesia and given better quality farmland. Special army units were formed after the deportations with the goal of uncovering any remnants of the Ukrainian underground and to verify that all Ukrainians or mixed families who might support UPA had been removed. The reported data indicate that approximately 140,000 Ukrainians had been deported by the end of July, but that the deportations actually continued until October. In the autumn, about 2,000 families in the Lublin Province and 5,000 in the Rzeszów Province[591] remained to be deported, totaling approximately 28,000 people. Perhaps 4,000 Ukrainians were incarcerated at that time, although most were eventually released and resettled. Some were deported in Jan-

---

589 Ibid, 463.
590 Ibid, 410–411.
591 Chojnowska, 57.

uary 1948 and 32 families from several villages in Nowy Targ County were sent west at the beginning of 1950. The total number of Ukrainians deported to the west amounted to about 172,000 people. After the final deportations, only a small number remained in the Ukrainian districts: those who possessed false documents, necessary skills, or were simply omitted during the operation.

The Polish army, hostile toward the Ukrainian people and fearful of partisan reprisals, rapidly herded large numbers of people to assembly points that resembled large temporary camps. The hungry and exhausted people were forced to remain at the points for a day or two, but the average length of stay increased over time. The initial transports on May 2 expeditiously deported 2,000 families who arrived in Szczecinek, and another 1,000 reached Olsztyn the following day. However, as the deportations continued, serious problems developed. People in many villages were removed very quickly, leaving grain, root crops, farm implements and other property, and although compensation for abandoned property was promised, it was never implemented. As more people arrived at the railroad stations, the delays lengthened due to the shortage of rolling stock since the authorities had grossly underestimated the number of people to be moved. The long delays and large numbers of people resulted in food shortages; most transports did not have adequate supply for an extended journey. Trains en route were to be re-supplied at the railroad junctions, but many junctions lacked adequate food supplies and feed for the livestock. The lack of railroad equipment and frequent breakdowns extended some trips by two weeks. Upon arrival, Polish authorities were faced with the daunting task of providing food and shelter and facilitating spring sowing and planting. The authorities harbored the illusion that upon arriving at their resettlement destinations, the deportees would begin farming immediately and become self-sufficient by autumn. In reality, many arrived too late to sow and plant and even early arrivals had limited success, since many lacked seeds, farm implements and horses. Early arrivals in Szczecinek County, for example, managed to sow only 70 hectares of barley and plant 230 hectares of potatoes.[592]

---

[592] Misylo, ed. *Aktsiia "Visla,"* 384.

Destruction of the Ukrainian Underground

On May 10, as the deportation was ending in the territory of Tactical Sector 26, Mossor issued a detailed plan for the final destruction of the UPA.[593] He considered partisans in that sector as "guards" or elite units, and therefore assigned more troops in that area compared to other sectors. The instruction outlined tactics against the Ren Battalion, but similar tactics were employed in other districts as well. Based on intelligence, Mossor identified nine locales (all with numerical designations) where the sotnias operated. Numerous bunkers containing grain and supplies had been found in the area, especially on the Chryszczata (Khreshchatyk) Mountain range, located just east of the village of Komańcza. Larger units had not been located, but Mossor's instruction contained erroneous intelligence information, including his belief that smaller Ukrainian groups each comprised of about 10 men were patrolling the area, and that the partisans were demobilizing as they prepared to depart for the west. The order emphasized that the UPA units in the area must be totally destroyed. Phase I of the operation was set to last through May 12. The Sixth Division, the 12th Regiment, and most of the Seventh Division were to clear the Baligród area, and other units in the region were apparently tasked with the deportations. Phase II was to commence on the morning of May 13 consisting of the Sixth Division (1,000 men), the Seventh Division (800 men) a Border Guard unit (100 men), the 12th Regiment (650 men) and a brigade of the Internal Troops Corps (800 men). Each regiment would be augmented by a sapper unit of 25 men equipped with explosives. By the afternoon, all units were required to position themselves in the newly designated areas and to continue searching for partisans. The following day, the Sixth Division would march to Krosno County and the 12th Regiment to Sanok. During the operation, radios would be used to signal preparations for an attack, to notify of an actual attack, and to request for help. Planes that spotted unknown troops were to fire red flares toward the unit, and for ground units identified as Polish, troops would fire yellow flares to identify themselves. Communication among units and identification signals were issued in a special addendum that is referenced but unavailable. The Quartermaster's units were to supply operational units with adequate fuel and

593 Ibid, 271–276.

enough food for three to four days, and were responsible for evacuating the sick and wounded to the hospital in Sanok. If a large bunker was located, the regimental commander had to be contacted who in turn would dispatch a special unit to destroy the bunker. Special units were instructed to encircle bunkers at a distance of about 300 feet, demolishing all exits except one, through which explosives would be fired into the bunker to deafen its occupants. After a bunker was destroyed, the units were instructed to search dry trees and stumps in the vicinity in attempts to locate additional hiding places. They surveilled creeks located near bunkers in order to watch for approaching friendly troops, and an approaching unit was to be identified before opening fire. Polish troops had a standing order to advance toward the sound of gunfire and precautions were taken to prevent friendly fire among its own units. The Sixth and Seventh divisions and the Twelfth Regiment each received five dogs and handlers provided by the Border Guard Division. Troops were warned that the partisans would fight hard to break out of the encirclements and were also known to climb trees whereupon they would fire on Polish troops.

On May 20, the State Security Commission met in Warsaw to discuss the results of Phase I of Operation Vistula. At the conference, major figures participating in the operation presented their findings, including General Mossor who delivered a lengthy report. The struggle against UPA, in Mossor's view, was proceeding according to plan.

> Presently, the partisans are scattered and avoid contact with the troops…their familiarity with the terrain enables them to survive. … Nevertheless, the civilian UPA network has been destroyed along with many bunkers containing food, supplies, and serving as archives. While the partisans sustained heavy losses, they have not been completely eliminated; the operation must continue until complete liquidation, otherwise they will continue to fight… it is their only means of survival. [594]

After the conclusion of Operation Vistula, General Mossor suggested that some units should remain in strategic locations and security forces should be expanded in the Ukrainian areas and the neighboring Polish districts. The general stated that three Border Guard battalions should remain in Baligród, Bircza, and Lubaczów, and the Eighth Division was to remain in the Sanok area until the spring of 1948. He advised the division to be well provisioned for what he anticipated to be a prolonged campaign. For added security, it was also necessary to establish police

---

594 Ibid, 297–301.

stations in Polish villages, with police strength totaling about 500 men. Since the territory southeast of Baligród was completely deserted by that point, Mossor decided that a maneuvering Border Guard battalion should be stationed there in order to pursue any remaining partisans. The general then evaluated performance of several units and military formations. Col. Wiktor Sienicki, Col. Jan Kobyliński, and Col. Jan Bielecki, commanders of the Sixth, Seventh, and Eighth divisions respectively, were evaluated as good commanders, especially Col. Sienicki. However, Col. Ignacy Wieliczko, commander of the Ninth Division, had not performed well in Mossor's estimation. The division of the Corps of Internal Security Troops gave a good account of themselves although some officers had been poorly trained, and the railroad troops had been equally effective, displaying initiative throughout the operation. Other participants at the conference agreed with the general that major objectives had been attained, but the fight with the UPA had not yet ended and it would require a considerable amount of time and effort before the underground was completely destroyed.

The elimination of the underground in Tactical Sector 26 was swift, in part because the underground had decided to conclude the insurgency. Contingency plans were actually made in the summer of 1946 by UHVR and the UPA High Command who anticipated a massive Polish operation against the underground in the winter of 1946–47, after a significant percentage of the Ukrainian population had been deported to the east. Under this plan, several sotnias were to head for West Germany at the beginning of the operation and the rest were instructed to conceal themselves in the underground bunkers. The anticipated operation occurred in the spring against both the underground and the civilians. At the end of May 1947, after the complete removal of the population had been accomplished, the Transcurzon OUN/UPA leadership decided to terminate the insurgency at the end of May 1947. The Lemko battalion was instructed to cross the border to Ukraine, while units from the Przemyśl were to enter Czechoslovakia and head for the American Zone in Germany.[595]

On May 23, the Operational Staff of the GOW issued instructions outlining tactical changes to be employed during Phase II.[596] The instructions first summarized the results of Phase I, noting that UPA had sus-

[595] Shtendera and Potichnyj, eds., *Litopys UPA*, XIII-XV.

[596] Misylo, ed. *Aktsiia "Visla,"* 302–304.

tained heavy losses and had its supply bases destroyed, including food losses that could not be replaced since the local Ukrainian population had been deported. Based on intelligence obtained through captured underground correspondence, the instructions noted that UPA units were constantly losing contact with each other and experiencing severe shortages of food, clothing, medical supplies, weapons and ammunition. The instruction then turned its focus to Phase II, requiring the formation of small reconnaissance units consisting of between 25 and 30 elite troops aided by security personnel and police dogs. Units were required to have one or two trucks and a radio in order to maintain contact with neighboring units. The troops were further charged with recruiting informants, destroying bunkers, capturing partisans, and identifying partisan haunts and escape routes based on the latest information. The reconnaissance units were to be augmented by using maneuvering units of up to 100 men which would be equipped with trucks and radios and capable of responding quickly when partisans were located. During the several years of partisan warfare, troops rarely received the promised amount of equipment, and this phase of Operation Vistula seemed to have followed the same pattern. The aforementioned units were to be backed by mobile units comprised of between 100 to 150 men, who were required to move quickly and destroy any partisan units that they located. Officers were required to read maps and select routes in a hilly terrain that the trucks could negotiate.[597] Finally, the instruction did not specify the number of units to be formed in each category, their total strength, nor their operational activities.

The Ukrainian underground literature during Operation Vistula in the Twenty-Sixth Tactical Sector (TS-26) is sparse, but from the available information, it is clear that OUN and UPA were constantly on the move.[598] Ren wrote monthly reports, usually more detailed than those of other commanders, but the last available report from his battalion covered events that happened in July 1946. It is reasonable to assume that he would have continued to submit reports until at least March 1947 when Świerczewski was ambushed and the Polish government subsequently

[597] There had been previous complaints that some high-ranking officers were unable to read maps, but there is no indication whether training courses had been organized to remedy the problem.

[598] It is likely that additional reports were written that did not survive Operation Vistula.

flooded the area with troops. The limited information available on Ren's Lemko Battalion after July 1946 comes from Khrin's memoirs and that of his platoon leader Ostroverkh. Khrin wrote two memoirs about his underground activities, but events that occurred from the autumn of 1945 to the spring of 1947 are omitted, suggesting that the monograph of this crucial period had been lost. After entering Ukraine, he wrote a chronology entitled "Winter in the Bunker" (*Zymoiu v Bunkri*) where he described events that unfolded from the spring of 1947 through 1948. The piece provides only general information on the fighting in the Lemko region and serves as an introduction to events on the Soviet side. He notes that that there were periods where the partisans were forced to go without food for three days, as was the case with the Lemko Battalion which consisted of Khrin's, Stakh's and Bir's sotnias. They crossed the Soviet border in the Carpathians on June 29, 1947. Other sotnias were sent to the west to demonstrate that Ukrainians were still fighting for an independent state. He wrote:

> They went on the orders of the Political Executive, the UHVR, and the UPA High Command to demonstrate to the whole world that the Ukrainian nation, through its armed formation, the UPA, and its revolutionary cadre, are fighting for an Independent, Sovereign Ukrainian State…even though peace is being built throughout (the rest of) the world, and even though the war ended two years earlier.[599]

In the extensive underground literature, the final order for some units to go to Germany has not been published, although it is possible that the order arrived when the underground was being destroyed and was therefore lost. Some preparations for the march west were made earlier since sotnias crossing Czechoslovakia had local currency, American dollars, and maps. A more detailed account was written by Ostroverkh who chronicled his UPA experience after crossing the border. The article describes events that occurred during the period of time between the Świerczewski ambush and the elimination of the Ukrainian underground in Poland. It notes how many underground members crossed the border in small groups, but provides only essential information for major events.[600] Referencing the intensified Polish anti-partisan campaign that immediately followed the Świerczewski ambush, he claimed that a regi-

599 Potichnyj, ed., *Litopys UPA,* Vol. 30, 375.

600 Ibid, 217–367; events during the summer of 1947 are described on pp. 319–51 by Ostroverkh.

ment of troops arrived in the area and began searching the villages and mountains for Ukrainian partisans. According to Ostroverkh's account, Khrin and Stakh headed south toward the Czechoslovakian border and pitched camp, and several partisans later left the camp to fetch meat. As troops began advancing toward the camp, the sotnias had left but the partisans who were returning with meat were attacked, two were captured, and a third disappeared. One captive revealed that it had been Khrin's sotnia that had killed Świerczewski. On the following day, April 1, the partisans crossed the border pressed by Polish troops, but were attacked by Czechoslovakian troops. Khrin headed east along the Carpathians and returned to Poland, and over the next several months, his partisans were constantly on the move evading troops. Stakh and Khrin usually operated together, while Bir moved about separately. Throughout this period, the partisans did not initiate fights, but avoided troops whenever possible, since any prolonged fights would have attracted additional troops. During this period, Khrin occasionally started bonfires to attract troops to a specific location while the partisans headed in another direction. When necessary, partisans crossed the Slovak border, but were met with increasing resistance from Czechoslovak troops. Several attacks were staged on Chryszczsata Mountain, which was about 3,000 feet high and covered with forest. The mountain was frequented by partisans and had many supply bunkers, and sustained numerous attacks as a result. During one operation, the Polish military used planes, artillery and tanks in an attempt to seek out the UPA's hiding places, but the partisans were located elsewhere at the time. Contrary to Polish intelligence reports, the Ukrainian partisans were not ordered to operate in smaller units, but during the incessant pursuits and numerous fights, some men had inadvertently separated from the rest and wandered about before making contact with their units. Ostroverkh reported finding the mutilated bodies of four unknown partisans, possibly from the Baida's battalion. The corpses hands were tied, their eyes were gouged out, they had been cut with bayonets, and there was dirt in their mouths. Another time he found the body of Petryk, a 15-year old boy who had served as a scout in Khrin's sotnia. He was wounded in battle, had lost contact with his sotnia, and was headed for the area usually frequented by the unit when he was apparently intercepted by the enemy. He was later found dead, clutching his rifle, and had three raw potatoes in his pockets. While it wasn't uncommon for boys in their late teens to serve in UPA sotnias, Petryk seems to have been the youngest.

In addition to the challenge of avoiding capture and execution, obtaining food was another major problem and the partisans occasionally went hungry for days. Food shortages began immediately after the Świerczewski ambush, when Polish troops roamed the countryside and forests destroying bunkers and blockading villages. After the deportations, there were enough potatoes, cabbage, beans and grain left to feed the partisans for the rest of the year, but they had difficulty gaining access to the villages. There are reports of partisans going to villages to secure food, and while they were gathering provisions, Polish troops would enter the village, forcing the partisans to flee empty-handed. At the time, meat was rarely available. The partisans lived principally on potatoes, an easily portable commodity that they could bake in bonfires, use to make potato soup, or fry to make potato pancakes. According to one report from Mossor, he states that the "...partisans are stealing under our noses," apparently referring to an incident when Khrin's men once stole sheep from Polish troops. Some meat was also acquired by slaughtering the livestock left by the deportees. Ostroverkh notes, "Many villagers purposely left grain and clothing in bunkers, and sheep and calves in cellars, or they drove them to the forest."[601] It is doubtful that an impoverished population would have purposely left valuable property, and more plausible that the deported people hid their valuables to prevent theft by the troops, perhaps with the hope of returning later. Moreover, many villages were evacuated quickly, people did not always have the time to take all their belongings, and some livestock may have wandered off to the forest. As the summer progressed, grain that had been sowed before the deportations began ripening, and the partisans collected grain, shelled and dried it, then milled it in what they dubbed a "Siberian Mill," which was not further defined in the UPA literature. The "mill" probably consisted of two stones used to grind grain into flour.

Despite the constant pursuits and encirclements throughout Operation Vistula, no sotnia had been completely destroyed, but there were incremental losses that had significantly reduced UPA's strength. As previously mentioned, crossing the Slovak border had become a dangerous al-

601 Ibid, 329.

ternative as Czechoslovak troops had been stationed along the border in large numbers. Medical care became another pressing problem. Throughout the duration of the insurgency, medical service had always been primitive, but some care was usually available. The sick and wounded were attended to in underground hospitals or placed with reliable families in isolated villages, visited periodically by Red Cross medical personnel. After the Vistula deportations, such support was no longer available and there is no available information to determine whether or not the wounded received any care. Despite the hunger and losses, the sotnias maintained their cohesion, but clearly had to leave the area since the men were exhausted by the constant pursuits and food shortages. Ren's Battalion left for Ukraine at the end of June. For reasons that are not entirely clear, a large numbers of partisans remained in Poland. Ostroverkh gathered 54 people, including a few women, and divided them into four squads that remained in Poland. When the senior officers left and the underground began unraveling, discipline slackened and contrary to their orders, some members were planning to head west. Ostroverkh was extremely angry at the OUN network and the SB who had earlier threatened deserters with execution; from his perspective, they had committed the same offense. Ostroverkh contacted Mar, the OUN district chief, to request supplies and obtain advice. Mar advised him to provide his people with a choice of where to go. Ostroverkh informed the 24 people in his group of the option, and all of them chose to go east. Interestingly, the OUN network in the area seems to have remained largely in tact. On August 16, one group with 35 people left for Ukraine, a second group followed on August 17, and Ostroverkh himself left on August 18 with 26 people in tow. Most people in Ostrovekh's group were locals, but there were also some partisans from the Baida Battalion who had separated from sotnias crossing the Lemko region en route to the west. Ostroverkh, a Lemko, found it extremely difficult to leave his native land, a feeling that was undoubtedly shared by other Lemko partisans. His group came under fire crossing the border but did not sustain any losses.

Baida's Battalion also experienced increased pressure from the army and security forces during the first months of 1947. More information is available for this battalion compared to others because both of his sotnia commanders—Krylach and Burlaka—kept diaries. Another sotnia commander, Hromenko, also wrote about his experiences during the spring of

1947 after reaching the West. Hromenko's account is less detailed than the diaries and, as in most memoirs, a brave face is put on a desperate situation. As they had done in the Lemko region, more troops began arriving in the Przemyśl County early in January. In one operation, some 1,000 troops swept through the forest inflicting significant casualties on the partisans. As more and more troops roamed the forest and countryside, the partisans rarely engaged in offensive operations and any fights that occurred were mostly defensive. Throughout this period, Burlaka, Krylach and Lastivka operated either together or in close proximity to each other. As the deportation date approached, more troops arrived, increasing the pressure on the UPA units in the area. Sotnias were constantly on the move, at times going for days without food. Hromenko, with whom Baida traveled at the time, headed south toward the Carpathians with the hope that the Poles were less active in that area. At the end of April, the sotnia crossed the San River from the east and headed toward the Slovak border, hoping to establish contacts with local units and obtain assistance. Hromenko soon discovered that there were even more Polish troops present on the border than had been stationed in the Przemyśl area, and was unable to make contact since the partisans were on the run. On May 21, he learned that Poland, the USSR, and Czechoslovakia had signed an agreement to jointly fight UPA. It was at this point that the courier service began faltering, unable to safely and reliably deliver messages within the OUN-UPA network. Baida finally received orders to take his battalion west in the middle of June. The decision to send some units to the American Zone in Germany was developed a year earlier in anticipation of a Polish blockade during the winter of 1946–1947. This view was based on the Soviet practice of using winter blockades when the partisans were most vulnerable and had greater difficulty camouflaging themselves. Units arriving in the West were tasked with informing the world about the Ukrainian struggle and the Polish and Soviet policies toward Ukrainians.[602] At the same time, OUN representatives abroad had been working with the American and British intelligence services. The arrival of armed units from the east would have strengthened their claims that a strong underground resistance existed in Poland and Ukraine. Marching from Poland through Czechoslovakia to get to Ger-

602 Shtendera and Potichnyj, eds., *Litopys UPA*, Vol. 9, 384.

many was the preferred route since the communists had not yet seized power in Czechoslovakia. In addition, throughout the duration of the insurgency, the Slovaks had been friendly toward the UPA and most importantly, the country bordered with Austria and Bavaria. The reasons for selecting Baida's Battalion are not indicated in the underground literature or elsewhere in OUN/UPA correspondence; however, in retrospect, it is clear that Ren's Battalion would have been a more logical choice since it was already operating on the Slovak border.

When Hromenko's sotnia reached the Carpathians, the health condition of most of his men was abysmal. Three-quarters of the men, including Hromenko himself, were swelled from hunger, and some were even forced to cut their shoes to fit swollen feet.[603] Based on instructions, Baida ordered Hromenko's sotnia to make their way to Western Europe. The sotnia rested for a while in the mountains, where most recuperated. They had been given Polish zloty, Czechoslovak crowns, and American dollars to make purchases in Czechoslovakia, although there is no information available as to the source of the assistance. Hromenko held a meeting with his officers to inform them of their new assignment. On June 17, after the sotnia had crossed the Czechoslovakian border, the rest of the partisans were informed of the final destination. After the crossing, the sotnia encountered a small Slovak unit who initially mistook the partisans for their own, and walked toward them until it was too late to turn back. Hromenko conducted a discussion with a Slovak officer who informed him that although Slovak units would not militarily engage the Ukrainian partisans, the Czech troops had orders to interdict UPA along the border. After an amicable meeting, Hromenko's sotnia and the Slovak unit parted peacefully. With the arrival of Czech troops and security forces, the partisans were again forced to engage in combat and their hunger returned, since it was difficult to procure food in the villages. Some men could no longer march due to hunger and injuries, including the battalion chaplain, Father "Kadylo."[604] The priest was acquainted with a Slovak priest who worked with the Slovak underground, and he and other partisans who were in poor condition went to the Slovak priest hoping to recuperate and later join other UPA units that were heading west. As Burlaka noted in

603 Hromenko, *U Velykomu Reydi,* 111, 113.

604 This was a pseudonym. In Ukrainian, "kadylo" is the name for a censer (incense diffuser) used in a religious mass or liturgy.

his diary, the group was eventually arrested. During the march, no serious contact was made with troops until June 30. During that fight, a platoon leader named Dmytro Bil'o ("Bartelia"), along with one-and-a half squads, were separated and did not rejoin the sotnia. Hromenko told his men afterwards that if they separated, they were to proceed west on their own. The situation worsened as his sotnia entered the Czech lands, since the largely hostile population refused to sell food to the partisans, informed on their movement, and even fired at them on occasion. As a result, the partisans sustained significant losses while moving through that portion of the country. On September 5, the sotnia crossed the Austrian border where they encountered a friendly population that provided food and guides through the country. Five days later, on the night of September 9, 1947, they entered Bavaria, a full 99 days after crossing the Polish-Slovak border. By then the unit numbered only 36 men, and surrendered to the Americans when they reached Bavaria.[605]

More detailed information was reported by Burlaka, who kept a diary from October 1, 1946 to August 2, 1947, but his daily entries were brief and generally laconic and unemotional, as if he was describing the distant past rather than tumultuous current events.[606] As Operation Vistula continued, the tone of the diary became more emotional as people were being deported and troops roamed the countryside forcing the partisans to fight and run. At that point, the sotnia was sustaining larger losses, the men were swelling from hunger, and their survival was uncertain. Describing the situation in one of his platoons, he noted:

> Besides the horrible physical conditions in which the unit has found itself, the soldiers cannot stand the nerve racking situation…in their view, the situation is hopeless. Each day, more enemy troops arrive and the situation is getting worse…fights, exhaustion, and hunger are causing desertions. The finest soldiers with strong character, who previously even in the most difficult situations wouldn't have thought of it, are now deserting.[607]

Burlaka's diary also provides some information on the operations of the Lastivka and Krylach sotnias at that time, describing how the three sotnias operated either together or in close proximity to each other. Ma-

605 In the spring, the sotnia reportedly had a total of 120 men. The number who reached Slovakia is not provided, nor is it clear how many who separated eventually reached Germany.

606 Shtendera and Potichnyj, eds. *Litopys UPA*, Vol. 13, 1–111.

607 Ibid, 55

jor fighting did not occur in the autumn of 1946, contact with the Poles resulted either in light losses or none, and unlike other commanders, Burlaka did not provide estimates on Polish losses. A costly engagement took place on October 3, when Polish troops surprised the partisans, killing six and wounding seven, and some died later from their injuries. A large attack occurred on November 16 when the entire battalion, supported by the SB and the Mriia sotnia from Ukraine, attacked the small town of Dynów in Przemyśl County. The principal objective of the raid was to empty the local apothecary for medical supplies, as well as obtain supplies from a cooperative and other stores. At some point during the raid, a small Polish unit charged with defending the town attacked the partisans. During the engagement, one partisan was killed. On December 23, Burlaka's sotnia raided a store with UNRRA clothing and managed to secure a variety of clothing items, including 60 pairs of shoes. At the beginning of 1947, troop activity began to increase, and on January 12, approximately 1,000 Polish soldiers made a sweep through the forest without making contact with the partisans. During the next month, numerous skirmishes took place with minimal losses to the partisans, but a major engagement occurred on March 4. Large numbers of troops attacked the Krylach and Burlaka sotnias, with Krylach's sotnia sustaining most of the losses: 8 dead and 8 wounded (a few of whom died later) and Burlaka also had several losses that were not enumerated. By this time, the partisans were constantly on the move as an increasing number of Polish troops arrived and began operating in larger units. On April 28, the Poles began the deporting the local Ukrainians. Over the next several days, additional villages were emptied, and UPA units began storing food, including meat, in the bunkers. On May 6, approximately 1,000 troops swept through the forest at dawn, using tanks and planes, Burlaka's sotnia concealed itself in a secluded section of the forest and remained undetected. Evasive maneuvers continued throughout the month; however, at the beginning of June, the three sotnias came under a major attack and were forced into a large defensive fight. Lastivka was killed on June 2, part of his sotnia entered Ukraine, and the remainder joined Burlaka's sotnia. In a minor skirmish on June 13, Krylach was killed. His men managed to take his satchel containing documents, including his diary, but were unable to take his body. UPA made great efforts to retrieve the satchels of fallen officers since captured documents would have provided valuable information for the Poles.

After the deaths of Lastivka and Krylach, Burlaka was appointed as battalion commander of the three units and received orders to march to western Germany, a difficult assignment in the face of constant pursuits. The order was accompanied by a personal farewell message, dated May 25, from Orlan (Vasyl Halasa), and addressed to "Commanders, My Friends". The Communication underscored the underground leaders' deep commitment to their cause:

> The time has come for which we have waited a long time. The time has come when the enemy has made his last move. He is mistaken, however. We will not abandon our struggle, I believe in you, my friends. You have won glory for yourself in the struggle for our future. You honorably carried the banner of the Revolution in your strong hands. Remember that with your deeds, you are writing the most glorious pages of our history. Now a difficult task awaits you, and you must carry out the order with honor. Go where the order directs you. I too am leaving for the distant shore where many of our friends died with heads unbowed, proudly and mightily raising our banners of liberation. Perhaps I too will fall on this road, but what does my life or yours mean, all of our lives, compared to our sacred Ideal? Farewell my friends. Hold high our unblemished banner of the revolutionary struggle until victory! I wish you glorious victories and much personal fortune."[608]

At the beginning of June, Burlaka began moving south toward the Carpathians under difficult conditions, including persistent hunger and increasing desertions. On June 14, he finally held a meeting with the partisans and gave them an alternative to desertion: he promised to give an honorable discharge to anyone who wished to leave. The 24 men who accepted the discharge were permitted to take their weapons, but on the condition that they would not join Polish forces. Afterward, the battalion continued to move south and west with considerable difficulty, finally crossing the San River near Lesko on June 17, and the Czechoslovakian border on June 22. Burlaka experienced much greater difficulty than Hromenko when crossing into Czechoslovakia, since by than, more troops were deployed and were aware that Ukrainian partisans were heading for Germany. Immediately after the border crossing, his unit was attacked and managed to disperse the troops, capturing five Slovak soldiers. During the subsequent interrogations, the captives revealed that two Slovak units, each comprised of 150 men, were pursuing them. They

---

608 V'iatrovych, *Reydy UPA*, 176.

insisted that the Slovak soldiers had not wished to fight with the Ukrainians, but were forced to do so by their Czech officers. After explaining the reasons for UPA resistance to the soldiers, the sotnia allowed them to leave. They returned their rifles but kept the machine guns and automatic weapons that they had confiscated.[609] Frequent skirmishes occurred during the march, occasionally resulting in light partisan casualties. They were able to obtain food because the Slovak population was generally friendly toward the partisans. They purchased and slaughtered cattle and acquired large quantities of cheese from local shepherds.[610] As the march continued, the number of troops deployed significantly increased, making the partisans' situation more difficult. Due to the intensity of the pursuits, the partisans even began the practice of walking in streams to avoid leaving trails. On occasions when they made contact with troops and managed to escape, new blockades were organized further west. On August 16, in an attempt to adapt to the new situation, Burlaka divided the 67 partisans (including two women) in his sotnia into seven groups. He personally took command of one group, and the others were led either by platoon or squad leaders. He rationalized that smaller groups would have a better chance of evading troops and acquiring food, and later some of the groups subdivided into smaller groups of three or four. Some partisans had reached the foothills of the mountains dividing Slovakia and Moravia, but were unable to cross due to the fact that approximately 15,000 troops and security forces had been deployed throughout the country and were highly concentrated in the mountains.[611] Small partisan groups probing the mountains in attempts to evade capture would occasionally rendez-vous. At one point, Burlaka's group and that of his warrant officer Burkun met. On September 2, while the groups were still together, they were attacked and forced to disperse, and Burkun took Burlaka's satchel during the attack. Subsequently Burlaka was captured, while Burkun, along with two other partisans, crossed the mountains and headed west. He reached the Austrian border on October 19, and later noted in his diary that it had taken 17 weeks to cross the Czechoslovakian border. The Soviet Zone in Austria was lightly guarded and the Aus-

---

609 Shtendera and Potichnyj, eds., *Litopys UPA*, Vol. 13, 68.

610 Sheep in the Carpathians were taken to the mountains for summer grazing. The shepherds milked them and made cheese.

611 V'iatrovych, *Reydy UPA*, 123.

trians were generally very helpful, providing food and guiding the partisans through the mountains. As a result, the three men entered Bavaria on October 23 without incident.

The Brodych sotnia faced difficulties similar to those of Baida's group, but fared significantly better. The sotnia was part of the Ren Battalion that had operated in the western Lemko region since the autumn of 1946, and had also received orders to go west. However, the orders were not received until September due to communication difficulties.[612] During Operation Vistula, the sotnia was constantly pursued, casualties increased, and key members of the unit deserted ranks, including a platoon leader. In the autumn of 1946, the sotnia had consisted of four platoons comprised of 120 men, but was reduced to two platoons by May 1947.[613] At that time, the two platoons operated independently and headed for Germany separately, a departure from the practice of Hromenko and Burlaka who entered Czechoslovakia as a unit. Upon receiving orders, Brodych and his group made immediate preparations and soon after, they crossed into ethnic Polish territory. The unit moved west along the northern slopes of the Carpathians with virtually no harassment by Polish troops. They had some money to make purchases and were therefore able to secure an adequate food supply. To throw the Polish army off their trail, they posed as Polish partisans, a task they were well suited for since most of the partisans spoke at least some Polish. If questioned about their accents, they were instructed to claim that they came from the eastern districts, in other words, western Ukraine. By late autumn, the sotnia had passed through Polish territory undetected, reaching the Czech borderlands located southwest of Cracow, and planned to cross the border and make their way through Moravia to Austria. From Polish newspapers, Brodych had learned about the UPA movement across Czechoslovakia. The news stories identified the Hromenko and Burlaka sotnias and reported that the partisans had been completely destroyed. Against the wishes of some of his men, he decided to divide the platoon into small groups. Unlike Burlaka, Brodych did not designate group leaders, instead allowing the partisans in each group to select their own leader. After

---

612 Information on the sotnia's odyssey is provided by two partisans who reached the West and wrote about their experiences: Ivan Dmytryk and Ivan Harasymiv in *Litopys UPA,* Vol. 29, 1992.

613 Dmytryk, *Zapysky Ukrainskoho*, 130.

making their preparations, the small groups entered Moravia. No longer inconspicuous, they encountered much more difficulty compared to what they had experienced in Poland. Unable to pose as Czechs, the partisans were easily identified by a hostile population that frequently reported on their movement, and who were further encouraged by a bounty of 10,000 crowns for each captured partisan. During the march, Brodych and many others were captured, although some managed to reach Germany. Ivan Harasymiv ("Palii"), a squad leader, reached Austria in the fall. The other platoon, comprised of 39 men, immediately divided into five small groups and headed west separately. Ivan Dmytryk's group essentially followed the same route as Brodych, posed as Polish partisans or smugglers, and reached the American Zone in November.[614] By autumn, Tactical Sector 26, the core of the UPA presence in the Transcurzon region, had been effectively eliminated. Three sotnias went to Ukraine and five others, or the remnants of them, attempted to reach the American Zone. Two sotnia commanders were killed on the Polish side, and two out of the three were captured in Czechoslovakia and extradited either to Poland or the Soviet Union. There they were brutally interrogated and most were shot. Others were sent to the gulag in the USSR or received long prison terms in Poland.

Information for Tactical Sector 27 ("Bastion") is sparse compared to other sectors since the battalion archive was flooded. Diaries, if they were kept, are not available, and the few members who did manage to reach the West did not write comprehensive memoirs.[615] Nevertheless, the events in the sector during 1947 were similar to those in others sectors. Troops began arriving at the beginning of January and organizing ambushes. By mid-February a 200-man unit began operating in the area. The soldiers captured by UPA reported that the troops did not wish to fight Polish partisans, but were eager to fight Ukrainians. The hatred for Ukrainians was reinforced by military incentives, such as extra pay and leave time for soldiers who captured weapons. On March 17, 1947, an interesting letter was sent by a high-ranking OUN member to a commander

---

614 In their later writings, the partisans who reached Germany generally reported having had unusually good luck in key situations, while the less fortunate were either killed or captured.

615 The available material for the battalion is printed in Potichnyj, ed., *Litopys UPA*, Vol. 40.

concerning the partial demobilization of the UPA, but neither the sender nor the recipient were identified in the document. The author noted that the matter had been discussed in June 1946, following the massive campaign that deported Ukrainians to the east. The author advanced his view that the better-educated and more capable partisans should be retained and the less qualified released. What the demobilized partisans would do remained unanswered, as the author noted. He further asserted that a smaller UPA would embolden the Polish army and security forces to search more aggressively and to deploy their forces in smaller units covering more territory. The author then noted that sensitive topics could not be discussed through written correspondence, but would be discussed orally at the next opportune time.[616] The writer was undoubtedly aware but did not discuss another implication of the demobilization: many of the released partisans would be captured, providing the Polish military with valuable information and endangering the survival of the rest of the Underground.

In some areas of the Tactical Sector 27, the deportations began in early April. In addition to Ukrainians, some Poles accused of working with the underground were deported as well, and sotnia commander Hryhorii Levko ("Kruk") began burning the vacated villages. Over the next few months, the area was flooded with troops, UPA losses increased to approximately 40 percent, and the underground began to disintegrate. Attempts by the OUN network to establish contact with the underground in the Carpathians were unsuccessful, and no one knew what was happening there. Orlan arrived from the Przemyśl area in May and informed the leadership that the insurgency in the Transcurzon region was ending. The partisans were advised to go either to Ukraine, Germany, or to the Olsztyn province in East Prussia, where many Ukrainians had been resettled. By the end of August, the Zalizniak Battalion ceased to exist as an organized unit when its sotnias divided into smaller units and fled in different directions. Information concerning Kruk or his men has not been found, but a Polish document dated July 27, 1947 reports that Kruk with 48 men and Kalynovych with 49 men were still operating in their areas.[617] Shum was killed on November 7, 1947, and some of his men subsequently headed east. In the late autumn, Kalynovych along with men from vari-

616 Ibid, 250–251.

617 Misylo, ed. *Aktsiia "Visla"*, 405.

ous sotnias and OUN members headed for Czechoslovakia. The group was attacked by Czechoslovak troops, and after running out of ammunition during the battle, some of the partisans shot themselves and others were captured. Kalynovych received a head wound over his right eye and was captured. After recuperating, he was sent to Poland on May 11, 1948 and executed on April 28, 1949. Mykola Taraban ("Tucha") and some of his men went to Olsztyn, and others headed east. He reached Germany in 1948 and eventually settled in the U.S., and a few underground members reached the West with him. In November 1947, Zalizniak and two of his men left for Slovakia, where his parents lived. Passing successfully as a Hungarian soldier released from the Soviet POW camp, he received the necessary documents that helped him to evade detection and capture. In the spring of 1948, he sent his two companions to retrieve the battalion archive, but when they located the bunker, they found that it was flooded and its contents were damaged beyond recognition. The two men eventually reached the West; one settled in the U.S. and another in Canada, while Zalizniak remained in Slovakia. A decade later, Czechoslovakian authorities learned of his true identity and sent him to Poland. There he was tried and received a death sentence, which was later commuted to a long prison term and he was finally released in 1981.[618]

Events in Tactical Sector 28 ("Danyliv") followed a similar pattern. At the beginning of 1947, larger contingents of troops and security forces began arriving in the region and staged sweeps throughout the countryside and forest without much success. These operations failed to destroy large partisan units but occasionally surprised a group of several men in a village. The battalion in the area was smaller compared to others in Transcurzon, operated over a much larger territory, and did not have good control of the countryside. At the same time, the OUN network was weaker than in other sectors. With more Polish informants and Soviet agents, the Polish authorities were frequently able to locate a few partisans in a particular village. The men normally did not post guards and when surprised, they were unable to repel attacks and many were killed; however, some managed to escape to the forests.[619] These attacks seem to have accounted for most UPA losses in this area. In addition to expanding their regular forces, the authorities began using more ORMO

618 Potichnyj and Viatrovych, eds. *Spohady Voiakiv*, 330–331.

619 Potichnyj, ed. *Litopys UPA*, Vol. 39, 551.

units in Polish villages to protect them against the UPA raids. During the first half of January, the attention of the military was divided between fighting the partisans and spreading propaganda for the upcoming parliamentary elections. Despite limited support, and through fraudulent means, the communists were able to secure a majority in the elections. The underground literature notes that Ukrainians did not participate in the elections. A large segment of the Polish population, which did not support the communists, was disappointed in the results and expected protests from Britain and the U.S.

After the election, the military threw its full weight against the Ukrainian partisans. In February 1947, they staged another unsuccessful sweep with 350 men and located two bunkers—one was completely empty and the other contained two blankets. The regular forces were now increasingly supported by ORMO units, largely made up of men who were recruited from Communist Party. The recruits performed police duties in towns and participated with troops in raids on Ukrainian villages, motivated by plunder. The February UPA report notes that Polish strength increased to about 600 soldiers and police. However, it appears that less troops had been committed to this sector compared to the other two. To cope with the growing threat, the battalion commander Berkut organized a meeting of sotnia commanders and other principal officers of the battalion.[620] The meeting did not propose operational changes, but sought to evaluate the current status, identify shortcomings, and in some cases, take remedial steps. The sotnia commander Vasyl' Iarmola ("Iar") stated that although his partisans were well-armed, properly clothed and in overall good condition, his unit was poorly concealed and the supply service was not organized well. Ievhen Ianchuk ("Duda") stated that qualified men had recently been transferred from other units, resolving his sotnia's shortage of squad leaders. Vasyl' Kral' ("Chaus") reported a lack of political instructors in his unit, especially battalion political officers who would develop and deliver political training designed to monitor and enhance morale. Low morale resulted in heavy drinking among some, a problem that UPA placed great emphasis on eliminating within its ranks. However, because this sector operated in smaller units, the leadership had a more difficult time enforcing disciplinary standards.

620 Ibid, 315–316.

Warrant officers reported that although clothing and footwear were currently satisfactory, additional supplies were lacking, and were consequently ordered to seek additional supplies from the Military District. As summer arrived, the deportation campaigns shifted north. The Ukrainian population of the Hrubieszów area was deported between June 15 and July 20. Polish troops roamed through the forest searching for partisans and bunkers, stationing small groups of soldiers around the forest and quartering the remainder in adjacent villages. Poorly camouflaged bunkers or those with tracks around them were quickly located, although the better-concealed bunkers usually remained undiscovered. Under the circumstances, the partisans were in survival mode and did not usually engage in offensive attacks on troops, nor did they make attempts to halt the deportations as they had done in the previous year. There were occasional attacks, however, when Poles settled in Ukrainian villages. An OUN report notes that 24 partisans, including the sotnia commander Semen Prystupa ("Davyd"), had been killed in the area. Davyd was wounded in the knee and hid in a barn, and when he was discovered by Polish troops, he killed one soldier and then shot himself. In another incident, 12 members were captured and interrogated, and some divulged information.[621]

There is a sharp decrease in the available underground literature covering the spring of 1947 when the Poles began deporting people and relentlessly pursuing the partisans. Berkut's last battalion report covers the month of March 1947, and subsequent information can be gleaned from occasional OUN correspondences. A letter dated August 16, 1947 states that Ukrainians were being rapidly deported and that Poles were being resettled in the vacated villages. Under such circumstances, the underground found it increasingly difficult to survive as the Polish army began organizing more ORMO units. To counter the trend, the weakened underground managed to disarm an ORMO unit on July 8, at which time they also burned some abandoned homes and attacked police who were guarding the new settlers.[622] Another OUN message relates that the struggle in Podlasie had ended and measures must be taken to save the cadre either by abandoning the area or preparing to spend the winter in bunkers. Because of the uncertainty, the writer gave instructions to pre-

---

621 Ibid, 773–774.

622 Potichnyj, ed. *Litopys UPA*, Vol. 39, 690.

pare for the winter by storing food in the forest, maintaining intelligence efforts, and increasing attacks on new Polish settlements.

Most Ukrainians from the Lublin Province were deported to the Olsztyn region that was located almost 200 miles north of Podlasie. During the deportation, some OUN members were transported along with the civilians and later established contact with the partisans in the Lublin province. In the autumn, small groups of UPA and OUN members assembled in Podlasie to plan the next course of action. Sick members were demobilized, provided with false documents, and sent primarily to the Baltic area, while others went to Ukraine (apparently those from the east who had families there.) The rest were divided into two groups: some would head for Olsztyn to spend the winter there, others were to conceal themselves and spend the winter in the Transcurzon area.[623] At the beginning of December 1947, 17 members divided into two groups and headed separately for the Baltic area. The first group, with 10 men, was headed by a platoon leader codenamed "Shepel," and the second, for which more information is available, was commanded by Ievhen Shtendera ("Prirva.") The winter march was difficult, but posing as AK, the partisans were assisted by local people who supported the Polish underground. Prirva, who managed to arrive safely, subsequently learned that the Shepel group had been completely wiped out. On January 6, he took his partisans to the home of a Ukrainian family for Christmas Eve, and they were subsequently divided up and distributed among other families. After Christmas, the group made contact with the three partisans who had been sent earlier to locate Ukrainians, but it is unclear whether Prirva had obtained address of the family from them or from another source. The Poles learned of the UPA arrival in the area and the local newspapers reported that "General Prirva" had arrived with a large partisan contingent, and a bounty of 100,000 zloty was offered for his capture or death. After spending the winter in the Olsztyn area, Prirva and his group returned to Podlasie at the beginning of May 1948 and found that the partisans had

---

623 Much of the population had identification papers that had been issued during the German occupation. The underground had German blanks and issued them to its own members but the documents had limited value. If authorities checked with the issuing office noted in the document, the holder would be arrested. At the same time, old papers were being replaced with new Polish documents and underground members had great difficulty acquiring passable identification cards after Operation Vistula. See Ibid, 869–875.

dwindled to a little more than a few dozen. Soon after, the partisans received orders to depart for the American Zone in Germany although the available information is limited to the journey of Prirva's seven-man unit. On June 10, the group began marching southwest through Poland without making serious contact either with Polish or Czech troops since the blockades that were deployed a year earlier had since been removed. In one situation, however, the partisans came under fire while crossing a bridge on the Czech territory and were separated. After unsuccessful attempts to locate the others, Prirva and three of his men continued to Bavaria separately, finally reaching the American Zone at the beginning of September 1948.

Throughout the insurgency, Polish military courts routinely executed captive UPA and OUN members. In preparation for Operation Vistula, a special military court was established to handle the expected flood of captives, and the first hearing was conducted in Sanok on April 22, 1947. Eventually, about a dozen regional courts were also established and received instructions to immediately execute those who were sentenced to death.[624] As a result, trials were short and perfunctory affairs, usually based on reports obtained through interrogations and beatings. The executions of those who were sentenced to death were normally carried out just days after sentencing, but in some cases, condemned prisoners were executed on the same day. Most who faced such trials were shot, but some (a very small minority) received life sentences or very lengthy prison terms. Although the criteria used for sentencing is not indicated in the available documentation, it is clear that at least some young partisans were spared execution because they were not of legal age. After de-Stalinization and Władysław Gomułka's rise to power in Poland in 1956, the prisoners were freed. Between 1944 and 1956, 573 underground members received death sentences. Only 31 of the 372 arrested in 1947 had their sentences commuted to long prison terms and the rest were shot. During the summer of 1947, Czech forces captured a large number of partisans who were heading for Germany. By all accounts, the captives were treated well and those who were wounded received the necessary medical care. After they recuperated, some were sent to the Soviet Union, but most went to Poland. On May 22, 1948, 112 were sent

---

[624] Misylo, ed. *Aktsiia "Visla"*, 309–310.

to Poland, and 75 of them received death sentences. [625] It appears that the captured partisans were more likely to be executed in Poland than the USSR, where many were sent to the Gulag. Some underground members managed to evade capture and scattered throughout Poland. Most, however, were eventually located and arrested, in part because a few underground members began cooperating with authorities. Among those captured was Myroslav Onyshkevych, commander of UPA's Transcurzon region, who was arrested June 3, 1950 and executed the following month.

At the conclusion of Operation Vistula, General Mossor issued a classified report detailing the events of the operation from April 20 to July 31.[626] He noted the dual tasks of the Operational Group: To destroy the Ukrainian underground and to deport Poland's Ukrainians. Initially, the operation was conducted in the southern portion of the Rzeszów Province and later extended to the rest of the province and subsequently to the Cracow and Lublin provinces. On July 17, Operational Group Vistula passed the responsibility for the campaign against UPA to the two military districts.[627] The Fifth District headquartered in Cracow was to continue the operation in the Cracow and Rzeszów provinces, and the Seventh District in Lublin was responsible for that province. On July 15, 1947, the State Commission for Security held a meeting in Warsaw and

---

625 Ibid, 503.

626 Ibid, 392–399. On July 10, as the operation was ending, the Politburo was informed of Mossor's compromising activities during the war with the suggestion that he be removed from the command and transferred to a teaching position at the Military Academy. The communist regime immediately arrested individuals under these circumstances, but Mossor was promoted to the rank of Lieutenant General and transferred to command Cracow Military District. He later served as Chief of Military Intelligence until his arrest in 1950. Born in Cracow in 1896, he joined the Polish Army in 1918, and between the wars he held various posts and was an instructor of tactics at the Warsaw Higher Military School. In 1939, he commanded a cavalry regiment and was captured by the Germans. While in prison, he wrote a report predicting the German-Soviet war. The report was smuggled out of prison and a copy reached the Polish delegation in London. In 1943, he headed a group of Polish Officers as part of a Red Cross Commission invited by the Germans to investigate the massacre of Polish officers by the Soviet police in the Katyn forest of Belarus. He joined the Polish People's Army after the war and again held important posts until his arrest in May 1950. At his trial, he received a life sentence for his activities during the German occupation, but was released after de-Stalinization along with many other prisoners in 1956. He died the following year of a stroke. See Misylo, ed. *Aktsiia "Visla"*, 58, 362.

627 Operational Group Vistula was formed on April 17, 1947 and disbanded on July 31, 1947. See Misylo, ed. *Aktsiia "Visla,"* 370–372.

General Mossor summarized the accomplishments of the Polish forces against the UPA during the campaign.[628] He noted that the operation first began against Tactical Sector 26 and Ren and Baida's battalions had been dispersed. Ren's units crossed the Soviet border to fight in Ukraine and Baida's sotnias crossed the Czechoslovak border, attempting to reach the American Zone in Germany. Mossor placed the underground strength at the beginning of the campaign at 2,400, a figure that included the regular UPA units, the OUN network, SKV, and SB. The strength of these supporting elements, however, was usually overstated. He then reported on the casualties of the two battalions and their flights to the USSR and Czechoslovakia. According to Mossor, the operation shifted north to the territory of 27th and 28th UPA Tactical Sectors, and during the second month, the resistance in those regions had been minimal. The Zalizniak and Berkut battalions totaled 789 partisans along with 249 persons in the OUN network, and both groups amounting to a total of 1,038 people. He noted that after the conclusion of the operation, the underground strength had been reduced to 472. Additionally, a large OUN unit was operating in Biała Podlaska (Bila Podliaska), but had disintegrated when the unit commander Ivan Romanchenko ("Volodia") and some of the other officers were killed. The general noted that 1,509 underground members had been killed or captured during the campaign, totaling approximately 75 percent of the total UPA strength in April. He concluded that large units had been broken up but small groups were still operating in the Ukrainian districts and posed a danger and therefore, the remnants must be pursued and completely eradicated. After summarizing the campaign against the Ukrainian underground, Mossor evaluated performance of the Polish Army and security forces. He noted that initially, Polish performance had been poor since the majority of the units were engaged in deportation, and the training of officers and conscripts had been inadequate. Some officers (including some regimental commanders) were unable to read maps or use a compass and the troops took scant precautions during marches and provided little security during encampment. During the three-and-one half-year fight with the UPA, the Poles had a habit of moving through hostile territory bunched together and rarely sending out point men or flankers. UPA's favored tactic was the ambush and when

628 Ibid, 364–365

properly executed, Polish troops in this configuration sustained heavy losses. Poor training was also reflected in the handling of weapons. The general reported that during the campaign, 29 soldiers had been killed and 97 were wounded as the result gun accidents. In contrast, 61 soldiers were killed and 91 were wounded as the result of fighting the partisans. Despite these self-inflicted casualties, UPA commanders noted that the Polish troops were fighting better than they had previously during Operation Rzeszów.

The evaluation of UPA's proficiency, as that of any other military formation, cannot be precise. Some writers addressing this issue seem to have been influenced by politics toward the insurgency and the underground. To that end, General Mossor's comments on UPA's capability is useful for evaluation since he was involved in the counterinsurgency since the beginning and had subsequently commanded Operation Vistula. These experiences gave him ample opportunity to evaluate their performance, and, of course, it is not likely that he would have exhibited a positive bias toward the UPA. At the beginning of Operation Vistula, he referred to the UPA as "well-armed elite troops with iron discipline" and there are several factors that support his conclusion. Every UPA squad had at least one machine gun, and the rest were armed mostly with rifles, although some units had automatic weapons. Overall, it was a reasonably well-armed light infantry force by World War II standards. At the same time, the partisans were volunteers who were more aggressive than conscripts and more committed since they were protecting their own people for a cause that motivated them. Moreover, the Polish policy of brutalizing captives made them more determined to resist. There are frequent reports of men shooting themselves to avoid capture, and ironically, the policy of mistreating captives strengthened their resolve. Furthermore, the partisans were experienced soldiers who had received military training, but more importantly, a large number had extensive combat experience having served for the duration of the insurgency. There are differences of opinion on the UPA's recruiting methods: some scholars claim that men were forced to join; however, this was not the typical recruitment method. When fighting broke out in the Volhynia and Lublin provinces in 1943, some men were conscripted into the service. After the war, UPA seems to have relied on volunteers, but at times, forcible recruitment was staged to protect the volunteers' families from Polish retribution. Ivan Lyko, who operated in the eastern Lemko region where Khrin had organized his sotnia, recounted in his memoirs that with some boys who had expressed the desire to join, the partisans would collect them by coming to their villages and making a show of "forcibly" taking them. The ruse enabled families to claim that their sons had been forced to join, although it is unclear as to whether or not this induction method was used in other areas.[629] Finally, UPA units operated in the same areas during the deportation campaigns, became familiar with the terrain, and therefore had a tactical advantage over Polish troops.

In the end, Polish casualty figures are likely the best measure of UPA's fighting capabilities. During the insurgency, the Polish Army, the Internal Security Corps and the Border Guards had 2,483 men killed. In addition, the police, ORMO, and public security personnel lost 603 men, making a combined total of 2,887.[630] These figures exclude the losses of railroad troops who had been killed while guarding stations and railroad lines—primary UPA targets. The figures indicate only the number killed but not a complete casualty count that included those who had been wounded, which is significant because those who are wounded in combat typically outnumber those killed by a wide margin. If the number killed and wounded were counted in the casualty rates, Polish casualties would have totaled about twice the maximum underground strength. The level of Polish casualties are remarkably high when considering that UPA had no outside support, fought with weapons and ammunition that they had captured or gathered on battlefields, and their only base of support was a small population of impoverished farmers. Despite their difficulties during the three years of fighting, the partisans had managed to be better organized and better armed than the Polish Army. In the end, they were simply overwhelmed by Polish forces and succumbed to sheer numbers during Operation Vistula.

At the conclusion of Operation Rzeszów in the summer of 1946, Ukrainians began returning from the forests to their villages and were no longer evading Polish troops. At this point the military realized that large numbers of Ukrainians still remained in Poland who were capable of supporting the underground. It initiated a campaign to conduct another

---

629 Potichnyj in Best and Moklak, eds., *The Lemko Region*, 158.

630 Szcześniak and Szota, *Droga*, 422–423.

deportation, this time to the newly acquired (former German) territories. During Operation Vistula, a more coordinated operation was organized compared to the earlier effort where each military district was charged with fighting the underground and deporting population on its territory. By the spring of 1947, a unified command was established to conduct these operations in all districts regardless of their territorial subordination. Designated military units and security forces along with relevant civilian agencies in the area were subordinated to the commander of Operation Vistula. The new command structure was also accompanied by tactical changes. Previously, operations were conducted in all Ukrainian districts simultaneously, but during Operation Vistula, only few districts at a time were targeted, enabling the army to inundate areas with troops and therefore prevent meaningful resistance by the underground as well as preventing the possibility of civilian flight. By the end of the summer, the task was accomplished and centuries of Polish-Ukrainian conflict had ended.

Chapter VII:
Resettling the Dispossessed

After six years of warfare, Eastern Europe had been devastated by both the German and Soviet fronts and the resulting occupations. Across the landscape, housing, transport, and manufacturing industries lay in ruins. In Ukraine, the destruction was more severe than in most other regions of Europe due to the numerous battles fought across the country, but particularly because of the methods that had been employed by both the German and Soviet combatants. The Red Army employed a scorched-earth policy while retreating eastward in 1941 and the German Army repeated similar processes a few years later as their troops were pushed west.[631] Ukrainian deportees of Operation Vistula were resettled in the German territories that had been ceded to Poland as part of the Yalta Agreement, and these regions had also sustained considerable damage to their buildings and infrastructures. In the ravaged landscape of the postwar aftermath, Ukrainians who were resettled to Ukraine as well as those who were resettled in Poland's new northern and western frontier lands all experienced extreme hardship in adjusting to their new circumstances.

Resettlements to Ukraine, 1944–1946

As the deportees left Poland, a majority was taken to eastern Ukraine between 1944 and 1946. On August 25, 1945, the NKVD issued a letter reminding Ukrainian officials that, per the instruction of NKVD chief Lavrenty Beria, migrants from Poland could not be settled within the 50-kilometer (31 miles) zone east of the Polish border.[632] The zone was established to prevent Ukrainians from returning to Poland, noting that the returning people were occasionally helped by the UPA operating on both sides of the border. Prior to the instruction, 924 families were

---

631 "The war destroyed 16,150 industrial enterprises, which employed 2.3 million workers. At the end of 1944, only 19 percent of the prewar enterprises and 17 percent of their labor remained intact in Ukraine." See Holubnychy, V. "Postwar Reconstruction," in Kubijovyč, ed. *Ukraine,* Vol. I, 894.

632 Serhiichuk, *Trahediia*, 288.

settled in the area, but eventually had to be relocated.[633] Although the establishment of the zone may have seemed a rational decision, shipping people to the eastern oblasts was not a necessary measure. Almost a million Poles had been driven out of western Ukraine, leaving behind abandoned homes and farms. The vacated properties would have provided more than adequate space for less than half a million new settlers coming from Poland, even if the strip along the border had been excluded. The available documents do not indicate the reasons for settling people in eastern Ukraine, but the political motives are clear. The NKVD was well aware that the Ukrainians had resisted resettlement, an action that was contrary to the official party line, and most had become more nationalistic in the struggle and therefore supported the underground. At the same time, the situation in western Ukraine still remained turbulent since the underground continued to operate there until the early 1950s. Deporting people to the eastern oblasts and scattering them among a population with limited national awareness was the preferred alternative and prevented flight to Poland. Still, illegal border crossings remained a problem until 1947 when the remaining Ukrainians were deported to the newly acquired German territories. In the spring of 1947, USSR NKVD chief S. Kruglov outlined the problem in a letter to Lazar Kaganovich, stating that during a two-week period, 666 people had been detained at the border.[634] The Ukrainian NKVD chief Tymofii Strokach wrote a more detailed letter on the flight to Poland, also to Kaganovich, who at the time had replaced Khrushchev as the party chief in Ukraine. He noted that 1,044 people were detained at the border from March to May 10, 1947. "Resettlers move toward the border using 5–8 wagons carrying between 30–50 people...some families of two or three people travel by railroad."[635] The first refugees who were settled in border regions had an opportunity to cross the border. Presumably, a significant number of these people were aided by the local population and were not reported to the authorities. Stokach then reported on the reasons that people were giving when interrogated for fleeing. One man said, "I was returning to Poland because after the poor year of 1946, I could not feed my family of seven people." Another man noted that he worked on a collective farm in the

633 Ibid, 286
634 Ibid, 342.
635 Ibid, 343.

Odesa Oblast but after the poor harvest, had not received anything for his work. He was advised to seek help from the county authorities. The county chairman advised him to go elsewhere because he could not help him. Still another detainee also worked on collective farm in Dnipropetrovs'k Oblast, but because of the poor harvest, he had neither food nor a place to live. Both reports are not critical of the people fleeing but simply state how many are leaving and for what reasons, implying that these people needed help.

Housing was the most immediate and daunting problem as described in a secret letter written by V. Abakumov, the USSR Minister of State Security, to Beria with a copy to Stalin, dated August 6, 1946. Abakumov wrote that 442,420 Ukrainians had arrived from Poland by July 15, 1946, who were "destitute and lack housing", and then provided a few examples.[636] Of the 2,210 families who had arrived in the Kirovohrad oblast of central Ukraine, only 111 had received some sort of dwelling. The remainder was assigned to live with collective farm families, resulting in the assignment of two to three families in woefully small cottages. Of the 1,749 families who were resettled in the Poltava Oblast, only 648 received housing and the remainder lived in very unsatisfactory conditions. Likewise, of the 4,942 families that had arrived in the Odesa Oblast, 3,337 received apartments and the remainder were assigned to dwellings not certified "for human habitation". The minister further stated that the lack clothing and footwear was preventing many people from going to work and children from attending school. Thus in Voroshilovhrad (present day Luhans'k Oblast), 360 children were unable to attend school and in one county of the Korovohrad Oblast, only 37 out of 630 able-bodied adults were able to work on the collective farms. Although local authorities were required to build housing, very little construction was actually undertaken. According to Abakumov, 275 dwellings were supposed to have been built in the Kivovohrad Oblast by mid-July of 1946, but only 14 had actually been completed. The authorities were not only tardy in building homes but also failed to provide the proper construction materials for people to build their own houses. The minister than noted that the new arrivals were writing alarming letters to

---

636 A number of letters related to the deportation of Ukrainians were sent either directly to Stalin or he was sent a copy. He certainly was well informed about the matter. See Ibid, 337.

their friends and relatives in Poland urging them not to leave, and included some excerpts from the intercepted mail. One man wrote to his parents "...our life here is very bad. If you are thinking of leaving, dear Papa and Mama, don't leave. Stay where you where you are now living." Abakumov noted that some deportees had even attempted to organize an anti-Soviet group with the aim of returning to Poland, and assured Stalin and Beria that the Ministry of State Security was eliminating traitorous elements from among the migrants.

In February of 1946, officials in the Sumy Oblast of northeastern Ukraine wrote a lengthy report that described the difficulties of accommodating the new arrivals, the same types of difficulties that were reported for the other oblasts of eastern Ukraine.[637] The new arrivals had not been given permanent dwellings but were instead assigned to live with collective farm families in small cottages or sent to live on collective farms or in the buildings of other organizations. The occasional references to these accommodations clearly indicate that they were not fit for human habitation. On a collective farm that was ironically named " New Life," six families comprised of 22 people had been assigned three hallways in a building. The dwelling was filthy, the air unbearable, as a result, some of the inhabitants developed sores on their arms and legs, yet the local officials had failed to provide any assistance. On the collective farms "Stalin" and "Progress" "...the dwellings are unheated and people do not undress. Many wear filthy clothing and some don't have underwear. Because there is a shortage of soap, people do not wash themselves, their clothing, or their underwear." [638]

In addition to the housing shortage, people were unable to feed and clothe themselves and take care of basic necessities. Deportees were able to work on collective farms during the summer, but many were unable to perform outdoor work in the winter due to the lack of warm clothing and proper footwear. Those who worked outdoors had to work in close proximity to their dwellings and periodically retreated indoors to warm themselves, reducing their earnings. The lack of warm clothing also prevented many immigrant children from attending school during the winter. Food

---

637 Information on the conditions in the Sumy Oblast is published in Ibid, 290–301. The conditions in the Sumy oblast typify the conditions described for the other oblasts where deportees were resettled.

638 Ibid, 291.

shortage was another dire problem since the meager collective farm earnings, amounting to about a pound of grain for a day's work, were inadequate and quickly exhausted. One report describes the experiences of one family who could not feed themselves: "A family of eight did not eat some days…the father had to sell his overcoat to buy potatoes."[639] The problem of shortages was compounded by the callousness, inefficiency, and corruption of local officials. A party document notes that in the Stalino Oblast in eastern Ukraine (present day Donetsk Oblast), 3,100 kilograms of grain that had been allocated for the new arrivals was sold privately. In another county (*raion*), local officials sold the construction materials assigned to build homes for the new immigrants. Officials in the Sumy Oblast wrote a lengthy report in February 1946 that described the difficulties of accommodating the new arrivals, a description that is also representative of the problems that arose in other oblasts.[640] Less than half of the new immigrants in the oblast were resettled on collective farms, although specific information on the remainder is not reported. Inspectors frequently discovered that grain allocated for the migrants had not been distributed among them. At the same time, people had not been compensated for the property they had left behind in Poland as specified in the agreement, and their horses had been confiscated by the collective farm administration without compensation. Due to the lack of adequate clothing, the report continues, the majority of school-aged children were not attending school and authorities were not providing aid.

In an August 31, 1945 letter to Anastas Mikoyan, Stalin's confidant, Ukrainian officials requested material assistance, noting that almost a quarter of a million people had arrived from Poland lacking clothing, footwear, and other basic necessities. The officials explained that because of the centralized distribution of merchandise by the All-Union organs, Ukraine was unable to provide the special assistance required by the new settlers. Officials requested 500 thousand meters of cloth (10 meters per family), 52,400 pairs of shoes (one per family), and 100 tons of soap for a five month period, amounting to approximately 400 grams per family or about three bars. There is no indication as to whether or not the request was granted.[641] Authors of such reports tended to blame local

639 Ibid, 292–293.

640 Information on the conditions in eastern oblasts is published in Ibid, 290–328.

641 Serhiichuk, Trahediia, 289.

officials for the difficulties that the migrants faced. Examples of some callous and corrupt officials can always be found, especially at times of great need. Nevertheless, the individual failings of local officials were actually a minor problem. Ukraine was gripped by a severe shortage of virtually everything, a condition that was caused by the devastation of war and the policies made by the highest levels of political leadership, which considered the welfare of the people an issue of secondary importance. Based on official Soviet correspondence, it appears that senior Ukrainian officials were not indifferent to the plight of the deportees, but were unable to provide substantial relief.

Along with the housing and material privations, the callous behavior of the local authorities and the indigenous population caused additional difficulties for the new settlers. New arrivals were occasionally called "Poles" and "Banderites." In Ukraine, the strained relations were partially caused by the noticeable linguistic and cultural differences between the two groups. Those coming from the west spoke a Ukrainian dialect influenced by Polish, while the speech of easterners was studded with Russian words. There were also cultural differences caused by divergent historical experiences; the easterners had lived in a Russian state for centuries, while westerners had been influenced by Polish language and culture. Galicia differed even more since it had been part of the Austrian Empire for a century and a half and the religion of the people had been predominantly Greek Catholic.

Famine in the Steppe

One of the most tragic aspects of the resettlement actions was the fact that they coincided with a famine that occurred in the southern oblasts of Ukraine between 1946–1948. Earlier in history, Ukraine had been dubbed "the bread basket of Europe", but during the Soviet period, Ukrainians had frequently endured food shortages and famines, largely exacerbated by Soviet policies. The most notable case occurred during the infamous *Holodomor* famine of 1932–1933 when millions of Ukrainians had perished as the result of Soviet agrarian policies. Famines related to the Civil War that followed the Russian Revolution and the collectivization of agriculture is a topic that has been widely discussed in numerous publications.[642] Another famine, albeit on a smaller scale than earlier famines, occurred in 1946 and added to the misery of the Ukrainian settlers who came from Poland. By that time of the resettlements, the agricultural sector was beginning to recover from the devastation caused by the war when a combination of adverse climatic conditions and draconian government procurement policies produced another famine. The famine was not limited to Ukraine but spread through much of the southern portion of the Soviet Union. Population losses due to famine have not been officially published, and indeed the government never admitted that there was a famine. Estimates placed the losses at one to one and a half million, but precise estimates are difficult for those years because of huge wartime losses and because physicians were ordered to misdiagnose the causes of deaths.[643] Symptoms related to starvation were to be reported as gastrointestinal disorders or heart problems.[644] The 1946 famine was a result of Soviet agrarian policy and climate conditions. During the Soviet period, the peasantry was the most exploited segment of the population. The government established annual procurement quotas for grain and other produce, and collective farms were required to deliver specified amounts at very low prices. To a considerable extent, the outcome of annual harvests depended on the weather, and delivery quotas did not always properly factor in the weather. In this area, that is an important consideration because the steppe does not have abundant annual precipitation and therefore occasionally experiences draught.

In eastern Ukraine, the winter of 1945–46 was unnaturally warm, resulting in a minimal accumulation of snow and periodic thaws followed by freezing weather, conditions that damaged much of the winter crops. Twenty percent of the winter crop was killed by frost "...in 120 counties of Kharkiv, Vorosholovhrad, Sumy, Odesa, Mykolaiv, and Kherson oblasts..."[645] A severe draught in the summer of 1946 resulted in another poor harvest, but was compounded by the fact that the delivery grain quota for Ukraine was raised from 726,000 tons to 1,080,000 tons

---

642 Discussion of both famines is presented in Conquest, Robert, *The Harvest of Sorrow*, 1986.

643 Ellman, Michael. "The 1947 Soviet Famine and the Entitlement Approach to Famines." *Cambridge Journal of Economics*, 2000, No. 24, 622.

644 Zima, V.F. *Golod v SSSR 1946–1947*, 66.

645 Voronov and Pyliavets, *Holod,* 31.

[646] Despite strenuous efforts by local officials, the plan was not fulfilled and had a deficit of approximately 50 percent. On November 26, 1946, Khrushchev received a telegram from Stalin and Andrei Zhdanov, a Politburo member, urging him to fulfill the plan and implying that he lacked "Bolshevik zeal" in the performance of his duties.[647] While Stalin was urging Khrushchev to fulfill the plan, people were writing frantic letters asking for help. Collective farmers from Vinnytsia Oblast wrote to Khrushchev: "Nikita Sergeievich, our dear father, our defender! Our lives are difficult, we are all in rags, naked and shoeless, filthy and hungry. We do not resemble people, but are worse off than the animals. It has never been as bad before as it is now. People are dying of starvation and children are coming down with crippling illnesses… if we implement this plan we will all drop dead."[648] In the same vein, the widow of a Red Army soldier with four children from the Odesa Oblast wrote to Mikhail Kalinin, Chairman of the Presidium of the Supreme Soviet, asking for help. One of her children had already starved to death and she was afraid that the other children would die as well.[649] Some assistance was eventually provided but by the time it arrived, it was usually too late. Notwithstanding the poor harvest, a sufficient amount of grain had been produced to prevent a famine, but just as in the 1930s, Stalin chose to export large quantities of grain while people starved at home. During 1946–47, 2.5 million tons of grain was exported, some gratis, primarily to the east European countries where Stalin was installing communist regimes.[650] As a result, the winter of 1946–47 was brutal in the steppe lands of Ukraine. "Famine gripped most of the territory of the republic. The situation was more or less satisfactory only in western Ukraine."[651]

There were numerous reports of people eating dogs and by January 1, 1947, ration cards had been issued to 331,600 people in rural areas. By the summer of 1947, over a million people were registered as suffering from dystrophy due to malnutrition, and this estimate is based on incomplete data.[652] The most horrific events of the famine were described by

---

646 Ibid, 32.
647 Ibid, 40–42.
648 Ibid, 30.
649 Zima, *Golod v SSSR*, pp. 67–68
650 Ibid, 149.
651 Voronov and Piliavets', *Holod*, p. 42
652 Ibid, 43–44

Nikita Khrushchev in his "Memoirs." At the time, he was First Secretary of the Ukrainian Communist Party:

> We began to receive indications that people were dying. In some places, cannibalism occurred. I was told, for example, that a head and a pair of human feet were found under a bridge in Vasilkov (a small town near Kyiv). In other words, a cadaver had been used for food. Later on, such instances became more frequent. A.I. Kirichenko, the first secretary of the party's Odesa province committee, reported that when he arrived at a collective farm to check on how people were getting through the winter, he was told to go to the house of a certain peasant woman. After his visit, he reported the following: I found a scene of horror. The woman had the corpse of her own child on the table and was cutting it up. She chattered away as she worked, "We've already eaten Manechka, and now we're salting Vanechka. This will last us for some time." This woman had gone crazy with hunger and butchered her own children! Can you imagine that?[653]

The rural population in severely stricken areas began illegally abandoning collective farms. Just as the serfs in feudal times, collective farmers were required to obtain authorization to leave their farms. Some fled to towns or less adversely affected areas in the east, but most traveled to western Ukraine. The region had been part of Poland between the wars and still had not been collectivized. Between January 1, 1946 and January 1, 1947, the number of working age women and teenagers older than 16 had decreased by 283,900 on collective farms. "It should be noted that a large share of this population died of famine and the figure does not include children or the elderly, the primary victims of the famine."[654] Into this misery arrived the destitute deportees from Poland who undoubtedly fared worse than the local people since they were not familiar with the Soviet system and they did not have any acquaintances who could assist them. Despite the pressure from the police and civilian authorities, the deportees also began abandoning the eastern oblasts and illegally traveled to western Ukraine. By the middle of 1946, over 4,000 families from Zaporizhzha, Mykolaiv, and Kirovohrad oblasts had left for western Ukraine.[655] It is likely that a relocation of this magnitude had at least the tacit approval of the local authorities, who were unable to provide for them and therefore permitted people to leave.

In addition to taking direct measures to prevent the new settlers from returning to Poland or fleeing elsewhere abroad, Soviet police also

---

653 Khrushchev, Sergei, ed. *Memoirs of Nikita Khrushchev*, 7.
654 Voronov and Piliavets', *Holod*, 43.
655 Serhiichuk, *Trahediia*, 339.

monitored their activities inside the country by conducting various types of surveillance in order to uncover incidences of agitation or disloyalty to the state. In a top secret letter to Beria dated August 6, 1946, Minister of State Security V. Abakumov identified a number of individuals "...who attempted to organize an anti-Soviet organization among the deportees and illegally return to Poland." [656] Abakumov assured Beria that "...the Ministry of State Security of the Ukrainian SSR continues to uncover enemy elements among the deportees from Poland." The surveillance also involved censoring the deportees' international postal correspondence. Abakumov even quoted a portion of a confiscated letter written by a deportee to relatives in Canada:

> ...Our life here is bad. We will not be able to live as we had done earlier. Before we worked and we had something, but here we work on collective farms and have nothing. People are moving around looking for something better, many have left for Volhynia. [657]

Abakumov, as other police officials, attributed the discontent to the difficult living conditions but adds that there are anti-Soviet elements among the deportees who were urging people to return to Poland. He then names several individuals accused of being former OUN members and one individual was accused of attempting to organize an underground. The letters to Poland were especially disturbing to both the Soviet and Polish authorities because after receiving the letters, Ukrainians who remained in Poland were even more determined to resist resettlement to Ukraine. The Lemkos received more attention than others from the Soviet officials due to their correspondence with numerous relatives in the United States and Canada. Since they spoke a partially Polonized dialect and had previously lived in a mountainous region, they experienced greater difficulties acclimating themselves to the hot, treeless steppe lands. Because there had been a high degree of emigration to North America around the turn of the twentieth century, many Lemkos had relatives in Canada and the United States, and wrote letters describing their situation in the Soviet Union with hopes of obtaining much-needed financial or material assistance.

---

656 Ibid.

657 Ibid.

N. Filatov, head of the All-Slavic Committee, an organization formed to generate support for the Soviet Union among Slavs, wrote a secret, detailed letter to Mikhail Suslov at the Central Committee.[658] In one section of the report, Filatov reported on the actual conditions that the new settlers faced in their resettlement locations. According to the letter, only between three to five families were assigned to a single collective farm and some families had been separated. Of the 34 families interviewed, only one resided with all members of their families, and the remaining families had their members scattered throughout Ukraine. Many had left their assigned places and traveled across the country to reunite with their relatives, usually in western Ukraine. On one collective farm in the Stalino Oblast, six families had left everything behind to reunite with relatives in the Ternopil' Oblast. In addition to longing for their relatives, many people in the Stalino oblast were facing severe difficulties: sickness due to the brackish water and starvation resulting from the poor harvest coupled with the high grain requisitions. They stated that local officials and party organizations had simply ignored their needs. Dmytro Ksenich was originally from the village of Nieznajowa (Neznaieva) in the Lemko region. In 1945, Polish bandits coerced the family to leave at gunpoint in the early stages of removal, which were carried out under the pretense of "voluntary" relocation. In a personal interview conducted in 2011, he described the desperate conditions that his family experienced on a state-run farm (*sovkhoz*) and the reasons why they subsequently fled to western Ukraine:

658 See Ibid, 329–337.

> They say that there was a drought in 12 different oblasts. Nothing grew, everything withered. We searched for potatoes in the ground which we had already planted and we boiled them and ate them. We even ate grass. I discovered some rotten beets growing at the *sovkhoz*, took them in my hands, and I didn't know from which end to start eating them. We were always hungry during 1946 and 1947. In 1948, there was no drought in western Ukraine. There we could find food. But how did we get here to Kalush from Donetsk oblast? You couldn't just get tickets. Through acquaintances, we had to buy them and we had to overpay. We couldn't take anything with us. We could each take a suitcase and took whatever we could fit into it. We arrived in Kalush but didn't receive a house. We got a place to live because my mother found a job at a pig farm and hired me out as a servant. As a 15-year-old boy, I worked as a servant for 21 hours per day and only slept for three hours a day and lived this way for a year. It's true that there was food there. But they only gave me a soldier's (meager) portion.[659]

Ternopil' Oblast on the other hand, had over 160,000 deportees, and since between 15,000–20,000 were Lemkos, the prospect of relocating offered significant advantages. A large number of Poles had been deported, having been forced to abandon homes and farms that could be made available to the new arrivals. The land was fertile and the climate more agreeable than in the east, and the cultural differences were not as sharp; however, Ternopil' and other areas in the west presented a new set of problems. Local authorities viewed the arrivals from the east as illegal immigrants and refused to settle them, and some local people were hostile to the new arrivals, hoping to take the Polish farms for themselves since collective farms had not yet been established in this part of Ukraine.

In the same report, Filatov described the visit of Dmitri Vyslotsky, whom he identifies as the former editor of the newspaper *Karpatskaya Rus'*, an organ of Lemko Soyuz (the Lemko-Association) based in Yonkers, New York.[660] Vyslotsky had been sent to Ukraine to report on how the Lemkos were adjusting to their new lives there. The organization was organized by Lemkos who did not consider themselves to be Ukrainians and supported Tsarist Russia and later, to a lesser extent, the Soviet Union. Filatov relates Vyslotsky's claim that "Lemko émigrés in the USA

---

659 Caudill and Sivak. Personal interview with Dmytro Ksenich. Kalush, Ivano-Frankiv'sk, Ukraine. October, 2011.

660 Vislotsky adopted a pen name, Vanio Hunianka, a diminutive name for Ivan Hunia. In the Lemko dialect, a "hunia" is a coat made of homespun wool cloth. He published an article about his trip in a 1947 issue of *Karpatorusski Kalendar*, a publication of Lemko Soyuz, although the article doesn't provide much information on the actual living conditions of the Lemkos.

and Canada are the left wing of the Ukrainian émigrés in America, they are sympathetic toward the Soviet Union and collected about $300 thousand for the Red Army during the war."[661] Filatov reported that up to 200,000 Lemkos lived in America at the time and virtually every deported Lemko had close relatives in the United States. According to Filatov, Vyslotsky ostensibly made the trip to collect information about their new lives in order to counter lies in "the Fascist Ukrainian press," a label that referred to the anti-Soviet Ukrainian press that operated in the United States and Canada at the time, which had reported on the abysmal living conditions experienced by the deportees. The Ukrainian press received much of its information from letters mailed by the deportees to their relatives in the United States. The two men visited some deportees living in Stalino and Ternopil' oblasts, part of the reportedly 100–120 thousand Lemkos who had been deported. The conversations were candid since some of the Lemkos knew Vyslotsky personally or through his writing (in which he used the pen name "Van'io Hunianka,") and many gave him letters to pass along to their relatives, unaware of his collaboration with Soviet authorities. The letters provide a firsthand account of the conditions these people actually experienced in the eastern and western oblasts.

In the report to Suslov, Filatov included four letters (two anonymous) that had been collected by Vislotsky. The letters paint a bleak situation, with some people complaining that they had been divided and scattered among collective farms rather than being settled in large groups as they had been promised in Poland. More importantly, one letter complains that people were unable to earn a living. One man stated that for a day of work, he received only 200–300 grams of wheat or rye, about half a pound. Another wrote that for a whole year of work, he received 37 kilograms of grains and 45 rubles. Another letter noted that packages sent from the U.S. containing clothing, footwear and flour were sorted by the authorities who kept the better quality goods and allowed the lower quality goods to be purchased by the people for not less than 120 rubles, despite the fact that the average Lemko deportee earned only 50 to 80 rubles a year.[662] Four letters were written by people living in the Ternopil' Oblast, all of whom seemed to have migrated there from initial resettle-

661 Serhiichuk, *Trahediia,* 333.

662 Ibid, 335.

ment in the eastern oblasts, but the letters suggested that their lives had not improved. One man wrote that he had no place to live and was told to dig a bunker; the family had no food and was reduced to begging among local people. Most letters describe horrible conditions and ask for help. One writer requested that Lemkos in the United States should work toward the goal of returning the deportees to Poland, otherwise, "... Lemkos, as a distinct ethnic group, will perish."[663]

Filatov closed the report to Suslov by recommending that the Lemkos should be resettled in large groups in western Ukraine, but under no circumstances be allowed to return to Poland or Czechoslovakia; some Lemkos in the Prešov area of Slovakia had migrated to Ukraine after the war. The returnees, he cautioned, would provide grist for anti-Soviet propaganda abroad. He noted that Lemkos in particular were receiving dollars from abroad, and proposed that a system should be established to exchange clothing for dollars, which would net the Soviet Union several million dollars of hard currency. Vyslotsky's later statement to communist party officials suggests that he was unmoved by the plight of his kinsmen and had deliberately withheld the Lemkos' letters from their intended recipients in the United States:

> It is unfortunate that Lemkos have half, if not more, of their population in America and are writing letters to their relatives. They thought that I was returning to America and so they gave me letters for their relatives, putting them in my pockets. If these letters were sent to America they would only provide material for Fascist propaganda."[664]

Vyslotsky published a lengthy article describing his trip that studiously avoided providing information on the daily lives of the deportees. He describes his travels in the Soviet Union, adds some history about Rus', Moscow, and Kyiv, and ends with his visit to the Stalino and Ternopil' oblasts of Ukraine where many Lemkos were relocated. He visited a number of collective farms in each oblast where numerous Lemko families had been resettled, noting their names and the villages from where they came. As for their personal lives, he stated that there were difficulties, without specifying what they were, and noted that the people were adjusting to their new lives. In the Stalino Oblast located on the steppe in eastern Ukraine, he wrote that some were having difficulties adjusting to

---

663 Serhiichuk, *Trahediia,* 334.

the flat, hot plains and longed for the Carpathians. As to the broader question of why these people were deported, he recites for his readers the standard Communist Party line:

> For the blessed future Slavic peace—it was necessary to resettle the Lemkos in their national country and Poles from our national country into the Polish national country. Lemkos in the Soviet Union, in Rus', will not perish but will merge with their own people.[665]

Despite the extremely difficult conditions and lack of assistance, most of the deportees survived and were eventually able to acquire basic material necessities, but there are limits to human endurance. A 2009 interview with Pelagia Volians'ka, who was seventeen years old when her family was deported from Wola Piotrowa, Sanok County in 1946, described her family's experience after being resettled in Monastyrs'kyi district of Ternopil' Oblast:

> We had been a poor people in Lemkivshchyna, but my father worked hard and had a very good house. We came to Ukraine and were given a Polish house that had no windows or doors. How could we live there? My father had a nervous breakdown.[666]

Eventually, people improved their lives through personal efforts and benefitted from the recovery of the economy from the ravages of war. A 1952 Party document notes that 93,207 people who emigrated from Poland lived in western Ukraine, 85.4 percent owned homes, 9.2 percent lived in apartments, and 5.4 percent lived with the local population in shared dwellings.[667] Ukrainian statistics do not provide separate socio-economic data for the migrants from Poland, but anecdotal information suggests that they eventually attained a standard of living comparable to the rest of the population.

Resettlements in Poland's "Recovered Territories" (1947)

The deportations to Poland's northern and western territories, specifically to the provinces of Pomerania, Prussia and Silesia, was a much more expeditious process compared to the resettlements to Ukraine.

---

665 See Vyslotsky, 44.

666 Caudill, Personal Interview with Pelagia Volians'ka Tzin'kalo, L'viv Oblast, Ukraine, June 2009.

667 Serhiichuk, *Trahediia*, 348.

Since there was no pretense of voluntary emigration, people were brought to railroad stations and placed aboard the next available train. At that point, in contrast to the earlier removals, the deportees were being screened for political loyalty. Individuals who were deemed to have connections with the underground were arrested and sent to Jaworzno. Families who were suspected of supporting the underground were assigned to category A, B or C and designated for resettlement in separate locations from other Ukrainians.[668] Once the sorting process had been completed, people were put in freight cars and shipped to the "Recovered Territories." One of the goals of the resettlement process in the new Polish territories was rapid assimilation, a policy that was implemented by dispersing Ukrainians in Polish communities rather than settling them together in contiguous locations. At the same time, the deportees were considered to be a hostile element and were therefore placed in restricted zones. Ukrainians could not be settled closer than 30 miles from a foreign border, 20 miles from the sea or a provincial capital or within about six miles from the 1939 western Polish border. Moreover, they could not comprise more than 10 percent of the population in any community. The allotted areas amounted to small strips of territory in the center of the western provinces.[669]

The deportees were initially sent to the Szczecinek County (in Szczecin province) in Pomerania and to the Olsztyn province in Prussia, but were later settled in other provinces as well because Polish authorities had grossly underestimated the number of people they would need to deport. Szczecinek was scheduled to receive a total of 8,000 families; however, by July 10, 1947, 9,677 had arrived, bringing with them 6,332 horses and 11,597 cows, and the number eventually increased to 11,000 families. Olsztyn was allocated 5,000 families, but 12,427 had arrived by mid-June with 9,095 horses and 15,436 cows in tow, and the population figure later increased to 13,300 families.[670] Olsztyn received about one-third of the Ukrainian population who faced more severe difficulties than those in other provinces. The provincial governor informed authorities that the zone restrictions had eliminated 60 percent of the territory in the

---

668 Halagida, Igor. *Ukraincy na Zachodnich I Polnochnych Ziemiach Polski, 1947–1957.* (Warszawa: Instytut Pamieci Narodowej, 2002), 36

669 Misylo, ed. *Aktsiia "Visla",* 408–410.

670 Ibid, 381.

province as being eligible for Ukrainian settlement. If, in addition, each community was to have less than 10 percent of Ukrainians, then only 20,000 were permitted to remain in the province and 34,600 would have to be transferred to other provinces. Moreover, of the 44,250 Ukrainians who had been resettled in restricted zones, some had already begun to farm. As the result of these conditions, the governor requested that the deportees remain in their current places, and was subsequently advised that the restrictions should apply only to people in the dangerous categories, allowing the bulk of Ukrainians to remain. The settlement restrictions were eventually modified in other provinces as well. Eventually, Ukrainians were settled in six provinces, as shown in Table 7: the majority were placed in northern provinces along the Baltic Sea and about 20 percent, comprised mostly of western Lemkos, were sent to lower Silesia.[671] People were dispersed over 3,000 villages, and only five percent were settled in urban areas, mostly in small towns.

Table 7 Settlement of Ukrainians in Poland's "Recovered Territories" After Operation Vistula, August 15, 1947

Province	Number of counties	Number of people	Percentage by village	Ukrainians by province
Total: 6	***66***	***140,660***	***10.1***	***1.9***
Bialostok	2	991	3.0	12.2
Gdansk	6	6,838	5.7	1.8
Olsztyn	17	55,089	16.9	11.6
Poznask	9	8,042	4.6	2.9
Szczecin	18	48,465	12.1	7.8
Wroclaw	14	21,235	6.7	4.7

Source: Roman Drodz, *Droga na Zachod*..."Tyrsa" Sp. z o.o. Warszawa, 1997, p.113.

The former German territories where Ukrainians were settled after Operation Vistula had come under Polish control as the war was ending. At that time, many indigenous Germans had fled before the advancing Red Army or had been driven out. Most left behind farm equipment, as well as a considerable amount of household items and in some cases livestock. After the war, Polish communist authorities resettled ethnic Poles who were deported from the Soviet Union into these regions and encouraged those from other parts of the country to settle the vacated land. Over the next two years, much of the land had been resettled by

671 Chojnowska, 72

Polish immigrants who took the better farmsteads, land plots, and available property. Some less desirable but habitable buildings remained empty; however, some of the buildings (especially those that were damaged) had been stripped of doors, windows, stoves and other removable equipment.[672] In 1947, Ukrainian settlers were placed in these buildings: the first wave was settled in the more habitable dwellings, but later arrivals were often placed in severely damaged buildings. Finding acceptable dwellings for the arrivals was a daunting problem: an estimated 14,000 farmsteads were available in the Olsztyn Province and another 12,000 in Szczecin, but a majority of the dwellings had sustained significant damage and at least 25 percent could not be repaired before winter.[673] A report issued in July of 1947 notes that 20,000 families lived in damaged buildings and lacked basic amenities. The conditions were survivable during periods of warm weather, but without repairs, the inhabitants would likely freeze during the winter. In response, the government allocated 450 million zloty for repairs, a grossly insufficient sum. Of approximately 10,000 dwellings that required repairs in the Olsztyn province, only about 2,500 had been repaired by December. Data in other provinces elucidate similar situations: only 700 out of 10,500 dwellings in Szczecin, 500 out of 1,300 in Poznan, and none in Gdańsk.[674] Undoubtedly, survival was extremely difficult for the Ukrainian settlers under these conditions. As one survivor noted, "It's better not to mention how we lived, what is there to talk about—instead of a window—a board, instead of a stove—a spot for a fire..."[675]

After acquiring some sort of accommodations, earning a living was the next pressing problem. Most arrivals were settled on private farms and the remaining people were placed on state farms (*Państwowe Gospodarstwo Rolne*, PGR). In the Szczecin Province, families with livestock were usually given private farms and those without livestock were settled on state farms.[676] Those who attempted to farm faced numerous difficulties: most had arrived too late in the season to sow and plant, and they received poor plots of land that hadn't been cultivated for many

672 Cited in Halagida, *Ukraincy*, 42.
673 Chojnowska, 60–61.
674 Ibid, 75.
675 Halagida, *Ukraincy*, 44.
676 Drozd in Hunczak, Taras ed., *Zakerzonnia*, p. 47.

years. To successfully farm this land, farmers required a team of horses, a good plow, and fertilizer. The terrain along the Baltic Sea is sandy, and the requirements to make the land arable were beyond the means of the deportees. Some people did cultivate small plots of land but the harvest was meager. The government provided some financial assistance and monthly ration cards for each individual. The amount of food people actually received was less than what had been specified on the ration cards and frequently arrived one or two months late.[677]

Beyond the problems of food and shelter, the deportees faced societal difficulties since they had been labeled as enemies of the Polish people.[678] Luka Wozniak, whose family was deported from the village of Binczarowa (Bil'tsareva) in the western Lemko region, described his family's experiences after being resettled in lower Silesia:

> The people already living in that town were from eastern Poland, beyond the Bug river. They were said to be Poles, but they spoke Ukrainian. They treated us like we were the worst people in the world. They said that we were *Banderivtsy* (Banderites) and that we were going to kill them during the night. Later they confessed that for two months, those people organized guards to keep an eye on us. They slept with axes because they were afraid of us. I started going to school there. The other kids there threw rocks at us. All of those antagonisms eventually passed, but then there were other misfortunes. We had to eat. There was a state farm in Polkowice and my father went to the administration there. He asked if there was any work available, and told them that he had small children to feed. Slowly they all obtained work: my father, my older brothers, and my sister.[679]

For the rural and conservative Ukrainians, church had always been a focal point of community life, but their dispersal precluded the re-establishment of viable parishes. As historian Roman Drozd described: "The deportees were under constant surveillance. They were forbidden to organize cultural and educational activities. They were also forbidden to restore Ukrainian Catholic parishes or establish Orthodox parishes."[680] Moreover, like the prewar Polish government before it, the new communist regime was hostile to the Eastern Church since historic religious differences had been the major impediment to the Polonization of the

677 Chojnowska, 76.

678 Horbal, *Lemko Studies*, 445.

679 Garbera, Personal Interview with Luka Wozniak in Legnica, Poland. July, 2012.

680 Drozd in Hunczak, ed., *Zakerzonnia,* p. 50.

Ukrainian population. Greek Catholic parishes reportedly had about 120 priests in the Rzeszów and Cracow provinces at the time of the deportation.[681] About one-half of that number accompanied their parishioners to the west and the remainder were arrested or turned over to the Soviet authorities. The Polish authorities unjustifiably accused the clergy of supporting the insurgency. In reality, a majority of Ukrainian priests simply performed typical parish functions and were not active supporters of the underground. As with any segment of the population, however, exceptions can be found, and certainly some priests had served as chaplains in the UPA. The Polish government was especially hostile to the Greek Catholic Church since it was associated with the rise of Ukrainian nationalism in Galicia, and they initially banned the establishment of the churches in the resettlement territories. The Orthodox Church, located largely in the Lublin Province, faced fewer restrictions. In 1951, it was permitted to establish 27 parishes in the west.[682] In 1952, Polish authorities permitted the establishment of a few Greek Catholic Churches, but heavily favored the Orthodox Church. The situation improved for Ukrainians after the de-Stalinization in the mid-1950s. At the twentieth Communist Party meeting Nikita Khrushchev denounced Stalin's excesses and the condemnation reverberated throughout the Soviet Union and communist Eastern Europe. Many draconian Stalinist policies were moderated if not eliminated. In Poland, Władysław Gomułka, a moderate by communist standards, was appointed as the First Secretary of the Party and introduced changes, some of which also benefited Ukrainians. The Ukrainian Social and Cultural Society was allowed to form with numerous local branches and had grown to about 7,000 members by the end of 1958. The organization sought to promote the civil and cultural rights of Ukrainians, including freedom of worship and education. Ukrainian language was taught in few schools but most children studied in Ukrainian language education centers, and by the 1959–60 school year, almost 3,000 students were receiving some type of instruction in Ukrainian.[683]

Most deportees had a strong desire to return to their homes in southeastern Poland, although doing so was illegal and people who at-

---

681 Ibid, p. 145.

682 Ibid, p. 55.

683 Ibid., pp. 65 and 69.

tempted this were subject to arrest.[684] A 1949 decree forbade the deported Ukrainians to return to the areas from where they had been deported. As the governor of Cracow Province stated, it was time to finally "re-Polonize the southeastern districts." A small number chose to emigrate to the USSR, and approximately 1,164 people left in 1948 alone..[685] The legal impediments notwithstanding, about 3,000 people had returned by 1952 and after de-Stalinization, return migration further increased with the number of returnees reaching approximately 20,000 between 1957 and 1958.[686] In time, the material well-being of the people improved but they remained a repressed minority, forbidden to establish cultural or religious life due to Poland's assimilation policies.

At the present time, most Ukrainians live in the same areas where they were deported and a small minority returned to their ancestral lands in southeastern Poland, but their reported share of the population is unrealistically low. The 2011 Polish Census reports that 36,000 Ukrainians and 7,000 Lemkos were living in Poland.[687] At the time of their deportation in 1947, the two groups totaled at least 175,000. This figure excludes approximately 14,000 Ukrainians who were transferred to Poland in 1951 as part of a Soviet-Polish boundary adjustment.[688] During the period between 1947–2011, the overall population of Poland increased 61 percent. If the deported group of about 175,000 increased at the same rate, the combined figure for Ukrainians and Lemkos should be approximately 282,000. Because the new arrivals were dispersed among Poles, substantial assimilation should be expected especially through intermarriages, but the huge deficit cannot be attributed to assimilation alone, since the deported group included a large number of embittered people who were not amenable to a rapid assimilation. As Drozd wrote: "The resettled Ukrainians had no interest in establishing closer ties with the Poles, and mutual dislike contributed to this attitude, ultimately causing the social isolation of both groups."[689] The unrealistically low figure is caused either by improper enumeration or census responses by Ukrainians who are willfully concealing their ancestry.

---

684 Misylo, ed. *Aktsiia "Visla"*, 36.
685 Halagida, *Ukraincy*, 51.
686 Drozd in Hunczak, Taras ed., *Zakerzonnia*, 67.
687 Glowny, 2012, p. 106.
688 Drozd in Hunczak, Taras ed., *Zakerzonnia,* 45.
689 Ibid, 51.

Whatever the reasons for the small share of Ukrainians in present-day Poland, which could be attributed to assimilation or abandonment of ancestral identity, the longstanding Polish policy of Polonizing Ukrainians had finally come to fruition. As was stated in a government document: "The fundamental goal of resettling of the Operation 'W(isła)' settlers is their assimilation in the new Polish environment. All efforts should be made to achieve this goal. Do not use the term 'Ukrainian' when referring to these settlers. In cases, where the intellectual element have been brought with other settlers to the Regaïned Territories, it is absolutely imperative to settle them separately and far away from the communities where the Operation 'W(isła)' settlers reside."[690] On August 3, 1990, after the collapse of the Communist regime in Poland, the Polish Senate condemned Operation Vistula.

690 Official decree cited in Ibid, 50.

Conclusion

The history of the Polish-Ukrainian conflict, from its medieval beginnings until its culmination with Operation Vistula in 1947, is a long history of competing political and territorial interests that intermittently erupted into violent conflicts. For centuries, Poles and Ukrainians fought to gain control of the same territory, and once the land had been incorporated into the Soviet Union and the new border was internationally recognized, the rationale for the struggle between them was eliminated.

Since the collapse of communism in Eastern Europe, Poland and Ukraine have had an exemplary relationship. Some scholars, such as historian Orest Subtelny, attribute the current good relations to the post World War II deportations that separated the two groups and effectively eliminated the hostilities.[691] An examination of contemporary Polish-Ukrainian relations seems to support that thesis. In 1991, Poland was the first country to recognize Ukraine as an independent state and has since become one of the staunchest supporters of a free Ukraine. Leaders of both Poland and Ukraine have denounced the mutual atrocities of the past and have since significantly improved their diplomatic relations since the collapse of the Soviet Union. In 1990, the Polish parliament apologized for Operation Vistula, and in 1998, Poland erected a monument to Ukrainians who had been imprisoned in Jaworzno. Similarly, in 1997, Ukrainian President Leonid Kuchma expressed regret for the 1943 ethnic cleansing in Volhynia.

There can be no doubt that the physical separation of Poles and Ukrainians has contributed to positive diplomatic relations between the two countries in modern times. The current leaders of both countries are now able to concentrate on broader geopolitical issues affecting both of their countries rather than focusing on internal ethnic strife. Nevertheless, the good relations must be heavily attributed to the current geo-political realities in the region. Both countries live in fear of a Russian reconquest, and nothing fosters strong relations between states better than a common powerful enemy. For Poland, the existence of an independent and viable Ukraine ensures a geographic buffer with Russia. In turn, Ukraine has gained a strong supporter in the European Union that has

---

[691] Ther and Siljak., p. 169.

urged other European countries to aid Ukraine in the event of a Russian threat. The harmonious relationship between the two countries is commendable after centuries of conflict; however, Polish support for Ukraine is largely the result of Poland's concerns about Russian encroachment into Polish lands and the need to have a geopolitical buffer between the Polish state and Russia.

Despite the excellent relations, there still remains an incongruence of Ukrainian and Polish historical perspectives and interpretations of historical events in the national narratives of both countries. These differences are deeply rooted in the more far-reaching history between Poles and Ukrainians. From the Polish perspective, the growth of Ukrainian national awareness in its eastern provinces resulted in the loss of historic Polish lands. Ukrainians interpret interwar Polonization policies and colonization efforts as an attempt to destroy their identity as a separate people. Although the current scholarly literature on the subject is more objective than it was in the communist era, each side steadfastly emphasizes its own grievances. Despite the fact that hostility between the two groups has abated, it has not been forgotten and those traumatic experiences have been passed down from generation to generation.

Although it is tempting for some scholars to imagine that the post-World War II conflict was born from the nationalist inspiration of the twentieth century, the antecedents of that conflict were demonstrably present throughout several centuries of Polish-Ukrainian co-existence. Poland's fourteenth century conquest of the Kyivan Rus' territories began the Polish claim to the historic territories, and until the mid-twentieth century, Polish elites would assert this claim in the form of religious and cultural repressions dovetailed with assimilationist (*Polonization*) policies. These actions, which were consistently applied throughout the various iterations of the Polish state, produced a Ukrainian reaction that occasionally turned violent and internecine. The Cossack rebellions of the seventeenth century, the peasant uprisings of the eighteenth century, and guerrilla warfare in the twentieth century were all violent and destructive clashes fueled by economic and social grievances and patriotic fervor. As the Russian and Austrian empires collapsed in the early twentieth century, Ukrainians sought to establish their own state both on the Dnieper and in Galicia. Their efforts failed, but national awareness increased noticeably. People no longer considered themselves "Little Russians" or "Ruthenians" but were increasingly identifying as Ukrainians and supporting the emergence of an independent Ukrainian state. The Poles viewed Ukrainian nationalist aspirations as an unforgivable manifestation of disloyalty toward the Polish state, and consequently, they increasingly came to view Ukrainians as a fifth column that required suppression.

During the interwar period, Polonization policies were more aggressively applied than had been the case earlier in history, and in pursuing such repressions, the interwar Polish government unwittingly prepared the groundwork for the ethnic strife that followed. The collapse of the Polish State, the formation of large partisan armies by both Poles and Ukrainians, and the Soviet and German deportations and exterminations all contributed to creating a climate where attacks and the wholesale deportations of civilians became commonplace. As the war was drawing to a close, the Soviet Union initiated the mass deportations of Poles and Ukrainians in the border regions while much of Poland was still occupied by the German Army. The age-old policy of the Muscovite tsars was pursued by the Soviet commissars and had multiple objectives. First, by moving the boundary further west, the Soviets brought nearly all of the former Rus' lands, and therefore Ukrainians, under their control. This action could be justified as reinforcing the new frontiers along ethnic lines and eliminating mutual violence. At the same time, bringing Ukrainians under Soviet control would eliminate the possibility of a future irredentist movement forming along the border.

Although archival materials that detail Stalin's thinking on the subject of the deportations are not available, if such documents ever in fact existed, his views can be surmised from an examination of Soviet policies. When the Red Army crossed the Polish frontier in the summer of 1944, Soviet officials began organizing meetings in Ukrainian villages and urging people to resettle in Ukraine. At the same time, the Soviet Union and Poland signed a border agreement on July 27, 1944, and a population exchange agreement on September 9th. They scheduled the actual deportation to begin on October 15 and to be completed by February 1, 1945, which implies that the Soviet Union was clearly in a hurry. The western allies agreed that the new border should approximate the Curzon Line, but urged magnanimity toward Poland. Specifically, Stalin was asked to cede the city of L'viv and some oil fields in the Carpathian foothills to Poland, adjustments that would have shifted the border about

50 miles to the east of its current placement. By deporting both groups prior to the post-war conference scheduled to finalize the border, Stalin presented the U.S. and Britain with a *fait accompli.* The Soviet version of the border had to be accepted since it neatly separated both nationalities.

In addition to justifying the new borders, another important consideration was the elimination of ethnic strife. Soviet officials frequently rationalized mass deportations as a necessary action to eliminate disloyalty and curtail violence; and therefore, their chosen method reflected Stalin's approach to settling ethnic differences. During the war, he deported about half a dozen nationalities in Crimea and the Caucasus for alleged cooperation with Germans and, according to Khrushchev's secret speech, Ukrainians escaped a similar fate only because they were too numerous.[692] As the Soviet Union re-occupied western Ukraine, it was confronted with two hostile populations who were also at war with each other. By deporting the Poles from the territories that became attached to Soviet Ukraine, Stalin eliminated one hostile group and quickly ended inter-ethnic strife in those regions, although the Soviets had to fight Ukrainian partisans for another five years. Certainly a less draconian policy would have achieved similar objectives with less bloodshed; however, neither the Soviets nor the Polish communists ever sought accommodation with their opponents. Deportation and extermination was the preferred method of dealing with separatism, disloyalty and ethnic strife. During the interwar period, Ukrainians in Poland had sought to nurture separatist views in Soviet Ukraine. After the war, Stalin incorporated Northern Bukovyna and Transcarpathia into the Soviet Ukraine and deported Ukrainians from Poland as well, effectively bringing all Ukrainians under his control.

The Polish side was receptive to the Ukrainian removal and did not need much Soviet encouragement. To justify the mass deportations to the west during Operation Vistula, Polish communist authorities invoked a Polish law from 1936 that permitted the removal of people from border regions for security reasons.[693] Centuries of conflict generated mutual hatred that extended beyond rational bounds. The removal of Ukrainians to the west was officially declared to be a necessity in order to destroy the UPA, but it cannot be viewed as the only motivator since in 1949, two

---

692 Jacobs, 1962, p. 111.

693 Misylo, 1997, p.36.

years after the partisans were driven out of the area, a decree was issued forbidding the deportees to return to their homes. Finally, in 1950, authorities found it necessary to deport 34 families living in three villages that had been missed in 1947, and located almost 100 miles west of the Ukrainian border.[694] Clearly, the Ukrainian partisans were not the only issue that the Soviet and Polish communist authorities had concerning the Ukrainians in Poland.

Ukrainian national awareness increased in the Transcurzon region especially during the German occupation, and most people supported the UPA for patriotic reasons. The ethnic violence and deportation, however, increased the bond between the people and the partisans since UPA was the only group that provided a measure of protection against the increasing violence of Polish gangs and troops. Had the Polish authorities removed the threat of deportation and issued an amnesty for the UPA after the Soviet-sponsored deportations to Ukraine were completed in the summer of 1946, it is possible that the insurgency would have withered away and the situation in the area would have naturally stabilized. The longstanding mutual hostilities and the possibility (albeit remote) of the formation of future irredentist movements prompted the authorities to deport the remaining Ukrainians and disperse them among the Polish population.

The mass deportations of Poles and Ukrainians ended centuries of conflict at a horrific human cost. Poles were removed from western Ukraine and most were resettled in the newly acquired German territory. Most Ukrainians in Poland were moved to Soviet Ukraine and the remainder were scattered throughout northern and western Poland during Operation Vistula. A small number managed to remain in Ukrainian districts by reinventing themselves Roman Catholics or claiming Polish nationality as the price for remaining. In the end, the Polish–Ukrainian resettlements reflected Stalin's obsession with deportations as a method of resolving ethnic conflicts. On the Polish side, the evolving communist regime continued a centuries-old Polish policy of assimilating Ukrainians within the Polish state.

---

694 Ibid.

Bibliography

Armstrong, John A. *Ukrainian Nationalism*. Second Edition. Littleton: Ukrainian Academic Press, 1980.

Barr, James, M.P. and Davies Rhys, J. *M.P. Report on The Polish-Ukrainian Conflict in Eastern Galicia*. London: House of Commons, September 1931.

Bell-Fialkoff, Andrew. *Ethnic Cleansing*. New York: St. Martin's Press, 1996.

Berkhoff, Karel C. *Harvest of Despair: Life and Death in Ukraine under Nazi Rule*. Cambridge, Mass.: Belknap Press of Harvard University Press, 2004.

Best, Paul, and Jarosław Moklak, eds. *The Lemko Region, 1939–1947; War, Occupation and Deportation*. Cracow and New Haven: Carpatho-Slavic Group and the Historia Iagellonic Press, 2002.

Bilas, Ivan. *Represyvno-Karal'na Systema v Ukraini, 1917–1953*, Knyha Persha. Kyiv: "Lybid"--"Viisko Ukrayiny," 1994.

Bilinsky, Yaroslav. "60th Anniversary of the Polish-Ukrainian Tragedy of Volyn." *The Ukrainian Quarterly*, no. 3–4 (2003): 236–254.

Bociurkiw, B. R. "The Orthodox Church in Ukraine Since 1917." In Vol. II of *Ukraine; A Concise Encyclopedia*, Vol. II, edited by Volodymyr Kubiovyc, 167–177, Toronto: University of Toronto Press, 1971.

Boiars'kiy, P. K. Vnutrishnia Polityka Organizatsii Ukrainskykh Nationalistiv. Geneva, 1947.

Bor-Komorowski, Tadeusz. *Armia Podziemna*. Warszawa: Bellona, 1994.

Boroschak, Elias. "Ukraine in the Russian Empire in the Nineteenth and the Early Twentieth Centuries (1800–1917)." In Vol. I. of *Ukraine: A Concise Encyclopedia,* edited by Volodymyr Kubijovyč, 667–689, Toronto: University of Toronto Press, 1963.

Budrowycz, Bohdan. "Poland and the Ukrainian Problem, 1921–1939." *Canadian Slavonic Papers*, XXV, 4. Toronto: 1983, 475–499.

Bulba-Borovets', Taras, Otaman. *Armiia Bez Derzhavy.* Winnipeg: Society of Volyn, 1981.

Chojnowska, Aldona. "*Operacja "Wisła" (Przesiedlenie ludności ukraińskiej na ziemie zachodnie i północne w 1947 r.)*" in *Zeszyty Historyczne—Zeszyt Sto Drugi*. Paryz: Instytut Litercki, 1992.

Chojnowski, Andrej. *Koncepcje polityki narodowościowej rządów polskich w latach 1921–1939.* Wrocław: Akademia Nauk, 1979.

Chojnowski, A. "Pacification." In Vol. III (L-Pf) of *Encyclopedia of Ukraine* edited by Danylo Husar Struk. Toronto: University of Toronto Press, 1993.

Chubaty, N. "The Medieval History of Ukraine: The Princely Era." In Vol. I. of *Ukraine: A Concise Encyclopedia,* edited by Volodymyr Kubijovyč, 581–617, Toronto: University of Toronto Press, 1963.

Conquest, Robert, *The Harvest of Sorrow*; Soviet Collectivization and the Terror-Famine. London-New York: Oxford University Press, 1946

Czaplinski, Władysław and Ladogorski, Tadeusz, eds. *Atlas Historyczny Polski.* Warszawa-Wrocław: Polskie Przedsiebiorstwo Wydawnictw Kartograficznych, 1993.

Dallin, Alexander. *German Rule in Russia, 1941–1945; A Study of Occupation Politics,* Second Revised Edition, Boulder: Westview Press, 1957.

Davies, Norman. *God's Playground, A History of Poland.* Vol. II. Oxford: Clarendon Press, 1982

Dmytryk, Ivan. *Zapysky Ukrainskoho Povstantsia v Lisakh Lemkivshchyny*. L'viv: Chervona Kalyna, 1992.

Drozd, Roman. *Droga na zachód. Osadnictwo ludności ukraińskiej na ziemiach zachodnich i północnych Polski w ramach akcji „Wisła"*. Warszawa: Tyras, 1997.

Drozd, Roman. "The Ethnic Policy of the Polish Regime with Regards to the Ukrainian Population in Poland." In *Zakerzonnia, Ethnic Cleansing of the Ukrainian Minority in Poland, 1944–1947,* edited by Taras Hunczak, *21–96*. Clifton, NJ: Organization for the Defense of Lemko Western Ukraine, Inc., 2012.

Dvornik, Francis. "The Significance of the Missions of Cyril and Methodius." *Slavic Review*, no. 2 (1964): 195–223.

Dvornik, Francis. *The Slavs; Their Early History and Civilization.* Boston: American Academy of Arts and Sciences, 1956.

Dzhula-Dovbush, Stepan. *Neperedbachyna Dolia, Spomyny*. 2005.

Eberhardt, Piotr. *Polska Granica Wschodnia 1939–1945*. Warszawa: Spotkania, 1992.

Eberhardt, Piotr. *Przemiany narodowościowe na Ukrainie XX wieku.* Warszawa: Biblioteka "Obozu", 1994.

Ellman, Michael. "The 1947 Soviet Famine and the Entitlement Approach to Famines." *Cambridge Journal of Economics, no. 24 (2000): 603–630.*

Gellner, Ernest. *Encounters with Nationalism.* Oxford, UK and Cambridge, USA: Blackwell, 1994.

Gieysztor et al. *History of Poland.* 2nd edition. Warszawa: Polish Scientific Publishers, 1979

Główny Urząd Statystyczny. *Raport z Wyników: Powczenchy Ludności i Mieszkań 2011,* Warszawa: Main Administration of Statistics, 2012.)

Gudziak, Borys, A. Crisis and Reform; *The Kyivan Metropolitanate, the Patriarchate of Constantinople, and the Genesis of the Brest Union.* Cambridge, U.S.: Ukrainian Research Institute, Harvard University, 1998.

Halagida, Igor. *Ukraińcy na zachodnich i północnych ziemiach Polski 1947–1957 T. 1.* Warszawa: Instytut Pamięci Narodowej, 2002.

Harasymiv, Ivan. *Litopys Ukrains'koi Povstans'koi Armii. Z iunatskukh mrii--u riady UPA*, Vol. 29. Toronto-L'viv: Litopys UPA, 1999.

Herasymovych, I. et al. "Education in Western Ukraine in 1919–44 and Abroad." In Vol. II of *Ukraine; A Concise Encyclopedia*, edited by Volodymyr Kubijovyč, 371–381, Toronto: University of Toronto Press, 1971.

Herasymovych, I. and Terletsky, O. *Ukrainian Lands Under Austria-Hungary*. In Vol. II of *Ukraine: A Concise Encyclopedia,* edited by Volodymyr Kubijovyč, 327–340, Toronto: University of Toronto Press, 1971.

Heymann, Frederick, G. *Poland & Czechoslovakia.* Englewood Cliffs: Prentice-Hall, 1966.

Himka, John-Paul. "The Construction of Nationality in Galician Rus': Icarian Flights in Almost All Directions." In *Intellectuals and The Articulation of the Nation,* edited by Ronald Grigor Suny and Michael D. Kennedy, 109–164, Ann Arbor: The University of Michigan Press, 1999.

Himka, John-Paul. *The Greek Catholic Church and the Nation-Building in Galicia, 1772–1918*. Harvard Ukrainian Studies, Vol. VIII, nos. 3/4, December 1984. 426–452

Holubnychy, V. "Postwar Reconstruction." In Vol. I. of *Ukraine; A Concise Encyclopedia*, edited by Volodymyr Kubijovyč, 894–911, Toronto: University of Toronto Press, 1963.

Horak, Stephan. *Poland and Her National Minorities, 1919–39.* New York: Vantage Press, 1961.

Horbal, Bogdan. *Lemko Studies: A Handbook*. East European Monographs. Columbia University Press, New York, 2010.

Hromenko, M. *U Velykomu Reidi*. Munchen: Do Zbroi, 1956.

Hrushevsky, Mykhailo. *History of Ukraine-Rus. Vols. I-VI.* New York: Knyho-Spilka, 1954.

Hvat, I. Istoriia "Pivnichnoii Lemkivshchyny Do Vyhnannia Lemkiv" in *Vol. I. Lemkivshchyna; Zemlia, Liudy, Istoria, Kul'tura,,* edited by Bohdan O. Struminsky, 149–211, New York, 1988.

Hunczak, Taras, ed. *Zakerzonnia: Ethnic Cleansing of the Ukrainian Minority in Poland, 1944–1947*. Clifton, NJ: Organization for the Defense of Lemko Western Ukraine, Inc., 2012.

Isaievych, Iaroslav, et al. *Volyn' i Kholmshchyna,1938–1947; Pol'sko-Ukrains'ke Protistoiannia ta Ioho Vidlunnia*. L'viv, 2003.

Israel, Fred, L. *Major Peace Treaties of Modern History, 1648–1967,* Vol. III. New York: Chelsea House Publishers, 1967.

Ivanchuk, Roman, et al. *Narys Istorii "Prosvita"*. L'viv: Prosvita, 1993.

Jacobs, Dan N., ed. *The New Communist Manifesto and Related Documents*. Harper Torchbooks, 1962.

Jasiak, Marek. "Overcoming Ukrainian Resistance: The Deportation of Ukrainians within Poland in 1947." In Philip Ther and Ana Siljak, eds., 173–194. *Redrawing Nations: Ethnic Cleansing in East-Central Europe.* Lanham: Rowman & Littlefield, 2001.

Jonca, Adam. *Polish Tracks & Wheels; French Tanks in the Army.* Sandomierz, PL: Polish Drukarnia Dieczjalena, 2009.

Kamenetsky, Ihor. *Hitler's Occupation of Ukraine (1941–1944); A Study of Totalitarian Imperialism*. Milwaukee: Marquette University Press, 1956.

Kantor, Marvin. *Medieval Slavic Lives of Saints and Princes.* Ann Arbor: University of Michigan, 1983.

Karpus, Zbigniew, "Chełmszczyzna w latach okupacji niemieckiej." In T.10 of *Polska-Ukraina. Trudne pytania. T. 10: Materiały XI Międzynarodowego Seminarium Historycznego "Stosunki polsko-ukraińskie w latach II wojny światowej."* Warszawa: 26–28 Kwietnia 2005. Karta, 2009.

Kersten, Krystyna. *The Polish-Ukrainian Conflict Under Communist Rule.* Acta Poloniae Historica, 73. Wydawnictwo Naukowe, 1996.

Khrushchev, Sergei, ed. *Memoirs of Nikita Khrushchev, Vol. 2, Reformer (1945–1964).* University Park: *The* Pennsylvania State University Press, 2006.

Kirkien, L. *Russia, Poland and the Curzon Line.* London: Cadra House Publishers, Ltd., 1944.

Knysh, Z. *Ukrainian Military Organization.* In Vol. V (St-Z) of *Encyclopedia of Ukraine*, edited by Danylo Husar Struk, 400–401. Toronto: University of Toronto Press, 1993.

Korbonski, Stefan. *The Polish Underground State; A Guide to the Underground, 1939–1945.* Boulder: East European Quarterly, 1978.

Kordan, Bohdan, "Making Borders Stick: Population Transfer and Resettlement in the Trans-Curzon Territories, 1944–1949." *International Migration Review*, Vol. 31, no. 3 (Autumn, 1997). 704–720.

Korowytsky, I. *The Orthodox Church in Poland.* In Vol. II of *Ukraine; A Concise Encyclopedia*, edited by Volodymyr Kubijovyč, 178–182. Toronto: University of Toronto Press, 1971.

Kosyk, Volodymyr. *The Third Reich and Ukraine.* New York: P. Lang, 1993.

Kozik, Jan. *The Ukrainian National Movement in Galicia: 1815–1849.* Edmonton: University of Alberta, 1986.

Krup'iakevych, Ivan, et al. *Istoriia Ukrayin'skoho Viy'ska Druhe Dopovnene Vydania.* Winnipeg: Ivan Tuktor, 1953.

Kryp'iakevych, Ivan. *Istoriia Ukrainskoho Viis'ka.* L'viv: Ivan Tuktor, 1936.

Kubijovyč, Wolodymyr, *Ethnographic Map of the South-Western Ukraine (Halycyna-Galicia).* London, 1953.

Kubijovyč, Volodymyr. "Ethnic Composition of the Population." In Vol. I. of *Ukraine, A Concise Encyclopedia*, edited by Volodomyr Kubijovyč, 208–214, Toronto: University of Toronto Press, 1963.

Kubijovyč, Volodymyr. *Ethnic Groups of the South-Western Ukraine (Halycyna-Galicia)*, 1.1.1939. Wiesbaden: Otto Harrossowitz, 1983.

Kubijovyč, Volodymyr. "Kholm Gubernia." In Vol. II (G-K) of *Ukraine, A Concise Encyclopedia*, edited by Volodomyr Kubijovyč, 480, Toronto: University of Toronto Press, 1988.

Kubijovyč, Volodymyr. "Kholm Region." In Vol. II (G-K) of *Ukraine, A Concise Encyclopedia*, edited by Volodomyr Kubijovyč, 480–485, Toronto: University of Toronto Press, 1988.

Kubijovyč, Volodymyr. "Podlachia." In Vol. IV (Ph-Sr) of *Encyclopedia of Ukraine*, edited by Danylo Husar Struk, 58–61, Toronto: University of Toronto Press, 1993.

Kubijovyč, Volodymyr, ed. *Ukraine, A Concise Encyclopedia,* Vol. I. Toronto: University of Toronto Press, 1963.

Kubijovyč, Volodymyr, ed. *Ukraine, A Concise Encyclopedia,* Vol. II. Toronto: University of Toronto Press, 1971.

Kubijovyč, Volodymyr. *Ukraintsi v Heneral'nii Hubernii; 1939–1941, Istoriia Ukrain'skoho Tsentral'noho Komitetu*. Chicago: Mykola Denysiuk Publishing Co., 1975.

Kubiiovych, Volodymyr. *Meni 70*. Paryzh-Miunkhin: Naukove Tovarystvo Im. Shevchenka, 1970.

Kubijovyč, Volodymyr. *Zakhidni Ukrains'ki Zemli v Mezhakh Polshchi, 1920–1939 (Etnografichni Vidnoshennia).* Chicago-New York: Ukrayins'kii Publitsistychno-Naukovii Institut, 1963.

LaFeber, Walter, ed. *Eastern Europe and the Soviet Union, Vol. II*. Part of Schlesinger, Arthur, M. Jr., gen. ed. *The Dynamics of World Power, A Documentary History of the United States, 1945–1973*. New York: Chelsea House Publishers, 1973.

Lanckoronska, Karolina. "Studies on the Roman-Slavonic Rite in Poland." (*Orientalia Christiana Analecta*, 161). Roma: Pont. Institutum Orientalium Studiorum, 1961

Landwehr, Richard. *Fighting for Freedom: The Ukrainian Volunteer Division.* Silver Spring, MD: Bibliophile Legion Books, 1985.

Lebed, Mykola. *UPA, Ukrains'ka Povstans'ka Armiia.* Second Edition, Suchasnist', 1987.

Lencyk, W. "The Ukrainian Catholic Church Since 1800." In Vol. II of *Ukraine; A Concise Encyclopedia*, edited by Volodymyr Kubijovyč, 181–195, Toronto: University of Toronto Press, 1971.

Luckyj, George, S. N. *Between Gogol and Sevcenko.* Cambridge: Harvard Series in Ukrainian Studies, Vol. 8. Munchen: Wilhelm Fink Verlag, 1971.

Lyko, Ivan, ed. *Litopys Ukrains'koi Povstans'koi Armii. UPA na L'vivshchyni i Iaroslavshchyni; Spohady i Dokumenty Voiakiv UPA TV Roztochchia 1943–1947.* Vol. 31. Toronto-L'viv: Litopys UPA, 2001.

Lypynsky, Viachyslav, *Ukrayina Na Perelomi, 1657–1659,* Vol. III. Kyiv-Vienna, 1920.

Madajczyk, Czesław. *Burżuazyjno-obszarnicza reforma rolna w Polsce (1918–1939*). Warszawa: Książka i Wiedza, 1956.

Madajczyk, Czesław. *Generalna Gubernia w planach hitlerowskich: studia.* Warszawa: Państwowe Wydawnictwo Naukowe, 1961,

Magocsi, Paul Robert. *A History of Ukraine.* Toronto: University of Toronto Press, 1996.

Magocsi, Paul R. "The Language Question as a Factor in the National Movement in Eastern Galicia." in *Nationbuilding and the Politics of Nationalism; Essays on Austrian Galicia*, edited by Andrei S. Markovits and Frank E. Sysyn, eds., 222–238. Cambridge: Harvard Ukrainian Institute, 1982.

Makar, Jurij. "Chełmszczyzna w latach okupacji niemieckiej." in *Polska-Ukraina. Trudne pytania. T. 10: Materiały XI Międzynarodowego Seminarium Historycznego "Stosunki polsko-ukraińskie w latach II wojny światowej"*, Warszawa, 26–28 kwietnia 2005. Karta, 2006. 203–237

Mańkowski, Zygmunt. *Między Wisłą a Bugiem 1939–1944 Studium o polityce okupanta i postawach społeczeństwa.* Lublin: Wydawnictwo Lubelskie, 1978.

Martyniuk, Mykola, ed. *Nadbuzhanshchyna; Sokalshchyna, Belzchyna, Radekhivshchyna, Kaminechchyna, Kholmshchyna i Pidliashia.* Tom I. New York: Obednannia Nadbyzhantsiv, 1986.

Medrzecki, Wlodzimierz. *Województwo wołyńskie.* Wrocław: Ossolineum, 1988.

Ministerstwo Spraw Zagranicznych. *Traktat Pokoju między Polską a Rosją i Ukrainą. Ryga, 18 marca 1921. 85 lat później.* Warszawa: F. Hoesick, 1921.

Mirchuk, Petro, *Narys istorii Orhanizatsii Ukrains'kykh Natsionalistiv,* Vol. I. Munchen: Ukrainske Vydavnytstvo, 1968.

Misilo, Eugeniusz, ed. *Repatriacja czy deportacja; Przesiedlenie Ukraińców z Polski do USRR 1944–1946; Tom I Dokumenty 1944–1945.* Warszawa: Archiw Ukrainski, 1996.

Misilo, Eugeniusz, ed. *Repatriacja czy Deportacja; Przesiedlenie Ukraińców z Polski do USRR 1944–1946: Tom 2, Dokumenty 1946.* Warszawa: Archiw Ukrainski, 1999.

Misylo, Evhen, ed., *Aktsiia "Visla", Dokumenty.* L'viv-New York: Naukove Tovarystvo im. Shevchenka, 1997.

Moklak, Jarosław. *The Lemko Region in the Second Polish Republic: Political and Interdenominational Issues, 1918–1939.* Kraków: Jagiellonian University Press, 2013.

Mokry, Włodzimierz. ed., *Problemy Ukraińców w Polsce po wysiedleńczej akcji "Wisła" 1947 roku.* Kraków: Szwajpolt Fiol, 1997.

Motyka, Grzegorz. *Tak było w Bieszczadach. Walki polsko-ukraińskie 1943–1948*. Warszawa: Oficyna Wydawnicza Volumen, 1999.

Motyka, Grzegorz. *Ukraińska partyzantka, 1942–1960; Działalność Organizacji Ukraińskich Nacjonalistów i Ukraińskiej Powstańczej Armii*. Warszawa: Instytut Studiów Politycznych PAN, Oficyna Wydawnicza „Rytm", 2006.

Motyl, Alexander, J. *The Turn to The Right: The Ideological Origins of Ukrainian Nationalism, 1919–1929*. Boulder: East European Monographs, 1980.

Mushynka, Mykola. "Trahediia Lemkiv Pol'shchi." *Suchasnist*, May 1991, 63–66.

Naimark, Norman M. *Fires of Hatred: Ethnic Cleansing in Twentieth-Century Europe*. Cambridge: Harvard University Press, 2001.

Naimark, Norman and Gibianskii, Leonid, eds. *The Establishment of Communist Regimes in Eastern Europe, 1944–1949*. Boulder: Westview Press, 1997.

Nawrocki, Zbigniew. *Zamiast wolności; UB Na Rzeszówszczynie, 1944–1949*. Rzeszów, 1998.

Paneyko, Basil. "Galicia and the Polish-Ukrainian Problem." *The Slovanic (and East European) Review*, Vol. 9. London: Eyre & Spottswoode, 1930–31.

Pasternak, Evhen. *Nartsy istorii Kholmshchyny i Pidliashshia*. Winnipeg, 1968.

Paszkiewicz, Henryk. *The Origin of Russia*. London: George Allen & Unwin, Ltd. 1954.

Plokhy, S. M. *Yalta; The Price of Peace*. Viking, 2010.

Pelenski, Jarosław. "The Incorporation of the Ukrainian Lands of Old Rus into Crown (of) Poland." In *American Contribution to the Seventh International Congress of Slavists*, edited by Anna Cienciala, 19–52. The Hague: Mouton, 1973.

Perfecky, George A. *The Galician-Volynian Chronicle*. Munchen: Wilhelm Fink, 1973.

Petrenko, Roman. *Slidamy Armii Bez Derzhavy*. Kyiv-Toronto: Doslidnyy Instytut "Studium", 2004.

Petrenko, Roman. *Za Ukrainu, za ii Voliu. (Spohady)*. Vol. 27. Toronto-L'viv: Litopys UPA, 1997.

Polonska-Vasylenko, N. "At the Dawn of Modern Age: Ukraine Under Polish and Lithuanian Domination." In Vol. I. of *Ukraine; A Concise Encyclopedia*, edited by Volodomyr Kubijovyč, 618–634, Toronto: University of Toronto Press, 1963.

Polonska-Vasylenko, N. "The Ukrainian Church in the Lithuanian-Polish Realm and the Kozak Hetman State." In Vol. II of *Ukraine; A Concise Encyclopedia*, edited by Volodomyr Kubijovyč, 143–160. Toronto: University of Toronto Press, 1971.

Polska-Ukraina: Trudne Pytania.; Materialy Miedznarodowego Seminarium Historycznego "Stosunki Polsko-Ukrainskie w Latach II Wojny Swiatowej, 10 volumes, Karta, 1999–2006.

Potichnyj, Peter. "The Lemkos in the Ukrainian National Movement During and after WWII." In *The Lemko Region, 1939–1947; War, Occupation and Deportation,* edited by Paul Best and Jarosław Moklak, 141–170. Cracow-New Haven: Carpatho-Slavic Studies Group, 2002.

Potichnyj, Petro and Ivan Lyko, eds. *Litopys Ukrains'koi Povstans'koi Armii, Taktychnyy Vidtynok UPA 26-iy "Lemko": Lemkivshchyna i Peremyshchyna., (Dokumenty i materialy)* Vol. 33. Toronto-L'viv: Litopys UPA, 2001.

Potichnyj, Petro J. and Volodymyr V'iatrovych. *Spohady Voiakiv UPA ta Uchasnykiv Zbroynoho Pidpillia L'vivshchyny ta Liubachivshchyna,* Vol. 4. Toronto-L'viv: Litopys UPA, 2003

Potichnyj, Petro J. ed. *Litopys Ukrains'koi Povstans'koi Armii, Pidpilni Zhurnaly Zakerzonskoii Ukrainy*. Vol. 16. Toronto: Litopys UPA, 1987.

Potichnyj, Petro J., ed. *Litopys Ukrains'koi Povstans'koi Armii, Kriz Smikh Zaliza;* Stepan Stebel's'kyi and Oleksa Konopads'kyi *(Khroniky),* Vol. 30. Toronto-L'viv: Litopys UPA, 2000.

Potichnyj, Petro J., ed. *Litopys Ukrains'koi Povstans'koi Armii, Taktychnyy Vidtynok UPA-- 27y "Bastion": Liubachivshchyna, Tomashibshchyna, Iaroslavshyna (Dokumenty i Materialy)* Vol. 40. Toronto-L'viv, Litopys UPA, 2004.

Potichnyj, Petro J., ed. *Litopys Ukrains'koi Povstans'koi Armii,Taktycnnyy Vidtynok UPA,--28--y, "Danyliv": Kholmshchyna I Pidliashshia*. Vol. 39. Toronto-L'viv: Litopys UPA, 2003.

Pritsak, Omeljan. *The System of Government under Volodimer the Great and His Foreign Policy.* Cambridge: Harvard Ukrainian Studies, Vol. XIX, 1995.

Rapawy, Stephen. *Ukraine and the Border Issues.* Center for International Research, U.S. Bureau of the Census, May 1993.

Rapawy, Stephen. *Personal Interview with Peter Szpynda*. Astoria, NY, 2000.

Reddaway, W.F., et al. *The Cambridge History of Poland.* Cambridge: Cambridge University Press, 1950.

Reshestar, John. S. Jr. *The Ukrainian Revolution, 1917–1920.* Princeton: Princeton University Press, 1952.

Ripeckyj, Modest, ed. *Litopys Ukrains'koi Povstans'koi Armii; Medychna Opika v UPA,* Vol. 23. Toronto-L'viv: Litopys UPA, 1992.

Romanowski, Wincenty. *ZWZ-AK na Wolyniu, 1939–1944*. Lublin: Redakcja Wydawnictw Katolickiego Universytetu Lubelskiego, 1993.

Rosman, M. J., *The Lords' Jews; Magnate-Jewish Relations in the Polish-Lithuanian Commonwealth during the Eighteenth Century*. Cambridge: Harvard University Press, 1990.

Rudnytsky, Ivan L. The Ukrainians in Galicia Under Austrian Rule. In *Nationbuilding and the Politics of Nationalism; Essays on Austrian Galicia*, edited by Andrei S. Markovits and Frank E. Sysyn, eds., 23–67. Cambridge: Harvard Ukrainian Institute, 1982.

Rudnytsky, Ivan L. *Polish-Ukrainian Relations: The Burden of History.* In *Poland and Ukraine; Past and Present,* edited by Peter J. Potichnyj, 3–31. Edmonton: The Canadian Institute of Ukrainian Studies, 1980.

Sadkowski, Konrad. "From Ethnic Borderland to Catholic Fatherland: The Church, Christian Orthodox, and State Administration in the Chelm Region, 1918–1939." *Slavic Review*, no. 4, 813–839, 1998.

Scaglione, Aldo, ed. *The Emergence of National Languages*. Ravenna: Longo Editore, 1984

Shapoval, Iu. *OUN I UPA Na Tereni Polshchi (1944–1947 rr.)* Kyiv, 2000.

Schechtman, Joseph B. *Postwar Population Transfers in Europe, 1945–1955.* Philadelphia: University of Pennsylvania Press, 1962.

Schonfield, Hugh, J. *The Treaty of Versailles.* London, Peace Book Co., 1940.

Serhiichuk, Volodymyr. *Desiat Buremnykh Lit; Zakhidnoukrains'ki Zemli u 1944–1953 rr. Novi dokumenty i materially*. Kyiv: Vydavnystvo khudozhnoi literatury "Dnipro", 1998.

Serhiichuk, Volodymyr. *Trahediia Ukrainstiv v Polshchi*. Ternopil': Vydavnytsvo "Ternopil'", 1997.

Shankovsky, L. *Ukrainian Auxiliary Police*. In Vol. V (St-Z) of *Encyclopedia of Ukraine*, edited by Danylo Husar Struk, 354. Toronto: University of Toronto Press, 1993.

Shpyl'ka, Panteleymon, *Vyzvolni Zmahannia Skhidnoii Lemkivshchyny v 1918 Rotsi.* Lemkivskiy Kalendar na 1967 rik. Toronto-Passiac, 1967.

Shtendera, Yevhen, and Petro Potichnyj, eds. *Litopys Ukrains'koi Povstans'koi Armii. Volyn i Polissia,* Vol. 2. Toronto: Litopys UPA, 1977.

Shtendera, Yevhen, and Petro Potichnyj, eds. *Litopys Ukrains'koi Povstans'koi Armii; Ukrains'ka Holovna Vyzvolna Rada; Dokumenty, Ofitsiini Publikatsii, Materiialy)* Vol. 9., Toronto: Litopys UPA, 1982.

Shtendera, Yevhen, and Petro Potichnyj, eds. *Litopys Ukrains'koi Povstans'koi Armii, Peremys'kii Kurin' UPA.* Vol. 13. Toronto: Litopys UPA, 1986.

Shtendera, Yevhen, and Petro Potichnyj, eds. *Litopys Ukrains'koi Povstans'koi Armii, Ukrains'ka Holovna Vyzvolna Rada; dokumenty, ofitsiini publikatsii, materially.* Vol. 8. Toronto: Litopys UPA, 1980.

Shtendera, Yevhen, and Petro Potichnyj, eds. *Litopys Ukrains'koi Povatans'koi Armii, Volyn' i Polissia,* Vol. 1. Toronto: Litopys UPA, 1978.

Shtendera, Yevhen, ed. *Litopys Ukrains'koi Povstans'koi Armii;, Volyn I Polissia,* Vol. 5., Toronto: Litopys, UPA, 1984.

Shtendera, Yevhen. "In Search of Understanding: The Ukrainian and Polish Underground Movements, 1945 to 1947; Co-operation Between UPA and the WiN." In *Poland and Ukraine Past and Present,* edited by Peter Potichnyj, 271–293, Edmonton: Canadian Institute of Ukrainian Studies, 1980.

Siwicki, Mikołaj. *Dzieje Konfliktow Polsko-Ukrainskich*, Tom Drugi. Warszawa: Tyrsa, 1992; Tom Treci, 1994.

Snyder, Timothy. *Bloodlands: Europe between Hitler and Stalin.* New York: Basic Books, 2010.

Snyder, Timothy, *The Causes of Ukrainian-Polish Ethnic Cleansing 1943.* Past & Present, no. 179, Oxford University Press, May 2003.

Snyder, Timothy. *The Reconstruction of Nations Poland, Ukraine, Lithuania, Belarus, 1569–1999*. New Haven: Yale University Press, 2003.

Snyder, Timothy, "To Resolve the Ukrainian Problem Once and for All": The Ethnic Cleansing of Ukrainians in Poland, 1943–1947." *Journal of Cold War Studies*. Series 1.2, 86–110, 1999.

Sodol, P. "Legion of Ukrainian Nationalists." In Vol. III (L-Pf) of *Encyclopedia of Ukraine*, edited by Danylo Husar Struk. 71–72. Toronto: University of Toronto, 1993.

Sodol, Petro R. *UPA*: *They Fought Hitler and Stalin.* New York, 1987.

Sokhan, P. et al., eds. Litopys UPA, New Series, Vol. 2: *Volyn' and Polissia: UPA ta Zapillia, 1943–1944, Dokumenty i Materially*. Toronto-Kyiv: Litopys UPA, 1999.

Stachiw, Matthew and Jarosław Sztendera. *Western Ukraine at the Turning Point of Europe's History, 1918–1923*, Vol. I. New York: The Shevchenko Scientific Society, 1969.

Starosolsky, J., "Ukraine Under Polish Domination in the Fourteenth to Eighteenth Centuries." In Vol. II of *Ukraine; A Concise Encyclopedia,* edited by Volodymyr Kubijovyčh, 44–49. Toronto: University of Toronto Press, 1971.

Stebelis'kiy, Ihor, "Heohrafiia Liudyny." In Vol. I. of *Lemkivshchyna*; *Zemlia, Liudy, Istoria, Kul'tura,* edited by Bohdan O. Strumins'kiy, 113–148, New York: Naukove Tovarystvo im. Shevchenka: New York, 1988.

Struk, Danylo, Husar (Ed.). *Encyclopedia of Ukraine.* Vols. III & V. Toronto: University of Toronto Press, 1993.

Strumins'kyi, Bohdan, O., ed. *Lemkivshchyna*: *Zemlia, Liudy, Istoria, Kul'tura*. Vol. I. New York: Naukove Tovarystvo im. Shevchenka, 1988.

Subtelny, Orest. "Expulsion, Resettlement, Civil Strife: The Fate of Poland's Ukrainians, 1944–1947." In *Redrawing Nations; Ethnic Cleansing in East-Central Europe, 1944–1948,* edited by Philipp Ther and Ana Siljak, Lanham: Rowman & Littlefield, 2001.

Subtelny, Orest. *Ukraine: A History*. Toronto: University of Toronto Press, 1988.

Sysyn, Frank E. "Ukrainian-Polish Relations in the Seventeenth Century: The Role of National Consciousness and National Conflict in the Khmelnytsky Movement." In *Poland and Ukraine: Past and Present,* edited by Peter J. Potichnyj, 58–82. Edmonton: The Canadian Institute of Ukrainian Studies, 1980.

Szcześniak, Antoni B. and Wieslaw Z Szota. *„Droga do nikąd. Wojna polska z UPA"* Warszawa: Wydownistwo Ministerstwa Oborony Narodowej, 1973.

Tarnovych, Iuliian, *Iliustrovana istoriia Lemkivshchyny.* L'viv: Na Storozhi, 1936.

Temperley, H.W.V., ed. *A History of the Peace Conferences of Paris,* Vol. I. London: Oxford University Press, 1920

Ther, Philip and Ana Siljak, *Redrawing Nations: Ethnic Cleansing in East-Central Europe, 1944–1948*. Lanham, MD.: Rowman & Littlefield, 2001.

Torzecki, Ryszard. *Kwesta Ukrainska v Polityce III Rseszy (1933–1945).* Warszawa: Ksiazka i Wiedza, 1972.

Treaty Series 1923, no. 261 (League of Nations). London: Harrison & Sons, 1920–1946.

Trukhan, Myroslav. *Ukraintsi V Pol'shchi Pislia Druhoi Svitivoi Viiny. 1944–1984.* New York: Lemko Research Foundation, Inc., 1990

Valasek, Paul S. *Haller's Army in France*. Whitehall Printing, 2006.

V'iatrovych, Volodymyr. *Reidy UPA Terenamy Chekhoslovachchyny.* Toronto-L'viv: Litopys UPA, 2001.

V'iatrovych, Volodymyr, "The Communist Alliance Against the Ukrainian Insurgent Army (UPA)." *The Ukrainian Quarterly*, Winter 2002, 326–341.

Voronov, I.O. and Iu.H. Pyliavets, *Holod 1946–1947 rr.* Kyiv: Znannia, 1991.

Vozniak, Mykhaylo. *Iak Probudylosia Ukrainske Narodne Zhyttia v Halychyni za Avstrii*. L'viv: Dilo, 1924

Vyslotsky, Dmitri. "U Lemkov v Sovits'kom Soiuzi." *Karpatorusskiy Kalendar,* Lemko Soiuz, Yonkers, NY, 1947, 21–46.

Vytanovych, I. "Agriculture in Western Ukraine Between 1914 And 1939." In Vol. II. of *Ukraine; A Concise Encyclopedia*, edited by Volodymyr Kubijovyč, 858–860. Toronto: University of Toronto Press, 1971.

Vytvytsky, S. and S. Baran. *Western Ukraine Under Poland.* In Vol. I. of *Ukraine; A Concise Encyclopedia*, edited by Volodymyr Kubijovyč, 833–850. Toronto: University of Toronto Press, 1963.

Vytvytsky, S. and S. Baran. "The Western Ukrainian Republic. In Vol. I. of *Ukraine; A Concise Encyclopedia*, edited by Volodymyr Kubijovyč, 770–781. Toronto: University of Toronto Press, 1963.

Wandycz, Piotr. "The Poles in the Habsburg Monarchy." Jn *Nationbuilding and the Politics of Nationalism; Essays on Austrian Galicia*, edited by Andrei S. Markovits and Frank E. Sysyn, 68–93. Cambridge: Harvard Ukrainian Research Institute, 1982.

Weiner, Amir. *Making Sense of War the Second World War and the Fate of the Bolshevik Revolution*. Princeton, N.J.: Princeton University Press, 2002.

Wheeler-Bennett, John W. *Brest-Litovsk: The Forgotten Peace, March 1918*. London: Macmillan and Co., 1938.

Widajewicz, Józef. *Południowo-wschodnie kresy Polski w X i XI wieku.* Poznań: Poznańskiego Towarzystwa Przyjaciół Nauk, 1937.

Wistrich, Robert S. *Who's Who in Nazi Germany*. New York: Macmillan, 1982.

Wojciechowski, Zygmunt. *Mieszko I and the Rise of the Polish State*. London: The Baltic Institute, 1936.

Yurkevich, M. *Organization of Ukrainian Nationalists*. In Vol. III (L-Pf) of *Encyclopedia of Ukraine*, edited by Danylo Husar Struk, 708–710. Toronto: University of Toronto Press, 1993.

Zahaykevych, B. ed. *Peremyshl'; Zakhidnyi Bastion Ukrainy*. New York-Philadelphia: Peremys'kyi Vydavnychii Komitet, 1961.

Zima, V. F. *Golod v SSSR 1946–1947 Godov: Proiskhozhdenie i Posledstviia.* Moskov, 1996.

Appendix I

The Lemkos

A number of Ukrainian groups living on the western edge of ethnographic Ukraine developed local dialects and cultural characteristics differing from Ukrainians further east, a common phenomenon for people in border regions. Polishchuks (Pinchuks) were located in the northwest, while Hutsuls, Boykos, and Lemkos lived in the Carpathians. All share common characteristics: they lived in less accessible (often wooded) areas or in mountainous or swampy territories in the northwest or along the Carpathians with some bordering with foreign language groups. Because of their comparative isolation, they retained many old customs and archaic words and developed dialects differing from Ukrainian speakers further east.[695] Ancestors of the eastern Lemkos lived on the western edge of the medieval boundary of Kyivan Rus' whose border extended west of Krosno (Korosno), but some migrated westward along the Carpathians into the mountainous and sparsely populated Polish territory. The village of Mszana (Mshana), for example, in the western Lemko region near Dukla Pass, was already thriving by 1366.[696] In modern times, the Lemko region, located to the north of the Carpathians, extended 80 miles from the San River in the east westward to the Poprad River with a few villages located to the west of the river. Before World War I, a Ruthenian/Russophile movement existed throughout Galicia, but it was confined largely to the western Lemko region during the interwar period, an area that was not a part of the Kyivan Rus' in the Middle Ages. In the east most people identified themselves both as Ukrainians and Lemkos, although some older people considered themselves Rusnaks, a local variation of Ruthenian. During the German occupation, a period when Ukrainians enjoyed more cultural rights, the Ukrainian orientation became more prevalent as the insurgency and deportations commenced. In the west, most people viewed themselves as Lemkos and also Ruthenians, Russians, or Ukrainians, with the Ukrainian identification more prevalent among the younger

695 For discussion of Ukrainian ethnic groups, see Kuzela, *Tribal Division*, pp. 280–285, in Kubijovyč, Vol. I, 1963.

696 Starchak-Vavrychyn, *The Lemko Village*, p.217, Best and Moklak eds., *The Lemko*, 2002.

generation. The percentage that each group comprised cannot be determined from available data.

Since the early nineteenth century a number of scholars have attempted to determine the Lemko boundary without reaching a consensus.[697] The difficulty arises because Lemko and adjacent Ukrainian villages frequently have similar speech patterns, and thus, determining linguistic demarcation lines between them can be problematic. Moreover, the Lemko dialect was not standardized and differences in speech may have been noticeable between villages that were merely a few miles apart. More than any other factor, the inroads of the West Slavic languages differentiated the Lemko dialect from Ukrainian dialects to the east. In the East Slavic languages (Ukrainian, Belarusian, Russian), the principal stress on a vowel varies from word to word and may even change in the same word depending on the grammatical case. The West Slavic languages, by contrast, have a fixed accentuation pattern, and in Polish and Slovak, the penultimate vowel in a word is emphasized. Because the Lemkos were wedged between Poles and Slovaks, they adopted the Polish-Slovak accentuation system.[698] The change in accentuation was accompanied by an extensive borrowing of words from the neighboring languages, and their cognates usually serve as synonymous.

In addition to accentuation patterns, there were internal changes within some words compared to standard Ukrainian, for example, *vohon'* (fire) in standard Ukrainian becomes *ohen* in Lemko. In fact, the very name of the people appears to be tied to the dialect since Lemkos use the word *lem* to mean "only" in place of the words *tilky* or *lysh* which are used in standard Ukrainian. The term is derived from the Slovak word *lem* meaning *only*[1]. The generally accepted theory is that Ukrainians to the northeast of the Carpathians would have been aware of the difference in the speech pattern and began calling people "Lemkos." In much of the eastern Lemko region, the word *lem* was replaced by the word *tivko*, a regional variation of *til'ky* in modern times which underscores the regional difference within the dialect. Furthermore, the dialect retained old Slavic words no longer used in modern languages. The Kyivan chronicle,

---

697 Attempts by researchers to determine Lemko settlements are discussed in Struminskyi, *Terytoria*, 1988, pp. 26ff and Stebelsky, *Heohrafiia*, 1988, pp. 117–135.

for example, refers to serfs as *chiliad.* In the Lemko dialect, the word signifies members of a household.

Identifying linguistic boundaries in the west is less difficult since Lemkos bordered with Poles, although some Ukrainian villages were located in the Polish areas and it is not clear whether they should be viewed as Lemkos. Further east, the situation becomes progressively more difficult since they border with Ukrainians and the problem is further compounded in the upper reaches of the San River. There, Lemkos border with Boykos, another Ukrainian Carpathian ethnographic group with a distinct dialect that bears some resemblance to the Lemko dialect. The two groups merged along the upper San River. For this reason, some researchers claim the river as a boundary between the two groups, while others place it on the Hoczewka River further west, and some on the Osława River still further west, where, in their view, the linguistic differences are more distinct. This study accepts the enumeration of Lemko villages by Ivan Zilyns'kyi, a Lemko linguist born in the village of Krasna in Korosno County. Zilin'skyi was a recognized authority on Ukrainian dialects and his academic background prepared him better than most researchers to identify subtle changes in speech patterns among villages. In addition to the counties typically identified as Lemko, he considered most villages west of the San River to be Lemko and included seven villages located in the neighboring Ukrainian counties.[699] Table below presents population figures on Lemko villages as identified by Zilyns'kyi, using Kubijovyč's statistics for all towns and villages in Galicia, who based his estimates on published statistics and surveys.[700] Figures for Lemkos in the table are presented as Ukrainians although not all considered themselves to be Ukrainians; however, data that distinguishes the regional variations are not available.

---

699 List of enumerated village are presented in Struminsky, *Terytoria,* 1988, pp. 39–41.

700 Ethnographer and geographer Volodymyr Kubijovyč presented statistics for seven groups: Ukrainians, Polish speaking Ukrainians, Poles, Polish colonists, Latinites(Ukrainian speaking Roman Catholics), Jews, and Germans combined with other groups. In the table Ukrainians are combined with Polish speaking Ukrainians totaling 1,210, the next three groups are presented as Poles. Description of the groups and statistical methodology are in Kubijovyč, *Ethnic Groups*, 1983, pp. XX-XX11

Table 8: Population of the Lemko Region, January 1, 1939

	Population (In thousands)	**Percent**
Total	258,365	100.0
Ukrainians	187,340	72.5
Poles	57,130	22.1
Jews	13,500	5.2
Others	395	0.2

Note: Data include Lesko County villages identified as Lemko, Sanok, Krosno, Jasło, Gorlice, Nowy Sącz, and Nowy Targ counties. Statistics are reported by counties, arranged alphabetically. In the Lemko region only the Ukrainian portion of the county is reported, villages in Polish sections are given the supplementary tables, pp.110–111, and included in the table, if identified as Lemko. Seven villages located in Brzozów, Rzeszów, and Terka counties, which were identified as Lemko and are also included in the table.

Source: Kubijovyč, *Ethnic Groups,* 1983.

Appendix II
Activities of the UPA Tactical Sector 26,"Lemko," by Sotnia

January 1946 to July 1946

Throughout the insurgency, all UPA sotnias submitted operational reports each month to their battalion commanders, summarizing their monthly activities. The reports were occasionally supplemented with diagrams of battles. Based on the sotnia reports, battalion commanders compiled battalion reports and sent them directly to the military district commanders. All sotnias and battalions maintained underground bunkers in the forest where the reports and other materials were stored. Most of the materials either perished or have not been found; however, some survived and provide considerable information on the operation of the organization. The most comprehensive documentation consists of the monthly reports of Tactical Sector 26 from December 1945 through July 1946. During this period, Polish authorities attempted to meet the revised deportation deadline of June 15, 1946 and remove all Ukrainians. In response, the UPA made a concerted effort to thwart this plan, resulting in some of the heaviest fighting that occurred during the insurgency. Partisan activities during this period are summarized chronologically in the chart below.

The two battalions of the Tactical Sector 26 were designated as "attackers" (*udarnyky*) and each sotnia had a numerical designation. The pseudonym of the sotnia commander is also shown in the chart. The two visiting sotnias from Ukraine were identified only by the pseudonym of the sotnia commander—Myron or Karmeliuk. There is a brief description of each engagement with approximate locations, if reported. There are casualty figures for both sides, figures for the loss or capture of weapons, if significant, and enumeration of the number of livestock that were taken. Typically, an entire sotnia engaged in partisan operations, but occasionally, some platoons fought alone.

Increased Polish efforts to remove all Ukrainians from the area increased UPA activities, and transportation and communications facilities were their primary targets. During the seven-month period, the two battalions engaged in 182 operations, and the most intense fighting took place in May with 35 engagements with the least number (16) occurring in April when Myron and Bir conducted propaganda raids in Slovakia, a mission that was evidently ordered by the OUN authorities in Munich. More surprisingly, during the height of deportation activities in June, TS-26 instituted a training course for future non-commissioned officers and assigned the Lastivka sotnia to provide security for the school. As Ukrainian civilians were being deported, the partisans began burning abandoned Ukrainian villages to prevent settlement by Poles or use by the military. Polish villages were attacked in reprisals for their participation in attacking Ukrainian villages. As the war was ending in the area, many Polish and Ukrainian villages formed self-defense units for protection against banditry. The Polish authorities later incorporated these units into *Ochotnicza Rezerwa Milicji Obywatelskiej* (ORMO), a voluntary reserve militia whose members frequently participated in raids on Ukrainian villages alongside the regular army. In turn, these actions provoked UPA partisans to conduct retaliatory raids against Polish villages. The following chart contains a list of events that occurred between January through July of 1946.

Table 9: Operations of Tactical Sector 26 at the Beginning of 1946

Date	**Sotnia Code and Commander**	**Type of Action**	**Page**
1/1/1946	A-2: Hromenko	Reprisal raid on two Polish villages, Dylągowa and Sielnica, for attacking neighboring Ukrainian villages. The villages were burned completely; there were no casualties on either side; thirteen head of cattle and four horses were taken.	p. 250
1/1/1946	A-6: Krylach	Firefight with Polish troops. Troops had four killed and four wounded; UPA had three killed and five wounded.	p. 261
1/2/1946	A-7: Lastivka	Firefight with Soviet Border Guards. Soviets had no losses; UPA had one killed.	p. 161

1/3/1946	A-4: Burlaka	Firefight with Polish troops. Troops had four killed and four wounded; UPA had eleven killed and nine wounded.	p. 257
1/5/1946	A-3: Bir	Drove off guards on railroad bridge over the River San and exploded the bridge. Another sotnia platoon destroyed two miles of telephone line. Poles had two killed and few wounded, UPA had three wounded.	pp. 254–255
1/6/1946	A-1: Didyk A-5: Khrin	Burned two former Ukrainian villages, Deszno (Doshno) and Woltuszowa (Voltushova), which were settled by Poles from Ukraine who were accused of attacking Ukrainians.	p. 248
1/7/ 1946	A-2: Hromenko; A-4: Burlaka; A-6: Krylach; A-7: Lastivka	Unsuccessful attack on the town of Bircza (Bircha) by the Peremyshl' Battalion. Poles had seventy killed, number of wounded not indicated. UPA had 23 killed including the battalion commander Konyk; the number of wounded was not indicated.	pp. 250–254
1/9/1946	A-3: Bir	Exploded railroad bridge and destroyed two miles of telephone line. No losses were indicated.	p. 255
1/9/1946	A-7: Lastivka	Fire fight with police in Łukawica (Lukavytsia). No Polish losses; UPA had one killed.	p. 262
1/10/1946	N/A: Myron	Attacked police station in Cisna (Tisna). One policeman was killed and a few were wounded; UPA had one killed and two wounded.	pp. 263–264
1/11/1946	A-6: Krylach	Ambush of troops. UPA had one wounded; Polish losses unknown.	pp. 261–262
1/11/1946	A-5: Khrin	Burned two deported Ukrainian villages settled by Poles from Ukraine and partially	p. 259

		burned one Polish village for attacking Ukrainians; seven Polish self-defense men killed; UPA had no losses.	
1/13/1946	A-4: Burlaka	Burned buildings in the villages of Kupiatycze, Sielec, Berendiowce, and Huwniki which were used to house Border Guards, and destroyed a bridge in Huwniki. No losses on either side.	p. 258
1/13/1946	N/A: Myron	Burned 14 buildings that once housed Soviet and Polish troops in the Baligród area; no losses for both sides.	p. 264
1/17/1946	A-3: Bir.	Sotnia platoons operating separately destroyed 13 bridges and five miles of telephone lines.	p. 255
1/19/1946	A-3: Bir	Ambush and firefight with troops; Poles had 44 killed, many were wounded and four were captured; UPA had no losses.	pp. 255–256
1/21–28/1946	N/A: Myron	Burned thirty-five bridges in the Lesko County.	p. 265
1/22/1946	A-3: Bir	Four partisans surrounded in a house fought to the last man. Poles had seven killed and two wounded; UPA had four killed.	p. 256
1/24/1946	A-1: Didyk	UPA attacked Polish troops near Wisłok. Troops had two killed and seven wounded; UPA had no losses.	p. 249
1/24/1946	A-7: Lastivka	Exploded railroad bridge near Sanok. No losses for either side.	p. 263
1/24/1946	A-5: Khrin	UPA attacked troops raiding Zawadka Morochowska (Zavadka Morokhiv'ska). Five soldiers were killed and nine wounded; UPA had one killed.	pp. 259–260

1/25/1946	A-1: Didyk	Platoon of the Sotnia attacked troops burning Karlików (Karlykiv). Two soldiers were killed; UPA had no losses.	pp. 249–250
1/26/1946	A-5: Khrin	Platoon exploded bridge near Zagórz (Zahiria); Poles had three killed; one UPA partisan wounded and captured.	p. 261
1/29/1946	A-7: Lastivka	Exploded railroad bridge on the line going to the USSR. No losses on either side.	p. 263
1/30–31/1946	A-1: Didyk	Raid on the sotnia camp. Poles had one killed and a few wounded; UPA had one wounded.	p. 250
1/30/1946	A-7: Lastivka	Exploded railroad bridge near the village of Stefkowa (Stefkova) and burned two bridges; No losses on either side.	p. 263
1/30/1946	N/A: Myron	UPA squad carting bread was ambushed. Polish losses unknown; UPA had no losses.	p. 265
1/31/1946	A-4: Burlaka	Destroyed railroad station, tracks, and 36 wagons in the Lesko area. No losses on either side.	p. 258
1/31/1946	A-7: Lastivka	Burned two bridges. No losses on either side.	p. 263
2/1/ 1946	N/A: Myron	Burned 10 bridges in eastern Sanok County.	p. 283
2/2/1946	A-4: Burlaka	Fire fight with Polish troops. Polish losses unknown; UPA had two wounded.	p. 276
2/3/1946	N/A: Myron	Destroyed telephone lines. Losses not reported.	p. 281
2/4/1946	A-7: Lastivka	Ambushed Polish troops. Poles had 20	p. 280

		killed and six wounded; UPA had five killed and one wounded.	
2/4/1946	N/A: Myron	Burned five bridges in Baligród area. No losses reported on either side.	p. 281
2/4/1946	N/A: Karmeliuk	Destroyed railroad bridge, water pumping station, road bridge, police station, administrative office and cut telephone line in eastern Sanok County. No losses on either side.	pp. 281–282.
2/5/1946	A-1: Didyk; N/A: Karmeliuk	Burned wooden bridge, exploded railroad bridge and railroad water pump. Destroyed un-occupied police station in eastern Sanok county. No losses on either side.	p. 273
2/10/1946	A-4: Burlaka	Exploded gas pipe that was supplying gas to Przemyśl, Rzeszów and Cracow. No losses on either side.	pp. 275–276
2/11/1946	A-7 Lastivka	Police station in the village of Nowosiółki (Novosilky) was disarmed and building destroyed. Police were set free. No losses on either side.	pp. 280–281
2/12/1946	A-2: Hromenko	Two sotnia squads captured five Poles involved in the massacre of Ukrainians in the village of Pawłokoma (Pavlokoma). UPA had no losses.	p. 274
2/16/1946	A-5: Khrin	Attacked 20 soldiers who were taking hay from deported Ukrainian homes. Poles had two killed, one captured and 10 horses taken; UPA had no losses.	p. 277
2/16/1946	A-5: Khrin	Fire fight with troops near Mokre. Poles had 24 killed, 35 wounded; UPA had no losses.	p. 277
2/16/1946	A-3: Bir	Sotnia platoon ambushed a wagon with	p. 275

		five soldiers. Poles had four captured, one wounded fled; UPA had no losses.	
2/18/1946	N/A: Myron	Road mined. Poles had two killed, one wounded. UPA had no losses.	p. 281
2/19/1946	A-6: Krylach	UPA transporting food was attacked. Polish losses unknown; UPA had one killed.	p. 279
2/21/1946	N/A: Karmeliuk	Fire fight with troops. No losses on either side.	p. 283
2/22/1946	A-1: Didyk	Polish troops ambushed in the village of Kamienne (Kamiane). Poles had five killed, one wounded; UPA had no losses.	p. 273
2/22/1946	A-2: Hromenko	Polish troops ambushed. Poles had seven killed, five wounded; UPA had no losses.	p. 274
2/26/1946	A-5: Khrin	Attacked Polish troops. Poles had two killed; UPA had no losses.	p. 278
2/27/1946	A-5: Khrin	Attack on Polish troops near the village of Wolica (Volytsia). Poles had four killed, three captured and released; UPA had no losses.	p. 278
2/28/1946	A-5: Khrin	Attacked troops in Kamienne. Poles had 26 killed, 30 wounded; UPA had two seriously wounded.	p. 279
3/1–3/1946	A-7: Lastivka	During the three days five bridges were destroyed in the Przemyśl area. No casualties on either side.	p. 308
3/3/1946	A-1: Didyk	Fire fight with troops in the village of Turzańsk (Turyns'ke), Poles driven off. No casualties on either side. Ten houses and two barns burned.	p. 290
3/3/1946	N/A: Myron	Ambushed six Polish soldiers. One soldier killed, five captured and released; No UPA	p. 309

		losses.	
3/5/1946	A-7: Lastivka	Ambushed troops taking people to a deportation point. Troops had four killed; UPA had no casualties. People returned home.	p. 308
3/5/1946	A-1: Didyk	Damaged bridge in Karlików. No losses on either side.	p. 291
3/7/1946	A-3: Bir	Destroyed a bridge on Solinka River. No losses on either side.	p. 300
3/8/1946	A-3: Bir	Destroyed two bridges on the Hoczew-Brzuska (Hochiv-Berezka) road. No losses on either side.	p. 300
3/9/1946	A-3: Bir; N/A: Karmeliuk	Fight with Polish soldiers, eighteen soldiers killed; UPA had one killed and one missing.	pp. 300–301
3/10/1946	A-5: Khrin	Two sotnia platoons drove 30 soldiers out of the Administration for Public Safety who were robbing Poles and Ukrainians in the village of Czaszyn (Chashyn) and taking Polish men to the army. One captured Pole was stripped of his uniform and released.	p. 305
3/11/1946	A-5: Khrin	Two bridges and telephone line destroyed near Bukowsko. No losses on either side.	p. 305
3/12/1946	A-4: Burlaka	Burned oil derrick and fought troops. Polish losses included the burned derrick but there were no casualties; UPA had one killed.	p. 304
3/12/1946	A-5: Khrin	Destroyed three railroad bridges, tore up some rail tracks and tossed them in the Osława (Oslava) River. No casualties.	p. 306
3/12/1946	N/A: Myron	Exploded a bridge over the River Wisłok.	p. 309

		No casualties.	
3/13/1946	N/A: Myron	Destroyed two bridges. No casualties.	p. 309
3/15/1946	A-1: Didyk	Engaged troops in the village of Turzańsk. No casualties.	pp. 291–292
3/15/1946	N/A: Karmeliuk	Engaged troops in the village of Bukowiec (Bukovets'). Poles had two wounded, one of whom died; UPA had no losses.	p. 310
3/16/1946	A-5: Khrin	Fire fight with troops. Poles had four wounded; UPA had no casualties.	p. 306
3/16/1946	N/A: Myron	Set up ambush near Jasiel (Iasel') and killed one Polish officer.	pp. 309–310
3/18/1946	A-1: Didyk	Saw mill destroyed in Szczawne (Shchavne). No casualties.	pp. 292–293
3/19/1946	A-1: Didyk	Prolonged fight with troops around Mokre. Polish losses included about five killed and many wounded. UPA had one killed, four wounded. Destroyed locomotive.	pp. 293–294
3/20/1946	A-1: Didyk; A-5: Khrin: N/A: Myron	Engaged troops on the Slovak border near the village of Wisłok. Poles had twent-four killed, six wounded and seventy-nine captured. UPA had two wounded and captured large quantity of weapons and supplies.	pp. 294–295
3/21/1946	A-4: Burlaka A-7: Lastivka	Ambushed troops, fourteen soldiers were killed, one captured. UPA had one killed.	pp. 304–305
3/22/1946	N/A: Karmeliuk	Cut down seventy-five telephone poles in the Wetlina-Strzebowiska (Vetlyna-Strubovis'ka) area, and cut up telephone wire. No casualties.	p. 310
3/23/1946	A-1 Didyk	Destroyed railroad station, 40 railroad cars, and other buildings and bridges in Komańcza (Komancha). No casualties.	pp. 295–300
3/23/1946	N/A: Karmeliuk	Ambushed soldiers on the Smolnik-Strzebowiska road. Two soldiers were wounded.	pp. 310–311
3/24/1946	A-5: Khrin	Raided Polish village of Bukowsko to cap-	p. 310

	N/A: Myron	ture bandits robbing Ukrainian villages. Some bandits fled, one was caught and paid UPA 30 American dollars.	
3/24/1946	N/A: Karmeliuk	Ambushed troops. Two soldiers killed, four wounded; UPA had no losses.	p. 311
3/25/1946	A-1: Didyk	Attacked and destroyed railroad station in Łupków (Lupkiv) and supporting facilities. Polish losses could not be determined, some Poles fled to Slovakia. UPA had six wounded and two missing.	pp. 296–298
3/26/1946	A-5: Khrin; N/A: Myron	Attacked 180 soldiers in Kożuszne – Wysoczany (Kozhushne-Vysochany). Thirty-one soldiers killed, 40 wounded, and nine captured; UPA had no losses.	p. 307
3/28/1946	A-1: Didyk	Ambushed troops near Osławica (Oslavytsia). Polish losses could not be determined. UPA had no losses.	p. 298.
3/30/1946	A-3: Bir A-5: Khrin N/A: Myron	Engaged large body of troops in a prolonged battle in Średnie Wielkie (Serednie Velyky) area. 106 soldiers were killed, 15 wounded, and eight captured. UPA had seven killed and six wounded.	pp. 301–303
3/31/1946	A-2: Hromenko A-4: Burlaka	Engaged Polish troops near Załuże (Zaluzhe*)*. Polish losses could not be determined; UPA had no losses.	pp. 299–300
4/2/1946	A-4: Burlaka; A-7: Lastivka	Ambushed troops near the town of Bircza. Poles had 32 killed and 10 wounded (four died); UPA had no losses.	pp. 321–322
4/4/1946	A-1: Didyk	Retaliatory burning of two Polish villages for burning Ukrainian villages. Nadolany and Nowotaniec were burned completely, 10 cows and six horses taken; No UPA casualties.	p. 319
4/5/1946	A-5: Khrin	Retaliatory raid on Bukowsko because civilians together with troops were robbing Ukrainian villages. No known losses on either side. Approximately 500 buildings (including 60 brick buildings) were destroyed.	p. 323
4/6/1946	A-5: Khrin	Engagement with troops near Surowica (Surovytsia). Poles had two killed and four wounded; UPA had no losses.	p. 324

4/6/1946	A-7: Lastivka	Burned three Ukrainian villages on the Soviet border while Ukrainians were being deported. No losses.	p. 324
4/12/1946	A-1: Didyk	Engagement with troops in Kamionki. UPA had no losses and Polish losses could not be determined.	p. 319
4/16/1946	A-4: Burlaka	Raided town of Krzywcza. Captured six soldiers and took livestock and goods from two stores; No UPA losses.	pp. 322–323
4/16/1946	A-6: Krylach	Propaganda raid on the Polish village of Jacienica. No additional information. No casualties, took some livestock.	p. 324
4/17/1946	A-1: Didyk	Destroyed railroad bridge on the Ko-mańcza-Łupków line. No casualties.	p. 319
4/18/1946	A-7: Lastivka	Burned deported Ukrainian village of Do-lina Dolna (Dolyna Dil'na). No casualties.	p. 324
4/19/1946	A-7: Lastivka	Troops attacked partisans in Koniusza (Koniusha). Two soldiers were killed, one wounded; UPA had nine killed and two wounded.	pp. 224–225
4/19/1946	A-1: Didyk	Destroyed two brick buildings in Baligród area to prevent their use by troops. No losses.	p. 319
4/25/1946	A-2: Hromenko	Attacked group of Polish civilians taking potatoes from deported Ukrainian village of Pawłokoma. One Pole killed, three cap-tured and released.	p. 321
4/26/1946	A-1: Didyk	Extended engagement with troops near the Slovak border. Twenty-five soldiers were killed and three died of wounds. UPA had nine killed and three wounded.	pp. 319–320
4/27/1946	A-1: Didyk	Burial of partisans killed the previous day in a common grave on the church grounds of the church in Smolnik (Smil'nyk). A birch cross was erected on the grave with a sign: "For the fighters of the Ukrainian In-surgent Army who died on the battlefield defending their native land."	pp. 320–321
4/30/1946	A-4: Burlaka	Brief fight between Burlaka's military po-lice and a small group of Polish soldiers. Two soldiers killed; UPA had no losses.	p. 323
5/2/1946	A-5 Khrin	Prolonged engagement with a large body	pp. 345–

		of troops in the village of Habkowce (Habkivtsi). The fight resumed in the area where more troops arrived on May 5th. Polish losses were placed at 37 killed and many wounded. UPA had 4 wounded, one died of wounds. Partisans captured numerous weapons including 75mm cannon.	346
5/4/1946	A-6: Krylach	Raided Polish village of Izdebki because of "hostile attitudes" (not explained.) After short firefight with the self-defense unit and police who fled, a meeting was held with the villagers. No casualties were reported, but some uniforms and a horse were taken.	pp. 351–352
5/4/1946	N/A: Myron; N/A: Karmeliuk	Firefight with Czech troops on the border near the village of Wetlina. According to Slovak sources, Czechs had one killed and two wounded. UPA had no losses.	p. 353
5/5/1946	A-6 Krylach	Short firefight with troops. Polish losses unknown; UPA had one killed.	p. 352
5/6/1946	A-2: Hromenko; A-4: Burlaka	Attack on the Polish village of Olszanica and the railroad station. Poles had eleven killed; UPA had one killed, two wounded. Destroyed three bridges, a railroad station, a gas pipeline, and a few buildings.	pp. 338–340
5/7/1946	A-5: Khrin	Polish attack on partisans taking potatoes from deported village of Darów (Dariv). Poles had one killed, two wounded. UPA had no losses but lost a wagon and two horses.	p. 346
5/8/1946	A-5: Khrin	Meetings with villagers of Wola Piotrowa (Volia Petrova), Karlików and Przybyszów (Prybyshiv) hiding in the forest. The subject of the talk was "The Struggle Against Resettling the Ukrainian Population in the USSR."	p. 346
5/10/1946	A-2: Hromenko; A-4: Burlaka	Burned the village of Leszczawa Dolna (Lishchava Dolishnia). In this mixed village, Ukrainians were deported and Poles from Ukraine were settled. Villagers together with troops raided Ukrainian villages. Four civilians were killed, and thirty	p. 340

		cows, seventeen horses and other goods were taken. UPA had no losses.	
5/10/1946	A-5: Khrin	Prolonged fight with troops in Płonna and Kamienne. In Płonna: Poles had nine killed, and the wounded were removed in three wagons. UPA had four wounded. In Kamienne, there were two Poles killed. UPA captured weapons and supplies in both villages.	pp. 346–348
5/11/1946	A-3: Bir	Ambushed troops near the village of Kołonice (Kolonychi). Poles had eight killed, four wounded, and four captured; UPA had no losses.	p. 342
5/13/1946	N/A: Myron	Ambushed a truck carrying troops near the village of Habkowce. Nineteen soldiers were killed; UPA had no losses.	p. 354
5/15/1946	N/A: Myron	Ambushed a column of about 300 soldiers led by two tanks. Troops with tanks were allowed to pass, partisans opened fire on troops riding in wagons at the end of the column; 26 soldiers were killed and 30 seriously wounded. UPA had no losses.	pp. 354–355
5/16/1946	A-1: Didyk	On the road to Baligród destroyed four miles of telephone line and two wooden bridges. On one bridge, the supporting beams were cut and the bridge was left standing. On the following day, a truck with troops going over the bridge fell into a creek as the bridge collapsed. Polish losses, if any are unknown; UPA had no losses.	p. 337
5/17/1946	A-5: Khrin	Day-long fight with a unit of about 500 soldiers in the forest between Wisłok and Przybyszów. Poles had 39 dead and an unknown number wounded. UPA had five wounded, and the three who were seriously wounded shot themselves.	pp. 348–349
5/18/1946	A-1: Didyk	One sotnia platoon ambushed troops on the road near Baligród. Poles had five killed; UPA had no losses.	p. 337
5/18/1946	A-1: Didyk	Another platoon in the Baligród area ambushed troops. Poles had 18 killed. UPA	pp. 337–338

		had no losses.	
5/18/1946	A-3: Bir	Ambushed truck carrying troops. Poles had one killed and four wounded; UPA had no losses.	pp. 342–343
5/19/1946	A-2: Hromenko; A-4: Burlaka	Fight with troops near the village of Huta Brzuska (Huta Berezka). Poles had 18 killed and 15 wounded; UPA had one killed and one captured.	pp. 340–341
5/19/1946	A-5: Khrin	Khrin conducted three meetings with villagers heading for Slovakia who were promised to be resettled in deported Hungarian homes. Khrin argued that it was a ploy to get them out of the forest. People did not believe that the Slovaks would deceive them and entered Slovakia.	p. 350
5/19/1946	A-6: Krylach	Burned deported Ukrainian village of Manasterzec (Manastyrets'). No losses.	p. 352
5/20/1946	A-2: Hromenko	Brief firefight with troops. Poles had one wounded; UPA had one killed.	p. 341
5/20/1946	A-5: Khrin	Khrin met with Czech soldiers on the border to inquire about Ukrainian civilians who entered Slovakia. After a brief discussion, UPA left.	pp. 350–351
5/23/1946	A-3: Bir	Destroyed four brick buildings in Myczkowce (Mychkivtsi) that were designated to house troops. No fight took place.	p. 343
5/23/1946	A-5: Khrin	One squad going for food was ambushed, fled after a short firefight. No losses.	p. 351
5/24/1946	A-3: Bir	Engaged troops deporting Ukrainians from Bereżnica Niżna (Bereznyts'ia Nizhnia). Troops had 10 killed and few wounded; UPA had no losses.	pp. 343–344
5/26/1946	A-6: Krylach	Burned the Polish village of Temeszów for robbing Ukrainian villages. Five Poles died fighting; UPA had no losses and took livestock and goods.	pp. 352–353
5/26/1946	N/A: Myron	Destroyed three bridges on the Krywe – Strzebowiska (Kryve-Strubovys'ka) road and mined it. No losses.	p. 355
5/27/1946	A-5: Khrin	Burned the deported Ukrainian village of Dudyńce (Dudyntsi) as it was being settled by Poles. No losses.	p. 351

5/27/1946	N/A: Myron	Fired on Polish patrol that fled. No losses.	p. 355
5/28/1946	A-3: Bir	Sotnia squad destroyed three brick buildings in Zabrodzie to deny use by Poles. No losses.	p. 344
5/28/1946	A-4: Burlaka; A-7: Lastivka	Engaged Polish troops near Wola Krecowska (Volia Kretsivs'ka) who were supported by two planes. Poles had 22 killed and two captured who were released; UPA had no losses.	pp. 344–345
5/29/1946	A-5: Khrin	Two platoons surprised by troops, and the partisans fled. No casualties on either side. UPA lost seven rifles.	p. 351
5/30/1946	A-1: Didyk	A platoon burned the deported Ukrainian village of Stary Łupków (Staryi Lupkiv). No casualties.	p. 338
5/31/1946	A-1: Didyk	Fell trees on the road to Wola Matiaszowa (Volia Matiashova) to thwart deportation. No casualties.	p. 358
6/1/1946	A-5: Khrin	A platoon destroyed two bridges, barracks, and some brick buildings in Szczawne. Another platoon had a fight with an AK unit. Polish losses uncertain; UPA had no losses.	p. 374
6/1/1946	A-7: Lastivka	Provided security for an NCO school during the month. Additional information not provided.	p. 376
6/2/1946	A-1: Brodych	Burned two deported Ukrainian villages of Wola Michowa (Volia Myhova) and Smolnik to prevent use by troops. No casualties.	p. 368
6/4/1946	A-3: Bir	Troops attacked UPA encampment and were driven off. Poles had one killed and three wounded; UPA had no losses.	pp. 372–373
6/6/1946	A-4: Burlaka	Destroyed three miles of telephone line and burned four bridges on the road between Rybotycze and Łodynka. No casualties.	p. 373
6/7/1946	A-6: Krylach	Brief firefight with troops supported by two tanks. Poles had no losses; UPA had one killed and one wounded.	p. 376
6/8/1946	A-4: Burlaka	Held a meeting with Ukrainians in the vil-	p. 373

		lage of Jureczkowa (Iurechkova). Additional information not provided.	
6/8/1946	A-5: Khrin	Attacked 30 soldiers in Mokre repairing railroad line, seven were killed. The remainder fled and were mistakenly attacked by Public Security Troops.	pp. 374–375
6/8/1946	N/A: Myron	Ambushed a truck carrying troops near Cisna. Sixteen soldiers were killed and four wounded. Truck was destroyed.	p. 378
6/9/1946	A-4: Burlaka	Propaganda raid on the Polish settlement of Chwanow and Polonized village of Sen'kov(as written) Additional information not provided.	p. 373
6/11/1946	N/A: Myron	Road near Kalnica (Kal'nytsia) was mined. Four soldiers and two wagons of deportees were killed. Another soldier was killed later by mines. A sotnia platoon ambushed three trucks with troops. Twenty eight soldiers were killed and 30 wounded; UPA had no losses.	p. 379
6/12/1946	A-6: Krylach	Firefight with troops near Trzcianiec (Trostianets'). Poles had 17 killed and four wounded. UPA had seven killed and one wounded who was captured.	pp. 376–377
6/13/1946	A-3: Bir; A-3: Karmeliuk	Mined road near Baligród. Two trucks carrying troops were destroyed. Forty soldiers were killed and 20 wounded; UPA had no losses.	p. 373
6/13/1946	A-2: Hromenko; A-4: Burlaka	Propaganda talk with people in the mostly Polish village of Winniki. No additional information given.	p. 373
6/14/1946	A-4: Burlaka	Captured 23 soldiers making hay in Koniusza. Soldiers were disarmed, their uniforms were taken, and then they were released.	pp. 373–374
6/14/1946	A-5: Khrin	Brief firefight with troops. Polish losses uncertain; UPA had none	p. 375
6/14/1946	A-5: Khrin	A platoon was ambushed by troops. After short skirmish, UPA had no losses. Polish losses, if any, are uncertain.	p. 375
6/16/1946	A-1: Brodych	Destroyed railroad station and repair shop in Łupków. No losses.	p. 368

6/16/1946	A-5: Khrin	A squad attacked ten soldiers at a dance in Kiełczawa (Kel'chava). Poles had one woman killed and one soldier wounded; UPA had no losses.	p. 375
6/18/1946	A-5: Khrin	Sotnia's military police destroyed rectory, school and a cooperative store in Czazsyn. No losses.	p. 375
6/19/1946	A-2 Hromenko; A-4 Burlaka	Burned eight deported Ukrainian villages. No casualties.	pp. 369–370
6/19/1946	A-5: Khrin	Brief fight by a squad with troops near Kiełczawa one soldier killed. UPA had no losses.	pp. 375–376
6/22/1946	A-2: Hromenko	A sotnia squad was attacked by troops. Polish losses unknown; UPA had two killed.	pp. 370–371
6/23/1946	A-4: Burlaka	Ambushed a small group of police and a soldiers near Sielec. Poles had four killed; UPA had no losses.	p. 374
6/25/1946	A-2: Hromenko	Brief fight with soldiers and armed civilians near Hroszowka. Poles had two killed and two wounded; UPA had no losses.	p. 371
6/26/1946	A-2: Hromenko	A platoon ambushed 15 soldiers. Poles had two killed; UPA had no casualties.	p. 371
627/1946	A-2: Hromenko; A-6: Krylach	Attacked deportation commission stationed in Dobra Szlachecka guarded by 40 soldiers. Poles had four soldiers killed; UPA had no losses. Fate of the commission was not indicated.	pp. 370–371
6/27/1946	A-3: Bir	Burned brick building in Berezka. No losses.	p. 373
7/2/1946	A-1: Brodych	Ambushed truck on the road near Baligród, eight soldiers killed and civilian women wounded. UPA had no losses.	p. 395
7/2/1946	A-4: Burlaka	Skirmish with three soldiers. Poles had two killed, one wounded; No UPA losses.	pp. 400–401
7/5/1946	A-5: Khrin	Burned deported village of Mchawa (Mkhava) and drove troops out of the village. Polish casualties are unknown; UPA had none.	p. 407
7/7/1946	A-2: Hromenko; A-6: Krylach	Attacked and destroyed police station in the town of Dubiecko. Poles had two killed and two wounded; UPA had no cas-	pp. 396–397

		ualties.	
7/9/1946	A-3: Bir	Destroyed some buildings in the Baligród area considered suitable for stationing troops. No casualties.	p. 399
7/11/1946	A-5: Khrin	In Średnie Wielkie, partisans captured a Polish soldier of the 34th Regiment who was executed after interrogation. (Note: the regiment had shot civilians in number of villages at the beginning of the year.)	p. 407
7/12/1946	A-1: Brodych	A partisan encampment was attacked by troops in the forest. UPA withdrew. No casualties on either side.	p. 395
7/12/1946	A-2: Hromen-ko; A-6: Krylach	Engagement with troops conducting raid on the forest. Poles had three killed and 12 wounded; UPA had three killed.	p. 398
7/16/1946	A-7: Lastivka	Brief firefight with troops. Polish casualties are unknown; UPA had none.	p. 41
7/17/1946	A-3: Bir	Retaliatory raid on Wołkowyja for killing 35 Ukrainians in Terka by Border Guards stationed in Wolkowyja and supported by village self-defense unit. Poles had 30 Border Guards killed and 25 wounded, along with 45 self-defense unit men who were killed; UPA had two killed and five wounded.	pp. 399–400
7/18/1946	A-5: Khrin	Destroyed four bunkers, two watchtowers, and 10 houses used by troops in Kulaszne (Kuliashne). Troops were not in the village at the time. There were no casualties.	pp. 407–408
7/19/1946	A-1: Brodych	Two squads ambushed Border Guards on the Szczawne-Komańcza road. One Guardsman was killed, two were wounded and two captured. The two captured were interrogated. One was released and the other executed.	pp. 395–396
7/20/1946	A-4: Burlaka	Ambushed a wagon with three people. Policeman was killed and two civilians captured and turned over to SB. After interrogation, SB determined that they had engaged in banditry and were "liquidated." UPA had no losses.	p. 401
7/20/1946	A-5: Khrin	Retaliatory raid on the Polish village of	pp. 408–

		Pobiedno for banditry. A fight broke out with troops in the village at the time and a self-defense unit. The number of Poles killed could not be determined but 32 wounded were taken to Sanok for treatment; UPA had one missing.	409
7/22/1946	A-4: Burlaka	Thirty-two head of livestock and 10 horses taken by Poles from Ukrainians were captured by UPA, near Babice. No casualties on either side.	pp. 401–402
7/23/1946	A-1: Brodych	Two squads attacked Polish troops and civilians harvesting in the abandoned Ukrainian village of Lubne. Two soldiers were killed, one was wounded, and one captured. After interrogation, the captured man was "liquidated." Civilians were released but their horses were taken. UPA had no losses.	p. 396
7/23/1946	A-5: Khrin	Firefight with troops in Komańcza. Four were killed and a bridge was destroyed. UPA had no losses.	p. 410
7/24/1946	A-2: Hromenko; A-4: Burlaka; A-6: Krylach	Prolonged engagement with troops who had 51 killed, 83 wounded, and 14 captured who after interrogation were "liquidated." UPA had six killed and three wounded who later died.	pp. 402–407
7/24/1946	A-5: Khrin	Ambushed four trucks carrying troops and Public Security Soldiers. Thirteen were killed and 14 wounded; UPA had no losses.	pp. 409–410
7/27/1946	A-2: Hromenko	Attacked group of soldiers taking cattle from Ukrainian village of Hroszowka, two soldiers were killed and five wounded. UPA had no losses.	p. 399
7/27/1946	A-5: Khrin	Mined Polish army bunkers and houses used by troops in Wisłok and destroyed five bridges.	p. 410
7/30/1946	A-5: Khrin	Attacked Polish troops and civilians harvesting in Surowica. Three Poles including one civilian were killed, and five were wounded; UPA had no losses.	pp. 410–411

Notes: *N/A: Not Applicable, Sotnias from Ukraine operating with a battalion but not given battalion designation.*

Sources: Potichnyj, Petro. J. and Ivan Lyko, Eds. Taktychnii Vidtynok UPA 26-ii "Lemko": Lemkivshchyna I Peremyshchyna (Documenty I materialy). Tom. 33. Toronto-L'viv, Litopys UPA, 2001.

Appendix III: Gazetteer Toponyms (Listed in Alphabetical Order)

	Polish Toponym	Ukrainian Toponym
1.	Baligród	Balyhorod
2.	Bielsk	Bels'k
3.	Bereżnica Niżna	Bereznyts'ia Nizhnia
4.	Biała Podlaska	Bila Podliash'ka
5.	Biłgoraj	Bilohrai
6.	Binczarowa	Bil'tsareva
7.	Bircza	Bircha
8.	Bodnarka	Bodnarivka
9.	Brzozów	Bereziv, Boroziv
10.	Bug	Buh
11.	Bukowiec	Bukovets'
12.	Chełm	Kholm
13.	Chryszczata	Khreshchatyk
14.	Cisna	Tisna
15.	Czaszyn	Chashyn
16.	Dąbrówka Ruska	Dubrivka Rus'ka
17.	Darów	Dariv
18.	Dezhno	Doshno
19.	Dobcza	Dibcha
20.	Dolina Dolna	Dolyna Dil'na
21.	Drohiczyn	Dorohochyn
22.	Dudyńce	Dudyntsi
23.	Dukla	Duklia
24.	Dynów	Dyniv
25.	Galicia	Halychyna
26.	Gładyszów	Hladyshiv
27.	Gorlice	Horlytsi
28.	Grodlo	Horodlo
29.	Habkowce	Habkivtsi
30.	Hoczew	Hochiv
31.	Hrubieszów	Hrubeshiv
32.	Huta Brzuska	Huta Berezka
33.	Huzele	Huzelia
34.	Jablonica Ruska	Jablonica Rus'ka
35.	Jankowce	Yankivtsi
36.	Jarosław	Iaroslav

37.	Jasiel	Iasel'
38.	Jasło	Iaslo
39.	Jureczkowa	Iurechkova
40.	Kalnica	Kal'nytsia
41.	Kamienne	Kamiane
42.	Karlików	Karlykiv
43.	Kiełczawa	Kel'chava
44.	Kniazie	Kniazi
45.	Kołonice	Kolonychi
46.	Komańcza	Komancha
47.	Koniusza	Koniusha
48.	Kożuszne	Kozhushne
49.	Królik Polski	Korolyk Pols'kyi
50.	Krasnystaw	Krasnystav
51.	Królik Wołoski	Korolyk Vols'kyi
52.	Krosno	Korosno
53.	Krynica	Krynytsia
54.	Krywcza	Kryvcha
55.	Krywe	Kryve
56.	Krzywowierba	Kryvoverby
57.	Łańcut	Lantsut
58.	Leszczawa Dolna	Lishchava Dolishnia
59.	Lesko	Lis'ko
60.	Lipowiec	Lipovets
61.	Lubaczów	Liubachiv
62.	Lubliniec	Liublynets
63.	Lubycz	Liubych
64.	Łukawica	Lukavytsia
65.	Łupków	Lupkiv
66.	Lwów	L'viv
67.	Manasterzec	Manastyrets'
68.	Mchawa	Mkhava
69.	Morochów	Morokhiv
70.	Mszana	Mshana
71.	Myczkowce	Mychkivtsi
72.	Nadolany	Nadoliany
73.	Nieznajowa	Neznaieva
74.	Nowosielce	Novosil'tsi
75.	Nowosiółki	Novosilky
76.	Nowotaniec	Novotanets
77.	Nowa Grobla	Nova Hreblia
78.	Nowy Sącz	Novyi Sanch
79.	Nowy Targ	Novyi Tarh
80.	Olchowce	Vilkhivtsi

81.	Osława	Oslava
82.	Osławica	Oslavytsya
83.	Paszowa	Pashova
84.	Pawłokoma	Pavlokoma
85.	Piskorowice	Pyskorovychi
86.	Płonna	Polonna
87.	Podlasie	Pidlichia
88.	Polany Surowiczne	Poliany Surovychni
89.	Postołów	Postoliv
90.	Przemyśl	Peremyshl'
91.	Przeworsk	Perevors'k
92.	Przybyszów	Prybyshiv
93.	Puławy	Pulavy
94.	Ratnawica	Ratnavytsia
95.	Rawa Ruska	Rava Rus'ka
96.	Rozdziele	Rozdill'ia
97.	Rychwald/Owczary	Rykhvald
98.	Rymanów	Rymaniv
99.	Rzeszów	Riashiv
100.	Sagarin	Sahrin
101.	San	Sian
102.	Sanok	Sianik
103.	Smolnik	Smil'nyk
104.	Średnie Wielkie	Serednie Velyky
105.	Stanisławów	Stanislaviv, Ivano-Frankiv'sk
106.	Stary Dzików	Staryi Dykiv
107.	Stary Łupków	Staryi Lupkiv
108.	Stefkowa	Stefkova
109.	Storoze Wielke	Strozhi Velyky
110.	Stroze	Storozhi
111.	Stroze Male	Storozhi Mali
112.	Strzebowiska	Strubovys'ka
113.	Surowica	Surovytsia
114.	Szczawne	Shchavne
115.	Szczawnica	Shchavnytsia
116.	Tarnogród	Tarnohorod
117.	Teljatin	Teliatyn
118.	Ternopil'	Tarnopol
119.	Tomaszów	Tomashiv
120.	Trzcianiec	Trostianets'
121.	Turzańsk	Turyns'ke
122.	Tylawa	Tyliava
123.	Uhnow	Uhniv
124.	Ułazów	Ulaziv

125.	Uluch	Uliuch
126.	Wańkowa	Van'kova
127.	Waręż	Variazh
128.	Wasilow	Vasyliv
129.	Wereszyca	Vereshchytsya
130.	Wetlina	Vetlyna
131.	Wierchowina	Verkhovyna
132.	Wisła	Visla
133.	Wisłok Dolny	Vyslok Dolishnyi
134.	Wisłok Górny	Vyslok Horishnyi
135.	Wisłok Wielki	Vyslok Velykyi
136.	Włodawa	Voldova
137.	Wola Jaworowa	Volia Iavorova
138.	Wola Krecowska	Volia Kretsivs'ka
139.	Wola Matiaszowa	Volia Matiashova
140.	Wola Michowa	Volia Myhova
141.	Wola Piotrowa	Volia Petrova
142.	Wola Sękowa	Volia Sen'kova
143.	Wola Wołodzka	Volia Voldovs'ka
144.	Wolica	Volytsia
145.	Woltuszowa	Voltushova
146.	Wysoczany	Vysochany
147.	Zablotce	Zabolotsi
148.	Zagorz	Zahiria
149.	Załuże	Zaluzhe
150.	Zamość	Zamostia
151.	Zawadka Morochowska	Zavadka Morokhiv'ska
152.	Zboiska	Zbois'ka

Appendix IV: Acronyms

#	Acronym	Name	English Translation
1.	AK	Armia Krajowa	Home Army
2.	AL	Armia Ludowa	People's Army
3.	BCh	Bataliony Chłopskie	Peasant Battalions
4.	GL	Gwardia Ludowa	People's Guard (Communist Partisans, 1943–1945)
5.	KBW	Korpus Bezpieczeństwa Wewnętrznego	Internal Security Corps
6.	MO	Milicja Obywatelska	Citizens' Militia (Police)
7.	NOW	Narodowa Organizacja Wojskowa	National Military Organization (Right-wing partisans)
8.	NSZ	Narodowe Siły Zbrojne	National Armed Forces (Right-wing partisans)
9.	MVD	Ministerstvo Vnutrennykh Del	Ministry of Internal Affairs
10.	NKVD	Narodnyy Komisssariat Vnutrenykh Del	National Committee for Internal Affairs
11.	GOR	Grupa Operacyjna "Rzeszów"	Operational Group "Rzeszów"
12.	GOW	Grupa Operacyjna "Wisła"	Operational Group "Wisła"
13.	ORMO	Ochotnicza Rezerwa Milicji Obywatelskiej	Volunteer Reserve of People's Militia
14.	OUN	Organizatsiia Ukrains'kykh Nationalistiv	Organization of Ukrainian Nationalists
15.	OUN (b), OUN (r)	Organizatsiia Ukrains'kykh Nationalistiv (Bandera)	Organization of Ukrainian Nationalists, Bandera Wing/Revolutionary
16.	OUN (m)	Organizatsiia Ukrains'kykh Nationalistiv (Mel'nyk)	Organization of Ukrainian Nationalists, Mel'nyk Wing
17.	PGR	Państwowe Gospodarstwo Rolne	State Farm
18.	PKWN	Polski Komitet Wyzwolenia Narodowego	Polish National Liberation Committee
19.	PPR	Polska Partia Robotnicza	Polish Workers Party
20.	PUR	Państwowy Urząd Repatriacyjny	State Repatriation Administration
21.	SB	Sluzhba Bespeky	Security Service
22.	SKV	Samoboronnyi Kushchovyi Viddil	Self-Defense Cluster Unit
23.	UB(P)	Urząd Bezpieczeństwa (Publicznego)	Department for Public Security
24.	UHVR	Ukrains'ka Holovna Vyzvolna Rada	Supreme Ukrainian Liberation Council

25.	UNO	Ukrains'ka Natsional'ne Obiednannia	Ukrainian National Association
26.	UNDO	Ukrains'ke Narodna Demo-kratychna Iuniia	Ukrainian National Democratic Union
27.	UNR	Ukrains'ka Narodna Respublyka	Ukrainian National Republic
28.	UNRRA		United Nations Relief and Reha-bilitation Organization
29.	UPA	Ukrains'ka Povstans'ka Armiia,	Ukrainian Insurgent Army
30.	UTsK	Ukrains'ki Tsentralnyi Komitet	Ukrainian Central Committee
31.	UVO	Ukrains'ka Viyskova Organizatsiia	Ukrainian Military Organization
32.	WiN	Wolność i Niezawisłość	Freedom and Independence
33.	WOP	Wojska Ochrony Pogranicza	Border Guards
34.	WP	Wojsko Polskie	Polish Troops (Army)
35.	ZUNR	Zakhidna Ukrains'ka Respublyka	Western Ukrainian Republic

Index

A

B

C

D

E

F

G

K

L

M

R

S

Stadion, Franz, Austrian count 58–59

T

U

V

W

Y

Z

About the Author

Dr. Stephen Rapawy was employed by the U.S. Bureau of the Census for over 34 years as a Statistician/Demographer writing reports focused primarily on demography, labor force, employment, and wages in the Soviet Union. During his tenure at the Census Bureau, he served as a Branch Chief of the Soviet Social Study Branch. After the collapse of the Soviet Union, Dr. Rapawy's research focused on Ukraine, spanning a broad range of topics including border issues, population, living standards, city profiles, demographics, and linguistic and ethnic re-identification. He received a Ph.D. degree in Russian Area Studies in 1977 from Georgetown University, and wrote his doctoral dissertation on "The Linguistic Shift Among Ukrainians in Ukraine Since Stalin." He has held a lifelong interest in the Ukrainian deportations since he personally experienced "Operation Vistula" in 1947, when he and his family were deported from a Ukrainian district in Poland and subsequently resettled to western Poland. After retiring, he pursued his research interests in the topic, which coincided with the opening of the Polish and Ukrainian archives after the collapse of Communism.

ETHONOGRAPHIC MAP OF UKRAINE

PRE - WORLD WAR II

JVN 12/01/15

Map 1: "Ethnographic Map of Ukraine, Pre-World War II"

POLISH - UKRAINIAN MEDIEVAL BOUNDARIES

Map 2: "Polish–Ukrainian Medieval Boundaries"

ibidem-Verlag / *ibidem* Press
Melchiorstr. 15
70439 Stuttgart
Germany

ibidem@ibidem.eu
ibidem.eu